D1569530

'KUBLA KHAN' AND
THE FALL OF JERUSALEM

'KUBLA KHAN' AND
THE FALL OF JERUSALEM

THE MYTHOLOGICAL SCHOOL IN
BIBLICAL CRITICISM AND
SECULAR LITERATURE
1770—1880

E. S. SHAFFER

Lecturer in Comparative Literature
School of European Studies, University of East Anglia

CAMBRIDGE UNIVERSITY PRESS
CAMBRIDGE
LONDON · NEW YORK · MELBOURNE

Published by the Syndics of the Cambridge University Press
The Pitt Building, Trumpington Street, Cambridge CB2 1RP
Bentley House, 200 Euston Road, London NW1 2DB
32 East 57th Street, New York, NY 10022, USA
296 Beaconsfield Parade, Middle Park, Melbourne 3206, Australia

Library of Congress Catalogue Card Number: 74–79141

ISBN: 0 521 20478 X

First published 1975

Printed in Great Britain by
Western Printing Services Ltd, Bristol

IN MEMORY OF F. K. N.

CONTENTS

ACKNOWLEDGEMENTS

I should like to thank Clare Hall, Cambridge, where I have been a Research Fellow during the writing of this book. I should also like to thank Peter and Ursula Dronke for their several fertile suggestions in the earliest phase of this book; and John Beer for many kindnesses and Coleridgean 'aids to reflection' during the time I have been in Cambridge. John Rosenberg sympathetically read and indispensably criticized the manuscript in its first, most tentative form. I am equally indebted to Michael Black for his painstaking and constructive reading of a later draft. Thomas McFarland kindly gave abundant advice on a number of points both before and after the publication of his own book on Coleridge. P. H. Gaskill generously permitted me to consult a portion of his thesis, then in progress, on Hölderlin's pietist milieu. Peter Dronke checked the accuracy of the translations from the Latin. The editors of Coleridge's *Lectures 1795 On Politics and Religion*, Peter Mann and Lewis Patton, and the English publishers of *The Collected Coleridge*, Routledge and Kegan Paul, were kind enough to make the text available to me before publication. Acknowledgement should also be made to the Librarian of Reading University, who permitted me to consult the microfilm copies of the Victoria MSS; and to the Librarian of Jesus College, Cambridge, who permitted me access to copies of Coleridge's notebooks. Mr A. H. B. Coleridge gave permission to quote from unpublished manuscript sources. George Whalley, the editor of the marginalia for *The Collected Coleridge*, generously helped to check my readings against the originals and his transcripts. I should like to thank him also for his kind permission to consult his thesis on Coleridge's reading (London, 1950). Kathleen Coburn kindly checked my readings of the MS notebooks against her authoritative transcripts. Some of the material in Chapter 3 was given as a paper delivered to the Congress of the Fédération Internationale des Langues et Littératures Modernes in 1969; a brief version of Chapter 5 was published in *Victorian Studies* (December 1972). Michael Loewe entrusted me with his handsome first edition of *The Works of Sir William Jones*. I should also like to express my gratitude to the Reverend Professor C. F. D. Moule, the Reverend John Sturdy, Dr Ernst Bammel, the Reverend Stephen Sykes, and especially Father Reginald Fuller, for their assistance on Biblical critical problems. Finally, to Lionel Trilling my debt of gratitude is longstanding and all-encompassing; any thanks I can render must be understood as truly apocalyptic abbreviation referring to the accumulated wisdom of the Fathers *symbolo aenigmatico*.

I wish also to acknowledge gratefully the help of Mrs Mildred Pickett, who typed out, against her conscience, the blasphemous matter of the higher criticism, and of Mrs Betty Sharp, who carried on when conscience struck again.

What I owe to the positive and present aid of my husband Brian Shaffer I might itemize at length; the depths of his forbearance I can only gratefully surmise.

Cambridge   E. S. S.
1972

INTRODUCTION

This book proposes, in effect, a new method of literary criticism, or, at any rate, a mutation of existing practice among English-speaking critics. The intention is to explore the possibilities of a literary criticism which can absorb and bring to bear on literature the work of other disciplines. A full history of the higher criticism as such is not intended; there is, however, every reason, both conventional and novel, to treat the higher criticism. Surprisingly, no full history of the higher criticism exists in English, and no full history of the higher critical movement in England exists in any language. Even the most authoritative English accounts are sketchy and partial, rely on Victorian sources, convey inadequate knowledge of the major German sources, show little grasp of the place of the higher criticism in a general European movement of ideas and equally little of the very specific local history of its reception and practice in England. They place their emphasis largely on the late, that is, the mid-nineteenth-century history of the movement without any indication of its lively earlier history in England. Accounts of current views are largely a-historical. From the literary point of view, the situation is, if anything, even less satisfactory: there is no treatment whatsoever of Coleridge's relation to the higher criticism, though he was, if not an innovator, one of its subtlest exponents, and his religious thought in general cannot be understood without it; nor is there any adequate treatment of the effects of the movement on George Eliot's practice as a novelist. Indeed, there is no satisfactory account of its effect on any English author, despite constant glancing allusions to it in critical and scholarly treatments of the Victorians.

No single book could hope to remedy all these defects at once. I shall be content if the present book does something to bring out the reception in England in the second half of the eighteenth century of the

I

mythological school of German criticism as it was shaped by Herder and Eichhorn, and the continuity with the more familiar history of Victorian controversy, while, on the literary side, illuminating the attitudes of a very few of its leading practitioners.

This book is, then, a history of ideas; it might even be termed 'literary sociology' in so far as it recognizes the need to consider the entire milieu of a work of art, in its intimate relations with artistic creation, and not simply to offer superficial and perfunctory 'background' history. This is perhaps the most pressing problem in criticism now, and it has been treated variously and suggestively by Continental critics: by Lukács everywhere in his work, by Sartre in *La Critique de la raison dialectique*, translated in part as *The Question of Method*, by Lucien Goldmann in *Le Dieu caché*, and by Roland Barthes, in a succession of works, especially *Critique et verité*, in a scintillating and challenging, rather than definitive or acceptable, fashion. English and American critics have approached these questions too, but in nothing like the depth or range or systematic intention of these writers.

As Goldmann has said,

In non-dialectical works, the chapters devoted to theory in sociological and historical studies, and conversely, the chapters devoted to social and historical reality in histories of ideas or of literature and the arts, are treated as extraneous bodies; they are usually inspired by an interest in pure erudition or offered merely in the interest of general information. For the dialectical thinker, however, doctrines form the integrating part of the social reality itself and can be detached from it only by makeshift abstractions; the study of them is an *indispensable* element of the effective study of the problem in the same ways that social and historical reality constitutes one of the most important elements for understanding the spiritual life of an age.[1]

It is not necessary to be an avowed dialectical thinker (nor, like Goldmann, to equate this with 'marxist') to be persuaded of the justice of this analysis; the history of ideas appears in our literary criticism, if at all, deplorably impoverished, mechanical, and trivial.

In *Le Dieu caché*, Goldmann stated the problem succinctly:

The methodological problem, as far as the humanities or the science of man is concerned, is principally this: that of dividing the immediately available facts into relative wholes which are sufficiently autonomous to provide a framework for scientific investigation.[2]

Neither the individual work nor the personality of the author forms a sufficiently autonomous whole to provide such a framework, he points out; biography in particular is 'of historical interest only to a *very limited* degree and in an *indirect* way', for whatever clarification it affords of the literary work.[3] Yet nearly all of our criticism treats either the individual work or the personality of the author, and when both are attempted, perhaps the most common case, the insufficiency of each merely reinforces the insufficiency of the other. If we move beyond this doubly distorted and poverty-stricken criticism into the history of ideas, Goldmann warns us further that 'none of the traditional fields of university study (law, political history, experimental psychology, sociology, etc.) is concerned with a sufficiently autonomous subject'.[4]

Goldmann's problem, the relation of the whole and its parts, belongs to dialectical thinking, and his perception of it as a problem comes from his adherence to that school; nevertheless, the problem can be solved, for many purposes apart from the strictly philosophical cruces of dialectic itself, more directly and with less apparatus than he himself employs and without resort to the terminology of a particular school. To clarify what is meant for our purposes by the isolation of 'a sufficiently autonomous subject matter', we may cite the successful example offered by Michel Foucault's *Histoire de la folie*, in which the history of views of madness in the Enlightenment impinges directly on literature and yet belongs genuinely to the subject-matter of both psychology and medicine.[5] Foucault is enabled by his disentanglement of just this subject-matter to exercise a literary criticism of surpassing interest and originality, and to produce at the same time a critique not simply of outmoded medical theories but of modern psychology at its roots. His subject-matter vividly exemplifies the unsolved antinomy at the centre of Enlightenment thought, the simultaneous existence throughout the period of the aspiration to full and unmitigated rationality and the aspiration to affective or intuitive experience. The isolation of the 'sufficiently autonomous whole', then, implies selection of a subject-matter which cuts across the boundaries of the traditional disciplines, yet which in practice, to be manageable, must be smaller than any traditional discipline; it implies a subject-matter which can be as clearly defined as a discipline, although defined uniquely and for this purpose alone, in order to illuminate the peculiar qualities of the period. It may be helpful to think of this subject-matter as an activity, rather than a solid body of knowledge. 'It is not then a question of relating the art to the society, but of studying all the activities and their interrelations, without any concession of priority to any one of them we may choose to abstract.'[6] The boundaries of such a subject-matter will readily be understood to be elastic; the Biblical criticism which in Coleridge's youth might appear an obscure, difficult, largely foreign scholarly technique confined to a handful of professors of Oriental languages becomes by George Eliot's time the medium of secular religious experience. In the best work of both Goldmann and Foucault, then, the distinction between the 'literary' and the 'other' disciplines which they bring into play effectively disappears; the new relative whole may be judged sufficiently autonomous precisely when this happens. There is no separation between 'background' and literary analysis; the separation, so familiar to us as to seem natural and unavoidable, is the result of arbitrary and conventional and therefore ill-considered selection of subject-matter. It is the result of an inadequate methodology of literary criticism.

Raymond Williams has criticized Continental literary sociology for failing to recognize an ally in the practical criticism of Cambridge. That the insights of Lukács and Goldmann do not get translated into critical practice is an overstatement – one thinks, for example, of Lukács's extended criticism of Thomas Mann, Goldmann's of Pascal – but it is true that their often brilliant literary insights, arrived at through philosophical and social analysis, are usually not worked out in detail or in relation to a particular work. It is tantalizing for those of us whose interest is primarily in literary criticism to have these hard-won insights abandoned at the very moment when their application could begin. Even Foucault, who often uses literary works at the inception or culmination of his analysis, grants us only a few splendid pages on, say, *Le Neveu de Rameau*, and then moves on. One would hope that in an expanded conception of 'text', 'theoretical' and 'practical' criticism would be reunited. I have therefore attempted here to conduct my analysis through specific works: Coleridge's 'Kubla Khan', Hölderlin's 'Patmos', Browning's 'A Death in the Desert', George Eliot's *Daniel Deronda*, all of which are marked and shaped by the higher critical movement.

Given that the history of ideas is inseparable from the history of poetry, what 'relative whole' shall we disengage? In one sense, I have deliberately chosen the hardest case: 'Kubla Khan' (and, in the second instance, the odes of Hölderlin), poetry often claimed to be 'pure poetry', poetry of extreme lyricism, emerging unwilled from a consciousness loosed from considerations of rational order, is brought into relation with Biblical criticism, a body of highly technical information and intricate, specialized, restricted practice.

But this is only an apparent opposition. Northrop Frye, in a well-known passage calling for a new literary criticism in our own time, has written,

> The absence of any genuinely literary criticism of the Bible in modern times (until very recently) has left an enormous gap in our knowledge of literary symbolism as a whole, a gap which all the new knowledge brought to bear on it is quite incompetent to fill. I feel that historical scholarship is without exception 'lower' or analytic criticism, and that 'higher' criticism would be a quite different activity. The latter seems to me to be a purely literary criticism which would see the Bible, not as the scrapbook of corruptions, glosses, redactions, insertions, conflations, misplacings and misunderstandings revealed by the analytic critic, but as the typological unity which all these things were originally intended to help construct. . . A genuine higher criticism of the Bible, therefore, would be a synthetizing process which would start with the assumption that the Bible is a definitive myth, a single archetypal structure extending from creation to apocalypse.[7]

Frye seems to be unaware of the fact that precisely what he is pleading for was accomplished by the higher criticism from Herder to Strauss; that romantic literary criticism is the higher criticism of literature, and that his own principle,

> that in every age of literature there tends to be some kind of central encyclopaedic form, which is normally a scripture or sacred book in the mythical mode, and some 'analogy of revelation'. . .in other modes

is a principle available to him because so much romantic literature adopted and is based upon it.

German thought in this period was seminal for all the romantic movements of Europe; René Wellek has shown the effect of this in literary history, and his views have been extensively corroborated in *'Romantic' and Its Cognates: the European History of a Word*.[8] The history of Biblical criticism exhibits in a very well-defined way the relations between German and English thought. The local dispute over

Coleridge's indebtedness pales into insignificance; it is only another
proof of Anglo-American parochialism that Coleridge should be
fancied to be culpably alone in his dependence on Teutonic speculation.
A movement of this significance and scope cannot be reduced to the
mechanics (or the moralities) of transmission. The 'collapse of the
ontological foundations of religion' (Lukács's phrase) and the consequent reinterpretation of the major religious text of the West is a
communal event. It is, of course, also a private event, and proceeds
through the inner struggle of individual conscience. 'Influence'
embraces both aspects of transmission, public and private. Harold
Bloom has characterized the history of English poetry since Milton as
an effort of each succeeding poet to grapple with a forebear whom he
experienced as greater than himself. Coleridge's sense of subjection to
greatness in others was one of many ways in which his sensibility
fostered the growth of a genuinely new literary and religious aesthetics
in which he himself is a figure of European stature.

The broad scope and great significance of an intellectual movement,
however, do not exempt us from knowing the mode of its transmission.
The 'archetypal' history favoured by some excellent literary critics is
impotent to render the fine shades of experience. M. H. Abrams has
written of the importance of the Bible in the period:

The concurrence in topics and design among these very diverse writers was
less the result of mutual influence than it was of a common climate of the
post-Revolutionary age, and of a grounding in a common body of materials –
above all in the Bible, especially as expounded by radical Protestant vision-
aries, many of whom had assimilated a modicum of Neoplatonic lore.[9]

But it is precisely the common experience of the Bible that was altered
in the period, and it was altered through a specific series of works that
did indeed become known to very diverse writers in different places
(whose experience of the 'post-Revolutionary age' was much more
diverse than their experience of revaluations of the Biblical text). The
importance of precise knowledge of the critical texts and their diffusion
is simply that the mood or tone of an age, as of an individual, is the
indirect expression of what questions of truth and falsity are held to
be at stake.

Despite the central importance for all of Coleridge's thinking of the
nature of religious verity, there is no study of Coleridge's interest in,

and contribution to, the higher criticism: German histories of the movement do not mention him; English studies tend to assume that the history of the movement in England begins with George Eliot's translation of Strauss's *Das Leben Jesu, Life of Jesus*. The inaccessibility of some of his most interesting work, which still lies concealed in marginalia on German theological works and in his late unpublished notebooks and manuscripts, has doubtless played a part in this neglect. It is certain, however, that his early knowledge of the new criticism was very great, and that it can be clarified by reference to the radical Unitarian circles he moved in during the early 1790s, which were fully aware of the new Continental work and among the first to espouse it without subterfuge; to text-critical work that was largely carried on in Latin rather than German; to translations of such important works as J. D. Michaelis's *Einleitung in das Neue Testament, Introduction to the New Testament*; and to his contacts with Germany through Dr Thomas Beddoes in Bristol. By the time he encountered Eichhorn personally in Göttingen in 1798, he was already an adept. I have by no means essayed a complete investigation of these early contacts; but I hope the notes offer some useful indications of them.

German philosophy has always been known to stand in the immediate background of Coleridge's criticism and even his poetry; yet it has never seemed possible to display the interrelations without appearing to over-systematize, and so to draw further from, rather than nearer to, Coleridge's poetic and critical habits. The higher criticism provides a solution to this perennial problem, for it is an intermediary between philosophy and literary criticism: shaped by philosophical considerations at every step, yet involved in the closest possible analysis of literary texts, it moves back and forth between the two worlds with ease. The Biblical critics in Coleridge's time, most particularly in the 1790s, were engaged in showing that the sacred text belonged to mythology. The new harmonizing of the Bible with other mythologies that emerged from the struggle between the claims of a scientific scholarship and the claims of traditional religion yielded at last a series of vital answers to the question of what system of the supernatural could be made viable in modern poetry. As the Renaissance argument about epic machinery was generalized to all poetry, the relations of epic to other genres altered, new content became available, and the poet was in some sort restored to his office as bard and seer.

Too often Coleridge's religious views, like his philosophical views, have been interpreted with a literalism completely foreign to the higher critical movement. The style of the apologists for Christianity partook of the subtle obliquities of their ironic Enlightenment opponents; often both the critical apologists and the Enlightened sceptics ran the same risk of denunciation by the orthodox. Their arguments were affected by the direction and the tone of the opposition with whom they had more in common than with the unthinking or the zealous traditionalist. As R. P. Blackmur has written,

Those who seem to be the chief writers of our time have found their subjects in attempting to dramatise at once both the culture and the turbulences it was meant to control and in doing so they have had partially to create – as it happens, to recreate – the terms, the very symbolic substance of the culture as they went along.

The apologetical style is a form of romantic irony. The literary perspective opens for us aspects of the higher criticism that have been largely lost sight of, by accident and by design, in the pretensions of the nineteenth century to make of it a 'positive' science and in the attempts of the present century to incorporate its unavoidable results in as bland and a-historical a manner as possible into orthodoxy. The fact that those histories that do exist of the higher criticism and its reception in England come from theological and ecclesiastical circles has ensured the loss of this perspective. Equally, the perspective of critical apologetics since Bayle opens Coleridge's prose style to us; current literary practice, in alienating him from his intellectual milieu, has alienated him from his style. No style exists *per se*.

J. L. Lowes's imposingly wrong-headed book *The Road to Xanadu* has for forty years stood in the way of comprehension of Coleridge's poetry. Lowes's associative theory of the imagination, belied by Coleridge's theory and practice alike, has been rightly dismissed; yet at the same time, illogically, his account of Coleridge's sources and his way of deploying them has been largely accepted and widely imitated. But if his theoretical account of Coleridge's imaginative process is wrong, as it egregiously is, we cannot accept his tale of how the 'hooks-and-eyes' of half-remembered phrases of charmingly exotic old folios arranged themselves into a great poem. We must even doubt that these were his sources. It was Lowes, not Coleridge, whose imagination worked on bits and scraps; perforce: Lowes simply did not do his homework. His jocose antiquarianism, dismissing as if on principle the immediate intellectual milieu, belongs to what Philippe Sollers has called the 'needle-work class' of literary criticism. We must turn afresh to Coleridge's intellectual biography.

'Kubla Khan' spans Coleridge's early intellectual history, never satisfactorily described. The first influences were of the comfortable Anglicanism that rode unthinking tandem with the dominant Newtonianism of the English eighteenth century; the second were of the more corrosive Enlightenment sort: Coleridge while still at school became an 'infidel sceptic', under the aegis of Voltaire's *Philosophical Dictionary*. At the same time, we hear, in Lamb's famous description, he was orating out of Iamblichus. At Cambridge began his Unitarian associations. No man was educated as a 'pre-romantic', that barbarous invention of literary historians. The collocation of Voltaire, and neo-platonism, and Unitarianism, we shall see, makes sense in its true context. The publication of Coleridge's early lectures and sermons and the editing of *The Watchman* have thrown light on the years until 1796; the present work does something to clarify the crisis of 1796–7 in which Coleridge cast off as inadequate the post-Newtonian defences of revealed religion and moved towards an idealist solution.

Goldmann, in expanding Lukács's notion of the tragic vision, deliberately discovered his own method in those of whom he writes: the dialectical element he locates in Kant and reads back to Pascal is for him comfortably at one with his marxist dialectics. I am not altogether persuaded by this as a method of analysis, though it is undeniably enticing as a mode of critical empathy and a way to a unified style. In the present case, the kind of philosophical thinking which lies behind the achievements of Biblical criticism at the beginning of the nineteenth century also forms part of the history of the analysis of 'consciousness' which Lukács and Goldmann have practised; indeed, Feuerbach's critique of religion, treated here as the major influence, with Strauss, on George Eliot, brings us straight to Marx himself.

It becomes evident too that the emergence of a modern form of religious belief within and through the higher criticism is one of the most conspicuous illustrations of the Hegelian conception of 'false consciousness', a study in the meaning of that phrase. Such conceptions can have their full meaning now only within a theory like Lukács's of reification or within Sartre's psychoanalytic technique. But the un-folding of this theme in the technical context of the higher critical views of the authorship of the Fourth Gospel should be of interest to those aware of the use of the conception of false consciousness in a variety of modern works, both as an analytic tool and as a literary model. And it is particularly important to see Victorian 'hypocrisy' as inseparable from the history of modernism, Browning and George Eliot from Gide and Brecht. We may see in this, moreover, a source not only of the brilliant reconstructive Protestant theology of the present century, but of all those efforts across a variety of disciplines, including natural science, to view language itself as the sole residence of truth.

Yet this continuity ought, it seems to me, to be a warning and a call to self-analysis rather than an affirmation of the method. In giving the history of our own thought, we must give a critique of our own thought, not a justification of the past in our own terms. I abstain, then, from the unquestioned use of the staple terms of their analysis (including such dilute forms as Raymond Williams's 'structure of feeling'), which raise the ghosts of insoluble dilemmas of particular schools of philosophy.

Foucault again suggests a solution: his critique of modern medical psychology implies his own critical standpoint, but arises directly out of his historical analysis of the origins of modern psychology. In the same way, I would hope, the historical analysis of the roots of modern Biblical criticism is a critique of all 'positive' claims for the objectivity of the interpretation of texts, Biblical or poetic. In this sense, all terms of formal analysis must always be abolished by their very use; and this, rather than an easy continuity of styles, must be the criterion of the autonomy of the created whole.

It may be that consideration of the methods of the textual critics (even in more detail than has been possible here) will serve both to further and to make more precise in new ways the immense expansion of the meaning of 'text' that has been accomplished by semiology. If in our time 'text' has been liberated from 'writing' and become a system of signs, so in that period text was liberated from the letter of divine inspiration and became a system of human significances. That social criticism should be conducted according to the same canons as Biblical criticism would have been congenial to the men of whom we speak in this book, and indeed it was part of their own armoury. 'Le commentaire est entré dans le texte': this is Sainte-Beuve, speaking of Ballanche.

For Goldmann, the 'possible consciousness' of a period (a notion he is prepared to call 'the principal instrument of scientific thinking in the human sciences'), is expressed in its highest artistic works: these are the limits of a class's achievement. Lukács, more interestingly, holds that 'class-consciousness' itself is opposed to the actual self-awareness of a class at any given time – as Goldmann points out, 'class-consciousness' is for Lukács 'apocalyptic'. It seems to me most useful to think of 'possible consciousness' as what might have been accomplished by any particular class without altering its nature; and this can be read at the margins of a period, as Georges Bataille and Barthes have read Balzac's story 'Sarrasine' as a 'limit-text' in which extreme possibilities open out into the future. Thus one can consider not only the fixed, the summarizing, the central, but the tentative, open extremes, the violent outbreak of the new, even in the midst of the centre. It is in this sense that my analysis often touches on the genre problems of more traditional literary history, for in these forms we find the best analogy with the other structures disengaged for analysis. The continuing concern with genres may be seen as the continuity of French literary history, despite the tone of the revolt of the modern purveyed by Barthes, and indeed as the continuity of aesthetic idealism, where genres are strictly parallel to, and expressive of, the development of consciousness, whether paradigmatically analysed as in Schelling or historically emergent as in Hegel. If this traditional approach is maintained and justified historically by its link with the poets here under discussion in a way that may seem theoretically unjustified (in so far as I have said that after all one's terminology must not be continuous with the situation under analysis), at least we shall examine the genres at their moments of greatest flux and uncertainty, as fixities and densities in the process of transformation, and so closest to abolition.

This is not to say that I espouse Raymond Williams's notion that 'changing structures of feeling' normally precede more recognizable changes of formal ideal, belief, and institution. I doubt whether 'structures of feeling' are separable from formalized change, and if they are, whether the question of priority is capable of solution. In practice, moreover, Williams's view leads to an all too familiar evasion of the

11

need for full analysis of formal changes. Nevertheless, the example of 'Kubla Khan' invites us to hold that on the one hand it is true that the advance to new forms takes place spontaneously, unconsciously, and that the critical justification for it comes later (in Coleridge's case, more than fifteen years later), and yet, on the other hand, that the advance is made possible by prolonged and painstaking thought directed precisely at the nodal points of intellectual difficulty of the period. At the same time, we must be aware that this is the romantics' own model of the creative process (which was itself part of the justification for the advanced form): in another period, the model, and the experience, like the form, might be quite different. As Leavis has rightly said, 'Coleridge was at the fine point of consciousness of his age.'

This approach to genre in the romantic period expresses my conviction that the radical break with the past came at that time, and not with the advent of 'modernism', however defined – in short, with 'Kubla Khan' and the lyric of Hölderlin, rather than with Poe or with Lautréamont's 'Chants de Maldoror' (1869). It is not accidental that Hegel, employing the aesthetic categories of romanticism, was able to predict with such accuracy the whole course of art since his time: its history was implicit in the art of his own day, its theory in his own.

Moreover, it is thus that we can see that the challenge to realism which critics have found in modern poetry must be located in the romantic movement. It is not surprising from this point of view, though it must be from their own, that Barthes and Sollers have found their text in Balzac, according to accepted categories the greatest of realist novelists. The scope of the nineteenth-century novel has been misunderstood and unduly limited by the placing of its achievement under the rubric of realism. The novel did not simply continue the realistic thread within romanticism, or inherit the functions of the 'objective' or Homeric epic, but carried on the complex but indissoluble connection between the extension of consciousness in all directions and the definition of the moment of realism within this extension. The novel is subjective or 'sentimental' epic in Schiller's terms, as well as a reconstruction (itself a subjective process) of a naïve or objective epic. In so far as epic itself ran into the lyrical impulse, indeed, the novel came to epic through the epic as lyric. The neglect, the dismissal, of Goethe's overarching achievement in *Wilhelm Meister* and

12

its influence on the English novel is one of the scandals of our criticism. It is in George Eliot, and most fully in her final, and, in this perspective, her greatest novel, *Daniel Deronda*, that these themes come to expression in a new form.

Only within such a newly considered and coherent whole can the enterprise of comparative literature be conducted, for comparative literature pulls apart the unconsidered groupings offered by the literary history of any one nation, where the sheerest geographical and temporal contiguity substitutes for serious interpretative tools. What looks self-evident within a familiar local context – the received schools, sources and analogues, influences, background events – is called in question when the same enterprise (logically no more and no less justified) is extended across national boundaries. The merest attempt to conduct the inquiry as 'comparative' reveals how little our familiarity with a period begins to comprehend or absorb or exhaust it, and how often even comparative enterprises suffer from established contiguities. To cite just one standard technique of comparative literature, the consideration of personal influences through actual encounters, the present attempt to examine the dissemination of Biblical criticism shows that such accepted treatments as Eudo Mason's *Deutsche und englische Romantik*, which confine themselves to encounters between literary men, overlook the wider contacts, religious, political, scientific, which may be even more decisive. The literary relations between England and Germany are illuminated by just the nexus of Biblical criticism, the new historical outlook, and the interest in folk literatures. And indeed the examination opens the way to comparison with works that ought to be known as a matter of course to specialists in the period, but often are not (Klopstock), as well as to comparison of works that would not normally be seen to be comparable (Coleridge and Hölderlin). One of the contributions of marxist critics has been to establish one kind at least of broader context in which European comparative literature could be carried on; more recently, the semiological critics have sought a more flexible way of creating the right context for a given analysis, and this together with structural anthropology offers the possibility of a still more widely-ranging comparative literature. But these are possibilities so far only barely adumbrated. To some extent the problem is merely one of persuasion, of bringing a provincial audience (and all of us are provincials) to regard the familiar as alien, and the alien as familiar. But one hopes that the increased awareness of method required for comparative literature will find its way back into the treatment of the 'great traditions' by their respective adherents.

It may be – I suggest this tentatively – that the view of 'Orientalism' taken in this book could serve as a basis for comparison of European with non-European literatures. Perhaps the most striking result of the conjunction of Coleridge's poetic plans with Biblical criticism is a revision of our notions of the sources and meaning of poetic 'Orientalism'. Orientalism in European poetry is very much more than a fanciful and ignorant borrowing from the translations of the *Arabian Nights* that began to appear early in the eighteenth century, or from the tall stories of the travellers, or a taste for Chinese gardens or bric-à-brac. It is closely bound up with the new textual and historical scholarship exercised on the Bible since the Reformation, and drew on a very considerable body of new and challenging knowledge, geological, chronological, and anthropological, though its interpretation was still moulded by Christian apologetics; it is interwoven with a movement of thought that perhaps more than any other ushered in the modern world. If indeed it created a 'pseudo-Orient', it did so not as escapism, but on the contrary, as a subtle harmonizing of the urgently conflicting readings of the significance of primitive religious experience.

A new light, moreover, is thrown on 'romantic Hellenism'. The Hellenism associated with Bible studies was a very much wider phenomenon than the interest in Greek classical antiquity. Its concern was with the Hellenistic period, the immediate environment of early Christianity both before and after Christ, with the meeting and synthesis of cultures and ideas out of which emerged a distinctive Christian world view. 'Orientalism' was one aspect of this broad Hellenism. This is the context of Coleridge's interest in neo-platonism and his syncretic style, the means to the imaginative synthesis achieved in Hölderlin's mature odes, and the basis of the form of *Daniel Deronda*.

From this standpoint, 'Orientalism' can be seen in conjunction with first-rate literature of the eighteenth and nineteenth centuries, with Coleridge, Hölderlin, Browning, George Eliot – and Blake, Novalis, Hugo, Tennyson, Arnold, among others – with literature often not considered under this rubric at all, not merely with the second-

and third-rate Collins, Landor, Southey, Moore, Rückert. A European criticism can still approach the literature of other societies from the vantage point attained by these first-rate writers, aware that their own civilization rested upon myth as fully as non-Christian societies (often the same myths), and by this very awareness maintaining the centrality and efficaciousness of their own myths. It may be that today we do not wish to maintain the centrality or efficaciousness of our own myths, except through criticism itself (and this 'crisis' is only a logical development from the view of myth examined in this book); but if so, it is all the more imperative to have a criticism capable of expressing not a nerveless and unconvinced repetition of outmoded values, but a new and systematic will to equality of our own with other mythologies.

CHAPTER I

THE FALL OF JERUSALEM:
COLERIDGE'S UNWRITTEN EPIC

In a volume 'E Libris S. T. Coleridge' the young poet noted that he had paid 'half a guinea' for it at Priestley's, High Holborn, and a later comment, inscribed under this, records that he has 'had, for years, the first volume, among my Odd Books':

– I should have so filled the Margins before this time, that it would have been fairly worth the $10\frac{1}{2}$ Blood-drops wrung from the pinched Hippocratic Nose of my Poverty (£0 , , 10 , , 6) to any Friend of mine of an Apocalyptic Turn – but the villanous [sic] paper, the spongy Goodwin Sands, that would suck in a Galleon of Ink-wit, baffled every attempt tho' you may still see sundry black Wrecks hulking shapeless in the Margins.[1]

The volume was J. G. Eichhorn's *Commentarius in Apocalypsin Joannis* (Göttingen, 1791), *Commentary on the Apocalypse of John*, and Coleridge, as was his habit, had in fact blacked the margins of another copy of the work (bound together with the second volume) with comments for which Coleridge's friends would gladly pay in blood-drops. For these notes on Eichhorn's interpretation of the Book of Revelation illuminate Coleridge's poetic plans, cherished and reiterated throughout his life, for the 'last possible' epic, *The Fall of Jerusalem*, and reveal the sources of the splendour and sheer magnitude which readers have always sensed in 'Kubla Khan'.

Eichhorn's Latin commentary, following a suggestion of Herder, his close friend, interprets the Book of Revelation as a dramatic poem, in the style of the Hebrew Apocalyptics, depicting the events of the historical fall of Jerusalem in A.D. 68–9. Eichhorn provides at the beginning a breakdown of the Book of Revelation into acts and scenes and sets out his detailed commentary on each verse under its dramatic heading. The 'grand prophetic drama', as Coleridge called it, has three acts.[2] In Act One, 'Jerusalem falls, or Judaism is conquered by the Christian religion.' In Act Two, 'Rome falls, or the Gentiles are conquered by the Christian religion.' In Act Three, 'The heavenly Jerusalem descends from the sky, or the bliss of future life which will endure forever is described.' Together these might suggest a *Divine Comedy*. Coleridge's notes, however, refer almost wholly to Act One, and there is other reason to suppose that his epic would have employed the historical events of the fall of Jerusalem to show the recreation of the ancient religious constitution of man in the new Jerusalem.

He first conceived of a full-scale epic, based, according to neo-classic precepts, on history, though history interpreted in a symbolic way; in the event, he produced something even more radical than a symbolic epic, an apocalyptic one, in which the entire action is concentrated, past and present and future, into one moment of vision expressed in wholly lyrical style. Coleridge's notes suggest that 'Kubla Khan' is based on his epic plan, and that his 'dreamwork' condensed the three Acts of the Apocalypse into the climactic moment of the First Act, when the sixth seal is opened. It is no wonder he never set pen to paper to write the 'last possible' epic; he himself had already gone beyond it and made it impossible. Nor is the Orientalism of the poem accidental or factitious; it is intimately connected with the world in which an epic fall of Jerusalem could still be conceived, but could no longer be executed as such. In 'Kubla Khan' we see before our eyes the translation of the two major classical genres, epic and drama, into their most romantic form. Kenneth Burke has remarked that

Yvor Winters' label, 'Reference to a non-existent plot', to characterize such usages as Eliot's in 'Gerontion', 'By Hakagawa, bowing among the Titians', helps us see that Coleridge's poem was already moving towards a later elliptical manner, at a time when Southey could have turned 'Kubla Khan' into a work as long as *The Ring and the Book*. In this sense, the poem was a fragment.[3]

We may indeed attribute it to Coleridge's prescience as a poet, his fine tact for the genuine and the possible, that he refrained from writing yet another Biblical epic; but the plot was still existent, and Coleridge did conceive of a poem that would have been as long as Southey's epics, or Cottle's Old Testament epic *Messiah: a poem in*

Twenty-Eight Books (1815), or *The Holy Baptist: a Scriptural Poem in
Five Cantos* (1843), just as Keats conceived first of a full-scale Miltonic
Hyperion, and only by default, as it seemed to him, produced a dream-
vision, just as Chénier wrote his unfinished epic *Hermès*, to him
merely a prose outline interspersed with lyrical fragments, which
enjoyed a brilliant later career as an 'Orphic epic'. The critical justification of the epic fragment was arrived at only after composition and
accompanied by a painful sensation of failure. In all these cases, the
'elliptical manner' could as yet be achieved only elliptically. Coleridge
retained a nostalgia for his original intention that obscured his real
achievement:

I have since my twentieth year meditated on an heroic poem on the Siege of
Jerusalem by Titus – this is the Pride, & the Stronghold of my Hope. But I
never think of it except in my best moods.[4]

'Kubla Khan' was written in a day, as Jerusalem fell in a day; but the
alteration of genre, like adjustment to loss, requires a protracted re-
education of consciousness. The conception of 'event' itself had to
alter before the epic fragment could be recognized as a form.

Coleridge's mind in the 1790s seethed with plans for works of
magnitude: the *Joan of Arc*, a historical, indeed a political, epic; the
epic *Mohammed* in hexameters; *The Wanderings of Cain*, corresponding to Goethe's proposed epic of 'Ahasuerus', the wandering Jew.
Much that Coleridge actually completed was connected with these
large projects: 'The Destiny of Nations' with the *Joan*, 'The Ancient
Mariner' with *The Wanderings of Cain*. And he wrote two dramas,
Remorse and *Zapolya*, whose links with the other works and with the
Book of Revelation were pointed out long ago by Wilson Knight.[5]
Of all these projects, however, the one that seems to have been nearest
his heart was *The Fall of Jerusalem*.

Coleridge had planned his great epic 'in his earliest days', and it was
still table-talk with him shortly before his death. His subject was to
have been *The Fall of Jerusalem:* for it is 'the only subject now left
for an epic poem of the highest kind'.[6]

Herder appears to have been the first to suggest, in a 1774 draft of
Maran Atha, that the Book of Revelation was the historical reaction
of the aged Apostle John to the destruction of Jerusalem and referred
to events during the reign of Nero.[7] Revelation had traditionally

been considered a cosmological 'history of the world', as well as a history of civilization and of the Church, and had time and again been considered a description of current events heralding the end of the world. The detailed reference to historical events in the first century A.D. is the basis of all modern interpretation of Revelation, though it is now thought to refer in an even more complex way to events of the time of the Book's composition, under Domitian or Trajan (A.D. 96–8), as well as to the destruction of Jerusalem.

De Quincey once remarked that 'the best notion I can give of Herder to the English reader is to say that he is the German Coleridge'.[8] Unwelcome as this might have been to Coleridge, whose notes often betray considerable irritation at Herder, there is no doubt that Herder's inventive enthusiasm often moved the more painstaking and scholarly Eichhorn to transform Herder's aesthetic insights into principles of criticism, as Coleridge was able to transform Eichhorn's principles into new aesthetic insights, indeed, a new poetry.

Herder's interest in Oriental poetry (among many other things) was intense, and his translations into unrhymed verse and oratorio (unlike Eichhorn's more pedestrian metrical translation of the Book of Job) were included in English anthologies of German poetry, with Goethe, Schiller, and Klopstock, throughout the nineteenth century.[9] His critical work *Vom Geist der ebräischen Poesie* (1782), *The Spirit of Hebrew Poetry*, took its cue from Robert Lowth's *Lectures on the Sacred Poetry of the Hebrews* (delivered in Latin 1749–50), which for the first time considered the Old Testament simply as literature, as Oriental literature.[10] As Meinecke has remarked, 'Lowth's book was perhaps the most significant intellectual achievement of the entire pre-romantic movement in England. Without intending to do so, he nevertheless contributed to the liberation of historical research from the bonds of theology, in that it brought the purely human and historical content and value of the Bible into view.'[11]

Of course, the comparison of the Scriptures, especially the Old Testament, with other Oriental religions was not new; Spinoza himself in the *Tractatus Theologico-politicus*, a seminal book in the development of the higher criticism, had dismissed the claim to inspiration as a piece of characteristically Oriental hyperbole, and the denigration of Christianity through its equation with the other Oriental religions became a favourite tactic of the Enlightenment. A phrase from Bayle will illustrate: he ranged the rationalists against 'Les Religionnaires (Permettez-moi de me servir de ce mot pour désigner en commun les Juifs, les Payens, les Chrétiens, les Mahometans, etc.)'.[12] When the Christians are distinguished from the other Oriental religionists, it is to the advantage of the Oriental sage or the happy pagan or the gnostic heretic.

Voltaire's remarks under 'Abraham' in his *Philosophical Dictionary*, the book that led the schoolboy Coleridge into the 'deserts of infidelity', nicely illustrate the technique of negative mythologizing (and the tone of levity):

'Abraham' est un de ces noms célèbres dans l'Asie mineure, et dans l'Arabie, comme Thaut chez les Egyptiens, le premier Zoroastre dans la Perse, Hercule en Grèce, Orphée dans la Thrace, Odin chez les nations septentrionales, et tant d'autres plus connus par leur célébrité, que par une histoire bien avérée.[13]

It remained for the apologists for Christianity to draw these same parallels in a positive spirit.

Herder and Eichhorn carried Lowth's work further. 'Eichhorn set the tone to his successors, by whom the Hebrew Scriptures were constantly treated, not merely as the vehicle of a revelation, but as in form Oriental books, to be interpreted in accordance with the habits of mind of Semitic peoples.'[14] Moreover, they soon extended the secular interpretation to the New Testament: 'It is from Eichhorn and his more celebrated friend Herder that the custom of referring to the "Orientalism" of the Scriptures is mainly derived.'[15] The orthodox belief in the uniqueness of the Scriptures and their 'inspiration' by God was substantially undermined by treating the books of the Bible as examples of Oriental literature.

If the books of the Old and New Testament were examples of Oriental literature, Herder with characteristic panache treated all modern Biblical poetry, for instance, Klopstock's epic, *Der Messias*, *The Messiah*, on the last days of Christ, as examples of contemporary Oriental poetry, 'Christian poetry in the Oriental taste'. Coleridge's epic *The Fall of Jerusalem* would have been by the same token an Oriental poem.[16]

What did Coleridge know of Eichhorn before he went to Göttingen in 1798? A preliminary question may be simply: Who is Eichhorn?

Eichhorn has never enjoyed the general renown his achievements merit, and he has been especially unlucky in England. His predecessor in the chair of Philosophy, J. D. Michaelis, 'a chief intermediary between English and German scholarship', had many English acquaintances and was instrumental in the translation of a number of influential English works, including Lowth's, to which he drew Herder's attention; Michaelis's *Einleitung in das Neue Testament, Introduction to the New Testament*, was translated by Herbert Marsh, who had studied with him in Leipzig, and read by Coleridge in 1795.[17] In the 1780s and the first years of the 1790s there was considerable interest in, and knowledge of, the German Biblical criticism; but as the political climate darkened, Biblical criticism fell under the general ban of radical opinions. A plan for translating Eichhorn, proposed by Marsh, later Professor of Divinity at Cambridge, and A. H. Lloyd, Professor of Hebrew, foundered for lack of subscribers in 1798–9. To this day there has been no translation of Eichhorn's work. The consequence has been a distorted view of the history of the higher criticism and of its reception in England, and a misreading of Victorian intellectual history. On the assumption that the publication of the partial translation of Niebuhr by Julius Hare and Connop Thirlwall in the late 1820s and George Eliot's imposing translation of Strauss in 1835 initiated the English reception of the higher criticism, attempts have been made to isolate a 'pure Coleridgean' strand in Victorian theological thought to set off against the 'German' strand.[18] This attempt is completely misconceived; the principles on which Strauss worked had already been evolved by 1795, and they were fully incorporated into Coleridge's own thought. The later theological work of Coleridge indeed ranges far beyond Strauss, and has never been appreciated for what it is; but it is built on precisely the same foundations as Strauss's.

'Eichhorn was probably the greatest single source in Coleridge's exegetical background', as Fr Barth rightly pointed out in *Coleridge and Christian Doctrine*[19] (though this is the only reference to Eichhorn in the book). As Coleridge himself put it, in recommending to his son Derwent Eichhorn's introductions to the Old Testament, the New Testament, and the Apocrypha, together with his commentary on the Apocalypse, 'these will suffice for your *Biblical* Learning'.[20]

It is not surprising that Eichhorn's commentary should have suggested to Coleridge the union of the sublime Biblical poem with the neo-classical historical epic. Eichhorn, often called the founder of modern Biblical criticism, or, as Coleridge put it, 'founder and head of the daring school', the first to use the phrase 'die höhere kritik', the 'higher criticism', was as much a man of letters as a theologian. He was Professor of Oriental Languages at Jena and it was as an Orientalist that he approached the study of the Old Testament; his earliest writings were on Mohammedan history and Arabic and Syriac literature. His *Einleitung in das Alte Testament, Introduction to the Old Testament* (1780–3), was the first full demonstration of the higher critical method. Coleridge recorded, in a series of notes on these volumes, his full agreement with Eichhorn's general conclusions while suggesting the direction of his own contributions to the new criticism. Eichhorn went to Göttingen, where he lectured on a great range of subjects, historical, literary, and Biblical; for years he was the only lecturer in literary history. He pursued his Orientalism also as a member of the famous Philological Seminar of the classical scholar C. G. Heyne, who did so much to forward the literary study of mythology; the Seminar was one of the great attractions of Göttingen, and drew more than one generation of literary men, including A. W. Schlegel and Coleridge. The connections among Oriental scholarship, Biblical criticism, and poetry were close indeed; Goethe, who in the notes to the *West-östlicher Divan, West-eastern Divan*, paid such handsome tribute to the English Orientalist, Sir William Jones, recalled gratefully that Eichhorn had introduced him to the works of Jones.

During the 1790s Eichhorn published a series of articles extending his treatment of Genesis as Oriental myth to certain parts of the New Testament. At the time Coleridge encountered him in Göttingen, he was lecturing over this dangerous ground. The full results were published only in the nineteenth century, in his *Einleitung in das Neue Testament, Introduction to the New Testament* (1804–18); so that Coleridge's knowledge in 1798 was actually ahead of the published work in Germany.[21] His commentary on Revelation formed part of his efforts throughout the 1790s to treat the New Testament according to the same principles as the Old. It is probable that this book gave Coleridge his first direct acquaintance with Eichhorn's method, as it was written in Latin and therefore accessible before Coleridge's knowledge of German was sufficient to enable him to read the *Einleitung in das Alte Testament*.

Coleridge's knowledge of German textual criticism of the Bible dated in all probability from his earliest Unitarian contacts at Cambridge. A new translation of the Bible had been planned by Priestley and his associates and announced in a *Prospectus* as early as 1788; William Frend, with whom Coleridge was in close association in Cambridge, was one of the major contributors, being responsible for the historical books of the Old Testament. Materials for it were destroyed in the Birmingham Riots of 1791, just as Coleridge came up to Jesus College. The 'Unitarian Bible' was finally published only in 1808 and was based not on a translation by Unitarian hands, as first planned, but on Bishop Newcome's translation of Johann Jakob Griesbach's text of the New Testament (1774–5); the introduction gives a compact but well-informed summary of German textual criticism, information that was widely disseminated among Priestley's collaborators during the period of preparation.

Of the wider implications of the new criticism Coleridge must also have known a good deal even before he became acquainted with the Beddoes circle in Bristol, and through Beddoes with the work of Michaelis, Lessing, Semler, and Eichhorn. There were a number of available sources in or near the Unitarian movement.

The Unitarian movement had a special affinity for Biblical criticism that needs exploration against the background of its well-charted contributions to social and political liberty. A reconstructive textual criticism was of course necessary to the full statement of the Unitarian interpretation of early Christian history formulated during the eighteenth century: the Bible itself had to yield evidence of the Unitarian (non-Trinitarian) nature of the first, pristine Christianity. This was connected with the struggle against priestcraft and obscurantism and increasingly against political oppression, the state and ecclesiastical authorities who had concealed the true nature of the text. The Unitarians were part of that group of Dissenters who have been identified as the bearers of the English Enlightenment, the group typified by Joseph Priestley and his friends, philosophic, scientific, and technological innovators closely allied to the growth of manufacturing industry in the eighteenth century, industrious, ambitious men, political radicals and religious liberals; these men, theists still, gave a resounding 'No' to the question that Schleiermacher would pose, 'Is the tangle of history to be unravelled by linking Christianity with barbarism and science with unbelief?' The science of criticism would be a weapon of the apologists when the work of destruction was done, and it was substantially done by the end of the eighteenth century: the recognition that orthodox Christian doctrine was mythological in character became the central position of the new theology of the nineteenth century. Criticism was 'internalized', as Welch has said, in theology after 1800: there was no other tenable defence. In the light of detailed studies of the relation between religious and political attitudes, for example E. P. Thompson's *The Making of the English Working Class*, a study of Methodism among the working classes of England, it is significant that German Biblical criticism was particularly in vogue among the predominantly middle-class Unitarians, while the working-class radicals not only at the time of the Revolution but throughout the nineteenth century continued to take their inspiration from French sources, De La Mettrie, Voltaire, and especially Volney. This cleavage was noticeable in Coleridge's immediate circle: Tom Poole, Coleridge's good friend near Bristol, the prosperous tanner, took up the French cause, learnt French, started a French book circle, and distressed his neighbours with his radical opinions. In this political context we must understand Coleridge's vigorous denial in 1822 that Volney's *Ruins of Empire* had ever influenced him; yet it was Volney's doctrine in more palatable form that he found in the school of mythological criticism. The German criticism was learned and technical, unsuitable to serve as the handbook of a working-class movement as Volney's Chapter 15 did; moreover, it was susceptible of many interpretations, among them a revisionist reform from within that left ecclesiastical and political institutions apparently intact, and real power where it was before. From the 1830s in England knowledge of the most advanced Continental scholarship was a stick to beat the Anglican academic Establishment, pictured by Unitarian journals as sunk in parochial ignorance, sloth, and obscurantism; but wherever it was accepted by the Establishment the new criticism gave rise to a flourishing new movement in theology of which the 'de-mythologizing' of the present century is only the latest phase. The nature of this mode of thinking tells us much about the double face of political Romanticism, and even more about the nature of the Victorian compromise. From one point of view it might be seen as a major intellectual monument to bourgeois hypocrisy. These tortuous apologetics were deeply congenial to Coleridge's temperament. Unitarianism, then, led Coleridge directly to the German higher criticism; the mythological school of German higher criticism enabled him to move away from the immediate reformist concerns of the radicals and towards a new apologetics that ultimately he would use to transform Anglicanism and make it viable for another century.

The leading Unitarian Thomas Belsham, founder of the Unitarian Book Society in 1791, and principal editor of the Bible, was one of the first in England to accept the results of the new Biblical criticism: composite authorship of the Pentateuch, the unhistorical nature of stories of miraculous birth, the unscientific, that is the mythological, nature of the creation story.

In 1792, moreover, Coleridge read the works of Nathaniel Lardner (1684–1768), a Nonconformist who, while his own professions were conservative, had incorporated the results of Continental scholarship into his work and often exercised a radical influence. Lardner was much respected in Unitarian circles and his works were used in the preparation of the new Bible.

The fullest and most widely publicized accounts of recent German Biblical criticism were those of the Roman Catholic Biblical critic, Alexander Geddes. In 1792 he published the first volume of his new translation of the Bible (announced as early as 1786 and supported by Bishop Lowth and a number of highly placed subscribers). After his European tour in 1783, Geddes had written to his cousin:

In Germany almost every man of learning is an Orientalist. In short, Sacred Criticism is everywhere the predominant study of the learned of all communions who seem to vie with one another which shall do most towards restoring the Scriptures to their primitive purity or as near to it as possible.[22]

Geddes's first publications, his *Prospectus* (1786), his *Proposals and Specimens* (1798), and the first volume of the Bible were widely and on the whole favourably reviewed, in England and in Germany. *The Monthly Review* praised him for interpreting the Bible as he would any other ancient literature. The current notion of Biblical inspiration, the reviewer remarked, had hitherto prevented many readers from assessing the merits of the Scriptures as literary compositions. The reviewer perceived the nascent apologetic possibilities of the new criticism, pointing out that Geddes's views on the Hebrew cosmogony of

Genesis rescued Moses from the attack of modern philosophers. *The Critical Review* also praised it, quoting the translation rather than the critical remarks. *The British Critic*, on the other hand, noticed indignantly the denial of inspiration and the interpretation of the early history of the Bible as mythology. This was, said the reviewer, how Dr Priestley spoke; it was alarming to think that the teaching on the origin of evil or the Sabbath observance might rest on a myth or fabulous history. Michaelis had reviewed Geddes's earlier publications in detail in the *Neue Orientalische und Exegetische Bibliothek*, *New Oriental and Exegetical Library*; now Eichhorn took up the task, and remarked approvingly on how closely Geddes's 'clear and enlightened ideas' on the Semitic cosmogonies approached to the progressive outlook of the German critics.[23]

Relations between Geddes and the Unitarians became more intimate as Geddes's opinions became more radical, and censure within his own communion increased. In 1787 Geddes and Priestley had been in controversy in a series of letters on the divinity of Christ. But in the early 1790s, Geddes gathered a circle of Unitarian friends – Dr John Disney, Dr John Mason Good, Theophilus Lindsey, George Dyer, and Gilbert Wakefield, who had been working on a translation of the New Testament; when Priestley came to London from Birmingham, Geddes met him. Some of these men were members of the Chapter Coffee House, started by Holcroft and Frend, and it was there that Dyer met Coleridge in 1794. Coleridge reported to Southey that in the list of subscribers to his proposed *Imitations from the Modern Latin Poets* 'I hear there are the names of Parr, Disney, Lindsay, Wakefield, and Bowles.'[24] His letters to Dyer in 1795–6 and to John Prior Estlin show that he knew Wakefield, had indeed made the acquaintance of Disney, and continued to send his 'affectionate Regards to Mr Frend'.[25]

The contacts among the radicals were undoubtedly more extensive than literary history has documented. Blake's acquaintance with these circles is well known (although the effects of the new criticism on his use of Biblical materials has never been explored). Wordsworth felt he had reason to minimize the intimacy of his acquaintance with Godwin; yet Godwin's diaries have shown that Wordsworth visited him repeatedly in 1794. It is probable that Coleridge met Geddes personally in 1794, perhaps in the Chapter Coffee House, as he met

Dyer; it is certain that he met Geddes before leaving for Germany, for he carried a letter of introduction from Geddes to Dr Paulus, the head of the German rationalist theologians, at Heidelberg.[26] Paulus had made an extensive stay in London in 1789, when he met Geddes. The letter, marked 'Favour of Mr Coleridge', now resides in the University library at Heidelberg.

If Coleridge had read nothing but the reviews of Geddes's Bible, he would have had a tolerable idea of the main heads of the new criticism; if he read Geddes, as it is hard to conceive he did not, he had an excellent conspectus of the higher criticism as it had developed in the hands of Herder and Eichhorn. Although Geddes did not in every respect follow Eichhorn, he was highly praised in Germany for his full knowledge of the German scholarship, and continued to be championed by Eichhorn himself after opinion in England had turned against him. Coleridge, then, was able without any German to form a quite accurate view of Eichhorn's previous work, both the *Einleitung in das Alte Testament* and the early paper on the mythological view of Genesis.[27]

Coleridge's association with Thomas Beddoes was a decisive one, for it opened to him Beddoes's intimate acquaintance with German literature, the resources of his private library of Continental books and periodicals, and his personal friendships with German scholars and scientists, in particular the Göttingen circle that had centred on Michaelis and after his death on Eichhorn. Coleridge's debt to Beddoes was not solely intellectual; as Beddoes made a place for the young Davy in his Pneumatic Institute, so it was on his recommendation that Wedgwood helped Coleridge to a reporter's job and afterwards set up the annuity for him.[28] It was with his encouragement that Coleridge undertook *The Watchman*, and in publishing Beddoes's piece on Pitt in the third number, Coleridge wrote:

To announce a work from the pen of Dr Beddoes is to inform the benevolent in every city and parish that they are appointed agents to some new and practicable scheme for increasing the comforts or alleviating the miseries of their fellow-creatures.[29]

Coleridge's heartfelt letters on Beddoes's death in 1808 show his respect, gratitude, and love, and are in marked contrast to some public notices that recalled him as an atheist.

Coleridge wrote to Davy, who was equally in Beddoes's debt, demonstrating his grief and regretting that the biography of Beddoes was not to be entrusted to him:

My dear Davy

I was deeply affected by the passage in your letter respecting Dr Beddoes. It was indeed the echo of my own experience. The intelligence of his departure from among us came upon me abruptly, and unexpectedly. I was sitting down to dinner, having quitted an unfinished sheet which I had been writing in answer to a long and affectionate Letter from the Doctor. There was indeed a depth and a flow of feeling in it, which filled me with bodings, but I had no thought that the event was so near at hand. The Note, therefore, sent from one of his Patients, who had placed himself at Clifton by mine & Wordsworth's advice, the day after his decease, struck me like a bodily blow, & was followed by long and loud convulsive weeping with scarce any inward Suffering – but when some half hour after I recovered myself, and my tears flowed slowly and with grief more worthy of the cause, I felt that more Hope had been taken out of my life by this than by any former Event. For Beddoes was good and beneficent to all men; but to me he had always been kind and affectionate, and latterly I had become attached to him with a personal tenderness. The Death of Mr Thomas Wedgwood pulled hard at my heart; I am sure, no week of my life – almost I might have said – scarce a day in which I have not been made either sad or thoughtful by the recollection. But Dr Beddoes's Death has pulled yet harder: probably because it came second – likewise too perhaps, that I had not been in the habit of connecting such oppression of despondency with my love of Him. There are two things, which I exceedingly wished, and in both have been disappointed: to have written the Life and prepared the psychological Remains of my revered Friend and Benefactor, T. W: and to have been entrusted with the Biography &c of Dr B. –[30]

Stimulated by Beddoes, Coleridge began to study German and planned his trip to Germany, discarding the Jena of Schiller for the Göttingen of Blumenbach and Eichhorn.[31] Before Beddoes had lost his readership in chemistry at Oxford through his sympathy with the French Revolution, he had addressed a 'Memorial' to the Librarian of the Bodleian, deploring the failure to acquire the important Continental works of the time. He named Haller, Meiners, and Heyne (his admiration for Heyne reappears again and again in his writings), and he exclaimed:

But how can such writers as Jerusalem, Doederlein, Michaelis, Reimarus, Mendelssohn, or Lessing be searched for new arguments on either side, while our highpriests of learning take no care to introduce their offering into her temples.[32]

These, of course, were the leaders of the German Enlightenment; and Beddoes himself, whose works were extensively reviewed in Germany and read even by Kant, was admiringly referred to as an *Aufklärungsmesser*, 'a gauge of Enlightenment', testing at every point his countrymen's readiness to receive further illumination.[33] Beddoes's own library included more than 1,000 works, mainly Continental, and a large number of periodicals, especially those emanating from Göttingen.[34]

Coleridge too came in for his share of critical notice in the German reviews. Reviewing *The Monk* in *The Critical Review*, he called attention to its derivation from Schiller's novella, *Der Geisterseher*, *The Ghost-seer*, but predicted that the sensational, although useful for German literature in its infancy, would surely be abandoned at a later stage of development.[35] The implied slur drew a reply from the editor Böttiger in a piece on foreign judgements of German literature in the *Neuer Teutscher Merkur* ('Wie urteilt das Ausland über teutscher Literatur?').[36] He pointed out the favourable review of Voss's *Luise* in the Supplement for May and August of *The Critical Review*, and remarked dryly that perhaps the Germans were not so far behind after all, as the English, to judge by Beddoes's essay, experienced such difficulties in understanding Kant. In these early exchanges, Coleridge's lifelong activity as intermediary between German and English culture began. He was not unique; the ground was well prepared for him, not by Beddoes alone, but by the dissenting milieu of which Beddoes was a part.

Through Beddoes, Coleridge was able to follow the current work of Eichhorn and his pupil Gabler in the theological journals, the extension of the mythological view to much of the Old Testament and the New. Beddoes, devoted to the Göttingen circle, could have given him a succinct, accurate, and dramatic account of developments, and from 1796 he was studying German himself. The reports of acquaintances from Germany in 1798 that Coleridge was respected by Eichhorn as a worthy disputant in Biblical critical matters were fully justified by Coleridge's knowledge and the progress of his own ideas.

Through Beddoes, Coleridge learnt to know Lessing as 'the most formidable infidel of them all', to know, that is, whose arguments he must answer if he was to construct a new defence of Christianity. Watson's *Apology for the Bible* might be accepted as an adequate reply to Paine, he wrote in April 1796,

but the most formidable Infidel is Lessing, the author of 'Emilia Galotti'; – I ought to have written *was*, for he is dead. His book is not yet translated, and is entitled, in German, 'Fragments of an Anonymous Author'. It unites the wit of Voltaire with the subtlety of Hume and the profound erudition of *our* Lardner. I had some thoughts of translating it with an Answer, but gave it up.[37]

These fragments, *Fragmente eines Ungenannten,* were the notorious *Wolfenbüttel Fragmente,* which aroused furious controversy in Germany in the 1780s. They were published by Lessing as written by another hand, but attributed by contemporaries to Lessing himself, though important sections were the work of Hermann Samuel Reimarus, teacher of Oriental languages in the Hamburg Gymnasium.

The context of Coleridge's interest was at once literary and theological. In the *Fragments* he had one of the most effective and historically important statements of the familiar 'impostor' theory of the nature of religious leadership, directed not, as in Bayle, at the Old Testament leaders, or, as in Prideaux, at Mohammed, but at Jesus and the apostles.[38]

The *Fragments* achieved a distillation of radical English deism and at the same time founded the investigation of 'the historical Jesus' that was a dominant concern of the higher criticism through the nineteenth century. Albert Schweitzer in *The Quest for the Historical Jesus* praises their 'grandiose historical achievement'. Although written in the sarcastic tone of the Enlightenment, the *Fragments* presented what became one of the most important apologetic themes: the reconstruction of primitive Christian history, of the Jewish milieu of Jesus, in order to sift what the apostles reported from what Jesus really said and taught during his lifetime. Jesus is portrayed as wholly Jewish, as assuming that his Messiahship implied worldly rule:

His thoughts were bent upon a grand entry into the city of Jerusalem, at the Passover, a time when all Israelites throughout Judea would be assembled there, and when it would be conducted in a festive manner, and when by the united voices of the populace he would be proclaimed King of the Jews.[39]

The *Fragments* point to the trickery of Jesus and John the Baptist, who are said to have pretended by prearrangement to visions; and to the trickery of the apostles, who, having tasted worldly power, stole Jesus's body from the grave and concocted the story of the resurrection.

Coleridge, then, in the mid-1790s was aware of the most extreme attacks on the historical factuality of both the Old Testament and the New, including the veracity of Christ himself, and he was aware of the new mythological approach to the Bible, which when it approached 'the historical Jesus' was to become at once the most formidable critical weapon and the foundation of a new apologetics. The view that Jesus was a purely mythological figure had been vividly stated in Volney's *Ruins of Empire* and in Dupuis's *Origine de tous les cultes* (both of which Coleridge had read by 1796), but without critical method and far from the context of Judaic history.

Coleridge's two major interests, Christian theology under the penetrating probes of Enlightenment criticism, and a new poetry of the supernatural, met in the need for a modern mythology. For Herder, Eichhorn, and Coleridge, the two interests were inseparable. Their common situation, if not their common character, was summed up shrewdly by G. H. Lewes: 'Herder had something of the Hebrew Prophet in him, but the Hebrew Prophet fallen upon Deistical times, with Spinoza and Lessing for teachers.'[40] Herder, Eichhorn, and Coleridge considered themselves 'critical apologists' for religion; but it was not easy for them to come to terms with the disintegrative effects of their own criticism. In order to salvage Christianity, historical criticism had to be made constructive as well as destructive; the result was a new form of history. If what was of prime importance was not the eternal message of the Gospels, but the particular historical circumstances of their origin, then these circumstances represented an enabling milieu in which sacred events of this kind could take place. If the sacred writings of other nations were examined in their historical setting, then one might arrive again at a general view of the conditions of religious experience. It was the work of several generations to grasp this possibility and to carry it out. But it was in such a mythologized history that the solution to both the literary and the religious problem was to be found.

We are dealing here not with an obscure or isolated phenomenon, but with the rise of the modern conception of history. As Herbert Butterfield has written of the new historical school of Göttingen, it offers 'the spectacle of the world as it stands on the brink of a great intellectual change'[41] – the change which brings us into the modern world. Although there were greater single figures elsewhere before and after – Winckelmann, for example, and Niebuhr – the Göttingen school was 'a broadly based movement exhibiting a continuous development', and from the 1760s onwards they speak as men who are conscious that they live in a new age of historical scholarship.[42] If the beginning of the new school can be dated from the appointment of J. C. Gatterer to the chair of History in 1759, it was in the field of Biblical studies that the new school had emerged, as the historians freely acknowledged. Many of them had been students of theology in the first place. Schlözer always quoted precedents for scholarly editions of German historical sources from Biblical or classical scholarship: 'the ideal examples are the critical editions of the NT, especially Griesbach's Greek testament', that work which the Unitarians used as the basis for their Bible. The Biblical scholars had expounded the rules; the historians followed suit. As Lord Acton pointed out in his well-known essay on 'German Schools of History', the critical method in historical study goes back to the Biblical and classical scholarship which before the rise of the German historical school of the late eighteenth century had been progressing at a faster pace than historical studies proper:

The truth of religion was so momentous an issue, and the controversies about it were so intense, that the critical methods were developing in ecclesiastical research before anybody thought of transposing them into the field of modern history.[43]

Or, as Acton put it even more succinctly, 'Kritik grew up on the lives of Saints'.[44] Although it rapidly applied itself to secular history, it continued to flourish in the area of ecclesiastical history well into the nineteenth century with F. C. Baur, whose *Die Epochen der kirchlichen Geschichtschreibung* (1853), *The Epochs of Church Historiography*, was a major work of the Tübingen school, and with Leopold von Ranke himself. English historians throughout the nineteenth century repeatedly expressed their indebtedness to the German historians.

Coleridge, then, in advancing into the critical school of Biblical studies, was indeed at the fine point of consciousness of his age. He was so far from being an antiquarian that he became an adherent of that school of history which abolished antiquarian research into 'evidences' of the truth of each separate event, whether Christian or secular, in favour of 'a new notion, both exacting and comprehensive, of human development' in which 'history is a reinterpretation of the past which leads to conclusions about the present.'[45]

The epics of great civilizations were seen as the vehicles of mythologized history, indeed, as the source of historiography itself, as Heyne wrote in 1799 in the Göttingen *Commentationes*.[46] Coleridge's epic theory strained towards such a conception of 'event'. His criticism of *Paradise Lost*, and of the other major epics, especially Tasso's *Gerusalemme Liberata*, *Jerusalem Delivered*, and Dante's *Commedia*, and, secondarily, of Spenser, and of Southey, for whose Arabian *Thalaba* and Celtic-American *Madoc* he was at one time prepared to write a supporting 'Essay of Epic Poetry', makes it clear why *The Fall of Jerusalem* was the only fit subject left, and how he would have liked to treat it.

Milton, in his wisdom, had taken 'a mundane theme – one common to all mankind'.[47] Coleridge felt that the 'national' theme of King Arthur, which Milton had considered and rejected, could no longer be made interesting even to Englishmen. Even the interest derived from the events of the *Iliad* itself, as opposed to Homer's artistry in creating them, he thought 'very languid to all but Greeks. It is a Greek poem.'[48]

The superiority of the Paradise Lost is obvious in this respect, that the interest transcends the limits of a nation. But we do not generally dwell on this excellence. . .because it seems attributable to Christianity itself; – yet in fact the interest is wider than Christendom, and comprehends the Jewish and Mohammedan worlds; nay, still further, inasmuch as it represents the origin of evil, and the combat of evil and good, it contains matter of deep interest to all mankind, as forming the basis of all philosophy whatsoever.[49]

Although the purely religious epic offered incomparable advantages, there were also advantages to be gained from a subject not so strictly Christian as Milton's, and these have primarily to do with the demand for universality. It is in a sense accidental, or at any rate contrived, that *Paradise Lost* 'comprehends the Jewish and Mohammedan worlds'; the classical references are all subordinate to the Christian theme, and Dr Johnson for one felt that they were out of keeping with the whole.

To centre on Jerusalem at the time of its fall would be to show the real convergence of the Jewish, the Christian, and the classical worlds upon each other, as well as upon the eastern empires of Egypt and Syria. The Mohammedan world would appear, if not directly, by implication of the future. Into 'The Flight and Return of Mohammed' Coleridge intended to

introduce a disputation between Mahomet, as the representative of unipersonal Theism with the Judaico-Christian machinery of angels, genii, and prophets, an idolater with his gods, heroes, and spirits of the departed mighty, and a fetish-worshipper who adored the invisible alone, and held no religion common to all men or any number of men other than as they chanced at the same moment to be acted on by the same influence – even as when a hundred ant-hills are in motion under the same burst of sunshine.[50]

Another idea for a poem, conceived at the same period as the *Mohammed*, displays the same fascination with the ingathering of different races and systems. To Southey he wrote that he had discovered 'in one of the ecclesiastical Historians' the curious fact that

the Oak which Abraham planted at Mamre, was still existing in the time of Constantine and destroyed by his orders; – a famous Mart being held there every summer, persons of all Religions, both Jews & Christians & Asiatic Gentiles in a general confluence doing honor thereto/ – What a delightful subject this for an eclogue, or pastoral, or philosophical poem.[51]

Coleridge suggests that Southey's friend, William Taylor of Norwich, the most active translator and reviewer of German literature in the 1790s, is the man to write it: 'His knowledge, his style, his all-half believing Doubtingness of all, his – in short, I wish that you would hint it to him.[52] We can better imagine Coleridge doing it, perhaps as a single scene, a 'field full of folk' for his *Fall*. Coleridge all his life was master and slave of the subtle lights and shadows of the state of 'all-half believing Doubtingness of all', the dusk of romantic Christianity.

The same streaming movement towards the centre, the intimacy of death with rebirth, appears in an example of the magnetic power of the Holy City that Coleridge recorded in his notebook:

Amongst us divers Jewish Women in the extremity of old age pilgriming the Desert to die at Jerusalem, with them the Bones of their Parents, Husbands, Children, & Kinsfolk.[53]

The great Eastern capital could have been presented as sumptuously and brilliantly as Constantinople in this further passage noted down by Coleridge from George Sandys, *A Relation of a Journey begun An: Dom: 1610*:

Now when he goeth abroad, which is lightly every other Friday (besides at other times upon other occasions) unto the Mosque: and when in state; there is not in the world to be seene a greater spectacle of humane glory, and (if so I may speake) of sublimated manhood. For although (as hath bene said) the Temple of *Sancta Sophia,* which he most usually frequenteth is not above a stones cast from the out-most gate of the *Serraglio,* yet hath he not so few as a thousand horse (besides the archers of his guard and other footmen) in that short procession: the way on each side inclosed within as without, with *Capagies* and *Ianizzaries* in their scarlet gownes, and particular head ornaments. The *Chauses* ride formost with their gilded maces, then the Captains of the *Ianizzaries* with their *Aga*; next the chiefetaines of the *Spachies,* after them the *Sanziaks*: those of the souldierie wearing in the fronts of their bonnets the feathers of the birds of Paradise, brought out of *Arabia,* and by some esteemed the Phoenix. Then follow the *Bassas* and *Beglerbegs*: after them the Pretorian footmen, called the *Solacchi,* whereof there be in number three hundred. These are attired in calsouns and smocks of callico, wearing no more over them than halfesleeved coates of crimson damask, the shirts tuckt under their girdles: having plumes of feathers in the top of their copped bonnets; bearing quivers at their backs, with bowes ready bent in their left hands, and arrowes in their right: gliding along with a marvellous celerity. After them seven or nine goodly horses are led, having caparisons and trappings of inestimable value; followed by the idolized *Sultan* gallantly mounted. About whom there runne fortie Peichi (so called, in that they are naturally *Persians*) in high crowned brimless caps of beaten gold, with coates of gold girt to them with a girdle called *Chochiach.*[54]

The seriousness of Coleridge's epic intention lent inner meaning to the gorgeous trappings of the East. The traditional view that the one original and universal monotheistic faith was transmitted from one central source in the Orient still dominated the eighteenth century; Hume's argument that religion was naturally and originally polytheistic was an anomaly. The theory of original monotheism required an explanation of the collapse of monotheism into polytheism; it also entailed a reconvergence of cultures in the sophisticated monotheism of Judaeo-Christianity. The reconvergence of cultures in the Hellenistic period was for Coleridge the decisive moment in the history of civilization. Coleridge has often been called a 'neo-platonist', and not wholly without reason; but the reason lies not in any direct adoption of the ideas of Plotinus or Proclus, but in his view, expressed at length and in detail in his *Philosophical Lectures*, that the fusion of ideas that took place in their time represented the real birth of European civilization.

The stress he laid on the early Christian period gave a special turn to his literary theory as well as to his history of philosophy: he did not, like Schiller and the two Schlegels, make the sharp break between the classical and the modern, the 'naive' and the 'sentimental', two antithetical modes that had to be defined and strenuously reconciled in contemporary literature; rather he conceived this blending already to have taken place in modern (that is, Christian European and preeminently English) literature.

His epic poem would turn on this moment of blending, the confluence of cultures accomplished in Christ. His subject presented the splendid, more than Miltonic, opportunity to exhibit the confluence of cultures at the symbolic historical focus of Christian civilization. The Hellenistic syncretism was, like the romantic, eclectic and willed, yet in the life and death of Jesus it attained a genuine fusion; Jew and Babylonian, Greek, Roman, and Egyptian, Christian and Mohammedan yet to be born, were conquered by and absorbed into Christianity in the great symbolic metropolis of the East that stood for the enduring significance of that life and that death.

Coleridge's 'Orientalism', then, is neither affectation nor antiquarian's fancy nor an escape into the exotic. It embraces his general concern for the primitive spring of faith in one God for all mankind, and his special concern for the seed-time of European civilization. The pride of the Enlightenment in universality culminated in a stratagem of doubt: although Coleridge always spoke in the name of Christianity, and did everything in his power to preserve its local forms, he tended in equal degree to press beyond its parochialism. If Christianity was to be preserved, it must be seen to include everything else of value in civilized history.

Coleridge wished to write a universal religious epic, as Dante had written a Catholic epic and Milton a Protestant epic. But was any religious epic possible in 1795? Tasso had enunciated the neo-classic principle that the poet must not make use of Biblical matter, because it is true, known, and sacrosanct, and so leaves no scope for poetic invention; instead, the poet should have recourse to the great martial stories from Christian profane history. But by now the reason for preferring the profane was simply that Christian mythology seemed as lifeless as the Greek. It was too late not only for Homer, but also for Milton.

Unlike the English, the French were not inhibited by national pride from considering Milton's subject – God and the devil – suitable only for 'des vaudevilles'.[55] Nor were they inclined to indulge in the Addisonian apologetics by which Milton's work, admittedly neither a classic nor a neo-classic epic, was dubbed a 'divine poem'. Voltaire pleaded for understanding, for a truly universal taste, based on the 'commerce mutuel d'observations' among nations. But despite the appreciation of Shakespeare that his English visit had taught him and his guarded half-defence of Milton, Voltaire's unmixed admiration was accorded only to the historical epic, to Tasso's *Gerusalemme Liberata*, Lucan's *Thebaid*, his own *Henriade*.

Tasso's subject, the liberation of Jerusalem, an army of heroes under a virtuous chief going to deliver from the yoke of infidels a land consecrated by the birth and death of a god, is 'the greatest that anyone has ever chosen'.[56] But the epic, in Voltaire's view, must now be free not only of the religious or the mythological, but even the legendary or marvellous; and Tasso's is full of Italianate frippery. Voltaire preferred Lucan, as showing how

the true grandeur of a real hero is above that of the imaginary hero, how thought strong and solid surpasses those inventions which one calls poetic beauties, and which persons of good sense regard as insipid tales fit to amuse children.[57]

Voltaire, in accordance with his anthropological principle of granting to each nation its own style, conceded that Homer had done well to introduce the gods. But Lucan had done well to pass them by:

The civil wars of Rome were too serious for these *jeux d'imagination*. What sort of figure would Caesar have cut in the plain of Pharsalia, if Iris had carried him his sword, or if Venus had descended in a cloud of gold to his aid?[58]

An actual historical subject is more serious, more worthy of epic treatment, than any myth.

Coleridge, as so often, shared – if only as a starting-point – the

Enlightened opinion. He repeatedly expressed his preference for the historical over the fanciful, quoting the following more than once:

How wishedly will some pity the case of Argalus and Parthenia; the patience of Gryseld in Chaucer, the misery and troublesome adventures of the phanatic Lovers in Cleopatra, Cassandra, Amadis de Gaul, Sidney & such like. Yet all these are as meer Romantick as Rabelais his Gargantua and yet with an unmoved Apprehension can peruse the lamentable murder of Edward the second of England, & James the first...[59]

Coleridge agreed too that sacred matters must not be fictionalized:

I object from principle to all fictions grounded on Scripture History – and more than all to any introduction of our Lord. Even the *Paradise Regained* offends my mind. Here what is not historic truth, is a presumptuous falsehood.[60]

Yet he is irresistibly drawn towards the religious subject: 'But if I dared dramatize so aweful a part of the Gospel Narrative, I seem to feel that I could evolve the Judas into a perfectly intelligible character.' He goes on:

After writing the preceding page it did strike me that it might be of use and for edification to compose a sacred drama, for the purpose of elucidating the character of Judas, and without attributing to our Lord any act or even works not authenticated by the Gospels. One advantage would be, the presenting of a consistent whole by strict adherence to the narrative of John, & availing myself of the other Gospels so far only, as they were evidently consistent and of a piece with it.[61]

In so far, then, as the poet treats the Gospels as historical sources, he may write of sacred events; only mere fiction in sacred matters is disallowed, not the sacred itself.

Coleridge's epic subject itself provided him with an initial solution. The fall of Jerusalem, after all, is an historical subject; it is Tasso's own. It requires the depiction of no sacred matter, no direct use of the Gospels, yet according to the new historical criticism it is embedded in the Book of Revelation, it is the stuff of the New Testament itself.

Apart from Eichhorn's own notes giving Biblical, neo-platonic, deistic, and patristic parallels, Coleridge's main historical source for the events of the fall was Josephus.[62] Josephus's history is a work of art that compares well with Lucan. Of special value for Coleridge's epic is Josephus's extraordinary position as a Romanized Jew, a partisan of both sides and of neither, a man who in one breath is exhorting the Jews as their general to further resistance at the siege of Jotapata, and in the next as Vespasian's favourite is calling for his countrymen's surrender before the walls of Jerusalem. For this man who valued the cosmopolitanism of the Roman dispensation, the origins of the war were to be traced not to the viciousness of the procurators, nor to the massacre of the Roman garrison, but to the Jews' sudden refusal to continue receiving the sacrifices of foreigners (including Caesar) at the temple. From this general intolerance follow the internal dissensions among the Jews and their cruel slaughter of each other. Moreover, the Jews' action undermines the uneasy protection of their minorities in other great Hellenistic cities, in Alexandria and Damascus, and they fall prey to the people of those cities. Thus the withdrawal of one party from the pact of tolerance unleashes the sectarian passions of all parties everywhere.

The intense war of parties, in Josephus as in the Book of Revelation, presages the end of the known world. The partisan sectarian spirit of Revelation has often repelled readers who find it 'unchristian' and can excuse it only by reference to the persecution of Christians by the emperors at the time of the writing of Revelation. But it is clear that the state of mind in which sectarian furies rage is precisely the herald of Anti-Christ.

A special terror pervades Josephus's history, the terror of the man caught in the middle. The siege of Jaffa provides an image of it. The defending Jews were forced back between the double set of walls by the Romans, and the Jews inside the city shut the internal gates to keep the Romans out; 12,000 men were caught and slaughtered between the walls of the city. Battering on the gates and calling to their friends inside by name, 'yet had they their throats cut in the very midst of their supplications.'[63] The terror and the pathos of this potential end characterized the citizen of the Empire, the classically educated barbarian, forever enclosed between double walls.

How different will be the universality of the new imperium, how different the peace of God from the *pax romana*? The popular notion that Josephus himself became a Christian in his later days adds to the sense that these terrible internecine battles, in state and in self, presaged the coming of the new Jerusalem. For Coleridge's epic purposes,

Josephus's Roman universalism is a kind of half-way house, a dim foreshadowing of the true universality that will arise through the destruction of Jewish sectarianism and the establishment of Christianity, when Jerusalem will be the holy city of all mankind.

The scene of the ingathering of the peoples that so appealed to Coleridge's imagination received poignant illustration in Josephus's history of the fall of Jerusalem. Titus received from his father the army of the East, and laid siege to Jerusalem just at the moment when the city was crowded with those who had come to celebrate the Feast of the Passover. On the day of the Passover – 31 March – Titus took up his position on Mt Scopus with three legions, while another occupied the Mount of Olives. John of Giscala held the Temple, the Antonia, and the new town of Bezetha, and Simon held the upper and lower city. According to Josephus, they did as much destruction from within as the Romans did from without.

In April, Titus broke through the third, the outermost wall; then the causeways and movable towers were made ready to move against the Hippicus Tower and the Antonia. John succeeded in destroying the works raised against the Antonia; the Romans thereupon surrounded the whole city with an earthwork of circumvallation to cut off all communication, and the city was gripped by famine. The suffering within the city was terrible. Even before the siege ended, 600,000 bodies had been thrown out of the gates. Finally, during the night of 20 June, a handful of Roman soldiers gained entrance to the Antonia by surprise. Titus had the fortress destroyed, to get material to build mounds against the Temple.

Josephus pauses to describe the Temple just before its destruction. Here he is as much the connoisseur as the *dévot*. He approaches the holy house gradually through the outer courts to the golden doors; but before these doors was a veil as large as the doors:

It was a Babylonian curtain, embroidered with blue and fine linen, and scarlet, and purple, and of a contexture that was truly wonderful. Nor was this mixture of colours without its mystical interpretation, but was a kind of image of the universe; for by the scarlet, there seemed to be enigmatically signified fire, by the fine flax the earth, by the blue the air, and by the purple the sea; two of them having their colours the foundation of this resemblance; but the fine flax and the purple have their own origin for that foundation, the earth producing the one, and the sea the other.[64]

For three weeks the Jews desperately defended first the outer porti-
coes, then the inner, which the Romans entered only at great cost. On
23 July, a Roman soldier threw a blazing torch into one of the halls
adjoining the Holy of Holies. The result was a frightful mass of intermingled corpses and ruins. Next day the Romans burned the lower
city. There still remained the third rampart, the formidable stronghold
of the upper city, where the defenders of the Acra, carrying their
booty with them, joined Simon. When after three weeks the battering
rams breached the walls, John and Simon fled secretly with their troops.

As this terrible history approaches its climax, Josephus seems to lose
his Roman urbanity and speak in the tones of the Jewish apocalyptics:
the Jews themselves had polluted the Temple, using it as a military
camp and refuge for the seditious faction and shedding each other's
blood there long before the Romans came, 'till the dead bodies of
strangers were mingled together with those of their own country, and
those of profane persons with those of the priests, and the blood of
all sorts of dead carcases stood in lakes in the holy courts themselves'.[65]
Ultimately, then, Josephus gives a Jewish interpretation of the destruction: history is a private matter between God and His people, and
they have brought destruction upon themselves, the Romans being
only His instrument: 'In reality it was God who condemned the whole
nation, and turned every course that was taken for their preservation
to their destruction.'[66]

He recalls earlier punishments:

Had the Romans made any longer delay in coming against these villains, the
city would either have been swallowed up by the ground opening upon them
or been overflowed by water, or else been destroyed by such thunder as the
country of Sodom perished by.[67]

The description is absolute, eschatological:

Neither did any other city ever suffer such miseries, nor did any age ever
breed a generation more fruitful in wickedness than this was, from the beginning of the world.[68]

Thus even the Romanized Josephus who hoped for a civil surrender
sounds in his pain the apocalyptic note of his countryman John in the
Book of Revelation. Coleridge followed suit: 'The age was more
wicked and abandoned than any upon record –.'[69] In the face of this
dissension, this iniquity, this savagery, and this destruction only the

42

coming of a New Jerusalem could satisfy the apparently modest and simply human demand of a Josephus for worldly peace and fraternity.

On 1 August, the city was in the hands of the Romans, after 143 days of siege. It had been one of the bloodiest sieges in history. Estimates vary, but somewhere between 600,000 and a million Jews died by sword, disease, or famine. The survivors died in gladiatorial combats or in slavery. Said Titus: 'It is not I who have conquered. God, in His wrath against the Jews, has made use of my arm.'

Before the beginning of the siege, the Christians, recalling Christ's prophecies, withdrew beyond the Jordan, led by their bishop, St Simeon; for had not Christ beheld the city, and wept over it,

Saying, If thou hadst known, even thou, at least in this thy day, the things which belong unto thy peace! but now they are hid from thine eyes.

For the days shall come upon thee, that thine enemies shall cast a trench about thee, and compass thee round, and keep thee in on every side.

And shall lay thee even with the ground, and thy children within thee; and they shall not leave in thee one stone upon another; because thou knewest not the time of thy visitation.

And he went into the temple, and began to cast out them that sold therein, and them that bought;

Saying unto them, It is written, My house is the house of prayer: but ye have made it a den of thieves. (Luke 19, 42–6)

And so the prophecies had been fulfilled; and after the fall of Jerusalem, the little group of Christians returned to the city, to the house of John Mark and his mother Mary, the scene of the Last Supper. They were still almost entirely converts from Judaism. Otherwise there were few Jews left in the city.

The epic writes itself. It would be historical indeed; but religious in a still more profound sense. Not legendary, not doctrinal, but true; a non-Scriptural but sacred drama. There are times in history when Providence appears to intervene, events which gather up into themselves the whole past and the whole future. The poet of *The Fall of Jerusalem* would have no need of supernatural personages, for the event itself, the city itself, is holy. His task would be to convey that atmosphere of the presence of divine ends in the temporal actions of men. Jerusalem is falling: but the Messiah has appeared; the Empire is victorious: but it will fall into the hands of the few Christians waiting beyond the Jordan for the destruction to be complete. The fall involves a sense of impending liberation for all the world from its previous bonds. Nor does liberation await the future; it has already been accomplished, and its first sign is the fall of old, corrupted, and strife-racked Jerusalem. Tasso had mistaken his subject: Jerusalem was liberated not by the Crusaders but by Christ.

Coleridge's reinterpretation of Tasso's epic subject approached a new solution to the difficulty of portraying the supernatural in a modern poem. When he attacked Tasso for attaching an allegorical explanation to the *Gerusalemme Liberata*, he attacked him not for allegorizing, but for having provided nothing within his poem to lead the reader to suspect any allegorical intention whatsoever. An allegory tacked on could be perfectly in harmony with the poem; but, if the poem has succeeded, it is superfluous. Voltaire, despite his admiration for Tasso's poem, had not refrained from sketching in a few ironic paragraphs of his best manner the corruption of the Crusaders. It was impossible without falsification to present the Crusaders as 'liberating' Jerusalem; and the history of Jerusalem since then has been so inglorious as to nullify even the falsified effect. As Dr Johnson put it:

From the Italian writers it appears that the advantages of even Christian knowledge may be possessed in vain. Ariosto's pravity is generally known; and though the Deliverance of Jerusalem may be considered as a sacred subject, the poet has been very sparing of moral instruction.[70]

Coleridge criticized Klopstock's *Messias* for the way it intermingled extravagant fictions with his sacred matter; and Klopstock's own theoretical justification of this displays the view of the nature of 'event' that the new mythological history would finally destroy. In his essay 'Von der heiligen Poesie', 'On Divine Poetry', translated into English with the epic in 1763, he wrote:

Nur müsste der Dichter die Erfüllung in eben dem Tone beschreiben, in welchem der Prophet die Begebenheit vorher verkündigt hat. Die Geheimnisse sind dasjenige, was mit der meisten Einfalt gesagt werden muss, ausser wo sie, dass ich so sage, zu Begebenheiten werden. Alles, was der Messias tut, ist Geheimnis, weil er der Gottmensch ist, aber dennoch ist es zugleich historisch.[71]

The poet must describe the fulfilment of the prophecies in the same tone as the prophet previously prophesied the event. Holy mysteries must be described with the greatest simplicity, except, as I say, where they become events. Everything that the Messiah does is a mystery, because he is God incarnate, but at the same time everything he does is historical.

Klopstock seems to commit two fundamental errors here, both of which are based on a rationalist notion of 'event'. First, the prophet by definition never describes the event as such – only as prophecy. To describe the event 'in the same tone', then, must be a mistake if Klopstock's distinction between prophecy and event is to be maintained. The new critics gradually eroded this distinction until all history became prophecy. Second, the notion that if prophecy is interpreted as event in Klopstock's way, rather than event as prophecy, then the poet has free rein in description, drives fact and fiction further apart than ever, and renders poetry mere fancy.

Coleridge, in his notes on Lessing's 'Über den Beweis des Geistes und der Kraft' (1777), 'On the Proof of the Spirit and the Power', in the *Kleine Schriften* (which Coleridge claimed to reread each year), disputed the pervasive eighteenth-century notion that there is something specially privileged about a perceived 'fact'. Miracles were the crucial case. Is a miracle an historical event? The deists argued straightforwardly that a miracle was an impossibility in nature. Lessing evaded the resulting dismissal of the Bible accounts by arguing that 'Zufällige Geschichtswahrheiten können der Beweis von nothwendigen Vernunftswahrheiten nie werden.'[72] 'Accidental historical truths can never be the proof of necessary truths of reason.' The argument over the possibility of miracles cannot, then, affect faith: but by the same token, the superiority of *Vernunftswahrheiten* over *Geschichtswahrheiten* led Lessing to doubt whether the Bible was capable of serving as the foundation of a rational faith. Moreover, he made a sharp distinction between miracles self-witnessed and miracles known only through historical testimony at a distance.

The alleged 'inspiration' of the Evangelists' testimony is no more than an historical truth. Lessing's emotion over this crux in his religious position is manifest:

Das – nämlich das historisch immer ungewiss Bleibende – das ist der garstige breite Graben, über den ich nicht kommen kann, so oft und ernstlich ich auch den Sprung versucht habe. Kann mir jemand hinüberhelfen, der tu es; ich bitte ihn, ich beschwöre ihn. Er verdient einen Gotteslohn an mir.

This – namely, what always remains historically uncertain – this is the foul gaping chasm over which I cannot leap, however often and earnestly I try. If anyone can help me over, please do so; I beg him, I implore him. He will earn God's reward for it.

Coleridge in reply argues that there is no such specially privileged class of witnessed 'fact'. *Vernunftswahrheiten* cannot be separated out in this way from *Geschichtswahrheiten*, because what we see or experience depends on expectations formed by what we accept as *Vernunftswahrheiten*. This being so, the distinction between what we see with our own eyes and what we see through others' eyes diminishes in importance. Our own eyes do not in any case see the event, the unvarnished fact, because there is no such thing. If we share with an eyewitness the same *Vernunftswahrheiten*, then our interpretation of the event will tend to be the same as his, at whatever distance in time or space the event may be. Sight alone cannot distinguish between an 'unusual phenomenon' and a 'supernatural phenomenon', i.e. a miracle. The judgement on the basis of doctrine (*Glaubensanalogie*) is a theological rule of the Reformation to which Coleridge often returns; but in conjunction with the independent judgement of natural phenomena and historical event insisted on by empiricists, it leads to a new view of the nature of perception and the nature of what is perceived. Interpretation is embedded in event.

Coleridge argues that, given the prior belief which certain events could be taken as confirming, historical testimony is, though weaker than eye-witnessing, proportionally valuable:

If (as Lessing admits) the sight of a Miracle or the present fulfilment of a known prior prophecy would be the sufficient ground of implicit faith in the assurances of the Prophet and Thaumaturge, the Belief of such an Occurrence in proof of such assurances on the strongest possible historical evidence must be the ground of a *proportional* belief in these Assurances. Less indeed and less impressive, but yet *a* ground. For suppose the historic evidence *not* the best possible, the Belief would be *less*. Now what is capable of sensible diminution must be a *sensible* quantity. . . Belief would not be rational Belief, if it did not bear some ratio to knowledge: even tho' I should grant what L. (*erroneously*, I think) assumes – that the *sight* of an unusual phenomenon is $=$ to the knowledge of its' being a miracle, i.e. a supernatural phaenomenon.[73]

Coleridge's argument reflects a long struggle of the new criticism with the idea that an eye-witness account must be of special value. If, by their own critical endeavour, it became clear that none of the Gospels was an eye-witness account, the status of the 'event' therein recounted must, on the old view, be diminished, its credibility undermined; but if there are no such privileged accounts, if all event is interpretation, than the Gospels need not suffer. Indeed, as we shall see, their value as literature is increased. For Coleridge, 'event' and 'mystery' must be expressed with equal delicacy, obliquity, and restraint. The miracle becomes the paradigm of reported historical event; the historical events reported by eye-witnesses represent instantaneous myth-making. 'Erkennen ist mythologisieren.'[74] 'To perceive is to mythologize.' The result of Klopstock's error is, as he admits, indeed boasts, that the appreciation of his poem depends on the degree of Christian faith of the reader; for on this depends the validation of the mystery as event, on which the entire fiction is grounded. It is the rationalist, not the romantic poet, who must have his audience trundle their faith up like a wagon on which alone the historical mysteries can be performed.

It was the need for such a radical solution as this to save the credibility of the Gospels that led Coleridge to turn to Berkeley just at this time. It is unlikely, though not impossible, that Coleridge was reading the *Kleine Schriften* in 1797; but he was familiar with Lessing's views on the problem of historical evidence both from his play *Nathan der Weise* (1778), *Nathan the Wise*, which had been translated into English, published, and performed by 1794, and from the *Wolfenbüttel Fragments*.

Nathan the Wise, a plea for religious tolerance, was also, in Lessing's own view, an Oriental poem; he employed English blank verse (its first appearance in German drama) because he felt the Oriental flavour of the play would be too strong in prose. At the heart of the play is the parable of the three rings, taken from the *Decameron*, Day I, No. 3, 'Melchisedek the Jew', but made to turn upon Lessing's view of the unreliability of historical testimony. Nathan, likening the three apparently identical rings to the three religions, Judaism, Christianity, and Islam, points out that they cannot be differentiated on the basis of their originating principles, because these depend on historical events of which we can have no certain knowledge:

> Denn gründen alle sich nicht auf Geschichte?
> Geschrieben oder überliefert! Und

Muss doch wohl allein auf Treu'
Und Glauben angenommen werden. Nicht?

Are they not all founded on history?
Written or handed down! – And history –
Must it not be on trust and faith alone
Received? Is it not so?[75]

Precisely because, then, we must all place our credence most fully in those nearest to us – 'Doch deren Blut wir sind', 'For we are of their blood' – each religion must subsist, and no judgement can be made of their relative value.

In the *Fragments*, Lessing demonstrates pungently that there is a 'gap' between any miracle and what it is supposed to prove, even if the miracle be accepted as in any sense genuine. As Reimarus on the miracle of 'speaking in tongues' (Acts, 2) put it:

And how bad the argument:
Certain persons have spoken in foreign tongues;
Therefore Jesus has arisen from the dead.'[76]

Pushed to its conclusion, Lessing's point meant that there can be no 'external evidences' of Christianity; all the contentions of the school of Paley fall to the ground. Coleridge turned to 'internal evidences', or rather, to ways of providing for external evidences to coincide with internal evidences. Berkeley might help him here; so might Kant, of whom he had already heard a considerable amount from Beddoes.[77]

Beddoes wrote a favourable account of Kant in his letter to *The Monthly Magazine* in May 1796, hoping for an early translation into English, and offering a specimen translation from the *Kritik der Urteilskraft, Critique of Judgement*. Although Beddoes did not attempt, at any rate in public, an explication of Kant's principles, he had certainly read some part of his works, as well as those of Reinhold, 'the most perspicuous expositor of the philosophy of Kant'. The significance even of the bare suggestion for Coleridge was very great, for he immediately grasped the possibility that the philosophy of Kant held out some hope of an entirely new defence of Christianity.

Since 1794, since his disgrace at Jesus College and the failure of the humane scheme of Pantisocracy before it had been well begun, Coleridge, we know, had been working slowly away from 'Necessarianism' and 'Optimism'. In 1794 he wrote to his brother,

I will pray nightly to the Almighty Dispenser of good and evil, that his Chastisements may not have harrowed up my heart in vain! – Scepticism had mildewed my hope in the Saviour – I was far from disbelieving the Truth of revealed Religion, but still farther from a steady Faith.[78]

And again:

I had too much Vanity to be altogether a Christian – too much tenderness of Nature to be utterly an Infidel. Fond of the dazzle of Wit, fond of subtlety of Argument, I could not read without some degree of pleasure the levities of Voltaire, or the reasonings of Helvetius – but tremblingly alive to the feelings of humanity, and susceptible of the charms of Truth my Heart forced me to admire the beauty of Holiness in the Gospel, forced me to *love* the Jesus, whom my Reason (or perhaps my *reasonings*) would not permit me to *worship* – My Faith therefore was made up of the Evangelists and the Deistic Philosophy – a kind of *religious Twilight* –[79]

During the following years he ransacked the literature of infidelity and the literature of apology. He sought materials to reconstruct a defence of Christianity from a dissenting position; he identified himself as a 'Unitarian Christian', but one considerably more radical than the Unitarian clergy, one who on his tour of the provincial cities to raise a subscription for *The Watchman* was prepared to preach in 'coloured clothes' and on political topics. He sought a heterodox justification for Christianity. He studied atheism 'deeply & widely – I cannot say, without prejudice: for when I commenced the Examination, I was an Infidel.'[80] No longer an atheist, a deist, nor, by temperament, a sceptic, it was nevertheless to atheists, deists, and sceptics that he addressed himself; it was they who must be convinced that Christianity was still defensible. Hartley played an important role for Coleridge in this transitional period, for in Hartley's *Observations on Man*, association theory and necessarianism were made to serve the ends of 'Christian philosophy'.[81] It is no accident that some of his best letters during these years are addressed to Thelwall, who represents the spirit that must be converted. For this reason too he undertook 'an Examination of Godwin's political Justice' which was to set the system of Godwin against the system of Jesus: 'In my book on Godwin I compare the two Systems – his & Jesus's – & that book I am sure you will read with attention.'[82] At the same time he wrote, 'Have you read over Dr Lardner on the Logos? It is, I think, scarcely possible to read it, and not be convinced –'.[83] Now, Lardner's *A Letter written in the Year*

1730, Concerning the Question, Whether the Logos supplied the Place o,
an human Soul in the Person of Jesus Christ returns a good Unitarian
answer: 'No'. Jesus was a man, 'having a human soul, as well as a
human body'.

And the making the Logos to be the soul of Christ, does really annihilate
his example, and enervate all the force, which it should have upon us.[84]

It was this pamphlet that was said to have made Priestley a Socinian,
though Lardner was never one. Coleridge, then, was seeking a conception of Christ that he could accept intellectually, in order to construct 'my Critique on the New Philosophy'.[85]

Coleridge's theological lectures of 1795, the *Lectures on Revealed*
Religion, its Corruptions, and its Political Views, offered what was to be
his last attempt at a defence of an optimistic and necessarian view of
revealed religion based on standard Unitarian authorities. All the
'external evidences' under discussion were on their way to non-literal
interpretation in his next phase; the question of miracles seems to have
proved decisive.

Priestley, on whom Coleridge leaned in these lectures, argued with
rationalist confidence that the 'evidence of Christianity. . .stand[s]
upon as good ground as that of any other history whatsoever'.[86]
But both Priestley and Paley surreptitiously introduced a circular
argument in which a prior belief in God supports the possibility of
miracles. Coleridge perceived this:

For the belief of any historical Fact we can require three things only. That
the Testimony be numerous & manifestly disinterested – that the Agent
be sufficiently powerful and the final Cause sufficiently great. These three
Requisites the Scripture Miracles will be found to possess by him who previously believes the existence of a God & his attributes.[87]

Coleridge was thus prepared to agree with Reimarus and Lessing, and
was already on his way to his later position, that miracles have their
place as part of Christianity taken as an organic faith but cannot be
considered 'external evidences'. By 1801 Coleridge had formulated
his mature view of miracle:

Miracles must be ~~confirmed~~ judged by the doctrine which they confirm not
the doctrine by the miracle.
The Romanists argue preposterously while they would prove the truth
by miracles, whereas they should prove the miracles by the truth.[88]

But why, then, should there have been miracles at all? In 1795 Coleridge replied as Hegel did in *Die Positivität der Christlichen Religion, The Positivity of the Christian Religion*, written at the same time as the *Lectures*:

But unsusceptible of the effects of Reasoning Understanding so depraved will yield only to the overwhelming of supernatural Intervention. The wisest of the ancient Legislators had recourse to religious Imposture a fact which proves that they felt the necessity of the Revelation which they did not possess.[89]

The necessity of a prior belief in God, and at the same time of a 'depraved' understanding among the earliest Christians, for the explanation of what Paley himself called 'how the story of the evidence arose', created a paradox which was typically resolved by the higher criticism through an analysis of the nature of the Jewish milieu in which Christianity appeared. Whereas Hegel emphasized the Enlightenment attack on the Jewish mentality, but turned it to his own purposes as an attack on Kantian ethics, likewise enslaved to an 'objective God', Coleridge adopted the defence of the Hebrew polity prevalent among Unitarians and radicals and further elaborated by Lowth, Herder, and Eichhorn.

Despite what Coleridge agrees is 'the extirpating spirit' of 'the Mosaic Dispensation',[90] he praises the property arrangements among the Hebrew tribes: political liberty is the expression of true monotheism, which is still progressing towards the total abolition of property. If the Jews are seen as children – one common defence of the primitive Oriental – they represent God's purpose in keeping 'one people free from Idolatry' to point the way towards the final significance of monotheism. Thus Coleridge made an early and crude explanation of how the story of the miracles could have arisen: this depraved (and childish) understanding yet was the repository of the prior idea of God.

Coleridge's literal political progressivism and his literal defences of Christianity broke down together in the following year. He began to attack the whole structure: for the first time he attacked Newton and the 'Newtonian' Christian apologetics represented by both Hartley and Paley, earlier admired, by 1800 dismissed as 'Pseudo-rationalist'. He realized that a new world view was necessary to salvage 'revealed religion'; it could not be reconstructed from shards of Newtonianism. His life's work began from this realization.

He took up Berkeley for apologetic purposes; 'Bishop Taylor, Old Baxter, David Hartley & the Bishop of Cloyne are *my men*.'[91] The 'acquisition of a clear knowledge of Mr. Kant's principles' which Beddoes reckoned would be 'a hard task for a whole year' Coleridge would take up in earnest only after his return from Germany; but it suggested to him even then a solution along idealist lines.

Not yet being able to read Kant for himself, he turned to Kant's forerunners in English philosophy, to Cudworth and especially to Berkeley.[92] The association of Kant's name with Berkeley's was common on both sides of the Channel, despite Kant's painstaking efforts to disentangle his views from Berkeley's, which at the time of writing the *Critique of Pure Reason* he knew only through James Beattie's *Essays on the Nature and Immutability of Truth in Opposition to Sophistry and Scepticism* (1770). Yet as Hamann wrote to Herder in 1782: 'This much is certain: without Berkeley there would have been no Kant.' It is clear from Coleridge's marginalia on the German philosophers that he continually turned back to his Locke, Berkeley, Hume, and Descartes in reading them, even when his German was excellent. Berkeley's *Works* he borrowed from the Bristol Library in March 1796. Very shortly he began to declare himself a 'Berkleian'.[93] Kant, he knew, had in some way made time and space subjective; could something serviceable along these lines be found in Berkeley in defence of the credibility of the reported experience of the authors of the Gospels?[94] Nothing less than a new theory of perception was required. Lessing drew the conclusion from Reimarus's list of contradictions in the Gospel narratives of the resurrection that the Evangelists could not have been the same people as those who witnessed the resurrection. The Gospels were thrown into the limbo of mere hearsay (though Lessing himself postulated an early documentation in the form of an Aramaic Gospel on which the Evangelists drew). Coleridge reached out for an even more radical solution that would be a justification as well, whatever the contingencies: a revision of the entire conception of the meaning of 'witness' which would have revolutionary implications also for the conception of 'the visionary character' that he was evolving at the same time. In Berkeley's *Alciphron* he found the view that in consequence of the nature of perception, our knowledge of the Gospel events, including miracles, is as good as our knowledge of any event. We know this argument well: the new view of the nature of event is at the root of the famous discussion in the *Biographia Literaria* of 'fancy and imagination'. There Coleridge's mature and subtle transcendentalism, formed under the tutelage of Kant, came to full expression; but the first crude idealism of 1796 vaulted him over the hurdle that Eichhorn was never to surmount into a fully mythological interpretation of the Bible. Coleridge belonged, by age and conviction, to the next generation of Biblical critics, the generation of De Wette and Strauss.

Coleridge's epic, then, would introduce none but historical facts. Yet, as he put it, the events themselves were 'the completion of the prophecies'. His allegory, not tacked on at the end nor superimposed throughout, but the sense of the action itself, was a mythology of the invisible:

As for the old mythology, *incredulus odi*, yet there must be a mythology, or a quasi-mythology, for an epic poem. Here there would be the completion of the prophecies – the termination of the first revealed national religion under the violent assault of Paganism, itself the immediate forerunner & condition of the spread of a revealed mundane religion; and then you would have the character of the Roman and the Jew, & the awfulness, the completeness, the justice; I schemed it at 25, but, alas! *venturum expectat*.[95]

The new conception of history bridged precisely that epic gap between 'fact' and 'sacred story' that so plagued the Enlightenment. History itself was neither fact nor revelation, but the mythological milieu enabling events of a particular society to take place. The reply to the onslaught against miracles, then, was fundamentally rational – there are no miracles, that is, breaches of natural laws – but what is natural is stretched to include not merely physical but anthropological and sociological laws. What would be miracle to one society may occur naturally in another. Nature is subjectivized; events are mental. The concern of history is not disembodied event, but human nature.

Coleridge found his new mythology not in a Hellenic polytheism, nor in an animated physics (though he was exceedingly interested in Erasmus Darwin's attempt along these lines, and even more in Schelling's *Naturphilosophie*), but in the Hellenistic history created by the new Biblical critics as they perceived with increasing clarity that Christianity is a mythology fundamentally the same in kind as the other Oriental religions. By taking the myths of the Bible as true histories, Coleridge said, 'the whole Bible had been surrendered to the ridicule of its enemies'.[96] By mythologizing history, the doubting faithful could still place their credence in the Bible narrative.

Unlike the critical exegetes, Coleridge worked out this position fully in philosophical terms, and explored its implications; this was to be the work of the rest of his life. His is one of the finest achievements of the new criticism, going beyond Schelling's *Philosophie der Mythologie, Philosophy of Mythology* and beyond Strauss himself in his comprehension of the mythological bases of the leading ideas of his society, and it has still not been properly appreciated either in England or in Germany. At the end of the 1790s, he had travelled with the higher criticism as far as it had gone, with Lessing, Herder, and Eichhorn, and he was prepared to place Christianity in its mythological setting.

The life of Jesus was the testing ground; and Coleridge's epic would in this crucial respect have given expression to the new historical-critical view of the sacred events of Christianity. How well adapted this view was to literary purposes the ensuing century was to testify.

The sacred history of Jesus would appear in *The Fall of Jerusalem* in a brilliantly oblique and indirect way, but suffusing the whole and supplying its meaning. The 'great moral earthquake' of the fall of Jerusalem, as Herder called it, took on special significance in the context of the new Biblical criticism. Critical deists like Reimarus felt that, even assuming apostolic authorship, a thirty-year gap between the events of Jesus's life and the writing of the Gospel was sufficient to impugn the 'eye-witness' evidence of their authors; defenders were prepared to affirm that their credibility would hold if they were written by the time of the fall of Jerusalem. Thus Reimarus says,

It was not until thirty to sixty years after the death of Jesus, that people began to write an account of the performance of these miracles, in a language which the Jews in Palestine did not understand.[97]

And again, with a nice insinuation of apostolic senility:

Luke imagined thirty years afterwards, when the age allotted to man was well nigh spent, that he could with impunity write miracles and unscrupulously circulate them in the world.[98]

Nathaniel Lardner's twelve-volume defence of *the Credibility of the Gospel History* (1730) claimed no more than that the Gospels were written 'before, or soon after the destruction of *Jerusalem*'.[99] At that stage, then, in the discussion of the meaning of 'witness', the date of the fall of Jerusalem was considered crucial: a history of Jesus written in A.D. 70 was just at the limit of authentic witness, at the point when memories were turning into legend. For Coleridge, this point in historical time could represent not merely the nature of memory, but the myth-making nature of all perception:

> Life is a vision shadowy of Truth;
> And vice, and anguish, and the wormy grave
> Shapes of a dream! The veiling clouds retire,
> And lo! the Throne of the redeeming God
> Forth flashing unimaginable day
> Wraps in one blaze earth, heaven, and deepest hell.[100]

The nature of the traditional epic hero, the religio-political leader, had been rendered problematic by a series of Enlightenment controversies. When and how had the one original and universal monotheistic faith begun to fall away into the variety of sects? The role of the national religious leader was highly ambiguous: must not the founder of a local cult be a subverter of the true universal religion? The deists, moreover, suggested that religious leaders were deceivers of the people who befuddled them with 'mysteries' or at the least played to the vulgar and debased popular taste and achieved national unity by permitting or fostering idolatry. Mohammed was known as 'the Charlatan'; nor was Moses spared.[101] Coleridge was very familiar with these arguments, particularly through Warburton's influential book *The Divine Legation of Moses*,[102] in which Moses appears as the heir to Egyptian priestcraft.

A letter to Poole in 1796 shows that his interest in the newly discovered Indian manuscripts translated by William Jones as *The Institutes of Hindu Law, or the Ordinances of Menu* (1794) lay in the light they cast on the quality of Moses's leadership:

Menu's Ordinances exhibit a mournful picture of an hideous Union of Priest-craft & Despotism. The man who told George Dyer, that it would furnish unanswerable arguments against the Divine Legation of Moses, spoke what he did not himself believe – or rather perhaps believed it because he wished it. The first Chapter contains sublimity – & next to the first the last is the best.[103]

Jones calculated that the *Institutes* were written down 1580 years before the birth of Christ and thus were 'older than the five books or Moses',[104] and that the laws themselves were older than those of Solon or Lycurgus.[105] By an extended mythological parallelism based on etymology (the dubious technique of Jacob Bryant, often cited by Jones, usually unfavourably, and well known to Coleridge), Jones was prepared to suggest that the *Institutes* were none other than 'the most celebrated system of heathen Jurisprudence', the Laws of Minos.[106]

Coleridge accepted that the claim of Moses to be 'the original law-giver' in a temporal sense had been effectively challenged, but maintained that his laws compare favourably with the oppressive ordinances of Hinduism. In the context of Oriental history, the claim of the Bible to be the origin and pattern of religious civilization was reduced to a moral and finally to a symbolic claim only.

Coleridge's early epic projects all had heroes of this ambiguous character, shortly to be defined by Hegel as 'world-historical': his *Mohammed*, his *Joan*, his *Robespierre*, his *Cain*, whose sin, according to Josephus's *Antiquities*, was the founding of cities. He never ceased to be concerned with the nature of leadership, with the peculiar conjunction of religious superstition, personal ambition, and national achievement, as his translation of Schiller's *Wallenstein* and his Shakespeare criticism show. Indeed, the course of literature since his time has overwhelmingly amplified his sense of the ambiguities of heroism.

These concerns were reflected in the plans for the epic *Mohammed*. He had acquired, by the autumn of 1797, a very extensive knowledge of Mohammedan materials, having read George Sale (one of the first of the British Orientalists, Professor of Arabic at Oxford, translator of the Koran, and author of the Oriental articles in Bayle's Dictionary), Gibbon, Thevenot, Harris's *Collection*, and the *Universal History*. When he moved to Nether Stowey, he had Gibbon with him and was perusing the notoriously ironic chapters on Mohammed. He read Purchas because its third book contains the life of Mohammed.

Whether Southey or Coleridge first conceived of the epic, there is no doubt that Coleridge thought of it in terms of apologetics. Southey was prepared to acquiesce in the widely held view of the prophet as 'impostor' (his interest was in Ali, the prophet's son-in-law: 'Ali is of course my hero').[107] Coleridge defended Mohammed, just as he approved Schiller's guarded defence of Moses in *Die Sendung Moses*, *The Mission of Moses*, as having good intentions and good ends, although to gain them he was obliged to lead his people through their baser superstitions. Coleridge, in good Baylean fashion, employed his defence of non-Christian sects as a stratagem against Christian corruption:

> Prophet and priest, who scatter'd abroad both evil and blessing,
> Huge wasteful empires founded and hallowed slow persecution,
> Soul-withering, but crush'd the blasphemous rites of the Pagan
> And idolatrous Christians. – For veiling the Gospel of Jesus,
> They, the best corrupting, had made it worse than the vilest.

But he implies that the leader serves providential ends, Heaven 'choosing good from iniquity rather than evil from goodness'.[108] Coleridge mentioned Mohammed several times in 1796, the period of his most intense reading of histories of religion. He was at the end of the year already experimenting with the hexameter that the German Biblical epics and idylls were using so effectively; in the year of the 'Dejection' ode he would again turn to German metres.[109] 'I will translate a passage from a German Hexameter Poem', he wrote to Thelwall in December; the poem was Voss's popular idyll, *Luise*. It was at this time that he most probably made his sketch plan of the epic, on the right-hand side of a sheet on which he had been practising his hexameters for the translation of *Luise*.[110]

Many legendary stories of Mohammed were to be introduced from the footnotes of Sale and from 'Maracci's curious prolegomena to his *Refutation of the Koran*'.[111] It was such legendary material, like the events of Jesus's infancy and His miracles, that the new apologetics would do most to defend, in a new sense, against its own critical analysis of it as legendary. Indeed, the comparison between Mohammed and Jesus was explicit: Jesus, for Coleridge, was 'the other Oriental prophet'.[112]

Lamb wrote to him in January 1797 urging him to write an epic, 'something philosophical, something more worthy of his friend's great powers than the spade'.[113] Coleridge's intention to do just this was shortly deepened by his new association with Wordsworth, his enthusiastic audition of 'The Ruined Cottage' and their plans for the philosophic epic on 'man, nature, and society' that Coleridge conceived as *The Brook* and Wordsworth would execute as *The Prelude* and *The Excursion*.

The new mythological impulse could run to a chaos of ill-digested parallels, as we know from Southey's poems and indeed from a host of French 'epics of humanity'.[114] William Taylor, knowing of the project for the epic on Mohammed, satirically suggested to Southey after the defeat of Tipu Sultan in 1799 an epic to be called *The Storming of Serringapatem*, intermingling Indian, Christian, and Mohammedan mythologies:

The taking of Serringapatem is a good subject for you epo-poets: I see Mahomet and all the monsters of the Koran confederated in its defence, and the ancient divinities of Hindostan, in alliance with the Christian sainthood, assisting the English army to conquer for the Tremourtee or Trinity new sanctuaries, and plant its tricoloured union flag on the shattered battlements of the unitarian metropolis. David and Krishna compose in concert the hymns of triumph; St. Cecilia and the Gopia in sweeter concert execute the aerial harmonies; Vishnu undertakes another incarnation to fight beside Captain Campbell; and the two St James's once more mount their coursers to announce a victory to Sir John Shore: to the emperor of the British isles – St Paul himself will have presented Brama and Sheva and Nayarena and Rama, and all his own protectors and protectresses, especially, Cuvera, the Plutus of the land; Cama will promise husbands to his daughters; Ganga will offer his waters for a new and holier baptism.[115]

Coleridge's gift, however, was for the perception of what was susceptible of genuine poetic development and critical justification of the highest kind. In considering the contemporary possibilities of the religious epic, he recast the arguments that had governed epic theory since the Renaissance.

To portray the founder of the Christian religion untouched by those doubts that must touch any literally historical character, the solution must be radical. From the point of view of the epic 'rules', Coleridge's subject, he knew, had one fault, the lack of a 'personal interest', a hero with a private action and end:

Yet, with all its great capabilities, it has this one grand defect – that, whereas a poem, to be epic, must have a personal interest, – in the destruction of Jerusalem no genius or skill could possibly preserve the interest for the hero from being merged in the interest for the event. The fact is, the event itself is too sublime and overwhelming.[116]

This defect could be turned to supreme advantage. There could have been no one hero, either Jew, Roman, or Christian, without sacrificing the symbolic import of the whole to a partisan interest. Rather there must be several 'heroes', whose interest lies precisely in the force they represent, and not in their personal predicaments.

Josephus's account of the Jewish leaders would have delighted any deist: they are indeed no heroes, but a set of bloody, deceitful, sectarian zealots, would-be founders of a new theocracy. John of Giscala in particular is represented as a deceiver of the people, going among them as a spy for the Zealots. He was 'a man of great craft, and bore about him in his soul a great passion after tyranny'.[117] Simon of Gerasa is the type of cruel martial vigour, 'not so cunning indeed as John. . . but superior in strength of body and courage'.[118] Together, the warlike leader and the cunning pseudo-priest, they exactly coincide with the notion of the Oriental theocracy graphically presented by Voltaire.

Coleridge's notes on Eichhorn's *Commentary* convey instead a generalizing cosmic sense of the leaders as representatives of forces beyond their own characters or destinies: 'The four first Trumpets denote the Evils that preceded and prepared the way for the Outbreak of the Zelotes, Terrorists, and Septembrizers of Jerusalem.'[119]

He equates the falling star of Revelation with the assumption of leadership rather than, as Eichhorn does, with an angel:

Thus the Star that shot from her Heaven, like a fiery Meteor (Shakespeare, Midsummer Nights' Dream, in the celebrated allusion to the Duke of Norfolk & Mary Queen of Scots) signified I doubt some Leader from one of the Princely Houses that put himself at the head of the Robbers that so frightfully infested Judaea – and in whom did this Calamity commence? Josephus tells us. In *Amarus* and Eleazar! Who does not at once see the Marah, Bitterness, the waters of Marah.[120]

By fully euhemerizing Revelation, personal particularities and astrological myths met in historical character. Milton had been much criticized for having no epic hero; the new epic would proclaim the absence of a hero, for behind the event would lie the life and death of Jesus as centre and cause and end of the event in Jerusalem. Coleridge's avoidance of the specific depiction of the details of Jesus's life has convulsive theological origins in the embarrassment and difficulty that in his day characterized the confrontation with Jesus. To dwell on history was to avoid the miraculous and to rationalize superstition, yet the historical Jesus was curiously difficult to locate. As dogma was psychologized, the personal experience of religious feeling became increasingly important; and this personal experience had to centre on Christ. Yet historical and psychological rationalism made the primary matter of Christianity – the Crucifixion and the Resurrection – repugnant to the young men of the 1790s. Their nascent mythological understanding told them inescapably that the vision of Christ was the fundamental experience of Christianity; and that their age was incapable of it. All the writers of the period flutter on this pin. Schleiermacher leads his hearers up to the intimate experience of Jesus, and then shrinks from it; Hegel's early theological writings twist and turn in their attempt to find a place for Jesus; Coleridge's own religious writings to the very end circle round and round the image of Christ but never face it, and the 'personeity' of God he could justify only by a tortuous and indirect argument. Strauss finally carried this tendency to its extreme point in his fully mythological history of Christ's life.

Even the boldest poets of the period felt this difficulty. Goethe had a way of falling upon the great themes of his time and giving them definitive form. Coleridge had the same instinct, though so many of his plans remained unexecuted. In the case of the Wandering Jew, both poets thought of epic treatment, and neither carried it out; its echoes are everywhere, yet they are of wanderings, not of the bold, direct collision with Christ. Goethe outlined his plan in his autobiography, *Dichtung und Wahrheit, Poetry and Truth*: Ahazuerus, the shoemaker, railed at Jesus, warning Him that there would be rebellion and Jesus would be forced, willy-nilly, to place Himself at the head of a party. Judas betrays Him in order to force this on Him. Ahazuerus's shop lies along the road to Calvary, and he emerges to attack Jesus once again. Jesus faints, Veronica holds the napkin to His face. Ahazuerus, still railing in his love for Jesus, sees the face imprinted on the napkin, and hears the words, 'Over the earth shalt thou wander till thou shalt once more see me in this form.'[121] The necessity of direct confrontation with Christ presented an insuperable obstacle.

In Jean Paul's dramatic *Rede des toten Christus, Speech of the Dead Christ*, Christ Himself announces the death of God. In a dream of a churchyard, Jean Paul related, he saw Christ rising at the day of Judgement to those assembled from the graves. They ask, 'Christ! is there no God?' and He replies, 'There is no God.' Christ describes His journey through the myriad worlds and the deserts of heaven and hell, crying on the way, 'Father, where are you?', but only the eternal storm replied.[122] The more the theology of the age came to stress Christ as the link between man and a distant God, or, like Schleiermacher, Christ Himself as man, the more He too became cut off from God. Coleridge's instinct was always to maintain Christ's presence through His partial banishment to historically grounded myth.

In Coleridge's epic Jesus would appear only as a recent and vivid memory in the minds of His disciples and of the Jews who had known Him, espoused His cause, or rejoiced in His death; as a legend gradually forming; and as the redemption implicit in the fall of the antique Jerusalem of pagan and Jew. And, as Coleridge noted, Jerusalem was Jesus's special care:

Did not Christ weep over Jerusalem, even as over Lazarus? He wept twice, once in justification of public, and once in justification of private affections.[123]

The intimate geography of Jerusalem may serve as a Brunonian 'art of memory' to recall Christ's life. But the symbolic presence is also an absence.

CHAPTER 2

THE VISIONARY CHARACTER: REVELATION AND THE LYRICAL BALLAD

As a newly mythologized history encountered the Divine Word of the Bible, it released one set of epic possibilities; another more stunning and novel set of possibilities was released when the Word in its most symbolically extravagant and impenetrable form came into contact with the cutting edge of modern historical criticism. The epic *Fall of Jerusalem* was not to be a history based on Josephus and rivalling Tasso, but the re-creation of a Book of Revelation in a time of reasoning doubt. As Carlyle proclaimed,

Every man that writes is writing a new Bible; or a new Apocrypha; to last for a week or a thousand years; he that convinces a man and sets him working is the doer of a *miracle*.[1]

The shape of romantic poetry, indeed of poetry to the present day, begins to be visible as the eighteenth-century Biblical epic emerges into the lyrical ballad.

Coleridge, we have already seen, was fully in agreement with the premises of the new Biblical criticism. The first premise, that criticism could not shirk bringing the Biblical accounts under the rational scrutiny of the new natural philosophy, had originated in a scathing attack from rationalists, deists, and sceptics on the whole range of supernatural claims made by and for the Bible. The second premise, that the Bible is to be approached like any other literary text, entailed the freedom to amend the 'Holy Spirit' by establishing an accurate text, sifting the historical sources, questioning the traditional ascriptions of authorship and date, scrutinizing the formation of the canon, and comparing the Scriptures coolly with the sacred and secular writings of other nations. The significance of this procedure, whether or not it was openly stated in any given case, was simply the abandonment of the claim that the Bible is 'inspired'.

At the same time, however, the literary treatment of the Bible opened the way to a new apologetics of free-thinking theism which was to salvage Christianity until very nearly the end of the Victorian era. It has been said that the higher criticism abolished traditional apologetics, only to establish a new apologetics *vis-à-vis* the Enlightenment. Coleridge's philosophical turn of mind led him to formulate the implications of the new criticism in the most general manner, and so made him both more radical than Eichhorn himself on several important issues and more sweepingly effective in creating a new apologetics.

The men who were prepared to apply the methods of secular literary criticism to the Bible were naturally quick to carry the results of their Biblical criticism back into secular literature. The intricate interrelationship between *critica sacra* and *critica profana* in this period has never been traced. Yet its overwhelming importance for nineteenth-century literature has never ceased to be proclaimed.

To take one example: the Old Testament prophets and the apostles of the New were now to be considered as secular authors; yet were they not in some sense 'inspired', though not literally dictated to by the Holy Spirit? What, then, is secular inspiration? This question came to focus in the figure of St John the Divine, the author of the Book of Revelation. The answers will give us an insight into the poet–seer with his 'flashing eyes and floating hair', and how he governed the final form of 'Kubla Khan'.

Of all the books of the Old and the New Testament, the Book of Revelation had a peculiar aptness and fascination in the 1790s for a young poet of Coleridge's inclinations. Coleridge's great aim and accomplishment in criticism as in poetry was to refine and authenticate a form of the supernatural. The literature of his youth was dogged by rationalist explanations and exposures as crude and as sensational as the 'Gothick' wonders and 'graveyard' sensibilities that passed for supernatural. An alteration in sensibility could only be wrought by a revolution in religious attitudes as well as in poetic modes. To poetize this book was to attempt the heights of Miltonic sublimity from a perspective dictated by the boldest results of criticism.

Milton, in the famous passage in *The Reason of Church Government* in which he reviewed the poetic genres of the Bible, including Job as the model of the 'brief epic', and 'the divine pastoral drama' in the Song of Solomon, spoke impressively of the Apocalypse:

And the Apocalypse of Saint John is the majestick image of a high and stately Tragedy, shutting up and intermingling her solemn Scenes and Acts with a sevenfold Chorus of halleluja's and harping symphonies.[2]

Not only does the enterprise of setting Revelation to poetry have the *imprimatur* of Milton, the highest of all authorities for the young poet Coleridge, but he envisages it in terms which suggest a wholly different approach from the neo-classical. If the versifying of the Bible according to neo-classical precepts was hedged about with dire warnings against the falsification of history and the mishandling of sacred doctrine, there was a longer tradition whereby Biblical poetry benefited not only from the solemnity of its subject but from a special freedom to invest a variety of genres. Biblical poetry in the eighteenth century was still able to accomplish the renovation and innovation of genres. It is in this sense that we may understand the words of Girard: 'L'épopée religieuse a été le grand rêve romantique.'[3]

The solemnity and weight of Biblical poetry were not owing to its sacredness only. The Alexandrian allegorical exegesis taken over by Christian apologists had located all knowledge whatsoever in the Bible. If this practice began as a defence against the superiority of pagan Greek learning in the Hellenistic world, the doctrine of the correspondence between secular and sacred wisdom became, by the time of Isidore of Seville's *Etymologiae*, an imperious claim for Israel's primacy in philosophy, science, and poetry, maintained, like the claim for literal historical primacy, well into the eighteenth century.

Thus, it was said, Genesis and Ecclesiastes are compendia of physics; ethics is summed up in the Proverbs of Solomon; in Job are to be found 'all the laws of dialectics'; and all of logic is set out in the Song of Songs, possibly the most astonishing of all the astonishing claims to be made for the Song of Songs.[4] Coleridge's *The Statesman's Manual* contains an only slightly more moderate contemporary variation on the theme: 'All the important truths and efficient practical directions of Thucydides, Tacitus, Machiavelli, Bacon and Harrington preexist in the Bible': and their 'particular rules and precepts flow directly and visibly from universal principles, as from a fountain'.[5]

The old view that the Bible contained all wisdom paradoxically took on new life through the historical-critical movement, for again all knowledge was brought to bear on it, and all human religious experience was to be found in it, not merely the special revelation of Christianity. Thus Herder wrote to Hamann:

Die 'magere' Bibel wird all sieben Wissenschaften der alten und tausend der neuen Welt wie die fetten Kühe Pharaos in sich schlucken, bis ein Tag kommt, der durch Facta und Acta alles entsiegelt.[6]

The 'lean' Bible will swallow all seven arts of the old world and a thousand of the new like the fat kine of Pharaoh, until a day comes that unseals all things in Facta and Acta.

No lean book of the Bible was better suited to become a Pharaonic cow, or a Trojan horse, of the new and the old knowledge than Revelation, which traditionally 'unsealed' the mysteries of the old world and a new to the eyes of the seer.

The Book of Revelation seemed to clamour for a free, an 'anti-classical', treatment. Older models for such a Revelation epic were the panoramic poems of the Patristic poets and the celestial cycle poems like Du Bartas's *Sepmaine*, treating the seven days of creation, and his unfinished second *Sepmaine* presenting the seven ages of man's restoration, Tasso's own *Il mondo creato*, and the epics of the three-phase celestial cycles that Milton drew on. Within the Biblical epic certain techniques grew up for both overcoming and taking advantage of formlessness. The earliest Christian manoeuvre, the typological interpretation of the Old Testament, whereby principal characters and events foreshadow their 'counterparts' in the New, made for great flexibility in time schemes, which was further extended by the Patristic adoption of the Virgilian prophetic dream and vision of the future, from then on a standard feature of Biblical epic. Typology succeeded in subordinating not only Old Testament, but also classical heroes to New Testament significance. As a whole series of Old Testament children – Abel, Isaac, Joseph, Samson – might be represented as types of Christ, so a variety of classical figures historical and fictional – the Curii, Socrates, Hercules – could equally well be types of Christ. Like typological linking, the dream-vision was particularly popular in the Middle Ages, and a striking epic example is the *Northern Passion* of the fourteenth century, which incorporated the matter of the Book of Revelation into the Passion story as a vision seen by John when he reclined on Christ's bosom at the Last Supper.[7] Indeed, the Book of Revelation can be taken as the climax and summation of the typological method, for coming at the end of the Bible it may be held to resume the whole structure, so that to unravel its symbols is to set before one the entire cycle from the division in heaven, to the creation of the world and the fall of man, to the reunion with the divine.

By the eighteenth century, Biblical poetry had attained a greater degree of freedom than even these epics enjoy. The necessity of finding formal elements outside the Bible had always been a source of freedom, for despite the claim that the Bible was the original of all forms, the poets, trained in the classics, looked even in the Bible for classical genres. The formlessness of the Bible by classical standards made it possible to impose almost any one of the panoply of classical forms on any book of the Bible.

Coleridge indulges in the sport:

It is quite wonderful, that Luther who could see so plainly that Judith was an Allegoric Poem should have been blind to the Book of Jonas being an Apologue, in which Jonas means the Israelitish nation![8]

The two most popular parts of the Old Testament, the Song of Songs and the Book of Job, were treated as 'models' – that is, as fit materials to have other forms imposed upon them – of an extraordinary range of genres. The Book of Job was sometimes thought of as a regular Greek tragedy. Milton, of course, considered it as the model of the 'brief epic'. Lowth devoted considerable space to arguing that it was not a classical tragedy: 'The Greeks would have called such a production a Monody, or Elegiac Dialogue, or anything but a tragedy.'[9] By then it sufficed as an accolade to call it simply the 'most sublime' of Hebrew poems.

Even more startling are the transformations undergone by the Song of Songs. Origen himself wrote a dramatic version of it. Bernard of Clairvaux's allegorical interpretation is one of the most brilliant works of the Middle Ages. Milton called it 'a divine pastoral drama'. In the eighteenth century, Herder, freed from classical genres by his comprehension of Hebrew poetry, broke new ground by considering it simply as a series of sensuous love songs, 'weltliche Liebeslieder', unconnected dramatically or allegorically, 'eine Reihe schöner Perlen auf eine Schnur gefasset', 'a series of lovely pearls strung on one thread'.[10] In 1775 Goethe did a translation in this spirit. At the time of the *West-östlicher Divan,* he still held that no connection could be found between 'these fragments'. But after the appearance in 1820 of K. F. Umbreit's translation and commentary, he described the connection once more as 'dramatic'; 'Und so löst sich der epische Unzusammenhang doch in einem Zusammenhange auf', 'And so epic disconnectedness resolves itself after all into a unity.'[11]

Coleridge similarly reshuffled the genres. He seems originally to have regarded the poem as an epithalamium on the marriage of Solomon to an Egyptian princess, a simple love-poem; but later returned to the view that it signified the Messiah's communion with the soul.[12]

The Bible, then, had always been a source for poetic genres, and lent itself to differing interpretations according to the popularity of certain genres at different times. The Sacred Writings, the literal Word of God, curiously became the most malleable of materials. No form, but an inspired formlessness, an infinite potentiality of form, or capacity to assume all forms, is suggested by the tradition of Biblical poetry.

The lyric poetry of the Bible, Milton had said in the passage in which he spoke of the Apocalypse, can rival the 'magnifick Odes and Hymns' of Pindar and Callimachus. With the introduction of the ode form late in the sixteenth century had emerged the figure of the inspired 'Pindaric' bard. In England, the Old Testament David the Harpist was quickly established as the poetic equal of the great classical odists. The Protestant hymnody of the Reformation adopted first the Old Testament psalms; the new Greek scholarship encouraged the many metrical translations of the Psalms of David, culminating, in England, in the classical humanist version of George Sandys in 1643. The new *Textkritik* of the Bible followed the same path, comparing first the New Testament Greek with classical Greek texts, and then moving on into Jewish–Hellenistic literature and, in John Lightfoot's work on the Gospels (1658–78), into the study of Biblical Hebrew. On this parallelism of Greek and Hebrew culture Milton built, accomplishing the first phase of poetic Orientalism.

Milton's *Samson Agonistes* combines tragedy with a sublime lyric art aspiring to outdo the Greek, and the preface to *Samson* describes the Book of Revelation as a precedent:

Pareus, commenting on the Revelation, divides the whole book as a tragedy, into acts, distinguished each by a Chorus of heavenly harpings and songs between.

The lyrical freedom won for Biblical poetry was exploited by Klopstock, the best of Milton's eighteenth-century imitators. His fine prose tragedy *Der Tod Adams*, *The Death of Adam*, versified in its English translation, is less a drama than an extended ode to death. In the *Messias*, he came close to combining the Miltonic epic with the Miltonic choric tragedy. As the theorist of 'heilige Poesie', 'sacred poetry', and a first-rate practitioner of the ode form, he adapted *geistliche Gesänge*, 'spiritual songs', to the purposes of the blank-verse hexameter epic. The actual events of the Passion being brief and iconographical, it is presented as a series of vast invocations, prophecies, visions, cosmic and individual prayers of praise, denunciations, lamentations, and seraphic rejoicings.

Klopstock was the champion of the possibility of a 'Protestant mythology' in poetry, and Coleridge sympathized with this, although he was able in practice to remove the note of sectarian controversy:

Are the 'innumerable multitude of angels & archangels' less splendid beings than the countless Gods & Goddesses of Rome & Greece?—And can you seriously think that Mercury from Jove equals in poetic sublimity 'the mighty Angel that came down from Heaven, whose face was as it were the Sun, and his feet as pillars of fire: Who set his right foot on the sea, and his left upon the earth. And he sent forth a loud voice; and when he had sent it forth, seven Thunders uttered their Voices: and when the seven Thunders had uttered their Voices, the mighty Angel lifted up his hand to Heaven, & sware by Him that liveth for ever & ever, that TIME was no more?' (Rev. 10, 1–6) Is not Milton a *sublimer* poet than Homer or Virgil? Are not his Personages more sublimely cloathed? And do you not know, that there is not perhaps *one* page in Milton's Paradise Lost, in which he has not borrowed his imagery from the *Scriptures*? – I allow, and rejoice that *Christ* appealed only to the understanding & the affections; but I affirm that, after reading Isaiah or St Paul's Epistle to the Hebrews, Homer & Virgil are disgustingly *tame* to me, & Milton himself barely tolerable.[13]

In view of the shape-shifting of Biblical texts in the direction of the lyric, it is hardly surprising that even Eichhorn's outline of the acts and scenes of the 'grand prophetic drama' of the Fall of Jerusalem, despite the euhemerizing commentary that follows, reads much more like Milton's 'seven-fold Chorus of halleluja's and harping symphonies' than like a dramatic action:

The Drama Itself

PRELUDE c. iv–c. viii. 5.

The Scene is set.

(a) God is seen sitting upon the throne. c. iv. 1–11.

(b) Jesus Christ is seen enthroned with God and in addition a volume containing future changes of things sealed in letters, and at the same time it is declared, no one but God and his companion on the throne knows the argument of the volume. c. v. 1–14. . .

(e) The horror of the omens increases, portending evils to the adversaries of the Christian religion. c. vi 12–17. . .

ACT I c. viii. 6–c. xii. 17.

Jerusalem falls, or Judaism is conquered by the Christian Religion

(a) Public calamity is prophesied. c. viii. 6–12.

Conclusion. The triple woe is proclaimed. c. viii. 13. . .

ACT II c. xii. 18–c. xx. 10.

Rome falls, or the Gentiles are conquered by the Christian religion. . .

Rome, the seat of idolatry, is described under the image of a sea monster, in order that an idea of idolatry should be excited in the souls of the readers. c. xii. 18–c. xiii. 10.

The preceding scene is set with another monster emerging from the earth which counterfeits the prophet, who, having arranged prodigies and miracles to deceive mankind, aids the sea-monster. c. xii. 11–18.

Conclusion. The happiness of the worshippers of God and the contented state and condition of their souls is contrasted with the rage of the profane Gentiles and tumult of spirit with which they burn. c. xiv. 1–5. . .

Rome at last falls. c. xvi. 17–21. . .

(c) Lament over conquered Rome. c. xviii. 1–24.

(d) Triumphal song. c. xix. 1–10.

(e) Triumphal march. c. xix. 11–c. xx. 3. . .

ACT III c. xx. 11–c. xxii. 5.

The heavenly Jerusalem descends from the sky, or the bliss of future life which will endure forever is described.

(a) The scene is set: namely, the dead are resurrected and honest men are assembled among the citizens of the heavenly republic. c. xx. 11–14.

(b) The New Jerusalem, seat of the rule of the Messiah and of the happiness of future life is described. c. xxi. 1–c. xxii. 5.[14]

The Book of Revelation, then, constituted the ultimate challenge to the writer of sublime poetry, to the bard aspiring to equal Pindar and David, and appeared so even in the hands of the soberest historical critic.

But what would be the character of an apocalyptic poem? If the Book of Revelation was the most sublime book of the Bible, it was also the most nearly uncanonical, the most suspect, the most questionable. It had been the first Biblical text (apart from the Pauline epistles) to be attacked by the early Fathers as unapostolic, and on literary grounds that were to be developed fully by the higher criticism, and most especially by Herder and by Coleridge himself. It could the more easily be breached: Eichhorn felt able to publish his commentary on it more than a decade before he dared approach the public with his work on the Gospels.

Moreover, the book's holiness was as heretical as its fraudulence. Its visionary character had rendered it a particular favourite of the extreme Protestant sects and those who like Boehme claimed a similar gift. To this day the standard Christian authorities are silent concerning a vast, subterranean, mystical, and sometimes half-mad literature of interpretation that fed on hermetic and cabbalistic sources and still flourishes in a variety of pseudo-scientific forms. Even those uses of it which were to become orthodox, the visions of the New Jerusalem in Protestant hymns, took root first in the sectarian fringes of Puritanism and in the Herrnhüter and finally in Wesleyanism. If Isaac Watts's hymns and John Wesley's translations from the Herrnhüter *Gesangbuch* now reside in Anglican hymnals, their development in Blake reminds us of the powerful idiosyncrasy of that Protestant claim to literal vision which rejoiced in the New Jerusalem:

> There is a land of pure Delight,
> Where Saints immortal reign;
> Infinite Day excludes the Night,
> And Pleasures banish Pain.

> There everlasting Spring abides,
> And never-withering Flowers;
> Death like a narrow Sea divides
> This Heav'nly Land from ours.

> Sweet Fields beyond the swelling Flood
> Stand drest in living Green:
> So to the *Jews* old Canaan stood,
> While *Jordan* roll'd between.   (Watts)

The Book of Revelation lent itself with particular pyrotechnic ease to the eighteenth-century conception of the epic as sacred song. At the same time, its purported author became the focus of the investigation of the nature of prophetic inspiration and the authenticity of the Biblical canon. Could John the Apostle, John the Evangelist, and John the Apocalyptic have been the same man? If not, what was the basis of the author's authority, and, by extension, of the canonical authority of the Book of Revelation and indeed of the Fourth Gospel?

Once again, it had been Herder who had begun to consider the Old Testament prophets not as receptacles of divine inspiration, but as men with a special gift for evoking the numinous; and all that Herder had enthusiastically suggested, Eichhorn converted into the hermeneutic norm.[15] In the 1790s their analysis touched the New Testament: as Christianity lost its claim to a unique revelation, the apostles themselves could be seen as prophet–poets, as bards of an antique saga. As the dating and the historical analysis of the contents of the Gospels proceeded, John was set apart from the three newly labelled 'synoptic' Gospel writers, as reflecting a Hellenistic, philosophized account of the original Judaic saga.[16] The traditional fondness for John as the young apostle who was Jesus's favourite merges oddly but impressively with his new importance as the carrier of pagan conceptions into the mainstream of Christianity. In John, the antique bard evolved into the sophisticated conscious poet; John became the New Testament equivalent of Pindar and David. John the Apocalyptic absorbed the new intensity of the Evangelist's image; and the scepticism attaching to his own identity, and therefore to his prophetic capacity, increased the ambiguous attractions and the poetic range of 'John'. In the context of Biblical criticism, the strange conjunction of the especially holy and the especially heretical that had always characterized the Book of Revelation was carried over decisively into the romantic seer. In the familiar yet uncanny figure of the holy man of 'Kubla Khan' we have one of the very first of a long line of apostles of poetry.

Herder's anti-supernatural view of prophecy, his Hebraic 'humanism', was prefigured in literature, as the new Biblical criticism was to have in turn a striking effect on literature. In Klopstock's *Messias*, the Book of Revelation is incorporated into the figure of the visionary apostle John, the most prominent and vivid person – perhaps the only person – in the poem, and indispensable to its theology: as Jesus is the merciful mediator between God and man, so John is the merciful mediator between the Son of God and man. The young friend of Jesus, like Goethe's Iphigenia, is the image of the humane, civilized man of feeling. It is precisely his humanity that makes him the beloved of Christ and opens to him the visionary experiences denied to the other apostles. This somewhat surprising collocation follows from Klopstock's treatment of prophecy as rational event, Coleridge's objections to which we have already noted. According to Klopstock, if John is seen as fully human, then his visions, being rationalized at their source, can be as extravagant as the poet pleases. But just as when he presents miracle as 'fact', so when he presents human feeling as prophetic, the gap is not narrowed but widened between nature and supernature. In the context of individual psychology, moreover, the technique works much more successfully than in a 'factual' fantasy of the miraculous. It is not the doubting audience that is witness to the vision in history, but John, and his credible human sentiments and tender susceptibility render his visions comprehensible and genuine, although they are in no sense self-induced, or 'psychological' in a modern sense. The technique works so well that the reader more than once wishes that Klopstock had imagined the whole of his epic through John's eyes. But in the epic tradition the inspired poet narrated events from outside the poem; he did not sing them from within. Klopstock still claimed objectivity of vision both for the bard and for the visionary character.

The first scene with John is the highpoint of that graveyard poetry over which Klopstock waxed so enthusiastic, holding up 'the prophet' Young's *Nächte* as his great model after Milton.[17] Unaccountable as this enthusiasm for the *Night-Thoughts* may seem to the English reader, we see here what could be made of it.

In Book I and the opening of Book II (in heaven) the imagery of light and dark has already been established on a cosmic scale. Jesus is first seen alone on the Mount of Olives, as the souls of Adam and Eve pray to Him for mercy for the human race.

> Jesus vernahm sie
> Fern in der Tiefe. Wie mitten in heiligen Einsiedleyen,
> In der Zukunft Folge vertieft, prophetische Weise
> Dich, in der fern herwandelnde Stimme des Ewigen, hören.[18]

The Messiah heard them in his deep recess, as in a sacred solitude, the holy prophet rapt in contemplation, hears, in soft whispers, the voice of the Eternal.[19]

He descends, seeking John. Raphael describes to Him how John in his sleep had visions of Jesus, and tells Him where to find John: among the sepulchres of human bones, caring for a man possessed by grief. Jesus, touched by Raphael's description of John as the type of humanity, approaches 'den Gräbern der Toten', the tombs of the dead.

> Unten am mitternächtlichen Berge waren die Gräber
> In zusammengebirgte zerrüttete Felsen gehauen.
> Dicke, finsterverwachsene Wälder verwahrten den Eingang,
> Vor des fliehenden Wandrers Blick. Ein trauriger Morgen
> Stieg, wenn der Mittag schon sich über Jerusalem senkte,
> Dämmernd noch in die Gräber mit kühlem Schauer hinunter.[20]

Jesus now drew near to the sepulchres hewn in the cliff of the rock, where thick and gloomy woods guarded the entrance from the view of the hasty traveller. Here the morning dawn lowered in chilly coolness, and the sun faintly shot his beams among the tombs.[21]

The terrible episode follows in which the 'possessed' man Samma kills his youngest and favourite son by dashing him against the cliff, and is overwhelmed again by his own grief. We recognize the world of Wordworth's 'Guilt and Sorrow' and 'The Mad Mother'. Jesus restores Samma:

> Ins bleiche Gesicht voll Todesgestalten
> Kam die Menschheit zurück, er schrie, und weinte gen Himmel.[22]

Life [in an earlier version, 'Humanität'] dawns in that face, which just before had the awful stamp of death. With a loud cry and streaming eyes, he looks towards heaven.[23]

The remaining son turns to John to ask that he and his healed father be permitted to follow the prophet Jesus. Jesus dismisses them gently, and remains with John among the graves of man, until later the apostles seek Jesus as night falls and the threats to His life increase.

Again at the Last Supper Jesus vouchsafes a vision to John, the only one of the disciples to see it, and again this is the direct result of his humanity. Jesus passed the bread and the sacred cup:

Da Johannes sich naht, und auf den glänzenden Kelch sah,
Warf er zu Jesus Füssen sich nieder, küsste die weinend,
Trocknete dann die Thränen mit seiner fallenden Locke,
  Lass ihn meine Herrlichkeit sehn! sprach Jesus und schaute
Zu dem Vater empor. Johannes erhub sich, und sahe
In der Tiefe des Saals der Seraphim helle Versammlung.
Und die Seraphim wüssten, dass er sie sahe. Johannes
Stand in Entzückung verloren. Er schaute Gabriels Hoheit
Starr, mit Erstaunen. Er schaute des himmlischen Raphael Glänzen.
Und verehrt ihn. Er sah auch Salem in menschlichem Schimmer,
Und mit ausgebreiteten Armen entgegen ihm lächeln;
Und er liebte den Seraph. Er wandte sich um, und erblickte
In des Messias rühigem Auge die Spuren der Gottheit;
Und er sank verstümmend ans Herz des erhabnen Messias.[24]

When John, seized with a sudden transport, sunk down at his feet, kissed them, and wetted them with his tears.

Jesus then, looking up towards heaven, with a gracious smile, cried, O Father! permit him to see my glory. John then arising beheld at the end of the chamber a bright assembly of angels, who knew that he saw them. Rapt in an ecstatic transport, he beheld the sublime Gabriel, with motionless astonishment: enraptured he saw the brightness of the celestial Raphael, and him he honoured: with delight unutterable, he also perceived Salem in an human form, who with a smile of friendship, opened his arms, and him he loved. Now, turning his ravished eyes, he discovered in the Messiah's placid countenance ['Auge'], traces of his celestial glory, and sunk speechless on his bosom.[25]

John's traditional pose in Jesus's arms is here the direct and immediate result of his having been overcome by a vision of Christ's glory. Vision and human love are inextricable. The intense preference for John over the other apostles in this contemporary form passed over, through Lessing and Herder, into Biblical criticism. The process by which the Evangelists became antique Oriental bards, and John the philosophic and poetic genius among them, is as complex as it is fascinating.

John was brought into special prominence by the investigation of the order and mutual relations of the four Gospels. J. D. Michaelis, whose *Einleitung in das Neue Testament, Introduction to the New Testament,* Coleridge read in translation in 1795, denied the mutual dependence of the three first Gospels, and attributed their similarities to a common use of 'anderer apocryphische Evangelia', 'other apocryphal Gospels', that is, he originated the idea that behind the existing Gospels stood an earlier text or texts. Lessing, in one of his *Kleine Schriften*, 'Theses aus der Kirchengeschichte', 'Theses from Ecclesiastical History', published only after his death, suggested that the *Urevangelium* or archetypal Gospel standing behind the three first Gospels was the Aramaic gospel of the heretical Jewish Christians (Nazarenes) reported by the Church Fathers. By tracing the synoptic gospels to a heretical Jewish original, Lessing increased the value of the Gospel of John. It was John who had rescued the Gospel out of the hands of an ephemeral Jewish sect and made it worthy to be the basis of a world religion:

Nur sein Evangelium gab der christlichen Religion ihre wahre Konsistenz; nur seinem Evangelio haben wir es zu danken, wenn die christliche Religion in dieser Konsistenz allen Anfällen ungeachtet noch fortdauert und vermutlich so lange fortdauern wird, als es Menschen gibt, die eines Mittlers zwischen ihnen und der Gottheit zu bedürfen glauben; das ist ewig.[26]

Only his Gospel gave the Christian religion its true consistency; we have his Gospel alone to thank if the Christian religion in this consistency still endures in spite of all onslaughts and continues to endure as we suppose it will as long as there are human beings who believe that they require a mediator between them and divinity; that is eternal.

Eichhorn carried out Michaelis's suggestion more fully, and it is usually with his name that the *Urevangeliumshypothese* is associated.[27] Eichhorn's attempt to go behind the existing documents had the effect of throwing interest back on the earliest historical conditions of primitive Christianity. Much of what the Gospels told of Jesus consisted of mere 'sagas', he held, late accretions drawn from pre-Christian legendary material.

If Eichhorn showed a certain rationalist contempt for sagas and legends, Herder fell on the suggestion enthusiastically. He agreed with Lessing that the *Jesusbild* of the synoptic Gospels was at odds with that of John, and that John was incomparably superior in literary value and theological sophistication. But he was prepared to accord the earlier Evangelists special value as primitive poets of the new religion. The oldest Gospel was Jesus's own preaching, and the apostles, like rhapsodes ('evangelische Rhapsoden'), composed out of their witness not a written Gospel, but an oral one, that gradually grew into a cycle, held in common by the community. He criticized his colleagues for applying the notions of a bookish age to the primitive unlettered society of the earliest Christians, and he analysed the style of the Gospels in terms of primitive bardic poetry:

Bei einer freien mündlichen Erzählung ist nicht alles gleich frei. Sentenzen, grosse Aussprüche, Parabeln erhalten sich eher in demselben Ausdruck, als kleine Umstände der Geschichte; Übergänge und Bindungsformeln wählet der Erzählende selbst. In unsern Evangelien ist dieser Unterschied klar. Gewisse, insonderheit starke, dunkle, parabolische Ausdrücke sind allenthalben, selbst mit verschiedener Deutung, dieselben; in Umständen, in Übergängen, in Ordnung der Begebenheiten gehen die Erzählungen am freisten aus einander. . .

Das gemeinsame Evangelium bestand aus einzelnen Stücken, Erzählungen, Parabeln, Sprüchen, Perikopen. Dies gibt die Ansicht der Evangelien selbst und die verschiedene Ordnung, in der diese und jene Parabel oder Sage gesetzt ist. . . . Es bürgt für die Wahrheit des Evangeliums, dass es aus solchen Theilen bestehet: denn Leute, wie die meisten Apostel waren, erinnerten sich leichter eines Spruches, einer Parabel, eines Apophthegma, das ihnen auffallend gewesen war, als zusammenhängender Reden. . .[28]

In a free oral narrative not everything is equally free. Maxims, great sayings, parables are more easily retained in the same form of expression than trivial details of history: transitions and connecting formulas the narrator chooses himself. In our Gospels this difference is clear. Certain particularly strong, dark, parabolic expressions are everywhere the same, even when they have various meanings; in circumstantial detail, in transitions, in the ordering of events the Gospel narratives depart from one another most freely. . .

The common Gospel consisted of separate pieces, stories, parables, sayings, pericopes. This is clear from the form of the Gospels themselves and from the differing order in which this and that parable or saga is placed. It is a guarantee of the truth of the Gospel that it consists of such fragments: for common people, as most of the apostles were, were better able to remember a saying, a parable, an apothegm than logically consistent speeches. . .

Although Herder agreed that John was superior both as theology and as literature to the other evangelists, he regarded these merits as derived from and developing the special qualities of the primitive bardic cycle. It was precisely the legendary basis of saga that made the Gospels

a testament of faith rather than a chronicle of the biographical facts of
the life of Jesus, and therefore opened the way for John's philosophical
treatment of the legendary material:

Überhaupt beweiset das Evangelium Johannes die Idee am besten, . . . dass
sie die Evangelien nämlich auf keine Weise Biographieen, sondern historische
Beurkundungen des christlichen Glaubensbekenntnisses seyn sollten, das
Jesus der Christ sey, and wie er es gewesen. Johannes Evangelium, als das
späteste, verfolgt diesen Zweck im bestimmtesten Umriss; eine eigentliche
Biographie verliert man dabei ganz aus dem Augen, an welche man auch, als
Hauptidee derselben betrachtet, bei den ältern Evangelien nicht denken
sollte. Sie sind, was ihr Name saget.[29]

The Gospel of John offers by far the best proof of the idea. . .that the
Gospels were not meant in any sense as biographies, but as historical witnesses to the Christian faith that Jesus was the Christ, and in the manner
described. John's Gospel, as the latest in date, pursues this aim most firmly;
it banishes all notions of an actual biography, as indeed, even in the earlier
Gospels, the leading idea ought never to be thought of as biographical. The
Gospels are, what their name conveys.

In Herder's formulation, there was no longer any need to choose
between the virtues of the primitive cycle and the virtues of the
sophisticated, self-conscious version of it; the sophisticated bard
unfolded more fully and theoretically, although in the same 'dark'
style, what the primitive bard had indispensably envisioned. The
opposites of primitive and sophisticate, of naive and sentimental, were
reconciled in the figure of the poet–prophet John. 'John' represents
a solution to Herder's life-long attempts to define the primitive state
in such a way that it clearly denoted the highest poetic quality.

Coleridge, following rather than initiating these developments,
took an independent course through them. He too regarded both the
Old Testament prophets and the New Testament evangelists as bards.
In his *Confessions of an Enquiring Spirit, or Letters on the Inspiration of
the Scriptures*, he subscribed with a fullness of enthusiasm that outdoes
even Herder to the poetic inspiration of the bard David:

But let me once be persuaded that all these heart-awakening utterances of
human hearts – of men of like faculties and passions with myself, mourning,
rejoicing, suffering, triumphing – are but as a *Divina Commedia* of a superhuman – Oh bear with me, if I say – Ventriloquist; – that the royal Harper, to

whom I have so often submitted myself as a *many-stringed instrument* for his fire-tipt fingers to traverse, while every several nerve of emotion, passion, thought, that thrids the flesh-and-blood of our common humanity, responded to the touch, – that this *sweet Psalmist of Israel* was himself as mere an instrument as his harp, an *automaton* poet, mourner, and supplicant; – all is gone, – all sympathy, at least, and all example.[30]

Vigorous defence of the bardic abilities of prophetic Orientals was encouraged by Enlightened sneers at the Pentateuch as an 'Arabian tale'. Coleridge held that the first eleven chapters of Exodus are 'of a later date, a distinct book, a traditional Life of Moses and his brother Aaron' and that they were compiled by the 'Rhapsodi, or Homerenoumenoi, the Bards or Prophets' who collected the cycle of war songs or ballads 'rudely organized in the Historical Book of Judges'.[31]

In his willingness to attribute the Books of Moses and other parts of the Old Testament to a series of bards and interpolators, Coleridge was more radical than Eichhorn. Eichhorn refused, through the four editions of his book, to entertain the idea that the Pentateuch was not all of a piece (though it might have been written by 'the Deuteronomist' rather than Moses); this has been accounted the major block in his Old Testament scholarship.[32]

Coleridge may well have been better prepared than Eichhorn to entertain the most radical hypothesis about the Pentateuch, for this had been an English speciality since Hobbes had first suggested in *Leviathan* that the Books of Moses were not by but about Moses.[33] He was of course familiar with Spinoza's attribution of the Pentateuch to Ezra. Moreover, from at least 1792 Coleridge was familiar with Geddes's 'Fragment-Hypothesis': the Pentateuch did not merely draw on earlier sources, but was put together by an editor out of a collection of independent and often conflicting fragments.[34]

The terms in which Coleridge puts his acceptance of the fragmentation, however, show how thoroughly he had absorbed Herder's notion of the communal experience as a unifying element. Thus he agreed with Eichhorn that interpolations in the Book of Daniel during the tyranny of Antiochus Epiphanes made it a 'political Pamphlet' and, as the deist Anthony Collins had pointed out, not prophecy at all;[35] but this in no way detracts from the authenticity of the Book, for the interpolations were made by 'men of genius' among the Maccabees who employed 'floating legends' well-known in the Jewish community and equivalent to ours of 'Merlin, Nostradamus, etc. and the Greeks and Romans of the Sibyls'.[36]

Coleridge was prepared to multiply interpolations, and to defend them, where Eichhorn denied them. On Genesis 36, 31 he remarked:

> But why *not* consider this as a gloss introduced by the Editors of the Penta-teuch, or Preparers of the Copy that was to be layed up in the Temple of Solomon? The authenticity of the Books would be no more compromised by such glosses, than that of the Book before me by this marginal Note of mine.[37]

In short, such additions, as long as they are indigenous, actually add to the Bible's value as a record of the community, political and folkloric as well as religious.

For Coleridge, this view of the Pentateuch banished the orthodox claim to the literal inspiration of the New Testament as well, for the doctrine of absolute inspiration, of supernatural dictation or theo-pneusty, was derived, he wrote, from the Rabbis, who 'confined this miraculous character to the Pentateuch. Between the Mosaic and the Prophetic inspiration they asserted such a difference as amounts to a diversity.'[38]

In the same way, he was more radical than Eichhorn about the documentary backing for the Gospels. He agreed with Eichhorn, against Schleiermacher, that there was some documentary backing from apostolic times for the Gospels as finally formulated in the second century (he may not have known Schleiermacher on Luke until he annotated Thirlwall's translation in 1825). He did not, how-ever, admit an *Urevangelium* in the literal sense of a manuscript drawn on by the writers of the Gospels, but sophisticated it rather through a Herderian conception of a community of oral, legendary material that helped shape the primary documents as well as the Gospels.[39]

The New Testament like the Old Testament was a 'cycle' which was held in common by the members of the primitive community, and which could always be added to or revised in the light of new circum-stances. The flexibility of the text under primarily oral conditions is appropriately transferred to the critical interpretation when the text becomes fixed in literate times. The piecemeal, traditional, inconsistent character of the text, and its construction out of mobile 'elements', is precisely the mark of its essential wholeness, its ability to maintain its most general purposes through no matter how much alteration of specific parts.

Nothing could better illustrate Coleridge's admiration for 'John' as the New Testament bard than his early attempts to poetize the Book of Revelation in the style of Klopstock:

> And blest are they,
> Who in this fleshly World, the elect of Heaven,
> Their strong eye darting through the deeds of men,
> Adore with steadfast unpresuming gaze
> Him Nature's essence, mind, and energy!
> And gazing, trembling, patiently ascend
> Treading beneath their feet all visible things
> As steps, that upward to their Father's throne
> Lead gradual – else nor glorified nor loved.
> They not contempt embosom nor revenge:
>   For they dare know of what may seem deform
> The Supreme Fair sole operant: in whose sight
> All things are pure, his strong controlling love
> Alike from all educing perfect good.
> Their's too celestial courage, inly armed –
> Dwarfing Earth's giant brood, what time they muse
>   On their great Father, great beyond compare!
> And marching onwards view high o'er their heads
>   His waving banners of Omnipotence.[40]

Herder made his own passionate attempt at conveying the style of 'John':

He who has eyes to see, or who is possessed of any genuine feeling, will trace in the apocalypse the same prevailing features which distinguish the Gospel. . . [T]he spirit which pervades it, is, after all, the greatest text. If I were to describe the writings of St. John, I should say they shewed a soul both strong and tender; an amiable anxiety to be perspicuous; a peculiar gift for leading his reader by the slightest indication; strong masses of light and shade; economy, and at the same time copiousness, of imagery; a constant recurrence to the main thought, through the slender threads with which it is insensibly connected. His Gospel is pregnant with poetical simplicity, and varies with most significant emblems. In the one you see the eagle, soaring to the sun; in the other you have the dove, with all its native mildness. The Revelations are like the royal aloe, pre-eminent above plants.

The Gospel is the lily and the rose, streaked with the blood of affection: the least word conveys the sentiment to the heart.[41]

Neither Herder's rhetorical description of the style nor Coleridge's attempt to reproduce it comes very near the mark; but their aspiration, at least, is clear. It is, indeed, the John of the Apocalypse who seems to fuse the Apostle and the Evangelist, and so sets a stylistic standard impossible to achieve: he sees both the historical milieu of Jesus and the milieu of the philosophized history of the Fourth Gospel as one visionary landscape.[42] Herder's *Blätter* on contemporary poetry contain a lively dialogue between a Christian and a Rabbi, under the heading 'Christian poems in oriental taste (Klopstock)' – notice the classification of Klopstock's New Testament epic *Messias* as 'Oriental' – in which the Rabbi complains that Klopstock has no sense whatsoever for the Jewish milieu of Jesus, and the Christian defends Klopstock on the equally historical grounds that the *Messias* is 'a song of the origin of our religion'.[43] From the Christian point of view, it is quite right not to depict the realistic historical milieu as it was known to contemporary Jews, but the 'mythological' milieu of the Gospels, the milieu of belief.

The Christian reinforces his point by exclaiming:

Hätte unser Johannes, der ihn bis an seinen Tod begleitet, und sein Plato ward, mit dem feurigen Pinsel der Apokalypse ihn schildern sollen; so hätte er ihm so viel individuale Bestimmung gegeben, dass jeder rufen müsste: 'Das ist er! Johannes hat ihn gesehen.'

Had our John, who accompanied Him until His death, and became his Plato, wished to depict Him with the fiery brush of the Apocalypse, he would have given him so much individual characterization that every one would have been obliged to exclaim: 'That is he! John saw him!'[44]

The Apostle John, then, who saw Jesus with his own eyes, and the Evangelist John who philosophized His teaching, merge in the apocalyptic style. Epic objectivity is transformed into the epic subjectivity of vision: intensity of perception and profundity of doctrine are one and the same. The extraordinary but typically romantic conjunction begins to emerge: primal historical fact can be known only through visionary eyes. The apocalyptic bard gives us the historical milieu and the milieu of Christian belief as the landscape of mythology.

The conception of the prophet–poet underwent a further crucial change before it could emerge in its fully romantic guise. As it became clear that the Evangelists were far removed in time and space from Jesus, not only the traditional idea of inspiration as coming directly from God, but the newer idea of historical authenticity was undermined. Doubts about the apostolic authorship of Revelation had always been voiced; but now, paradoxically, the very value that Lessing and Herder placed on John helped to undermine the Fourth Gospel; for towards the end of the eighteenth century their insistence on the Hellenistic–philosophic tone of the Gospel gave grounds for suspecting that it could not have been written in apostolic times nor even in a Judaic milieu. Further burden was thereby placed on the 'visionary' element in the historical experience; yet what was the source and authority of the visionary element? Moreover, the Orientalism of the Scriptures was overwhelmingly confirmed by this new development; the increasing remoteness from the immediate environment of Jesus extended the range of Oriental references in the New Testament far beyond what had been meant by speaking of the 'Orientalism' of Hebrew poetry. The Word of God and His prophets became more and more tenuous, non-literal, and a-historical. Eichhorn and after him Coleridge undertook to restore 'John' and canonicity in terms that were a monument to the end of dogmatic authority. The bard of the Gospels was created once again new, his historical inauthenticity the essence of his character.

Doubts about the authorship of the Book of Revelation had begun with Origen, who pointed out what bad Greek the Apocalyptic wrote, in blatant contrast to the learned and elegant Evangelist. Dionysius had cuttingly suggested that he was the John Mark who was servant of Barnabas and Paul (Acts 12, 25); this would account too for his familiarity with Jewish legendary and heterodox material. Luther had rejected it; as had Semler. Michaelis, reviewing the entire tradition in his *Introduction*, concluded that the Book of Revelation should not be accounted canonical.[45] Nearer home still, Coleridge found the view that the author of the Apocalypse could not have been John the apostle and evangelist: Lardner, for whose learning he had the highest respect, had written, 'I must acknowledge that the Revelation, when compared with the apostle's unquestioned writings, has an unlikeness not easy to be accounted for.'[46]

A more popular suggestion, and one which is still accepted by the reputable commentator Austin Farrer, was that the author of Revelation was 'Presbyter John'. In Farrer's view, the Apostle John wrote nothing; Presbyter John wrote the Book of Revelation; and the Evangelist wrote the Epistles but was neither John.[47]

The attribution to 'Prester John' gives the greatest possible range to the undeniable Oriental provenance and connotations of the Book of Revelation. 'Prester John' was thought to rule over an immense and vague area of 'the East', until the Portuguese explorations had begun to show otherwise. He was held to be the Christian king of India; the Portuguese when they first landed assumed that the Hindu temples were a local form of Christianity. Indeed, most non-Muslim Asiatics were thought to be some kind of fallen Christians, so literal was the 'monotheist' hypothesis.[48] In the same way, because Alexander had penetrated to India, many local phenomena were interpreted as results of the Greek conquest; even Asoka's column was thought to have bastard Greek writing on it. As so often, the imposition of a Christian interpretation on Oriental cultures was paralleled by the imposition of a Hellenic interpretation.

Yet the vast extent of Prester John's possessions linked Christianity with numerous genuine if still half-legendary Asiatic phenomena. There was even a medieval tradition that St John himself was 'the wandering Jew', the result possibly of the extension of his Oriental travels through the 'Prester John' stories.[49] 'Prester John' was identified in J. Ludolphus, *A New History of Ethiopia* (1682) as an Asian king – 'Prester-Chan' – who had been driven out of his kingdom by the king of the Tartars and was later wrongly regarded as an African king.[50] Apparently the refugee king took up his abode in Abyssinia, for in Herbert's *Travels*, his chief fort was described as being at Amara, and he was given a Jewish connection: as a descendant of 'Maqueda the Sabaean Queen', whose people became Jewish proselytes through the affectionate offices of Solomon. The specific place of conflict between the Tartars and the Christian king and bishop was not in China, where Kubla Khan ruled, but in India, where under the Mughal descendants of Kubla one of the great Moslem civilizations of the world developed, adorned by the wonderful 'pleasure domes' described by Jones and the English returning from their struggles with Tipu Sultan, the last of the dynasty.

The author of the Book of Revelation, then, Christian, Moslem, and Jewish, Indian, Abyssinian, and African ruler, sage and magician, victorious and defeated, is the compendium of Oriental Christianity. Even if 'Presbyter John' is stripped of his legendary empire, and is simply an historical bishop of Ephesus, he stands guard over the earliest Eastern outpost of Christianity, and is the appropriate author for the 'Asiatic book' of the Bible.

Indeed, even if the author is taken to be John the Evangelist, it has been shown in overwhelmingly convincing and erudite detail from Herder to C. H. Dodd, how thoroughly permeated is the Fourth Gospel with Hellenistic thought of all kinds: with the pagan hermetic philosophies, with the work of Philo, in which the fusion of Greek with Judaic thought had already in the first century been effected, with Greek and Coptic gnosticism.[51] On whatever view, the Gospel of John presents a striking synthesis of Oriental thought, whether of the period just before, just after, or considerably after, the Fall of Jerusalem. As Beckwith says in his commentary, 'Whoever the author of the Book of Revelation, the Book's origin is always "Asian".'[52]

Eichhorn still held that the author is John the Evangelist and Apostle. His grounds for maintaining the orthodox position, however, are of the greatest significance for the development of the mythological view of Christianity. If John the Apostle is today generally deprived of the authorship of the Book of Revelation, the way this is stated by the authoritative *Lexikon für Theologie und Kirche* ('from a dogmatic point of view' the question is declared 'open') sums up the new and subtle way of handling these unsavoury facts suggested by Eichhorn and extended by Coleridge.[53]

Eichhorn proposed a new solution to the problems raised by Michaelis over the authenticity of the Book of Revelation. Michaelis had made it a major issue, and one that threatened to block the progress of historical criticism, by holding that canonicity (and therefore inspiration) should in all cases depend on the authentic apostolic origin of the text. If this test had been applied, the resulting canon could have been hardly larger than Marcion's heretical gnostic canon of the second century comprising Mark and three Pauline letters. If historical criticism was to hold the Gospels non-apostolic, then it had to find another test of canonicity, or put historical criticism altogether beyond the pale of theological respectability.

Eichhorn's procedure displays his usual mixture of boldness and conservative intention. He declined to enter into the controversy that had raged since the third century, saying evasively that 'the *canonical authority* of the poem does not depend on the name of the author, but rather on the testimony of the early church and on its argument', 'Carminis enim "auctoritas canonica" non pendet ab auctoris nomine, sed a testimoniis potius veteris ecclesiae et ab eius argumento.'[54]

In short, Eichhorn, like Schleiermacher, reversed Michaelis's rule. Canonicity was not to depend on apostolic authorship, but authorship on canonicity, in two senses, first, the tradition within the church, and second, the conformity of the doctrine with apostolic teaching. As Schleiermacher put it, a person in agreement with an Apostle's teaching 'es eine ganz erlaubte Fiction ansehen konnte, dass er seine Schrift unter des Apostels Namen herausgab', 'could regard it as a completely permissible fiction to publish his writings under the apostle's name'.[55] The reliance on the argument of the poem went back to Semler's rather crude, though authentically Lutheran literary test of the authenticity of the contents, on the basis of which he denied the authorship of Revelation to John: it gave him no 'Nährung für sein Herz', 'nourishment for his heart'.[56] The doctrine of the weight of tradition is related both to Herder's stress on communal feeling rather than fact, and to the Reformation's theological bias. But tradition is understood in a totally new way: it is neither the unquestioned authority of the Church nor the unquestioned authority of the Biblical text on which tradition rests, but the perpetually shifting sense within the Christian community of what has the power to persuade its members and strengthen them in the faith. Coleridge was to develop these two, still embryonic, approaches into one in his later writings: whatever the literal, documentable truth might be found to be, the historical experience of conviction within the Christian community was in itself a form of validation, and this experience could be maintained and reawakened through an imaginative grasp of what that experience had been. Apostolic authorship depended on canonicity, and canonicity ultimately on inspiration in the new sense of the capacity to recreate imaginatively the experience of faith.[57]

These concerns were, of course, at the centre of romantic aesthetics. The need for imaginative reconstruction of events which could not be reliably known in any other way led directly to the elaboration of the poet's power to recreate and the audience's ability to share in the poetic process. The issue was raised in the classic essay on Biblical hermeneutics, J. A. Ernesti's *Institutio Interpretis Novi Testamenti* (1761), translated in 1832 as *Principles of Biblical Interpretation*. Hermeneutics is the general principles of interpretation of texts; interpretation is exegesis, or application of principles. Ernesti wrote simply:

Interpretation is the art of teaching the real sentiment contained in any form of words, or of effecting that another may derive from them the same idea that the writer intended to convey.[58]

Schleiermacher, meditating on Ernesti early in the nineteenth century, posed the question at a more philosophical level: What is it to understand? Under what conditions is *Verstehen* possible?[59] Until Schleiermacher, hermeneutics was only 'ein Gebäude der Regeln', 'an edifice of rules', as Dilthey put it.[60] Even Ernesti, although he started from purely linguistic considerations, suggested the scope of the enterprise: the interpreter must not only know the Biblical languages, he must possess 'distinguished attainments, in antiquities, history, chronology, in short, in all liberal knowledge and critical art'.[61] Schleiermacher called for an 'allgemeine Hermeneutik', a 'general hermeneutics'. This required not simply the application of textual rules, but the 'Nachbildung eines fremden Lebens', 'the reconstruction of alien experience', the experience of the author within his historical milieu. Schleiermacher drew on Winckelmann's art criticism, on Herder's mode of empathy with earlier periods, and on the new aesthetic philosophy of Heyne and F. A. Wolf, as well as on Friedrich Schlegel, who had planned an *ars critica* grounded in a theory of the productive literary capacity, illustrated by his essays on Greek poetry, on Goethe, and Boccaccio. The philosophical underpinnings of his general hermeneutics he borrowed from Schelling, especially the *Vorlesungen über die Methode des akademischen Studiums* (1802), *Lectures on the Methods of University Studies*. Briefly stated, 'art is *the* instrument whereby empirical history is possible'.[62] To put it another way, only art can hold out the hope that 'Past thoughts can be re-enacted in the minds of the historians.'[63]

Dilthey described the major accomplishment of Schleiermacher's hermeneutics in these terms:

Sie soll gegenüber dem beständigen Einbruch romantischer Willkür und skeptischer Subjektivität in das Gebiet der Geschichte die Allgemeingültigkeit der Interpretation theoretisch begründen, auf welcher aller Sicherheit der Geschichte beruht.[64]

The function of hermeneutics, as against the continuous intrusion of romantic arbitrariness and sceptical subjectivity into the domain of history, is to provide a theoretical grounding for the general validity of the interpretation, on which all historical certainty rests.

But Dilthey spoke as the founder of the *Geisteswissenschaften*, of the modern social sciences, as one concerned with finding an 'objectivity' to rank with (though not identical with) that claimed by the natural sciences. Dilthey, then, distorted Schleiermacher in borrowing romantic techniques of empathy and of recreation in order to ground a new claim to objectivity for the historical sciences. For the romantics there was no guarantee of objectivity; sceptical subjectivity was at the basis of the need to have recourse to the poetic reconstruction of past experience.

The recourse to art for explanation, for *Verstehen*, became a programme for art. In 'The Ancient Mariner', Coleridge drew a visionary character belonging clearly to the primitive milieu in which apostolic credulity could flourish. These were the apostles as the *Wolfenbüttel Fragmente* described them – poor, deprived, ill-educated men, subject to accesses of superstitious fear and reverence. And these were the apostles as Herder described them, primitive bards telling a tale destined to be repeated over and over again, and winning an audience in the most unlikely places. The poem wholly conveys the authenticity of the incredible event in the psyche of the teller, which is unassailable, and has the power of communicating itself to others.

Coleridge could not have known Schleiermacher's lectures on hermeneutics directly, for they were not published until 1838; but he had the same background in Biblical criticism, and there is no doubt he attempted to find an historical art of interpretation that would lend the poise of objectivity to the subjective process of 'Nachbildung eines fremden Lebens'. In the *Aids to Reflection*, Coleridge attempted to reconstruct the mode of thought of Archbishop Leighton, and with it the milieu of seventeenth-century Christian belief, in order both to point up what was out of reach of contemporary Christianity, and exactly in that measure to restore it. Taking contemporary reason as his guide, he could convey the inwardness of doctrine only through reconstruction of a remote experience.

The peculiar connection of dubiety and creativity is summed up in the character of the apocalyptic. The apocalyptic is by definition a false prophet. In Jewish thought 'there was no true apocalyptic until prophecy failed'.[65] The writer of apocalyptic uses the methods and style and tone of the true prophets, and often he borrows the very name of a genuine prophet. The 'prophecy' is written after the fact: it uses a known occurrence of destruction, an undeniable doom, on which to base its predictions of still greater catastrophe, or the end of the world. Its accuracy about the 'predicted' but past event buys the prophet credit.

Those who wished to maintain the authenticity of Revelation have always narrowed the distinction between true prophecy and apocalypse as much as possible, even in some cases claiming superiority for apocalypse as a form developed relatively late in Jewish history.[66] Eichhorn, and even more Coleridge, gave another twist to this. By extension, all the Biblical rhapsodes become 'apocalyptics' if none is apostolic. In short, all are poets assuming an apostolic name. The Book of Revelation is placed on a par with the Gospels, is canonical once more in this entirely new sense of the word. Canonicity depends on the capacity of the text to undergo and to call forth continued imaginative reconstruction of the *Urevangelium* within it.

It is here that the poet Coleridge soars out beyond the rationalist Eichhorn. In opposition to the deist contention that ancient religious leaders were tricksters, Eichhorn offered a still rationalist though historicized defence: they worked in the spirit of their age; they were not fraudulent, but unavoidably credulous. Eichhorn treated the great prophets as conscious artists, bridging the gap between the Enlightenment charges of deliberate fraud and straightforward orthodox claims to divine inspiration. This was a brilliant solution. Yet there is more than a trace of the notion of deliberate trickery left in Eichhorn's conception of the artist. Ezekiel he praises as the greatest artist of the prophets – and therefore the least authentic visionary: 'Alle Entzückungen und Visionen sind, meinem Urtheil nach, blosse Einkleidung, blosse poetische Dichtungen.'[67] 'All these raptures and visions are in my judgement mere cover-up, mere poetical fancies.' Coleridge protested against this unwarranted distinction between the artist and the visionary:

It perplexes me to understand how a Man of Eichhorn's Sense, Learning, and Acquaintance with Psychology could form, or attach belief to, so cold-blooded an hypothesis. That in Ezeckiel's Visions Ideas or Spiritual Entities are presented in visual Symbols, I never doubted; but as little can I doubt, that such Symbols did present themselves to Ezekiel in Visions – and by a Law closely connected with, if not contained in, that by which Sensations are organized into Images and Mental Sounds in our ordinary sleep.[68]

Ezekiel's vision of God, Eichhorn claimed, is 'so magnificent, varied, and great that the presentation can hardly be an impromptu, but must have been planned and worked out with much art'.[69] 'So mahlt, z. B. Ezechiel seine Gotteserscheinung so prächtig, vielseitig und gross, dass schwerlich ihre Darstellung ein Impromptu sein kann, sondern von ihm mit Kunst angelegt und ausgearbeitet sein muss.' In a splendid marginal note, Coleridge demurs, offering his own experience as evidence:

From the analogy of Dreams during an excited state of the Nerves, which I have myself experienced, and the wonderful intricacy, complexity, and yet clarity of the visual Objects, I should infer the contrary. Likewise, the noticeable fact of the words descriptive of these Objects rising at the same time, and with the same spontaneity and absence of all conscious Effort, weighs greatly with me, against the hypothesis of Pre-meditation, in this and similar Passages of the Prophetic Books.[70]

He made the same objection to Eichhorn's dismissal of certain passages of Revelation as mere poetic embroidery. Where the tradition and the training of the seer is sufficiently strong, where he is saturated in the spiritual experience of his community, his visions can be spontaneous, not artfully premeditated. So too the poet's imagination, steeped in its own subject, may compose as if inspired.

The claim Coleridge made in his Preface to 'Kubla' to a form of spontaneous composition is not an excuse for a fragment, but a presentation of his credentials for writing apocalyptic, for assuming the prophetic role. In however small a degree, he could claim to have shared the experience of the great prophets, of Ezekiel, and of the great apocalyptic, John. These experiences were in one form or another so persistent with Coleridge, and figure so largely in his theory of the imagination, that his account of the writing of 'Kubla' should not be dismissed as a figment. Each rift of his mind loaded with the ore of the Apocalypse, Southey's Oriental enthusiasms, his own epic plans and hopes, the first tentative notions of the lyrical ballads, and experiments in versification, it is perfectly possible that he should have dreamed the whole in this vivid compressed form in which all the major images are concentrated and blent, and the action concentrated at the point most pregnant with its own significance: the creation of the holy city threatened with destruction and promised its recreation. The prefatory 'Vision in a Dream' becomes a kind of authentication of the poet's right to present the prophetic lays of a 'John'.

Now that inspiration was not directly divine, now that it must take place without miracle, 'without any sensible addition or infusion', the sources of vision must be such as would satisfy the Enlightenment rationalists as well as fulfil some part of the traditional expectations.[71] Coleridge's Preface is apologetical, in that it claims none but natural phenomena behind a psychological curiosity, while the state described approximates as nearly as possible to illuminated trance and supernatural dictation.

Among the forms of suspension of the conditions of ordinary perception which played so important a role in Coleridge's theory of the imagination, sleep (or waking dreams) is prominent:

In the paradisiacal World Sleep was voluntary & holy – a spiritual before God, in which the mind elevated by contemplation retired into pure intellect suspending all commerce with sensible objects & perceiving the present deity–[72]

Sleep (and anodynes for physical pain) are most readily grasped by the Enlightened mind as altering mental conditions, yet all such suspension, with the insertion of the vivid but ultimately vague (alliterating) detail – the haunting 'person from Porlock' – strengthens the visionary claim, and is part of the apocalyptic method.

In the new secular theory of inspiration, then – and this was its triumph – there was no difference between the brief note on the Crewe MS of 'Kubla' and the later, more elaborate prefatory 'Vision in a Dream'.[73] Still later, in his *Confessions*, Coleridge wrote of the welcome confirmation that the Bible tradition gave to the visitations of the 'phantom self':

The Bible has been found a spiritual World, – spiritual, and yet at the same time outward and common to all. You in one place, I in another, all men somewhere or at some time, meet with an assurance that the hopes and fears, the thoughts and yearnings that proceed from or tend to, a right spirit in us, are not dreams or fleeting singularities, no voices heard in sleep, or spectres which the eye suffers but not perceives.[74]

Coleridge never wished to exploit this element of falsehood and pose (the irony appealed to some poets of his time and after), except in so far as it rendered prophecy, like all the bardic gifts, remote and un-attainable in its true form. Strain and yearning characterized the poetic assumption of the prophetic attitude. Just as Coleridge refused to hold that the great religious sages and leaders had deliberately deceived the people, so the illicit and deliberate assumption of powers by the traditional apocalyptic was represented only in the great con-tortions and involutions of the poet seeking a vision closed to him.

The romantic longing to approximate the seer reached its apotheosis in Rimbaud's famous letter:

I say that one must be a *seer*, make oneself a *seer*. The poet makes himself a *seer* by a long, prodigious and rational *disordering of all the senses*. Every form of love, of suffering, of madness; he searches himself, he consumes all the poisons in him, and keeps only their quintessences. This is an unspeak-able torture during which he needs all his faith and superhuman strength, and during which he becomes the great patient, the great criminal, the great accursed – and the great banned one! – among men. For he arrives at the *unknown*![75]

Rimbaud spoke somewhat contemptuously of the earlier generation:

The first romantics were seers without quite realizing it: the cultivation of their souls began accidentally: abandoned locomotives, but with their fires still alight, which the rails still carry along for a while.[76]

But this was hardly the case: Coleridge's generation first grasped rationally the necessity to 'cultivate their souls', and stoked those fires as assiduously as Rimbaud, while pretending, at times, to be carried along on the rails. The apocalyptic seer, while claiming more than the poet, is closer to the poet than to the true prophet; he perfectly represents the romantic union of despair of true vision with the inflation of the poetic imagination. Prophecy having failed – the true visionary having vanished – the poetic genre of apocalypse must take its place, and the false prophet, the poet, do his best to speak truth, though only in symbols figuring the throne and face of God he cannot see, and dimly reminiscent of the origins of prophetic and poetic knowledge in the first radiance of mythological prehistory.

And yet, were not the first apocalyptics and rhapsodes of the Gospel in the same position as the poet? The direct apostolic vision was only a shred of memory long after a 'fact' that had never been. The romantics achieved a new comprehension not only of their own historical position, but of the problematic nature of all the seers of the past. In the terms of their own analysis, they were able genuinely to revive the conditions of inspiration.

Thus Coleridge's prophet–poet, if still Greek, still 'Pindaric' in feeling and reference, is equally the Renaissance David, the classic David of Michelangelo, and the Christian John, humane and sophisticated; and in his anonymity, behind these great Oriental figures, is visible the universal primitive bard, the bard of the Tartars and of the Celts and of the Americans, the bard of the neo-platonic mysteries and of the early Christians, a bizarre, rapt creature maintaining for his community their touch with the nether and the upper worlds. And the modern poet justly stands here too: for romanticism calls all vision in question, while affirming it.

If, then, we accord to Coleridge the poetic vision of the apocalyptic as he redefined it, the form in which he accomplished his epic of revelation is not difficult to understand. If religious epic in the eighteenth century had taken on the characteristics of the ode, on the model of *Samson* or the *Messias*, the brief, almost static action, interspersed with choric song, the theory, authoritatively formulated by Wolf in his *Prolegomena ad Homerum* (1795), that the *Iliad* was not Homer's, but a redaction of a series of lays handed down in folk tradition, offered an obvious new form for the deliberate production of epic, especially to a masterly practitioner of the ballad, the 'obvious British equivalent of the hypothetical Homeric rhapsodes'. As Albert Friedman has pointed out in *The Ballad Revival*,

In the neo-classic period, the ancient writings about bards and rhapsodes, about commemorative and chronicle verse, were used to comment on the ballads; but after the ballad had actually been found in tradition, the flow of instruction was reversed, and the balladry emerged as a striking clue to the perplexing problem of Homer and the homeridae.[77]

In the same way, balladry emerged as a striking clue to the problem of the composition of the Bible.

For apocalypse, where one could expect no straightforward consecutive narrative, the ballad-lay was the ideal solution, excising all epic flats and bringing the bard figure to the fore. Scott in the 'Lay of the Last Minstrel', so notoriously inspired by 'Christabel', and Macaulay's 'Lays of Ancient Rome' tried to do just this: to take a historical and heroic matter, fit stuff for an epic, and render it in the 'original' folk form of the lay. Macaulay based his 'Lays of Ancient Rome' (1842) both on Wolf's Homeric ballad theory and on Niebuhr's argument in his *Roman History* (1811–15, translated in part by Coleridge's 'disciples' Thirlwall and Hare in 1828–30) that traditional lays were the source of the legendary portions of Roman history in Livy's *Annales*, 'broken and defaced fragments of the early poetry', as Macaulay put it.[78] Thomas Arnold, who helped make Niebuhr's a powerful influence, espoused this idea, and Macaulay undertook to recast Livy's legendary material in what must have been, according to Niebuhr, its original form.

As Friedman has remarked, 'Both Wolf and Niebuhr were aware that their theories reflected on the composition of Holy Scriptures.'[79] Their theories ultimately rest on Herder's argument in *The Spirit of Hebrew Poetry* that the creation story had evolved from primitive folksongs, from isolated ballads 'On the Sabbath', 'On the Destruction of the World', and so on. Coleridge's substantial agreement is shown by his proposal for 'a metrical translation of all the odes and fragments of odes scattered throughout the Pentateuch and the Historical works of the O. Testament.'[80] This conception of Homer as bard connected him intimately with the Prophets.

Macaulay's notion of the ancient lay is represented by this strophe:

> And nearer fast and nearer
> Doth the red whirlwind come;
> And louder still and still more loud
> From underneath that rolling cloud,
> Is heard the trumpet's war-note proud
> The trampling and the hum.

And plainly and more plainly
   Now through the gloom appears,
Far to left and far to right,
In broken gleams of dark-blue light,
The long array of helmets bright,
   The long array of spears.   ('Horatius', XXI)

In the English tradition, the ode had tended to be closer to the ballad than elsewhere. Drayton in a minor lyric gives the history of the ode, including the Greek, the Druid, and the ancient British Harper. His own 'Agincourt' is a sophisticated ballad, a welding together of native and foreign elements. Moreover, he wrote that though he called his poems 'odes', they might be called 'ballads'; this seems to have been the result of a confusion of 'ballad' with 'ballade': 'For both the great Master of Italian rymes [sic], PETRARCH, and our CHAUCER and others of the Upper House of the Muses, have thought their Canzons honoured in the title of a Ballad.'[81] Thomas Warton's influential *History of English Poetry* referred to some Anglo-Saxon and Middle English poems as 'odes', especially the 'Battle of Brunanburgh' and the 'Poema Morale'.

Donald Davie was evidently mistaken in asserting that there is 'no precedent in English' for the marriage of the ode and the ballad that Ezra Pound effected in *The Confucian Odes*.[82] Rather Pound discovered in the ancient Chinese confirmation of the romantic enterprise of the lyrical ballad.

Given the Apocalypse as epic matter, the new theory perfectly accounts for the form of 'Kubla': a fusion between a traditional ballad form, with its sense of essential rhythms and consonances, and the irregular, 'sublime' ode forms, which raised the minstrel into a rhapsode.

The combination of ballad-lay and ode conforms to the two-fold nature of the new romantic bard. The ballad preserves the contact with the original primitive folk community out of which epic, whether the *Iliad* or the *New Testament*, sprung, embodying its mythologized historical experience; the ode expresses that society's highest pitch and reach of religious development. In Wordworth's hands, the lyrical ballad never attained the same fusion; it tended to separate out into the familiar eighteenth-century forms of the pseudo-popular ballad and the meditative ode.

Coleridge's dream-vision tale is substantially true, then, and he wrote not one lay of his intended epic, but a kind of symbolic summary of its entire action and significance. It was indeed a fragment of a vast intention; and yet a whole poem. Just as Coleridge developed a method of asserting the unity of Bible texts despite their disintegration in time and space, so he created a new epic unity despite the fragmentary 'lay theory' of Homer. 'Kubla Khan', the apocalyptic epic, is the apotheosis of a new form: the lyrical ballad.

CHAPTER 3

THE ORIENTAL IDYLL

The romantic epic is the 'little epic', the pastoral or 'minor epic' to which Porphyry in 'The Cave of the Nymphs' had assigned a higher, theological level of meaning. It is concerned with the cosmic aetiological drama that is one form of myth. That this level of meaning has been so impressively represented in modern poetry is owing in large part to the reformulation of the significance of myth in the Christian context carried out by the Biblical critics in the 1790s. 'Kubla Khan' is one of the first poems to represent the new views of myth and so to usher in a new poetic age.

Lent impetus by Greek studies, the idyll became the most popular form of the eighteenth century, and aesthetic theory confirmed its position. Even major epics, major in length, scope, and intention, tended to have an idyllic core. Schiller spoke of idyll as one of the most characteristic forms of modern poetry, praising Milton's depiction of Adam and Eve as the finest example of it. Its excellence depended not simply on 'primaeval communion with the springs of Being', but on suggesting the progress, refinement, and end of Being as well. Schiller suggested the range of the modern poet of idyll:

Er mache sich die Aufgabe einer Idylle, welche jene Hirtenunschuld auch in Subjekten der Kultur und unter allen Bedingungen des rüstigsten feurigsten Lebens, des ausgebreitetsten Denkens, der raffiniertesten Kunst, der höchsten gesellschaftlichen Verfeinerung ausführt, welche, mit einem Wort, den Menschen, der nun einmal nicht mehr nach *Arkadien* zurück kann, bis nach *Elysium* führt.[1]

Let him [the modern poet] make it his task to create an idyll which carries out that pastoral innocence also in subjects of culture and in all conditions of the most active, passionate life, the most strenuous thought, the most subtle art, the highest social refinement, which, in short, leads man, who cannot any longer return to Arcadia, forwards to Elysium.

The romantic epic operates through a 'picture' technique. This was at first tied to the painterly picturesque, as in Lessing's *Laokoon* and in Uvedale Price's theory, well-known in England in the 1790s; but it rapidly acquired greater freedom.

Coleridge was very familiar with these developments, and practised the picturesque method of Gilpin in his notebook descriptions of Germany. A recent critic has commented:

The picturesque artists' was the wider range of experience that could be managed by discontinuity and planned irregularity, but they kept to the picture-like single perspective. The interior landscape, however, moves naturally towards the principle of multiple perspectives, as in the first two lines of 'The Waste Land', where the Christian Chaucer, Sir James Frazer, and Jessie Weston are simultaneously present.[2]

In fact, the exterior landscape, becoming a mobile location, mobile in time and space, developed 'multiple perspectives' and so became capable of serving as an interior landscape. The accomplished inter-changeability of exterior and interior landscapes is perhaps the most significant achievement of Biblical Orientalism for poetry in the nineteenth century.

The idyll was indeed to be a major nineteenth-century form; one need think only of those two Victorian 'apocalyptic epics', Tennyson's *Idylls of the King* and Hopkins's *The Wreck of the Deutschland*. If Tennyson's idyll is the 'miniature epic in a luxuriant natural back-ground', as Douglas Bush puts it, Coleridge's is the most miniature epic in the most luxuriant natural background of all. Coleridge's syncretist use of myth, moreover, is echoed everywhere in Victorian poetry, not in direct emulation, but as a response to the same move-ments of thought. 'Kubla Khan' accomplishes the poetic revolution that in France occupied the period from Chénier's Orphic epic to the 'Parnasse'. In Germany, not surprisingly, the step from Hölderlin to Rilke scarcely seems to need the mediation of a century.

The visionary tradition had a picturesque perspective built into it. Eichhorn could with justification interpret the Apocalypse as a drama, for, in theory, the visionary prophet is actually seeing the events played out in the heavens, as all events are rehearsed before they take place on earth. The heavens are a stage on which he sees the drama unroll:

Quod autem in his visorum descriptionibus prophetae legebantur in statu ecstatico in coelum abrepti res futuras, ante eventum ad actum revocatas et repraesentatas, suis oculis obiectas conspexisse, id hanc vim habuit et effectum, ut ex eo colligeretur, nihil in orbe terrarum evenire et contingere, quod non antea coram Deo coelitumque congressu in theatro.[3]

But that in these descriptions of visions, prophets, rapt into heaven in ecstatic state, were read to have beheld with their own eyes things to come, realized and represented before the event – this had the power and effect that from it could be concluded, nothing happens in the universe which is not first given to be played and watched in the celestial theatre in the presence of God and the heavenly assembly.

The mythological Bible critics adapted the visionary theatre, in which the seer was to see the future, to the historian's view of the past. As Strauss put it,

In the absence of any more genuine account which would serve as a correcting parallel, [the historian] must transplant himself in imagination upon the theatre of action, and strive to the utmost to contemplate the events by the light of the age in which they occurred.[4]

Coleridge's marginalia on Eichhorn's *Commentarius* cluster about the climactic point in the history, that is, around Rev. 9, 13–15, the second of the three woes, when the sixth angel sounds its trumpet. Here the Roman army invades the centre of the city; the destruction of the Temple is imminent, though not to be accomplished until the blaring of the seventh trumpet: 'But in the days of the voice of the seventh angel, when he shall begin to sound, the mystery of God should be finished, as he hath declared to his servants the prophets' (Rev. 10, 7).
This moment in the Book of Revelation –

'And the sixth angel sounded, and I heard a voice from the four horns of the golden altar which is before God,
'Saying to the sixth angel which had the Trumpet, Loose the four angels which are bound in the great river Euphrates'

– is the 'pregnant moment' of Lessing's 'picture' technique, when the prophetic Laocoön and his sons are seen not in their death agony, but

98

calm in the very toils of the serpents. We do not see Troy burn; we are not aware that it will burn, though after the fact the fate of Laocoön is an unmistakable portent. So here, the world is for the first and last time on the brink of a destruction that has been accomplished again and again.

At this idyllic moment in the 'little epic' vision of Revelation we see the geography of the city whole – its vertical as well as its cross-section – the corrupt city, the place of the imprisonment of the demons and the dead; the Holy City of men; and the celestial city of the New Jerusalem, which Zechariah and Ezekiel envisioned as pre-existing and descending into the earthly city with the Messiah's coming. They are united as never before, yet separating out at the trumpet call to judgement, and signalling their final reunion, the single tripartite cosmos of Dante.

As in Shelley's *Prometheus*, a critic tells us, it is the 'fusion of outer and mental worlds that become the Romantic substitute for little epic narrative. For them the arresting of a vivid moment of experience, or "spot of time" in Wordsworth's phrase, took precedence over any ritual order of events.'[5] But in 'Kubla' we see that the romantics did not 'substitute' for the little epic narrative – such a substitution would be inexplicable – but transformed the epic narrative itself into a spot of time that stood for and absorbed the whole. Ritual is not so much abandoned as transfixed at the gesture that implies the necessity of its past and future repetition.

Eichhorn's interpretation of these verses, and Coleridge's dissent from it, carry us from the neo-classic epic and the apocalyptic lay to the centre of the sacred geography of 'Kubla'. Eichhorn gives the historical interpretation: the Roman army enter the *theatrum* and find the 'demon' enemy, some of whom they imprison. ('Angel' may be 'demon' in Hebrew folklore.) The Jews, then, are imprisoned. In the Euphrates? Eichhorn comments,

Qui carceris locus soli debetur poetae ingenio, nullamque patitur ex historia excidii Hierosolymitani interpretationem. Poesis enim prophetica postulat, ut singula in carmine declaranda ad loca certa personasque certas revocentur. Quid? quod nec Romanus exercitus, ad Judaos coercendos ab Euphrate progressos dici poterat; is enim ex Achaia profectus Alexandriam petiit et legionibus Ptolemaidis et Caesareae auctus in Judaeam irrupit, vid. Josephus de bello Judaico lib. 3. c. 1. 3.[6]

The place of imprisonment we owe solely to the fancy of the poet, and it allows of no interpretation in accordance with the historical destruction of Jerusalem. Indeed, prophetic poetry postulates that each thing to be declared in the song must be related to specific places and people. Which ones? The Roman army could not be said to have proceeded to surround the Jews from the Euphrates; for it had set out from Achaia, reached Alexandria, and, increased by legions of Ptolemais and of Caesarea, invaded Judea. (See Josephus, *The Jewish War*, Book 3, chap. 1. 3.)

He points out that in Old Testament passages 'the Euphrates' appears in apposition with 'the great river' (Genesis 15, 18; Deut. 1, 7; Jos. 1, 4).

Coleridge condemns the method that makes Eichhorn impotent to interpret this and a variety of other passages: 'Eichhorn's great error is in carrying his general meanings, & his resolutions of particular passages into mere poetic garnish, to an excess.'[7]

Eichhorn, in short, allegorizes too fully in a historical sense, and when allegory fails him, he gives up, and attributes the passage to mere poetic fancy. This misses the real sense and significance of the apocalyptic style.

Coleridge justifies the apocalyptic poet's imagination. He protests:

I wonder at this assertion from so acute and ingenious a Man as Eichhorn.

First, as I have noted – as Rome was to be symbolized as *Babylon*, the River must be Euphrates. But that the four mighty Destroyers were bound in the great River 'up a great River, great as any Sea' is according to the code of popular Beliefs – the bad Spirits are sent bound to the bottom of the Red *Sea* – But a *Sea* would not have been appropriate or designative of the Roman Power – while the Tyber was a perfect Synonime of Rome, and the trite poetic exponent of the Roman Empire – Now the Tyber could not but be changed into the Euphrates – Therefore the ἐπὶ τῷ ποτάμῳ τῷ μεγάλῳ 'Ευφράτῃ is no mere poetic ornature; but a very significant & requisite amplification.

Four giant Dæmons could not be imagined bound or chained up in a vast *City* – this would have been far too indefinite – But neither in any Dungeon or Tower in Babylon – That would have been as much too narrow, & besides too gross an outrage to probability, & above all, too little ghostliness – with great judgement therefore the sublime Seer transfers their prison to the River but amplifies the River into all the magnificence of a Sea for the imagination of the Readers. Only read the Greek words aloud ore rotundo: and you will feel the effect. – Add to this the Hebrew Associations with the Euphrates – Captivity after bloody Wars, and the Siege, Sack, and utter Destruction

of their chief City & Temple! – Is it not, I again say, wonderful that
Eichhorn should overlook all these so striking and exquisite proprieties in a
'soli debetur poetæ ingenio'!!⁸

Now it is not impossible that Eichhorn is right. But what Coleridge
does here is characteristic of the symbolism of 'Kubla'. First, the three
great sacred cities – Jerusalem, Babylon, and Rome – are blended; the
symbolism is not sequential, as in Eichhorn's scheme, but simultaneous.
Because Rome too must fall, and the city of wickedness is Babylon,
the captive demons in Jerusalem may be imprisoned in 'the Euphrates'.
Coleridge's note exclaims: 'As Rome was to be Babylon, the River
must of course be Euphrates!'⁹ The references are interchangeable,
they flow in and out of each other. Geographical mobility is uncannily
combined with exact location, timelessness with precise and known
history. The superimposition and blending of meaning is perfect.

Nor is the method far from Revelation itself: 'And their dead bodies
shall lie in the street of the great city, which spiritually is called Sodom
and Egypt, where also our Lord was crucified' (Rev. 11, 8). All great
cities are places of corruption, and may be called by their names; and
in all places of corruption was, and is, the Lord crucified. This is unstated typology of immense extent.

Especially characteristic of 'Kubla' is the way the river expands at a
touch into a sea – size is as immaterial as place and time – while re-
taining all the connotations of that particular named river and acquiring
all those of the sea. Both river and sea are prominent in the Apocalypse.
Babylon's seat is also 'upon many waters' (Jeremiah 51, 13). As Farrer
remarks, 'we may suppose the side-streams and canals of Euphrates
spreading around her'.¹⁰ Farrer points out too that John's river of
blood at the time of the destruction 'even unto the horses' bridles' is a
reference to Ezekiel 47 and 48, 20 where in the vision of Jerusalem the
river of life issuing from it is measured, on all four sides equally, by the
depth of the stream on the body of a man trying to ford it.

The sea is of course, as Lowth put it, the 'place where the wicked
after death were supposed to be confined; and which, from the destruction of the old world by the deluge, the covering of the Asphaltic vale
with the Dead Sea, etc. was believed to be situated *under the waters*'.¹¹
Moreover, the sea is a 'ritual name'. John's vision begins with a
presentation of the great 'Sea' of the heavenly temple (Rev. 4, 6)

which refers to the laver in the Temple, and, in Christianity, to baptism: 'Baptism is a "sea", indeed, it is the Red Sea water through which the people of God are saved, and separated from heathen Egypt (I Cor. 10, 1–2).'[12]

The Old Testament context of 'caves of ice' is even more striking. In the fourth of Herder's *Oriental Dialogues*, which marks the high point in his splendid dithyramb on nature in Oriental poetry, and its dependence on the One God, he shows the connection of God's creativity with His destructive powers, using the Book of Job as his text. The abyss, the unfathomable ocean, is both the place of the dead and the vast region of the unborn. The abyss, or destruction, 'hath no covering before Him'. 'The abyss where light had never pierced, stands uncovered – this is the awful, the dark moment, when CREATION begins.' Herder follows the steps of the creation in Job 38: first the founding of the earth, then the formation of the sea:

The earth is represented as an edifice, founded and measured by the Almighty; and no sooner are its foundations laid, and the corner-stone fixed, than all the *sons* of God and the *morning-stars* raise an acclamation of joy and a song of praise to the great Creator. Now comes the formation of the ocean:

> Who shut up the sea within doors,
> When it brake forth, as it were, from the womb?

Herder cites the passage, 'Hast thou entered into the springs of the sea? . . .Hast thou entered into the treasures of the snow?'

> Hath the rain a father?
> The drops of the dew, who hath begotten them?
> Out of whose womb cometh forth the ice?

> The waters rise into mountains, and become as stone,
> And the surface of the waves is bound in frost.

Herder glosses the passage:

Above, the light comes forth in streams, and the east-wind carries them over the land: the Father of heaven and the earth forms canals for the rain and marks out a course for the clouds. Below, the waters become a rock, and the waves of the sea are held in chains of ice.[13]

The 'caves of ice', then, mark a most dramatic moment in the creation: the emergence at once of solidity and variety out of the sea's abyss. The primaeval relation between creation and destruction is the main formal principle of Revelation, as well as of 'Kubla'. Coleridge, of course, had no need of Herder to remind him of these passages from the Book of Job. But Herder sets Coleridge's enterprise in its context, even ending his chapter with poems of Ossian: 'To the Setting Sun', 'To the Morning Sun', 'To the Moon', 'Address to the Evening Star'.

And of course one could go on in this vein: a woman presides over each phase of Revelation, and in each of her incarnations she is familiar in the annals of the Old Testament.[14] Jerusalem wails for her imprisoned 'demon' leaders (no mere 'Gothick' touch this, although 'demon-lover' undoubtedly owes something to the vogue for Bürger and perhaps Wieland).[15] In the note previously quoted referring to the Jewish leaders, Coleridge spoke of the Hebrew 'Amarus', a link to the 'Amahra' of the first draft of 'Kubla' and to Milton's Mt Amara, which critics have agreed was a major reference point for 'Kubla' (though no such link is needed), as well as connecting with the sea itself, the bitter waters.[16] The 'cedarn' cover of the sacred mountain of Lebanon is proverbial. The 'ancestral voices prophesying war' are not a trivial detail filched from Purchas about the priests of the Khan, but the heart of the apocalyptic warning of the seer echoing his great prophetic forbears Jeremiah and Ezekiel, distant and unattended.[17]

The number symbolism which is so conspicuous a feature of Oriental systems was also given a Biblical origin or at least sanction: through one verse from the Apocrypha, Wisdom of Solomon 11, 21: 'omnia in mensura et numero et pondere disposuisti', 'number was sanctified as a form-bestowing factor in the divine work of creation'.[18] The very idea of the Bible as containing all wisdom is a recommendation of brevity. Again the range is from the popular-sententious – like the numerical apothegm from the *Arabian Nights*, 'Always use the toothpick for two and seventy virtues lie therein' – to the systematic holy mystification of the prophets. 'Kubla Khan' contains a considerable amount of sacred numerology, though in a very refined form. The main examples – 'So twice five miles of fertile ground/ With walls and towers were girdled round' and 'Five miles meandering with a mazy motion' – may well have been suggested by Ezekiel's measurements of the Holy City.

In apocalyptic mysticism, the Book of Ezekiel, with its vision of the throne-chariot in the first chapter, and its measurements of the celestial city in the last, was of particular importance. Indeed, St Jerome mentions a Jewish tradition which forbids the study of the beginning and the end of the Book of Ezekiel before the completion of the thirtieth year.[19] It is, of course, the model for the New Jerusalem of Revelation. In Coleridge's Notebooks for May 1799 appears the significant collocation of 'The Tarter Chan' and 'The Fable of the Four Wheels', that is, the chariot from Ezekiel.

[Y]e shall offer an oblation unto the Lord, an holy portion of the land: the length shall be the length of five and twenty thousand reeds, and the breadth shall be ten thousand. This shall be holy in all the borders thereof round about.

2. Of this there shall be for the sanctuary five hundred in length, with five hundred in breadth, square round about; and fifty cubits round about for the suburbs thereof.

3. And of this measure shalt thou measure the length of five and twenty thousand, and the breadth of ten thousand: and in it shall be the sanctuary and the most holy place. (45, 1–3)

The incantatory numbers, based on five, continue throughout the measuring of the sacred river waters on the body of the prophet:

15. And the five thousand, that are left in the breadth over against the five and twenty thousand, shall be a profane place for the city, for dwelling, and for suburbs: and the city shall be in the midst thereof. . .

20. All the oblation shall be five and twenty thousand by five and twenty thousand: ye shall offer the holy oblation foursquare, with the possession of the city.

21. And the residue shall be for the prince, on the one side and on the other of the holy oblation, and of the possession of the city, over against the five and twenty thousand of the oblation toward the east border, and westward over against the five and twenty thousand toward the west border, over against the portions for the prince: and it shall be the holy oblation; and the sanctuary of the house shall be in the midst thereof. (48, 15–21)

It is not surprising that this obsessive five, a holy number, ambiguously indicating the sanctuary and in the centre the most holy place, the city and the suburbs, and then the entire surrounding area of land, in the prophet who provided the pattern for the Book of Revelation, should be used by Coleridge as a sign of the tradition of the coming of the New Jerusalem.[20]

To go on allegorizing 'Kubla' in this vein would not be quite futile, for the Christianized Old Testament context was certainly the primary one for Coleridge. Nevertheless, it is inadequate to the poem, as all interpretations of 'Kubla' have been, for it fails to take account of the method of simultaneous Oriental contexts developed in half a century of Biblical and literary studies.[21] In rejecting our simple allegory of Revelation, we shall see the process by which the renascence of allegory in Biblical criticism modulated into romantic symbolism.

The impetus to a new mythological understanding came from many sides: from explorers' and travellers' reports, from Sir William Jones's *Asiatick Researches*, from the *philosophes*' speculations on the nature of primitive man. But the most profound alteration in attitudes and ideas was brought about when Christianity faced the fact of its own mythological character. The Biblical critics' new views of myth, clearly stated by Eichhorn and Gabler in the 1790s, represent the most subtle and influential, if desperate, Christian apologetics. In myth, the legendary, the monstrous, and the traditional could be accommodated by historical scholarship; in myth, 'fact' and 'fiction' could be merged into a new form of truth.

The visionary Oriental landscape of poetry bears the traces of this whole difficult history; it emerges at the end of the century in a new form, nowhere so fully or so gracefully achieved as in 'Kubla Khan'. Far from reflecting ignorance about the Orient, far from any mere search for the exotic, the ornamental, or the artificial, far from being a mere 'expressive' reaction in favour of the primitive, the new mythical landscape has absorbed the vast quantity of new information and the insights of an Oriental scholarship gradually freed, almost against its will, from the literalism both of inherited tradition and of rationalist historicizing.

As the new view of myth began to emerge, the Edenic scene intensified in significance through the multiplication of simultaneous reference: the primordial myths persist not only through all the stages of Christian thought, dressed up anew at each major religious metamorphosis, they appear in all religions and nations. 'Kubla' represents in its eighteenth-century form the great primordial myth of the origin and end of civilization in the religious spirit of man.

What 'spot' is it we actually see in 'Kubla' at the pregnant visionary moment? The landscape of Revelation is there, certainly: the sacred river, the fountain, the sea where the forces of darkness are imprisoned, the woman both holy and demonic, the sacred enclosure of the Temple. But the immediate impression is of course primarily pastoral, paradisaical, and Oriental, and the imagery has always been felt, rightly, to have been displaced from the undeniable Biblical base. Yet the first clues are in the Bible. Goethe reminds us that 'Da wir von orientalischer Poesie sprechen, so wird notwendig, der Bibel, als der ältesten Sammlung, zu gedenken.' 'In speaking of Oriental poetry, we must take note of the Bible, as the oldest collection.'[22] One of Goethe's favourite books of the Bible was the Book of Ruth, the 'lieblichste kleine Ganze das uns episch und idyllisch überliefert worden ist', 'the most charming little unity, epic and idyll, that has been handed down to us'.[23]

One of the most charming little epic–idylls of the eighteenth century was the pastoral poet Salomon Gessner's *Der Tod Abels*, *The Death of Abel*, a poem to which Coleridge often referred admiringly. It is a good poem, deserving of the vast popularity it enjoyed in Germany and in England; even in the poor English translation by Mrs Collyer, in its ninth edition by 1768, something of its virtue is preserved. Gessner made a skilful fusion of the religious epic, the idyll, and the Oriental setting.

Just before the most likely date for the composition of 'Kubla Khan', 18 November 1797, Coleridge and Wordsworth on their walking tour planned to make the Valley of Stones the scene of a prose tale in the manner of Gessner's *Death of Abel*, and probably within a few days *The Wanderings of Cain* was begun and, as a collaborative enterprise, abandoned.[24] At the same time, certainly in the course of the tour, the idea of the *Lyrical Ballads* was conceived. Coleridge retired to the farm between Porlock and Linton with the setting of the Biblical idyll and the idea of the lyrical ballad uppermost in his mind.

The setting has much in common with that of the Song of Songs, as Goethe described it (and for that matter with the Book of Ruth):

Durch und durch wehet eine milde Luft des lieblichsten Bezirks von Kanaan; ländlichtrauliche Verhältnisse, Wein-, Garten- und Gewürzbau, etwas von städtischer Beschränkung, sodann aber ein königlicher Hof mit seinen Herrlichkeiten im Hintergrunde. Das Hauptthema jedoch bleibt glühende Neigung jugendlicher Herzen, die sich suchen, finden, abstossen, anziehen, unter mancherlei höchst einfachen Zuständen.[25]

Through and through the poem wafts the mild breeze of the loveliest district of Canaan; rural circumstances of mutual trust, vineyards, gardens, groves of spices, something of urban confinement too, but then a king's court with its formal splendours in the background. The main theme nevertheless remains the burning love of two young hearts, who seek, find, repel, and attract one another amid circumstances of exceedingly great simplicity.

This landscape, at once rural arcadia, city, and court, is an archetype of Oriental poetry.

These descriptions of the small 'city-kingdom' (Newton's phrase) are a commonplace of the numerous eighteenth-century efforts to write a complete universal history of civilization, sacred and profane. Newton, Vico, Boulainvilliers began with a universal pre-history based on the old notion of 'the four ages of the world'. They mused on the condition of the first men after the Flood, prior to the founding of cities.

The first men after the flood lived in caves of the earth & woods & planes well watered by rivers for feeding their herds & flocks, such as were the planes of Babylonia, Assyria, & Egypt. By degrees they cut down the woods & learnt to build houses & towns of brick in the planes of Assyria, Babylonia & Egypt. Thence men spread into places less fertile.[26]

They described the gradual formation of human communities, from the isolated units of the mobile desert patriarchs through the establishment of religious centres and the agglomeration into larger urban, national, and finally the vast imperial monarchies of Egypt, Assyria, Persia, and Greece. All empires were held to have shown the same pattern of growth. Newton, equally interested in precise calculations and in general laws of development, tried to plot the size of the ancient city-kingdoms, and he held them to have been very small, comparable with contemporary English villages and corporation towns. He computed that before the victory of the Israelites there had been about

1000 walled cities in the land, the large number indicative of their puny dimensions. He illustrates the particulate origin of empires by 'the small size of the army, hardly more than a collection of retainers, that Father Abraham had arrayed against the kings of Sodom and Gomorrah'.[27]

On the one hand, these were scientific descriptions, laws of growth, intended as a counterpart to the physical history of the world; on the other, they were celebrated, as De Bougainville, secretary of the Académie des Inscriptions et Belles-Lettres, celebrated Newton's, as 'l'histoire de l'esprit humain'.[28] A modern treatment like Lewis Mumford's *The City in History* is remarkably similar in spirit and in detail to its eighteenth-century forerunners.

In Gessner's poem, we find the ancient city-kingdom described at the point of its Biblical origin: the settlement built by Adam and Eve after their expulsion from Eden. We are shown the still lovely landscape of a holy mountain, reminiscent of Eden, still visited by spirits, yet new and bleak, a wholly human settlement, a raw stockade barely maintained against the wilderness, an altar visited as much in despair as in reverence. Adam and Eve echo their situation, wonderfully combining their original patriarchal dignity, simplicity and virtue with new labours, plaints, and pains. Gessner with great success and delicacy created a world half original paradise, half fallen nature.

Just this landscape, combining still-remembered paradise, wilderness, enclosed city, and cultivated court, is captured in 'Kubla'. City and country, rural yet populous, idyllic yet threatening, holy yet secular, sacred yet fallen, court and cot – it is tempting to see the stereotypes of the eighteenth century merging into those that will dominate the nineteenth. Just for this moment, in this exotic setting, they exist simultaneously, and express a permanent condition of man.

In the Biblical poems of the eighteenth century, this primeval Oriental scene recurs in a dazzling variety of forms. 'Eden' was an immensely diversified scene, a mobile location, not merely of the Creation and the Fall, but of that characteristically eighteenth-century *topos*, the founding state of civilization in general, the centre of *Urmonotheismus*, archetypal monotheism. Typically, as in Gessner, the scene was paradise displaced, paradise already lost though still visible, paradise beset by the ambiguities of human culture. Only with the Fall could civilization begin and develop. Eden had taken on new significance for a century that liked to believe in the progress of civilization and yet profoundly knew its corruption.

After the first night spent outside Paradise, Adam gathers new courage:

Seest thou, EVE, that river, which, like a huge serpent, winds in bright slopes through the meadows? The hill on its bank, seems, at this distance, like a garden full of trees, and its top is cover'd with verdure.[29]

Adam and Eve approach the brilliant scene:

We now advanc'd to the eminence. Its gentle ascent was almost cover'd with bushes and fertile shrubs. On the summit, in the midst of fruit-trees, grew a lofty cedar, whose thick branches form'd an extensive shade, which was render'd more cool and delightful, by a limpid brook, that ran in various windings among the flowers. This spot afforded a prospect so immense, that the sky was only bounded by the dusky air; the sky forming a concave around us, that appear'd wherever we turn'd, to touch the distant mountains.[30]

Here, then, are two natural domes, suggesting the presence of a celestial infinity, in a spot which, as Adam says, is 'a faint shadow of Paradise, whose blissful bowers we must never more behold'. He concludes: 'Receive us, majestic cedar, under thy shade.' Coleridge had a wealth of fully developed and directly relevant poetic description of fallen paradises at hand.

If Gessner maintained a sense of the patriarchal dignity of Adam and Eve even in their fallen state, Klopstock in *Der Tod Adams, The Death of Adam*, made palpable the fear of what must happen to the race when the memory of paradise is finally extinguished. In the morning the Angel of Death appears to Adam and tells him that he will die that day when the sun sinks onto the cedar forest that covers the slopes of Eden. The geography is exactly and imposingly generalized: on one of the mountain peaks surrounding that of Eden, the altars of the fallen Adam and Eve still face, over the chasm, a dimming Eden. Adam addresses Seth:

Es ist fürchterlich, Sohn! Zwar diese kühle Erde, in der auch die duftende Rose und die schattende Zeder wächst, ist es nicht! Aber hier soll ich verwesen![31]

How dreadful looks this earth, my son! no more
That fertile earth, which I of late beheld
O'erspread with roses, or in whose deep bosom
The branching cedars struck fantastic root.[32]

Adam looks in the direction of Eden, no longer able to see it:

Ihr schönen Gefilde! Ihr hohen quellvollen Berge! Ihr schattenden kühlen
Täler, und ihr Kinder der Berge und der Täler! die ihr euch unter dem Fusse
des Wandrers biegt, oder eure Gipfel über die hohe Wolke emporhebt! ihr
segenvollen Gefilde, wo ich gewandelt, wo ich Leben und Freude eingeatmet,
wo ich all meine Kinder, so viele Lebendige um mich gesehen habe!... Ich
will mich wegwenden, mein Sohn, denn ich kann den Strom kaum mehr von
der Ebne unterscheiden.[33]

　　　　　　　　　　　　　　O ye happy plains,
Ye lofty mountains, where a thousand springs
Rise; and, with streams luxurious, pour down
The steep declivities; ye vales eternal,
With cooling shades and laughing verdure crown'd
　　　　　　　　　...Let us depart,
My son; my feeble sight can scarce discern
Distinctly ought, nor from the river's stream
Knows the firm earth.[34]

These 'Forests elder than the Sun', as Coleridge called them, become
an obsessive image in the poem. Adam, looking in the direction of
Eden:

Adam. Hast du die Sonne gesehn, da du zurückkamst?
Seth. Sie war mit Wolken bedeckt, doch war sie nicht ganz dunkel einge-
　　hüllt. Wenn mich mein Auge nicht trügt; so war sie – weit herunter-
　　gestiegen!
Adam. Weit herunter. – Sieh aus, mein Sohn, ob die Wolken nicht weg
　　sind?[35]

　　　Adam.　　　　　　　　Alas, my child,
　　　I see them not. The sun perhaps with clouds
　　　Is darken'd o'er.
Seth. The clouds are thick; yet shade not
　　All the sun's brightness.
Adam. From the cedar's forest,
　　Seems it far distant yet?[36]

Again, in Act III, Seth looks out towards Eden:

Seth. Die Sonne steigt hinunter! die Zedern fangen schon an zu decken. Gib uns deinen Segen, mein Vater!
Adam. Sie steigt hinunter?[37]

> *Seth.* The sun declines apace and the tall cedars
> Fade on the eye: – oh father, father, bless us.
> *Adam.* The sun already at the cedar's forest![38]

Thus Eden, now screened by the cedars' cover and veiled by failing vision, becomes the seal of death for the fallen Adam.

This mountainous, cedar-covered scene is, of course, the Hebraic, the Palestinian paradise reflected in Coleridge's lines:

> And here were forests ancient as the hills
> Enfolding sunny spots of greenery.
>
> But oh! that deep romantic chasm which slanted
> Down the green hill athwart a cedarn cover!

In Klopstock's *Messias*, there is a transcendent or astronomical Eden, based, in its locale at least, on Young. The eternal Idea of Eden exists on another star. God descends, pausing to view His works, among them a star where lives a race of rational, unfallen men, an innocent Adam and Eve. In Klopstock's best 'Hebraic' style, Adam utters an invocation to the presence of God in Eden:

> Sprich, Ceder, und rausche!
> Reissender Strom, steh!
> Steh dort! Denn da ging er hinüber. Du sanfteres Athmen.
>
> Stille Winde, lisple von ihm, wie du lispelst, als Er,
> Ach der Unendliche! lächelnd von jenen Hügeln
> herab kam!
> Steh vor ihm, Erd', und wandle nicht fort, wie
> ehmals du standest,
> Als er über dir ging, als sein erhabneres Antlitz
> Wandelnde Himmel umflossen, als sein göttlich Rechte
> Sonnen hielt, und wog, und Morgensterne die Linke![39]

Speak, ye cedars, rustling speak – speak, for under your branches I saw him walk! Stay, thou rapid stream – stay, for there I saw him pass thy waves! Whisper, ye gentle gales, as when with smiling grace he descended from those towering hills! Stand still before him, O earth, and suspend thy course, as once thou stoodst still, when he passed over thee; when round his face sublime the moving heavens flowed! when his right hand poised the glowing suns, and in his left he held the revolving planets!⁴⁰

As popular as the creation story was its repetition in reverse at the time of the Flood, when degraded civilization was destroyed and patriarchal simplicity restored. More than one theorist of the origins of religion chose this as the crucial historical moment: whether in Vico's compelling descriptions of the distressed state of post-Diluvian man, out of which rose his worship of ferocious gods, or in Boulanger's mild, suffering, melancholy, and beneficent post-Diluvian primitive, this second Fall seemed to usher history in, to be a testing-place for man's secular psychology when the last authentic memory of pre-lapsarian Eden had been dispersed. 'Kubla', with its perfected simultaneities of reference, shows us both: the Eden of the first creation and the Eden of God's wrath on the rising verge of the Flood waters, where the ancestral voices prophesy in vain.

J. J. Bodmer, the translator of *Paradise Lost* into German, wrote an epic, *Noah*, which attempted to depict the rise of civilizations after the Fall and their decline to the Deluge. It so roused Southey's enthusiasm even in translation that he declared his intention to learn German, write on the subject of the Deluge, and so 'take my seat with Milton and Klopstock'.⁴¹ The myth of the Flood is still treated literally. But there is a real feeling in the poem for the glory of the decadent civilizations and their monuments that strew the plains round the lost Eden. How can the flowering of civilization be so vile? This puzzle of the theodicies exercised Bodmer, and he makes an almost Byronic lament over the deserted great cities after the Flood recedes. The evil city of Thamista, dwelling-place of Og, goes down thus: 'Now was the city encompass'd by the prevailing flood, and the lustre of its structures of polish'd marble, amidst the turbid deep, resembled the silver moon, in a gloomy sky.'⁴²

Bodmer attempted to map literally the geographical multiplicity of the complex set of centres of civilization on the eve of the Flood. Noah and his three sons live in a displaced Eden at the foot of the mountain of Eden; unknown to them, the true Eden still exists. As the poem opens, a path from the foot of the mountain becomes visible to

Japhet and he follows it back to Eden, where he discovers the sage Sipha (Noah's wife's brother) and his three daughters. This is the scene adapted by Wieland in his chivalric Oriental tale of *Oberon*, also known to Coleridge, probably in the original.[43] In Book II, Noah is taken by Raphael on a lightning tour of all the degraded kingdoms; like the hidden Eden, the true lore is everywhere enslaved by 'hell-born superstition', yet still survives in a higher sense.[44]

Eden is never wholly lost in this poem – that is the reward of Noah – but as the Deluge comes, Eden perforce takes new forms. The dome of the ark is lined inside with divine paintings, a revelation of a future Eden:

The ceiling seem'd to rise into a lofty dome, in the centre of which, was a wheel'd throne of sapphire, animated by an indwelling spirit, attended by cherubs. The wheels were studded with glittering beryl, and between them, fire blazed prompt for vengeance. On the throne sat a judge, arm'd with thunder; terrible his visage, terrible the front of his throne, and terrible the thundering wheels, whence, with irresistible rapidity issu'd destruction, hurling down myriads of beings, for whom open'd a flaming abyss, while round the judge, flew multitudes of bright spirits, shining with all the effulgence of celestial glory.[45]

Among these unfamiliar forms, Noah catches sight of a radiant figure:

How my heart beats, surely this is the precious Redeemer, and each piece in prophetic painting, displays the glorious work of redemption. Oh what comforts shall I receive in the rolling ark, when encompassed with the waters of the deluge, if the benevolent angel. . .will instruct me, by explaining these hidden mysteries![46]

In all these poems, the Old Testament setting has got to be linked with the New, and the means taken are usually unsatisfactory. Here the vision has to be literally pictorial for the Enlightenment poet; but it is symbolically vivid as well. We may perhaps think of Kubla's 'stately pleasure-dome' riding upon the shadow of the waters as carrying a revelation and a ravishment as great at least, and scarcely more exotic and obscure, than Noah's at these scenes of a future unknown to him yet stirring him to recognition. The patristic and medieval rhetorical technique of *figura* – the prefiguration of the New by the Old Testament – amplified and extended to other mythologies, and removed

from time and space, is just discernible at the heart of the new mythological poetics.

There is yet another vision of Eden in Bodmer's poem: Japhet's
prophetic dream of the garden of unborn souls. He sees an Eden-like
scene:

a plain, profusely adorn'd with flowers; streams clearer than crystal water'd
the luxuriant soil, and a grove laden with all the rich exuberance of autumn,
spread along the sloping hills, receiving the morning's genial light.[47]

This dream-light, in which he sees the unborn souls of various leaders,
is 'bright day', and when the dream-day wanes, he wakes. Bodmer's is
clearly a classical scene, a platonic 'soul-dwelling'; Eden is projected
backwards and forwards, before and after human time.

There was a lively argument among theologians as to whether the
scene of the creation was spring or autumn. The two versions of
Genesis, separated out by Jean Astruc, who noted in his *Conjectures*
of 1753 that some parts of Genesis are devoted to a god 'Jahweh' and
others to a god 'Elohim', give opposing pictures, the one based on the
Babylonian spring at the recession of the flood waters, the other on the
fertile and moist harvest season of Palestine after the parched summer.
'Kubla', without specifying the season, clearly represents both these
Oriental seasons: the waters are both rising and receding. The superimposition of two unfamiliar and opposed seasons breeds timelessness
more effectively than Bodmer's autumnal dream-light.

A vision in a dream of Eden as the New Jerusalem is granted to
John, ending Book 12 of the *Messias*. John is transported by his guar-
dian angel, first to Lebanon, where cedars wave, on a beautiful morning, when the purling of the brook in the vale below was as sweet as
the music of the temple. Then he hears the celestial harmony; and in a
darkened grove he sees a huge cedar cut down and fashioned into a
cross; but then it shoots forth palms. He is transported again, to Eden:

>Da war der Jünger nicht mehr in Libanons Haine.
>Ach, er war in Eden, und sah von dem Himmel ihm glänzen
>Mehr, also Purpur und Gold, und vernahm er erhabnere Chöre,
>Und es schlug ihm das Herz von der Wonne vollem Gefühle.[48]

The scene of the disciple's vision was now removed from Lebanon to Eden,
where he beheld a celestial glory that infinitely exceeded the splendour of

gold and purple. He now heard more sublime choirs, and his heart was filled with the sweetest sensations of joy.[49]

In a dazzling variety of forms, then, Eden appears in eighteenth-century poetry, a highly specified physical scene, yet a highly mobile one, whose marks and meanings can be transferred to a platonic pre-world, to outer space, or to a ceiling painting.

This Oriental scene of the origin of civilization, already so mobile, was gradually released from its Jewish, Christian, and Greek moorings and located in Mohammedan and Hindu settings. The most striking example is William Beckford's 'Arabian tale' *Vathek* (1782), whose scrutiny of this scene, at once Voltairean and sensuous, consciously organizes a large body of scholarly and literary material in which these familiar motifs are brilliantly reinforced in the exotic imagery of Islamic faith and superstition. The Caliph Vathek had a pleasure-palace upon a mountain; down the 'green declivity' of the mountain near four fountains, was a 'dreadful chasm', a 'vast black chasm' in the plain, where the Giaour, or Infidel, appears to the Caliph and 'in accents more sonorous than thunder' promises to bring him to the Palace of Subterranean Fire, which hold the 'talismans that control the world'.[50] Vathek is commanded to go from his city of Samarah to the ruined city of Istakhar, or ancient Persepolis. After making his way, with great vicissitudes, through the forests of cedar and the waste mountains, he finds in the ruins of great civilization a Hell that evokes 'l'ambiance persane de l'Arabie sous la dynastie des Abbassides, l'atmosphère même de *Vathek* tout entier' and yet is instantly recognizable to the Christian reader.[51] Beckford's Hell is justly renowned for the Miltonic sublimity of its Satanic ruler Eblis, the fallen angel of Islam, and the Dantesque vision of the tortured worshippers of the dark powers of knowledge whose hearts are perpetually aflame in their transparent breasts, chief among them the Princess Carathis, the Caliph's mother, whose demonic arts earn for her a perpetual circean whirling that renders her invisible.

Throughout the century Islam had continued to be considered a Christian heresy; so in *Vathek* the familiar motifs are printed in the negative. This negative printing has given *Vathek* a special place in romantic poetry, admired as it was by the masters of the darker vein, Byron, Poe, Swinburne, Mallarmé, and echoed in *Les Fleurs du mal* and the Carthage of Flaubert's *Salammbô*. In the ironic mode perfected since Bayle, the heretical context makes possible a free reference back to Christianity. Thus in *Vathek*, if Mohammedanism is a Christian heresy, by the powerful and unexpected superimposition of motifs, and their culmination in a mutual hell, Christian civilization is itself revealed as a heresy.

Ambition and lust had been seen as the ruling traits of Mohammed throughout the century. As Prideaux had written (defending Anglicanism against the deists):

It is to be observed that *Mahomet* began the *Imposture* about the same time that the *Bishop of Rome* first assumed the title of *Universal Pastor*. . .so that *Antichrist* seems at the time to have set both his feet upon *Christendom* together, the one in the *East* and the other in the *West*.[52]

In *Vathek*, the devils of Mohammed figure as the authors of civilization, which originates in the insatiable craving to grasp the roots of cosmic power. Religious civilization is Hell; and there is no alternative to it in Beckford's world but the gratifications of the child-like Gulchenrouz, whose innocence resembles Rousseau's pleasurable state after first being chastised by his nurse. As Raymond Schwab has said, 'La Renaissance orientale est l'avènement de l'humanisme intégrale';[53] but already its integrity is threatened from within.

Sir William Jones further extended, indeed systematized, the mobility of the primeval scene, first in his translations of poems from several Oriental languages, already published when *Vathek* was written, then in his own free imitations of them, and in his *Asiatick Researches* (1794), and finally in his brilliant letters from India of the end of the century; and he gave new scholarly grounding to the Biblical critics' insistence on the 'Oriental' nature of the Scriptures.[54] The fantastic, as Parreaux has noted, moved in the same direction as erudition and philology.[55] The work of Jones was of particular importance, as Schelling later acknowledged in the *Philosophie der Mythologie*, in the development of the syncretic view of mythology.

Jones was a representative and to some extent a victim of the cross-currents of the 1790s. His interests were primarily secular: law, poetry, Oriental languages; his enthusiasm for Persian and Arabic poetry and for the refinements of Hindu thought carried him very far from any orthodox Christian concerns. Yet he was aware of the bearing his researches had on his religion, and while insisting on untrammelled historical and linguistic investigation, on an 'analytic' method as opposed to Jacob Bryant's 'synthetic' one, the *Researches* nevertheless culminate in a defence of the traditional valuation of the Bible as superior in antiquity, in wisdom, and in literary value to the sacred writings of any other nation. He is aware of the revolutionary implications of his work on the antiquity of Hindu civilization and on the parallelism of mythologies, but rejects them. His resolutions of difficulties are often altogether too facile, yet lacking in conviction. His work is a strange mixture of a new and self-professed accuracy, geographical, linguistic, historical, with unfounded traditional views.

Jones's wide-ranging mind and graceful, flowing prose create a sense of the immediacy, accessibility, and disposability of the whole of Asia:

When I was at sea last August, on my voyage to this country, which I had long and ardently desired to visit, I found one evening, on inspecting the observations of the day, that *India* lay before us, and *Persia* on our left, whilst a breeze from *Arabia* blew nearly on our stern.[56]

In this same easy manner he commands all of Asia, from whatever centre he chooses:

Considering *Hindustan* as a centre, and turning your eyes in idea to the North, you have on your right, many important kingdoms in the Eastern peninsula, the ancient and wonderful empire of China with all her Tartarian dependencies, and that of Japan, with the cluster of precious islands, in which many singular curiosities have too long been concealed: before you lies that prodigious chain of mountains, which formerly perhaps were a barrier against the violence of the sea, and beyond them the very interesting country of Tibet, and the vast regions of Tartary, from which, as from the Trojan horse of the poets, have issued so many consummate warriors, whose domain has extended at least from the banks of the Ilissus to the mouths of the Ganges: on your left are the beautiful and celebrated provinces of Iran or Persia, the unmeasured, and perhaps unmeasurable deserts of Arabia, and the once flourishing kingdom, of Yemen. . .; and farther westward, the Asiatick dominions of the Turkish sultans, whose moon seems approaching rapidly to its wane.[57]

Jones prefers the term 'Asiatick' to 'Oriental', which is a merely relative term 'and though commonly used in Europe conveys no very distinct idea'.[58]

Yet his combination of traditional doctrine with the new historical accuracy is nowhere more striking or more influential than in his nomination of a candidate for the geographical centre and origin of monotheism.

Examining in turn the Hindus, the Arabs, the Tartars, the Persians, the Chinese, and 'the Borderers, Mountaineers, and Islanders of Asia', he reached the conclusion that the Hindus, Arabs, and Tartars are three separate races by whom most of Asia has been peopled; the other Asians are mixtures of these races. He nevertheless held to the traditional view that there was an original primitive monotheism which deteriorated into polytheism, and to the view that there was one literal geographical centre in which this first arose. Opposing Baillie's theory that the seat of civilization was Tartary, mainly on the grounds that its cold climate rendered it unfit, he opts for Iran as the centre from which all other civilizations radiated: Persia, the home of that refined and elegant poetry he so loved.

We may therefore hold this proposition firmly established, that *Iran*, or *Persia* in its largest sense, was the true centre of population, of knowledge, of languages, and of arts; which, instead of travelling westward only, as it has been fancifully supposed, or eastward, as might with equal reason have been asserted, were expanded in all directions to all the regions of the world, in which the Hindu race had settled under various denominations.[59]

This solution of course presents difficulties: for one, Jones adduces as proof that 'mother' Sanskrit was present in Iran, as were the other two 'independent' languages, Arabic and Tartar. In what sense can there be 'one' geographical centre from which everything emanated and 'one' mother language when there are by his own reckoning three races independent racially and linguistically?

Whatever the awkwardness of the theory, however, it incomparably enriched the idea of the single monotheist centre for civilization, by exploring the whole range of actual locations for such a centre and then selecting the most inclusive of them. It proved decisive for the romantic epic. The excitement aroused, especially in Germany in the 1790s, by Jones's *Asiatick Researches* and by his translation of the *Sakuntala* (and later by the publication of the *Ramayana* and the *Mahabarata*) maintained Herder's emphasis on the 'original' religious epic of mankind. The notion of Sanskrit as the general Indo-European mother language was turned to nationalist purposes in the search for the 'Indo-Germanic' epic, located with exhilarated inaccuracy in the *Nibelungen-lied*. As Heine remarked drily of the German romantic school, in particular Friedrich Schlegel, 'In the *Mahabarata* and the *Ramayana*, thay saw a Middle Ages in the shape of an elephant.'[60]

Although Jones opted for Iran, his own remarks support another possibility: Abyssinia, the scene of Milton's false paradise, Mt Amara. 'Ethiopia and Hindustan were peopled or colonized by the same extra-ordinary race', the people said by Apuleius to have 'received the first light of the rising sun'.[61] Jones cites the tradition (treated by D'Her-belot as a fable, but by Newton as genuine) that colonists from Edom had carried the arts and sciences of astronomy, navigation, and letters into Italy; and since the invention and propagation of letters and astronomy were widely agreed to be of Indian origin, the Idumeans must have been a branch of the Hindu race.[62] The 'goddess with many arms', representing the powers of Nature, dominated both Egypt (as Isis) and Bengal (as Isani).[63]

Abyssinia was noted for its wisdom; Aesop was an Abyssinian, and his apologues are related to the Hindu. Lowth and Eichhorn both credited the great culture of the Book of Job to its origin in Idumea, 'von jeher der Sitz morgenländische Weisen', as Eichhorn put it, 'from time immemorial the seat of Oriental sages'.[64] The links of Abyssinia with the Bible were stronger still: for many had argued in the eighteenth century, among them Bishop Warburton, that Moses, for better or for worse, had gleaned all his wisdom from the Egyptian priests. Jones adduces a linguistic connection as well, holding that 'the Jews and Arabs, the Assyrians, or second Persian race, the people who spoke Syraick, and a numerous tribe of Abyssinians, used one primitive dialect' which was wholly distinct from that of the first race of Persians and Indians, Romans, Greeks, Goths, Egyptians (or Ethiopians).[65]

If, then, one were seeking a geographical centre of Oriental civili-zation as closely linked with Mosaic history as possible, Abyssinia would be a more attractive choice than Iran. Coleridge in 'Kubla Khan' distributes his favours almost equally between the icy Tartary of the Khan and the Abyssinia of the 'damsel with the dulcimer'; Abyssinia as the only actual place named in the poem carries the day. The

Christian implication is still uppermost, though deliberately obscured and merged with its equivalent myths:

> A damsel with a dulcimer
> In a vision once I saw:
> It was an Abyssinian maid,
> And on her dulcimer she played,
> Singing of Mount Abora.

The Nile and India were thus connected by a stronger link than 'a hook of memory' between two isolated passages of Coleridge's reading; Jones even pays tribute to Bruce's modern description of the Nile, in the course of his discussion of the primal origin of civilization and the reasons for universal moon worship. Coleridge had no need to make 'free associations' in the manner of Lowes: the context was well established.

Jones's choice of Iran, one feels, was largely governed by his great love and knowledge of Persian poetry. It is his own imitations and pastiches of it that he offered to Europe as a treasury of new images, rather than the real but difficult splendours of his translation of the Arabian *Mu'allaqât*. The pieces he offered are stylized and schematic summaries of the main topics and images he felt could be most usefully and easily absorbed by European poetry. Although 'Kubla' gives Abyssinia precedence over Iran as the origin of civilization, and although the scene of the poem is fundamentally the rugged Palestinian topography of eighteenth-century depictions of the immediate post-Edenic world among the cedar-covered mountains and chasms, there is no doubt it is overlaid and refined by Jones's exquisite Persian Orientalism, by the beguiling, enamelled landscape of pleasure-dome, fountain, maidens, musky odours, and clear running waters:

> And there were gardens bright with sinuous rills,
> Where blossomed many an incense-bearing tree.

The perfumed trees – 'incense-breathing gales perfumed the grove' – are as obsessive an image in Jones's imitations as the cedarn cover in the Biblical epics.[66] The range of examples shows once again how Coleridge toned down any extravagance that would immediately have identified and so limited him to a particular kind of Oriental poetry:

'*Yes, I rejoined*, when those two damsels departed, musk was diffused from their robes, as the eastern gale sheds the scent of clove-gilly-flowers.'[67] The avoidance of extremes permits simple syncretic inter-leaving to pass unremarked.

Jones insisted on the confirmation his purely analytic examination offered to the Mosaic accounts: 'We cannot surely deem it an incon-siderable advantage, that all our historical researches have confirmed the Mosaick accounts of the primitive world.'[68] This is so even if Genesis is merely 'a preface to the oldest civil history now extant';[69] but if the Bible is inspired, then his, Jones's, theories are completely confirmed:

If MOSES then was endued with supernatural knowledge, it is no longer pro-bable only, but absolutely certain, that the whole race of man proceeded from Iran, as from a centre, whence they migrated at first in three great colonies; and that those three branches grew from a common stock, which had been miraculously preserved in a general convulsion and inundation of this globe.[70]

His reason for holding the Old Testament to be inspired (apart from the confirmation it lends to his theories) is particularly interesting:

The connection of the Mosaick history with that of the Gospel by a chain of sublime predictions unquestionably ancient, and apparently fulfilled, must induce us to think the Hebrew narrative more than human in its origin, and consequently true in every substantial part of it, though possibly expressed in figurative language; as many learned and pious men have believed, and as the most pious may believe without injury, and perhaps with advantage, to the cause of revealed religion.[71]

There is a kind of hedging in this passage which is immediately recog-nizable as belonging to the intelligent man of the Enlightenment who has no desire to undermine Christianity, whatever his appraisal of the worth of its evidences. For Jones, the essential 'proof' lies in historical accuracy: if the Book is literally accurate, then it is genuinely prophetic, i.e. inspired. Jones's faith has a kind of rationalist pathos about it: the Bible as accurate history, and prophecy as prediction, was doomed to extinction, in part by his own researches.

The crucial step towards the acknowledgment that the Bible is mythological was being taken at that very moment in Germany, with

Eichhorn and Gabler's explication of Genesis as myth. Jones, denying that Genesis is a myth, put clearly what was at stake:

Either the first eleven chapters of *Genesis*, all due allowance being made for a figurative Eastern style, are true, or the whole fabrick of our national religion is false.[72]

Jones adds that 'if any cool unbiased reasoner will clearly convince me, that MOSES drew his narrative through Egyptian conduits from the primeval fountains of Indian literature', he will be prepared to help circulate the truth.[73] But some pages further on he announces:

There is no shadow then of a foundation for an opinion, that MOSES borrowed the first nine or ten chapters of *Genesis* from the literature of *Egypt*: still less can the adamantine pillars of our *Christian* faith be moved by the result of any debates on the comparative antiquity of the *Hindus* and *Egyptians*, or of any inquiries into the *Indian* Theology.[74]

Eichhorn and his school, including Coleridge, thought otherwise. One feels a kind of constriction as one moves back from the imperial, Enlightened world of Jones, ruler and dilettante, into the world of the German protestant Biblical critics, the academic Orientalists. Yet theirs were the bolder minds, pursuing the implications of their work into the bone and marrow of Christian revelation. As Strauss noted,

The most hollow natural explanation, did it but retain the slightest vestige of the historical – however completely it annihilated every higher meaning, – was preferable, in the eyes of the orthodox, to the mythical interpretation.[75]

Again the origins of the higher critical analysis lie in literary studies, in the researches of Heyne into classical mythology and of Herder into Persian and Hebrew; and again their analysis issues immediately into literature. Coleridge's scheme for writing hymns on the sun and the moon is one of its fruits.

As early as 1779, Eichhorn had brought Heyne's ideas on myth to bear on Genesis, in his anonymous *Urgeschichte*, published in his *Repertorium für biblische und morgenländische Literatur*. His pupil, Johann Philipp Gabler, published a new edition of it in 1790–3, with a lengthy introduction and full commentary, which greatly extended its influence, and ushered in the mythological analysis of the rest of the Old Testament and the New.

It was, of course, nothing new to trace all religion to worship of the heavenly bodies; indeed, it was a stock Enlightenment procedure. Jones wrote:

Although I cannot believe with NEWTON, that ancient mythology was nothing but historical truth in a poetical dress, nor, with BACON, that it consisted solely of moral and metaphysical allegories, nor with BRYANT, that all the heathen divinities are only different attributes and representations of the Sun or of deceased progenitors, but conceive that the whole system of religious fables rose, like the *Nile*, from several distinct sources, yet I cannot but agree, that one great spring and fountain of all idolatry in the four quarters of the globe was the veneration paid by men to the vast body of fire, which 'looks from his sole dominion like the God of this world;' and another, the immoderate respect shown to the memory of powerful or virtuous ancestors, especially the founders of kingdoms, legislators, and warriors, of whom the *Sun* or the *Moon* were wildly supposed to be the parents.[76]

In 'On the Gods of Greece, Italy, and India' Jones gave a more cautiously eclectic summary of the 'four principal sources of all mythology':

I. Historical, or natural, truth has been perverted into fable by ignorance, imagination, flattery, or stupidity. . .II. The next source. . .seems to have been a wild admiration of the heavenly bodies, and, after a time, the systems and calculations of Astronomers. . .III. Numberless divinities have been created solely by the magick of poetry; whose essential business it is, to personify the most abstract notions, and to place a nymph or a genius in every grove and almost in every flower. . .IV. The metaphors and allegories of moralists and metaphysicians have been also very fertile in Deities.[77]

Coleridge was well acquainted too with Dupuis's reduction of Jesus to a solar myth, the twelve apostles to twelve astrological 'houses'. Moreover, there had been a century of active speculation in many quarters about the motivation and degree of comprehension of primitive man in arriving at his earliest religious conceptions.[78] But what was new was the attempt to harmonize these diverse accounts through the application of Heyne's view of mythology, gleaned from Greek literature, to the Bible considered as literature. The result was a deepened mythological hermeneutics that touched all literature.

One of Heyne's principles was: 'Man versetze sich ganz in das Zeitalter der Geschichte', 'Transplant yourself wholly into the period of the story.' Eichhorn developed this, demanding of the reader of Genesis:

Vergiss das Jahrhundert, in dem du lebst, und die Kenntnisse, die es dir darbietet, und kannst du das nicht, so lass dir nicht träumen, dass du das Buch im Geiste seines Ursprunges geniessen werdest. Das Jugendalter der Welt, das es beschreibt, erfordert einen Geist in seine Tiefe herabgestimmt; die ersten Strahlen des dämmernden Lichtes der Vernunft vertragen das helle Licht ihres vollen Tages nicht; der Hirte spricht nur einem Hirten, und der uralte Morgenländer nur einem anderen Morgenländer in die Seele.[79]

Forget the century in which you live and the knowledge it offers you, and if you cannot do that, do not imagine that you can savour the Book in the spirit of its origin. The youth of the world which it describes demands a spirit steeped in its depths; the first rays of the dawning light of reason cannot bear the bright light of its full day; the shepherd speaks only to the soul of a shepherd, and the ancient Oriental only to the soul of another Oriental.

A second principle of Heyne, equally familiar to us from its Biblical critical use, the 'necessary unity', 'nothwendige Einheitlichkeit', of interpretation, was used to unify the two originals that had been discerned in Genesis.

In Heyne's view, clearly formulated in a lecture to the Göttinger Akademie in 1764, myths were philosophemes about the cosmos. Thus far they were philosophical, even metaphysical; but in primitive times there was no adequate conceptual language in which to express these insights; they had to be expressed in the language of the senses, the *Bildersprache* that became a byword of Herder's. *Homo mythicus* had a native idea of God, however undeveloped. Heyne offered a psychological explanation of the process, similar to Kant's in his *Beobachtungen über das Gefühl des Schönen und Erhabenen, Observations on the Feeling of the Sublime and Beautiful* and equally derived from the Longinian revival: the immensity of nature places primitive man in a state of religious awe, and in this emotional state his imagination becomes active and forms his objective perceptions into an imaginative construction.[80]

As Eichhorn paraphrased Heyne's version:

Die Einbildungskraft bleibt nicht in den engen Grenzen der mündlichen Überlieferungen stehen, sie schweift noch weiter ins Reich der Möglichkeiten aus und erhöht vieles, was sie im Nebel der Zeit sieht bis zu einer Riesengrösse und verwandelt also Sagen in wahre Zauberideen.[81]

The imagination does not remain within the narrow bounds of the oral transmission, it ranges yet further in the realm of possibilities and raises much of what it glimpses in the mists of time to gigantic proportions and transforms sagas into truly magical ideas.

The foundation of mythology is ignorance of the causes of the appearances; whatever needs explanation, every event, order and, especially, disorder in nature and the psyche are attributed to the direct intervention of God. But the note of Enlightened condescension begins to disappear: of the causes of appearances, the 'witnesses' are always ignorant.

Heyne harmonized the two major and conflicting views of myth: that it is intellectual in character and that it originates in primitive ignorance. Myth was genuinely intellectual, he affirmed; yet allegorical exegesis was improper unless it was clearly indicated by the author as his intention, and we must always remember that we do not have the myths in their original form. Myth was genuinely primitive; yet it was not ignoble, not beast worship or fetishism, not the result of fear and 'superstition', nor was it imposed by unscrupulous priests or kings. Moreover, while Heyne's view lends itself to transcendentalist theories of perception, it had the virtue of appearing not as philosophy or psychology, but as a canon of criticism.

Heyne very well represents the early stage of the transition from Enlightenment ideas of an abstract natural religion indwelling in all men to romantic views of mythical symbolism as the paradigm for all thought. His sense of the philosophical nature of mythical expression which nevertheless takes a form quite different from abstract rationalism became both the problem and the solution for the new philosophy.

The Biblical critics tried, by applying Heyne's analysis of the mythic mode of thought, to reconstruct the process by which the Biblical 'histories' had been arrived at. For them, the important thing in Heyne's view of myth was that myth was no longer mere fable, unworthy fiction, or even poet's fiction in the sense of departure from truth; myth was 'the oldest history and the oldest philosophy', and one could respectably call, as Gabler did, for a 'mythologica sacra', a higher, or Biblical mythology.[82]

Eichhorn and Gabler had at first retained some elements of Genesis as historical (the eating of a poisoned fruit; the existence of a tree), in order, as they afterwards admitted, to make their analysis more palatable to the public; but in the new edition, Genesis 1–3 was stated to be, in Heyne's sense, a purely philosophical myth, that is, one in which 'the historical' is merely a vestment for the philosophical idea. The systematic comparison of extra-Biblical myths with Biblical ones, and the application of the principle of unified interpretation, made it impossible to maintain any element of historical fact whatsoever in Genesis. Thus the treatment of the Old Testament as Oriental literature led logically to the full relinquishing of the claim to historical factuality.

Herder had pointed out that there were four Oriental *Wundergeschöpfe* in Genesis, the two trees, the talking snake, and the cherub. Eichhorn had already explained the cherub and the tree of life as mythical. Gabler went further:

Und nun sollen doch die damit genau verbundenen zwei übrigen Wundergeschöpfe, der schädliche Baum, der ohnehin nach seiner offenbar mythischen Schilderung als Weisheitsbaum das unverkennbare Gepräge asiatischer Dichtung an sich trägt, und die Schlange, die als redend vorgestellt, offenbar auch ein Produkt der asiatischen Phantasie ist, im Paradies *wirklich* existiert haben?[83]

And now should the other two marvels that are closely connected with them nevertheless be held *really* to have existed in Paradise, the injurious tree, which, according to its manifestly mythical description as a tree of wisdom, bears the unmistakable stamp of Asiatic poetry, and the snake which is represented as speaking, manifestly also a product of the Asiatic fantasy?

The reference to familiar Greek literature emboldened the critics; as Gabler put it:

Sucht wohl ein Heyne mühsam den Prometheus, Epimetheus, die Pandora und ihre Büchse zu retten, und nur das notwendig-mythische von ihnen abzustreifen; oder hebt er nicht vielmehr den Hauptsatz der zum Grunde liegt: 'Mit den Künsten kommt Ungemach und Elend in die Welt' aus dem ganzen Mythos heraus und erklärt alles Übrige für nichts als für mythische Philosopheme, da ja selbst Prometheus, Epimetheus und Pandora offenbar etymologische Wesen sind? Sehen nun nicht Adam (Mann) and Eva (Männin) ebenso etymologisch aus, wie Prometheus und Pandora? Hat wohl je ein verständiger Ausleger der griechischen Mythen die Götterspeisen Nektar und Ambrosia so in Schutz genommen, wie der Theologe sich der Elohimspeisen, des Weisheits-und Lebensbaumes, annimmt?[84]

Does a Heyne really seek laboriously to salvage Prometheus, Epimetheus, Pandora and her box, and to strip away only the necessary mythical trappings from them; or does he not rather lift out of the myth as a whole the principle that lies at the base of it: 'With the arts disorder and suffering come into the world', and declare all the rest nothing but a mythical philosopheme, since even Prometheus, Epimetheus, and Pandora are clearly etymological beings? Do not Adam (Man) and Eve (Woman) look just as etymological as Prometheus and Pandora? Has any reasonable interpreter of the Greek myths ever defended (as real) the divine diet of nectar and ambrosia as the theologian defends the food of the Elohim, the tree of wisdom and life?

Gabler puts the fateful question: '*Is not the primitive world everywhere the same?*' '*Ist die Urwelt nicht überall gleich?*' The myths of the Bible have no claim to special protection.

The approach to full mythologizing was made step by step during the 1790s. Immediately following the republication of the *Urgeschichte*, Eichhorn began to apply his method to the New Testament, in a series of papers: the 'Versuch über die Engelserscheinungen in der Apostelgeschichte', 'Essay on the Appearances of the Angels in the Acts of the Apostles'; the 'Ausgiessung des Geistes am Pfingstfest', 'The Outpouring of the Holy Ghost at Pentecost'; and, especially, an essay on the 'Versuchungsgeschichte Jesu', the 'Temptation of Jesus', which rapidly became a model for mythological exegesis.[85] Eichhorn's method was to select the incidents most obviously dictated by preexistent mythological explanation and to reconstruct from the situation of the narrative the corresponding underlying natural process. He is most successful, as Sachs has noted, when he can provide a psychological motivation which is transposed, in accordance with the mythical outlook of Jesus's time, into the miraculous or supernatural. Each element of the narrative is given a naturally understandable psychological equivalent. In short, this is a thoroughly rationalistic method, though an 'advanced' one, in that mythical expressions are understood as historically necessary, rather than as the result of error, superstition, or deception.

Strauss, in the history of the mythological approach to the Bible that forms the introduction to *Das Leben Jesu,* summed up Eichhorn's achievement:

The mythological researches of a Heyne had so far enlarged his circle of vision as to lead Eichhorn to perceive that divine interpretations must be alike admitted, or alike denied, in the primitive histories of all people. It was the practice of all nations, of the Grecians as well as the Orientals, to refer every unexpected or inexplicable occurrence immediately to the Deity.[86]

Indeed, the celebrated *Das Leben Jesu* which created a scandal all over Europe on its publication in 1835 was only an uncompromising extension of Eichhorn's method to the whole fabric of the New Testament.

During the 1790s, Gabler published his own series of papers; he did not go beyond Eichhorn's method, but openly formulated their common canons of interpretation. Gabler pointed out explicitly that the method was not really conducing, as Eichhorn had hoped, to a critically sharpened conception of the *Tatsächliche,* of actual fact, but was postulating a narrative art 'bei welcher Objektiv-Tatsächliches und subjektives Räsonnement darüber eine ungeschiedene Einheit bilden', 'in which the objectively factual and the subjective rationale for it form an undifferentiated unity'.[87] The higher criticism had already moved from a mythology of history to a history of mythology.

This radical shift was nevertheless still grounded in Orientalism; the new narrative art, according to Gabler, was precisely the Oriental mode of thought:

Es liegt in dem Charakter des Orientalers, eine Begebenheit nie nackt zu erzählen, sondern so, wie er sich dachte, dass es dabei zugegangen oder wie sie erfolgt sein möchte. *Räsonnement war immer in Geschichte eingeschlossen, und wurde selbst als Faktum dargestellt*; weil der Orientaler sichs gar nicht denken konnte, dass etwas anders vorgefallen sein konnte als er sichs gerade vorstellte. Das Faktum und die Art, sich das Faktum zu denken, floss bei dem Morgenländer in Ein unzertrennliches Ganze zusammen.[88]

It is rooted in the character of the Oriental never to relate an event barely, but rather as he supposed that it happened or might have happened. *Rationale was always included within the story, and was itself represented as fact*; for the Oriental could not imagine that something could take place otherwise than just as he conceived it to himself. The fact and the way of conceiving the fact flowed together for the Oriental into an inseparable whole.

There is no mistaking the still rationalist primitivism of this description of the Oriental mind, much inferior to Herder's insights into the Christian Orientalism of the Evangelist. The decisive step had nevertheless been taken; the symbolist mythographers would now hold that not only was the Bible completely mythological, but that 'the Oriental mind' was the mind of Everyman.

Coleridge recalled his youthful enthusiasm for the mythological poetry of Genesis:

I interpreted the Chapter as a Morning Hymn, in which the Creation is represented under the analogy of the daily emergence of visible Nature out of Night thro' all the successive appearances till full Sun rise and thence explained the posteriority of the Sun & the visible Orb, to the Light, it's far earlier Harbinger.[89]

This may represent Coleridge's earliest view of the matter, in its straightforward Enlightenment pungency, its rational 'natural' explanatory power, and its Herderian affirmation that the Book is a set of Oriental songs. It is worth noticing, however, that Coleridge again finds means to resist the disintegrative effects of Biblical criticism through subtler modes of interpretation which themselves become part of his canon of criticism, sacred and secular. There are not necessarily two different accounts of the Creation merged in Genesis 1–3, Coleridge is saying, providing one applies Eichhorn's tools less crudely than Eichhorn does. He notes that Eichhorn would find his own interpretation 'too refined':

surely Eichhorn would denounce the separation of the Vegetable from the Animal Creation by an intermediate Creation of the present Solar System, Forests elder than the Sun, as a Chimaera κατ' ἔμφυσιν.[90]

Indeed, Coleridge is only applying more strictly one of Eichhorn's own rules: primitive man explained phenomena in the order of their sensuous appearance, not in order of their logical causes. 'Forests elder than the Sun' are not *Wundergeschöpfe*, nor are they signs of an overlapping of two Creation accounts, they are the great primeval trees that rise up in the early morning light to the eye of ancient man before he sees the actual orb of the sun come over the heavily wooded horizon. Again the poet's mind is able to credit the myth fully; and therefore he straightaway bounds ahead of the painful, crabwise progress of Eichhorn towards a grasp of the Bible as a whole as myth.

Coleridge takes Genesis as a proof of the high possibilities in primitive man, against those debunkers who insisted on his savage state. He inveighs against the

arbitrary and in many respects improbable Hypothesis, that the Human Race commenced in Savagery. Most unscriptural at all events is the Supposition: and in my humble opinion not less unphilosophical. If we credit the Book of Genesis (& what other historic document have we that comes near to it in age & authenticity?) we must admit, that the most important of the Arts were discovered or invented before the Flood and that a Monarch had risen before the dispersion of the Human Race. I can find nothing in Job, that might not have been written by a contemporary of Abraham: tho, if I were to fix on any period, it would be between the times of Joseph and Moses.[91]

In Coleridge there is no trace of the rationalist contempt for the 'Oriental mind' that still lingered in Gabler and Eichhorn even while they placed that mind at the basis of their own religious culture.

Coleridge's rejection of the notion of primitive *Spracharmut*, the poverty of language attributed to early man, made it possible for *Bildersprache* to attain the full reach of allegory. Gabler wrote, restating Heyne's view:

Bildersprache ist noch lange nicht Allegorie – nur dann konnte sich aus Bildersprache Allegorie bilden, als die Bildersprache nicht mehr *unvermeidliche* Folge der Spracharmut war, sondern üppiger poetischer Schmuck, freier Erguss des überströmenden Witzes und *absichtliches* Kunstwerk einer reichen Dichterfiktion wurde.[92]

The language of images is very far from being allegory – allegory could take shape from the language of images only when the language of images was no longer the *unavoidable* consequence of poverty of language, but had become *deliberate* poetic ornament, the free outpouring of a brimming intellect and the intentional artifact of a rich poetic fiction.

For Coleridge, the capacity for allegory was not confined to rational man; rational man simply made the mistake of using it in isolation from the spontaneous creative power of the *Bildersprache*.

The history of the development of the concept of the Logos (to Unitarians, the prime example of Oriental thought within Christianity) that Coleridge gave in the Introduction to his MS 'Logic' attempts to show how the poetic primitive transforms itself into the philosophical and finally the theological insight, producing along the way all literary genres.

The method and tone of this Introduction, although it is attached to much later thinking about transcendental logic, are quite distinct from that thinking and hark back to the mythological speculations of the 1790s. Coleridge gave a splendid description of the unmethodical, 'promiscuous' learning of childhood and of primitive communities. All that we need to know comes to us in

a gay & motley chaos of facts & forms, & thousand-fold experiences, the origin of which lies beyond memory, traceless as life itself & finally passing into a part of our life more naked than would have been compatible with distinct consciousness and with a security beyond the power of choice! Or shall we call this genial Impulse a Will *within* the Will, that forms the basis of choice and the succedaneum of instinct, which the conscious choice will perfect into knowledge?[93]

For individuals and communities, 'This is the happy delirium the healthful fever of the physical, moral & intellectual being, – nature's kind & providential gift to childhood.'[94]

In the *Aids to Reflection*, Coleridge, discussing the element of Oriental allegory in Genesis, makes it clear that primitive 'spontaneity' in no way precludes complexity of conception:

As to the abstruseness and subtlety of the Conceptions, this is so far from being an objection to this oldest *Gloss* on this venerable Relic of Semitic, not impossibly ante-diluvian, Philosophy, that to those who have carried their researches farthest back into Greek, Egyptian, Persian and Indian Antiquity, it will seem a strong confirmation. Or if I chose to address the Sceptic in the language of the Day, I might remind him, that as Alchemy went before Chemistry, and Astrology before Astronomy, so in all countries of civilized Man have Metaphysics outrun Common Sense.[95]

Coleridge's view is like Herder's both in its acclaim for the spontaneous motley of the primitive condition and in the subtlety with which the primitive state is made the foundation of all further development: as the 'Oriental tales' of the early Gospels are woven into and raised to a higher power by 'John', so a philosophical etymology of the Logos, the prime theological concept of St John, generates poetry. For Coleridge, myth could not be, as for critics tied to Heyne, an inarticulate allegory, for primitive language was supremely rich and ready; it is much more an implicit, an evolving allegory, as for Kant the aesthetic idea is always asymptotic to logical expression. 'Kubla Khan' renders the primitive language of myth in the form of a poetic artifact: poetry is not rationalizing and ornamental, but the achievement without loss of the evolution of the human race.

Herder, in his popular *Oriental Dialogues*, showed how the mobile location could be used as a method of literary criticism, how, that is, the myth as historical milieu could mediate between literal event and free allegory. Herder tried to establish a general context and landscape for 'Oriental poetry', extending Lowth's work on Hebrew poetry to Persian and Arabic poetry as well. He regularly illustrated his points both from the Old Testament and from Persian poetry; indeed, he sometimes illustrated points about Hebrew religious views from Persian poetry. Ultimately, his purpose was to show what a modern German poetry must be, and how it could escape from sterile imitations of classical or Oriental models by translating their spirit fully into the modern world.

He composed a generalized description of Paradise, which even in the Arabian and Persian bards expresses the ideal 'of human joy and felicity'.[96] In response to Alchipron's objection that the scenery is no doubt enchanting, but is it not likely to attach men too much to the pleasure of the senses? Eugenius replies:

On the contrary, I feel a sincere delight, when I find the eastern Bards, in their national songs, representing the verdant plains, the trees that project a deep and refreshing shade, the crystal lakes and purling streams, as the remains of the ancient Paradise, and the presage of its restoration in a future scene, which they call the *land of Eden*, the happy region of tranquillity and contentment. How different are these views of a future destination from the sordid notions of those northern Bards, the sons of *Edin*, who place their departed heroes in lofty halls, daubed with gold, and loaded with hogsheads of metheglin and beer, which they swill out of the skulls of their slaughtered enemies!

We must give up trying to choose among the multitudinous traditions of the location of Paradise, Herder concluded, and instead adopt Moses's own representation of it 'as a sort of *enchanted land*, unknown to him'.[98]

Although Palestine, Persia, and Abyssinia were the heartland of Orientalism for Coleridge, he drew examples for his 'enchanted land' from further afield. On the extreme western edge of the Orient is another example of the sacred landscape. Jotted down in his notebooks while reading *A Relation of a Journey begun An: Dom: 1610. Foure Bookes. Containing a description of the Turkish Empire, of Aegypt, of the Holy Land, of the Remote parts of Italy, and Islands adjoining* is a reference to this passage by Sandys, the translator of Ovid's *Metamorphoses*, as of the Psalms of David:

And as the Papists attribute an extraordinary holiness to *Rome*, so doe the Greekes unto *Athos*, a mountaine of *Macedonia*; so named of *Athon* the sonne of *Neptune*, dekt with still-flourishing trees, and abounding with fountaines; called also The Holy Mountaine by the Christians. A place from the beginning dedicated to Religion: lying directly West from Lemnos; and so high, that though it be seven hundred furlongs distant; yet it is said a little before the setting of the Sunne to cast a shadow on that Island. Whereupon the proverbe: 'Aspiring Athos hides/The Lemnian heifers sides.'[99]

Of all the forms of Oriental thought, Coleridge had least sympathy with Hinduism, at least in his later years.[100] The familiar passages in the *Philosophical Lectures*, probably echoing Friedrich Schlegel's polemic in *Die Weisheit der Inder* (1808), *The Wisdom of the Indians*, are confirmed in later manuscripts. Yet even in his last writings, in the midst of attacking Sir William Jones for comparing the *Bhagavad-gita* with Milton, this *topos* retained its power for him:

Their next neighbours of the North the temple-throned infant of Thibet with the Himala behind and the cradle of the Ganges at his feet, convey to my mind an impressive likeness, seems to me a pregnant symbol, of the whole Brahman Theosophy.[101]

Here is that same Oriental landscape again, the landscape of 'Kubla': the temple with the sacred mountain behind and the sacred river at its feet.

We have, then, in 'Kubla Khan' a perfectly generalized Oriental setting. It was not Coleridge's 'association' of isolated patches of reading that merged these Oriental landscapes into one, but a recognized literary technique. The 'picture' method employed upon an existing, in principle locatable, but invisible, natural landscape created an interchangeably internal and external vision.

The generalized Oriental setting achieved for Coleridge's poem what he admired as the chief technical virtue of *The Faerie Queene*: that it is enacted 'truly in the land of Faery, that is, of mental space'.[102] This was Spenser's means of achieving unity and 'harmonizing his descriptions of external nature and actual incidents with the allegorical character and epic activity of the poem'. His images are not picturesque, but are 'composed of a wondrous series of images, as in our dreams', and these images exist 'in the marvellous independence and true imaginative absence of all particular space and time'.

Herder pointed to the meaning of the unity achieved in this way. Ultimately, the superimposition of Oriental images depends on loosing the myth of the founding of civilization from specificities of date and place. Speaking of the 'essential and distinctive character of Man, and that which places him above all classes of beings merely animal, that he is *susceptible of religion*', Herder showed how man's religious susceptibility made possible the development of knowledge itself.[103] The idea of the unity of God led men to look for unity of design, for general laws of nature, and so delivered them again from 'polytheistical disorder and anarchy'.[104] Hebrew poetry, through its method of 'the parallelism of heaven and earth', was the 'first bulwark against idolatry'.[105]

But Herder failed, in Coleridge's view, to live up to his own insight. Herder's Oriental landscape was avowedly merely human, merely poetic, merely an 'Arabian tale' (or a Hebrew one) after all. The atmosphere of charmed sleep in Spenser existed not for itself, Coleridge pointed out, but to enable the allegory to work. Coleridge defended allegory in the Bible against Herder's disposition to interpret it all as *menschlich*, as if, Coleridge tartly remarks, we were to interpret 'Plato Kant Leibnitz, etc' as 'Esop's Fables for Children':

How can Herder have the effrontery to assert that there is no Tone of ALLEGORY in the Tree of *Life*, and the Tree of the Knowledge of Good and Evil – & a talking Serpent – &c &c. If these do not possess all the marks of

Eastern Allegory, of allegory indeed in genere, what does? And why should not Moses introduce historical Persons in an allegory, as well as the Author of the Book of Job? – History was for instruction – no such cold Divisions then existed, as *matter of fact* Chronicles, & general Gleanings of the Past, such as those of Herodotus.[106]

Coleridge here is making it very clear that the equality of all mythologies does not reduce them to a merely 'human' story; on the contrary, it must give rise to the profound sense for their spiritual truth that the Hellenistic age experienced. History itself must be understood anew in this light. For finally what was significant about the Oriental *topos* was not that being 'exotic' it could lend itself to mental topography, but that having acquired the status of mental topography, it was not absolved from the encounter with facts of time and place.

The way 'historical persons' are absorbed into mythical significance becomes plain in Coleridge's discussion of Origen's allegory of Genesis. In the notebooks where Coleridge discussed most searchingly various issues arising out of Eichhorn's work, he offered a profounder view than Herder, Gabler, or Eichhorn of the nature of myth and its application to Genesis. We are dealing now with the later Coleridge, Coleridge writing in full knowledge of Creuzer's *Symbolik* (1808–12) and of Schelling's early 'Über Mythen, Philosophemen, und Sagen' (1793), 'On Myths, Philosophemes, and Sagas', and the splendid essay, 'Die Gottheiten von Samothrake' (1815), 'The Gods of Samothrace'. Coleridge's early grasp of myth matured into a conception of intellectual activity as myth-making.

He criticized an anonymous German writer on the pagan Mysteries for rendering Origen's μύθους καὶ γράμματα as

fables and letters, instead of symbolic Stories and sacred Books – from not knowing the true import of *Mythes* or Philosophemes, which Sallust, the Greek Platonist, happily conveys when he describes the Kosmos or Material Universe as the μυθος κατ᾽ εξοχήυ – and the creative Logos as *mythologizing*.[107]

Coleridge's knowledge of Origen undoubtedly goes back to the earliest period of his intellectual life; the Church fathers, with the neo-platonists, were among his earliest reading. His Hellenistic orientation is an historical construction in an almost Hegelian sense;

but it is also a specific and learned reference to the authentic roots of Christian exegesis. Origen's criticism indeed throws light on Coleridge's. His strong doctrine of the inspiration of the Bible and his strong doctrine of the 'accommodation' of the Biblical revelation to the capacities of the audience make equally, though in opposite directions, for the strenuous application of allegorical techniques of interpretation. Ultimately, the conviction of the plenary inspiration of the Bible depends (wonderfully covertly) on the force and subtlety of the interpretation. Origen exemplifies in an earlier form the mutual dependence of the critical and the constructive that we have noted as characteristic of the higher criticism. Origen undertook to defend the Bible against pagan charges of crude and fabulous simplicity by developing a highly refined allegory. Coleridge, absorbing the historical–critical fragmentation of the Bible text, reasserted the substantial spiritual unity of the Bible through the idea of communal experience. Looking away from the historical situation of the two men, we may discover the necessary circularity of the commentator on a sacred text: he must find difficulties in it – inconsistencies, incoherences, barbarisms, absurdities – and having pointed them out, he must overcome them. For the best critic of Holy Writ, sacred or secular, to discover faults is to proclaim inspiration.

Coleridge went on to speak of the later chapters of Genesis, of Adam and Eve as a myth:

Thus too in Origen's belief the transgression of Adam and Eve was a Muthos, εν γραμμασι εβραΐκοις – an Idea shadowed out in an individual Instance, imaginary or historical – The truth remains the same. It did take place – and the Individuals, in whom it first took *place* (realized itself in space, & a fortiori in *time, place* implying both: for space cannot be particularized but in connection with Times, as the sole Measure of Space) were Adam and Eve – 'In Adam we all die' – or Adam and Eve were the Individuals, in whom it *first* took place: in this alone different from all other Men and Women/In the former the Individuality is rightfully assumed – in the second, it is recorded – the Truth is the same in both, and both alike are Mythic, and belong to Mythology.[108]

This is a brilliant solution: the radical dissolution of time and space, far more radical than in Herder, is converted into a defence of the historicity of mythological characters and events. The wheel comes full circle: when history is fully understood as myth, then myth can be rediscovered as history.

Coleridge's reference to Origen's controversial views on Genesis is as much an interpretation as a quotation of authority – as indeed quotation by Coleridge always is. Did Origen intend to jettison the literal sense of the story of Adam and Eve, as Philo had done, comparing the talking serpent with 'bogies and monsters'? Origen cited as a parallel the myth of the conception of Eros in Zeus's garden in the *Symposium*, suggesting that Plato may have learnt the myth from Jewish savants when he visited Egypt. As Hellenistic allegory derived from Greek reinterpretations of Homer after the attacks by Plato, the use by Biblical critics of methods developed for Greek literature was time-honoured but dangerous practice, subject to the same charges of unorthodoxy that have again and again been levelled at Origen. Christian defenders of Origen have sometimes tried to argue that he never sacrificed the literal meaning of the text to his allegorical interpretation; Coleridge, on the contrary, admits that Origen's passage on Genesis is spiritual allegory of the kind that is concerned with permanent meaning rather than historical literalism, praises him for it, and adopts it as a precedent for the equation of myth and history. This is typical of Coleridge's supposed orthodoxy: he embraces heresy and elevates it into tradition.[109]

The crucial point, however, is the nature of the distinction between 'allegory' and '*muthos*'. On the one hand, it is clear that Hellenistic allegory was an extremely important source for Heyne and the Biblical critics who adopted his method, and that this helps to explain the revival of allegory in the eighteenth century and its long survival into the romantic period. On the other hand, it is clear that 'myth' as used by the new critics was substantially different from allegory; and the difference lay precisely in its ability to mediate between the timeless moral or spiritual allegorization and the specific historical milieu in which a myth has its roots. The myth critics do not abandon but incorporate the historical interpretation of the Bible. Yet the 'historical milieu' becomes itself a mobile location like the paradise of the epics: it is a product of the historical experience not of one place and time but of the entire Christian community, and like an allegory, can be reconstructed and transported over the whole range of that experience.

Thus Coleridge:

The whole Jewish history, indeed, in all its details, is so admirably adapted to, and suggestive of, symbolical use, as to justify the belief that the spiritual application, the interior and permanent sense, was in the original intention of the inspiring Spirit, though it might not have been present, as an object of distinct consciousness, to the inspired writer.[110]

Daniélou has written that it is possible to hold to the historical reality of the events, 'because typology consists precisely in showing that it is the history itself that is figurative, and not in substituting allegory for history'.[111] Eichhorn and Gabler banned *figura*: the Old Testament did not pre-figure the New. But they developed a new kind of *figura*: the New Testament contained the whole of the Old Testament. This was historically rational; yet it preserved the traditional fictional possibilities. Now they take their start in Revelation after the fact, in short, in apocalypse, not in 'prophecy'. Prophecy is no longer the prediction of actual events to come, but the renewed vision of the meaning of the past for the future. Within the New Jerusalem is contained the progressive history of Eden from the Creation. This conception of *figura*, by renewing the typically figurative blend of historical reality and spiritual interpretation, pointed the way from allegory to symbolism.

Schelling, whose very earliest writings, in 1792, demonstrate his intimate knowledge of the work of Heyne, Herder, and Eichhorn, in his *Philosophie der Mythologie* extended and summed up the development of Biblical Orientalism. Mythology is the mark of humanity; without it, no community, no people can exist, for a people is 'die Gemeinschaft des Bewusstseyns', 'a community of consciousness'.[112] Poetry, he said, does not give rise to mythology, but mythology to poetry:

Poesie [ist] wohl das natürliche Ende und selbst das nothwendig unmittelbare Erzeugniss der Mythologie, aber als wirkliche Poesie. . .nicht der hervorbringende Grund, nicht die Quelle der Göttervorstellungen seyn könnte.[113]

Poetry is indeed the natural end and even the necessary direct product of mythology, but, as genuine poetry,. . .cannot be the cause nor the source of conceptions of the gods.

Poetry, then, is the higher stage of mythology; and Schelling's own conception of symbol is such that the fullness and perfection of any potentiality depends on and embraces the 'abyss' from which it evolved.

Schelling reviewed the history of the movement. Before Hume, it had been assumed that monotheism was original, by revelation, and that polytheism arose only through corruption and falling away from revelation. Hume's view that polytheism, based on the animation of nature, was the source of the conception of God, was combated in various ways.

Lessing in *Die Erziehung des Menschengeschlechts, Education of the Human Race*, attributed polytheism to the exercise of reason which 'zerlegte den einzigen Unermesslichen in mehrere Ermessliche', 'analysed the single uncommensurable object into several measurable ones'.[114] G. Voss thought the gods of all nations were euhemerized in the Old Testament, a modern version of the theory that all genres were to be found in the Bible, which if not the origin of all mythologies, was a compendium and synthesis of them. This theory was systemized through Baillie's idea that all peoples had split off from an *Urvolk*. But such an *Urvolk*, with an *Uroffenbarung*, Schelling says, cannot be one nation, but must in some way stand for all mankind; the Hebraic teaching must be pieced out with the various mythologies of other nations. The first to do this was William Jones.

Herder's attempt to describe a generalized Oriental landscape, then, was not merely a literary and critical device, it was part of the much larger undertaking to show that all human society is founded on the same religious need or instinct, a sense for God without which it would be impossible to see gods in nature at all; the undertaking to piece together the one *Urvolk* again.

Schelling was able to reconcile the notion of natural polytheism with the notion of original revelation: the first monotheism was only a potentiality, still unconscious, a 'relative monotheism', a servitude from which polytheism liberated men by teaching them to discriminate and to seek the enduring amidst alteration. Original monotheism was not a revelation for all time, but the beginning of the long process of education of the race; and the medium of that education was mythology.

Like Schiller, Schelling held that one does not and cannot find or explore the religious consciousness simply by going back to a primitive state of man; revelation is a process taking place in history, not a single event taking place at the commencement of the race, though it culminates in Christ. It teaches the race not only its origins, but its end, what Kant called our 'moral destination'. Mythology is the preparation for religious revelation, both historically and psychologically; the taste – or the distaste – for the bizarre or passionate primitive is irrelevant. 'Das Heidenthum ist uns innerlich fremd, aber auch mit dem unverstandenen Christenthum ist zu der angedeuteten Kunsthöhe nicht zu gelangen.'[115] 'Paganism is inwardly alien to us, yet with an uncomprehended Christianity we can never attain to the highest level of art.' Not only the underlying unity of the religious sense, but the many forms it takes must be honoured. Although we seek the reason of things, we must not merely allegorize them. 'Die Absicht muss vielmehr seyn, dass auch die Form als eine nothwendige und insofern vernunftige erscheine.'[116] 'We must rather consider the form too as necessary and therefore rational.'

Schelling, although in the *Philosophie der Kunst* (1802–3) he rejected the notion that allegory was the essence of mythology, which he defined as a form of symbolic thought attributing to the gods an independent value, still maintained that Christian thought was allegorical. This last vestige of Christian privilege is banished in the *Philosophie der Mythologie*, apparently in reaction against Creuzer, whose *Symbolik* maintained a dualism of sense and sign that went against the grain of Schelling's idealism. Schelling was dissatisfied even with the term 'symbol', which he thought suggested the dissociation of image and sense almost as much as allegory, and adopted instead Coleridge's conception of tautegory, which he quoted in a long footnote: in that mythology is not allegoric, but tautegoric, the gods do not signify anything outside of themselves, but simply what they are.[117] All revelation by the same token is tautegory.

The result of this levelling of Christianity to mythology is the triumph of critical apologetics: for now Christ is endowed with an historical reality again, the Incarnation is to be taken at face value, the bread and wine are not symbols but the flesh and blood of Jesus. The new mythological truth of Christianity is immediate, unconditional, 'lived'; it is the reality not of representation of doctrine, but of a train of historical events which have taken truly place, even if they have existed only in the history of consciousness.[118]

The literal historical event in the sense of the Enlightenment – which it had become abundantly clear the Christian story was not – was effectively transformed into a metaphysical event. For Schelling this carried the implication that ritual, rite, the re-enacting of the metaphysical event, took precedence over doctrine; for Coleridge, as in his interpretation of the Genesis myth, the metaphysical event enacts its doctrinal significance. Schelling continued to stress the difference between myth and poetry, because he had still to combat the school of Heyne and Eichhorn, for whom poetry itself, artificial, intellectual, was tied to the allegorical tradition. But Coleridge identified poetry with myth; this being so, he could absorb allegory into his scheme of development, not as characterizing Christian thought as against myth, but as one legitimate phase of mythological poetry. This, of course, does not mean that poetry reproduces primitive myth, but rather that it creates, at each stage of the development of consciousness, the metaphysical event.

The old attempt to demonstrate the priority and superiority of Judaeo-Christian revelation through the comparison of the religious imagery of the Greeks, the Hebrews, the Egyptians, the Persians, the Indians, became the attempt to comprehend the fundamental psychology of the human race. Man looking into his primaeval religious history finds the depths of his present psyche. At the same time, though only by an immense expansion of Christian terms of reference and a complete re-casting of the meaning of historicity, symbolic mythologists could defend Christianity as the culmination and expression of the whole range of human religious demands.

Schelling expressed the insight of the universality of the original significance of mythology in these romantic terms:

Man konnte die Mythologie etwa auch mit einem grossen Tonstück vergleichen, das eine Anzahl Menschen, die allen Sinn für den musikalischen Zusammenhang, für Rhythmus und Tact desselben verloren hatten, gleichsam mechanisch fortspielte, wo es dann nur als eine unentwirrbare Masse von Misstönen erscheinen konnte, indess dasselbe Tonstück, Kunstgemäss aufgeführt, sogleich seine Harmonie, seinen Zusammenhang und ursprünglichen Verstand wieder offenbaren würde.[119]

We can compare mythology with a great musical composition, which a number of men who had lost all sense for musical connexion, for rhythm and for measure kept on playing as if mechanically, so that only an inextricably confused mass of discords could result, whereas the same composition, artistically performed, would at once reveal again its harmony, its connexion, and its original meaning.

Coleridge in 'Kubla Khan', having not yet reached his own mature views of the nature of symbolic unity, was able to use the syncretist technique of 'piecing out' from a diversity of culturally uprooted mythologies to create a unity of superimposed, overlapping images whose not quite exact correspondence sets their edges shimmering and revives each nation's failing gods into authentic universal life. In 'Kubla', Coleridge gives us both the echo of the half-forgotten meaning of the races of the world, and a sense for the whole composition fully harmonized.

In his critical remarks on Cottle's epic *Messiah*, made in 1815, just after preparing the new preface to 'Kubla Khan' for the first publication of the poem, Coleridge expressed fully the romantic theory of the fragment as genre. The union of essential epic brevity with universal scope that he had described as the Miltonic idea of his own proposed epic in 1797 reappears, in the wake of his reading of Schelling, as a fully formulated aesthetic defence of the epic fragment:

The common end of all *narrative*, nay, of *all*, Poems is to convert a series into a Whole: to make those events, which in real or imagined History move on in a strait Line, assume to our Understandings a *circular* motion – the snake with it's Tail in it's Mouth. Hence indeed the almost flattering and yet appropriate Term, Poesy – i.e. poiesis = *making*. Doubtless, to *his* eye, which alone comprehends all Past and all Future in one eternal Present, what to our short sight appears strait is but a part of the great Cycle – just as the calm Sea to us appears level, tho' it be indeed only a part of a globe. Now what the Globe is in Geography, *miniaturing* in order to *manifest* the Truth, such is a Poem to that Image of God, which we were created into, and which still seeks that Unity, or Revelation of the *One* in and by the *Many*, which reminds it, that tho' in order to be an individual Being it must go forth from God, yet as the *rece*ding from *him* is to *pro*ceed towards Nothingness and Privation, it must still at every step turn back toward him in order to *be* at all – Now a straight Line, continuously retracted forms of necessity a circular orbit. Now God's Will and Work CANNOT be frustrated.[120]

History 'real or imagined' is a linear series of metaphysical events bent by ultimate ends into the cyclical form that assures those ends.

The original monotheistic unity, loosed from time and space, formally achieves the status of symbol; but it refuses the title as long as 'symbol' does not maintain a link, however tenuous, with an 'event'. Schelling redefined symbol, through Coleridge's 'tautegory', so that it would do just that; and this too is the sense of the 'reality' which in Coleridge's familiar definition of symbol is visible through its translucence. The achievement of 'mental space' controlled by a firm unity that is a reminiscence of an only-just-abandoned claim to literalness depended on an Orientalism evolved through the exigencies of the higher criticism.

Kathleen Raine has said that with 'the Hellenistic revolution' set in train by Thomas Taylor and culminating in Shelley,

Polytheism had become the natural language of English poetry, not in the purely decorative sense in which Pope or Dryden adorned country squires and their elegant daughters with the names of gods and nymphs, but as a language of qualitative and metaphysical discourse.[121]

This is half right. It was indeed a language of qualitative and metaphysical discourse; but it was so precisely because it was not the language of polytheism (any more than Plato's mythological language was). The new mythology, while honouring and incorporating the diversity of forms, specifically denigrated polytheism and sought a basis, historical and psychological, for an underlying 'monotheism' or unity of numina.

Mythological interpretation depends on an already existing tradition whose terms can be used to 'place' new events. Scholem, in *On the Kabbalah and its Symbolism*, points out that this is true of the whole mystical tradition – that whether it presents itself as radically reforming or as confirming ancient authority, its revelations are always in terms of its orthodox tradition.[122] To put it crudely, Buddhists do not have visions of the Virgin Mary. Strauss falls back heavily on Jewish tradition for his explanation of the events of the life of Jesus. No one in England did more than Coleridge to show the nineteenth century the way to its form of vision: the imaginative renewal and maintenance of the past. But the dependence on tradition for explanation leaves its real sources obscured and finally buries the tradition itself. Coleridge's strong objections to Eichhorn's referring the art of John solely to pre-existing usage in the other books of the Bible display his intense certainty that the springs of mythology must always rise freshly from the experience of the single seer.

As Empson has said of pastoral, 'It is felt that you cannot have a proper hero without a proper people, even if the book only gives him an implied or magical relation to it.'[123] Coleridge carried pastoral to its outward bound, for the 'hero' is the visionary poet who renews and reminds a people of the mythology without which they are not a people at all, but tribes of animals. And 'the people' in this instance is humanity, the original humanity before the polytheistic dispersion. Traditionally, the hero was 'half outside morality, because he must be half outside his tribe in order to mediate between it and God, or it and nature'.[124] The element of magic is inherent in this relation. 'Magic' was whatever could restore humanity's sense of its own nature, which was bound up with its sense of the supernatural. This lost, the entire edifice of civilization, including the prized rationality, comes tumbling down.

Coleridge's syncretism, even working within the bounds of Christianity, gave him a range and depth and sympathy hardly to be found in any orthodoxy. It is just possible that a Buddhist might have a vision of the Virgin Mary – or of an Abyssinian maid. In that primitive yet cosmopolitan dawn just before the beginning of the nineteenth century it was not so evidently necessary that 'The gods of China are always Chinese', as Wallace Stevens put it for our own tribal times in 'Two or Three Ideas'.[125] Coleridge's transcendental enterprise was to lay bare the source of mythology, the sense for a God in the human race. In 'Kubla Khan' we see the enterprise making its earliest and most attractive appearance, as we find there the sense for a God in its first pristine form, before articulation, before all tradition. It is first revelation, as it is last.

CHAPTER 4

HÖLDERLIN'S 'PATMOS' ODE AND 'KUBLA KHAN': MYTHOLOGICAL DOUBLING

For Friedrich Hölderlin as for Coleridge, the Book of Revelation opened the way to an Oriental syncretism that answered religious and poetic needs and finally passed beyond syncretism into a new mythology. For Hölderlin, the way was more agonized and more deeply concentrated on the reconciliation of Greek mythology with Christianity, two modes of thought held to be dramatically opposed by a series of German critics; but for both men, the way to reconciliation led through the current interpretations of the mystery rites as enacting the primal significance of all religious culture.

In the long poems Hölderlin wrote in the two years after 1802, the great hymns, his culminating achievement before the final *Umnachtung* (he lived out another thirty years in his strange but appealing 'madness'), the primary poetic influences are Pindar, whom he was translating – those superb translations that capture the quality of the Greek ode for German – and the Bible, especially the Book of Revelation.

In one of the finest hymns, 'Patmos' (1803), his most complete poetic resolution of his characteristic themes, he presents a vision within a vision, of one of the Greek islands, the *Inseln* that are the most recurrent symbol in all his poetry, this time of Patmos, nearer Asia Minor than Greece, and through Patmos, of St John's intense memory of his encounters with Christ in Jerusalem. As in 'Kubla', the complex and indirect form of vision open to a dark Enlightened age, the time-scheme of the Apocalypse, a magical psychic geography of civilization, and the relation of Christian to other mythologies dominate the poem.

Hölderlin and Coleridge were almost exactly of an age. Of Hölderlin it has been said, 'He is a descendant of the age of Enlightenment of the era of Kant... It was one of the early errors of Hölderlin criticism to identify him too closely with the Romantic tendency in German literature.'[1] I should rather say that both Coleridge and Hölderlin show how much of Enlightenment thought was carried over in transmuted form into romanticism. They absorbed the poetry of the late eighteenth century and were midwives to romantic poetry at almost the same moment in time, 1797–8. Both were men of high intelligence, close to the philosophic life of the time, bred in the Enlightenment, familiar with Kant and with the new idealism; Hölderlin took a degree in philosophy, heard Fichte lecture and of course was the friend as well as the schoolmate of Schelling and Hegel. Both men, concerned with old forms – the epic, the Greek ode – founded new forms and made metrical departures. Hölderlin's form was the ode, or hymn, Coleridge's perhaps more fundamentally the ballad, but all forms were translated into the meditative and visionary lyric: Hölderlin's 'novel' *Hyperion* is a wonderful poetic prose, his 'tragedy' *Empedokles* is lyric monologue and chorus. Not least, both men worked out in theory and in practice a public, mythological art suitable for a rational age, and so produced a private, idiosyncratic system.

The two poets' later development was similar: as Kempter has said of Hölderlin, 'the Jacobin became a royalist, the pantheist became a dogmatist, the friend of Greece became a Christian and German poet'.[2] Moreover, both men in their long years under medical supervision, Hölderlin in his madness and Coleridge in his opium retreat in Highgate, kept on writing, and what they wrote, though rarefied and obscure, is still rising in critical esteem.

The context in which we have discussed 'Kubla', largely unfamiliar in Coleridge criticism, was Hölderlin's immediate intellectual background. Intense admirer and friend of Schiller, earnest reader of Kant and pupil of Fichte, visitor to Paulus, student (like Schelling) of Heyne's work on Greek myths and philosophemes, collaborator with Hegel on his early theological work (including *Das Leben Jesu* (1795), *The Life of Jesus*), enthusiast for Schleiermacher's *Reden*, and deeply indebted to Herder, Hölderlin was a participant in those developments whose reverberations reached Coleridge to so much effect.

Orthodox, rationalist, and pietist strands are difficult to disentangle in the Germany of Hölderlin's youth, and the very attempt to disentangle them shows how closely and often unexpectedly linked they were. Hölderlin is often regarded as the heir of Swabian pietism, and so in fact he was. But in the Württemberg of his childhood, only a few radical pietist elements had left the Lutheran church, and his own home was not among the sectarians, dissenters, chiliasts, or *schöne Seelen*. His Denkendorf and Maulbronn years were 'initially responsible for the alienation from the established church of any religious feelings Hölderlin may have had', and he fled not to pietism but to Schiller's dramas, the fight against tyranny in France, Kant's philosophy, and ancient Greece.[3] The Tübinger Stift, the famous school which Hölderlin attended in the company of Schelling and Hegel, had been known for its pietist interests; a former Chancellor of the school, J. F. Reuss, had in 1757 defended Johann Albrecht Bengel, whose *Apokalypse* or *Erklärte Offenbarung Johannis oder vielmehr Jesu Christi, Commentary on the Revelation of John or rather of Jesus Christ*, republished in 1788, had preached that a new era of the world was at hand in which the God would return. Semler took Reuss to task for his championship.[4] In the background of pietism also stood Christoph Friedrich Oetinger, continuator of Boehme and source of much romantic mystical speculation. The leading poet of pietism was Philipp Friedrich Hiller, whose book *Geistliches Liederkästlein* (1762), *Little Treasury of Spiritual Songs*, Hölderlin received as a school prize.[5] It has been said that Hölderlin was educated in an atmosphere of literal apocalypticism that lent an urgent expectancy to the German humanistic Renaissance and the Napoleonic upheavals of Europe. In the early 1790s the second coming of Christ and the return of the Golden Age could seem identical and imminent; the times were repeatedly likened to the milieu in which Jesus appeared. For Hölderlin, history and mythology could fully merge. There is no mistaking this note in Hölderlin's poetry. But the Tübinger Stift in his day was past the peak of pietist influence; indeed, the dominant tone was rationalist, and it was by rationalist means that Christianity was defended. The teacher with whom Hölderlin and Hegel read Euripides in 1790 can be seen as a pietist, but only 'indirectly, as an advocate of Herder with a Swabian bias'.[6] Some authorities, including Ritschl, go so far as to say that Swabian pietism was in any case 'Enlightenment in a religious mantle'.[7] Any attempt at a purely pietist, as at a purely orthodox or a purely rationalist, reading of Hölderlin's poetry, is certain to come to grief.

The strands of orthodoxy, rationalism, and pietism were able to merge most successfully in the 1790s, as we have seen, in the conception of the Bible as a poetic mythology. The connection between the new mythological inquiries of the Biblical critics, the influence of Herder, the work of Greek scholars, the current views of the Mysteries, and the pietist revelations gave Hölderlin's development a direction which has not been traced in Hölderlin scholarship. The failure to do so has led to unnecessary conflict and even deadlock over Hölderlin's religious views, especially in the late poems. The movement in Biblical studies brings us a great deal closer, undeniably difficult though these poems are, to the exact shades of Hölderlin's faith. As Schleiermacher wrote in *Über die Religion: Reden an die Gebildeten unter ihren Verächtern, On Religion: Speeches to its Educated Despisers*, 'When the God and immortality of my childhood vanished from my doubting eyes, religion still remained to me.'[8]

Current views on the Mysteries gave both Coleridge and Hölderlin an opportunity to unite the historical–critical movement with the stream of the occult and mystical views of Revelation. The 'Mystery' stands at the centre of both their poems, and their interpretations of it, while highly individual, are part of the same history. Comparisons between the pagan mystery religions and either the initial or a later phase of ancient Christianity have been common for 200 years. Coleridge and Hölderlin were both well acquainted with the involved and fascinating history of these comparisons, though for Coleridge the question arose through his attempts to reconcile Unitarian with Anglican views, and for Hölderlin through his Hellenism and his close association with Hegel's early theology.

Coleridge in his lecture of 1795 on the corruptions of Christianity followed Priestley's *Early Opinions of Jesus* in laying the corruptions of early 'unitarian' Christianity at the door of the gnostic philosophers – a view deriving from Bayle and a commonplace among the English deists. Priestley's aim was to support the Unitarian view of the mere humanity of Jesus, and to show that the Trinitarian position had sprung from the gnostic opinion that, as Coleridge put it, Christ was 'a Spirit distinct from the man Jesus entering into him at his Baptism, and quitting him before his Agony.'[9] In all Coleridge's early lectures, 'Mystery' is a term of Enlightenment opprobrium attaching to the deceptions of priesthood: the doctrine of the gnostics 'produced all the Mysteries, Impostures, and Persecutions, that have disgraced the Christian Community'.[10]

As Coleridge made his way back towards the Church of England, he had to revise the Unitarian view that Trinitarianism was a gnostic corruption of early Christianity; and the most striking change comes in the value he attached to the Mysteries. Instead of standing in the deist manner for all forms of mystification that obscure the simple, natural, and universal content of Christianity, the Mystery is a fully developed rite that acts as an historical synthesis of paganism and Christianity, and supplies the dramatic expression of the meaning of 'tautegory'.

It was Coleridge's high, philosophical, and 'spiritualized' notion of the essence of religion that made the Mysteries of such importance to him, for the esoteric gnosis, the original revelation, a priestly and philosophical secret in the best sense, must be safeguarded against the superstitious mythologies of the masses; yet it must be visible, it must be enacted.

Not popular mythology, but its esoteric interpretation in the Mysteries was directly allied with poetry. In his 'Prometheus' lecture, Coleridge wrote:

The earliest Greeks took up the religious and lyrical poetry of the Hebrews; and the schools of the prophets were, however partially and imperfectly represented by the mysteries derived through the corrupt channel of the Phoenicians. With these secret schools of physiological theology, the mythical poets were doubtless in connection; and it was these schools which prevented polytheism from producing all its natural sensualising effects. The mysteries and the mythical hymns and paeans shaped themselves gradually into epic poetry and history on the one hand, and into the ethical tragedy and philosophy on the other.[11]

Just as Coleridge never abandoned the Unitarian sense of 'atonement' (it appears in the Kantian setting of the *Aids*), however, he was able to combine his new attitude towards the gnostic and platonic importations into early Christianity with the stress placed by the Unitarians on the Jewish sects, both before and after Christ, who kept safe the essentials of monotheist revelation. The higher criticism offered him the means: for it placed the safekeeping of the Gospel stories, in the period in which they had not yet been put in their final written form, in the hands of those same Jewish Christian sects that the Unitarians considered their 'orthodox' ancestors. Moreover, it suggested, by its emphasis on the Jewish milieu of Jesus, that much of the material that eventually found its way into the Gospels pre-existed in various forms inside the Jewish community or in heterodox Jewish sects like the Essenes. Later he made this relation more explicit. Where the Christian doctrine was not clearly present in the orthodox Jewish community, he held, it was part of the lore of the heterodox community. The idea of Christ's ascension and descent – the descent of the Logos or Son of Man into nature – was 'part of the Jewish *cabala* or idea of the Messiah by the spiritualists before the Christian era, and therefore taken for granted with respect to Jesus as soon as he was admitted to be the Messiah.'[12]

The spiritual lore was part of original revelation; and knowledge of it had passed from the Jews into the Mysteries. Coleridge cites Origen in favour of 'the opinion of those who regard the Original Doctrines of the Initiated as *refractions* of the Light of the ante-Mosaic or Patriarchal Revelation. –'

The only fair ground of complaint is that Arnobius, who knew nothing of the Mysteries but by Hear-say. . .does not at all distinguish the fabulous additions of poets and popular tradition from the actual representations in the more August Mysteries, the Eleusinian, Samothracian, Persian and Egyptian, nor even from the Sacerdotal which held a mid place between the inner Mysteries and the popular Legends. Origen, who had studied the subject, speaks very, very much more respectfully – & favours the opinion of those who regard the Original Doctrines of the Initiated as *refractions* of the Light of the ante-Mosaic or Patriarchal Revelation – [13]

In short, the gnosticism which in 1795 he condemned as the source of all corruption he transformed into a permanent tradition of esoteric heterodoxy that periodically emerges and is adopted into the orthodox cult. The monument to this is the Mystery.

Thus Coleridge succeeded finally in uniting the two irreconcilable views, the standard Unitarian condemnation of gnostic Orientalism and the Trinitarian necessity to give credence to the gnostic–platonic importations into the Gospel of John. The break in the continuity between Old Testament and New Testament and within early Christianity was mended. The higher criticism was the mediating factor, and its broader view of Orientalism – the inclusion of Jewish with gnostic and platonic Orientalism – made this possible.

One of the influences on the higher criticism was a still more radically mythologizing school of thought, whose views, though rejected then and now with indignation, eased the way for a more moderate Oriental syncretist mythologizing. These were the views of Dupuis and Volney, and to a lesser extent Richard Payne Knight and before him d'Hancarville. In 1795, Coleridge singled Volney out for condemnation; but in 1796, we know, he read through all of Dupuis. It has been convincingly argued that Dupuis suggested to the German critics that a large quantity of legendary material had found its way into the Gospels, though they refused to go the whole way with him and consider Jesus himself as mythical, like Osiris or Attis.[14]

Coleridge mentioned Volney's *Ruins* in the 1795 lectures in the course of his argument against the view that the Gospels were forgeries. Although not accepting it in its extreme form ('This same learned Infidel has likewise asserted the Book of Genesis to be an Astronomical & Geographical Allegory, and Jesus Christ to be the same with Bacchus, Krisna, and the Chinese God Fo!')[15] the claim that Jesus was sheerly mythological was a spectacular way of casting doubt on the evidence of the Gospels; like Conyers Middleton's argument for the continuity between pagan and Roman practices, also well known to Coleridge, it was not simply an extravagance to be dismissed, but a step in the serious arguments as to the historical validity of various kinds of testimony that followed from taking the Gospels as human productions.

Dupuis argued that just as Genesis was a conscious allegory, so the life of Jesus was also an allegory, composed by a Jewish sect, the Therapeutae or the Essenes ('de grands allégoristes'), based on other resurrected gods invented by Egyptian hierophants and the like. This argument, however extreme, provided the Biblical critics with an explanation as to how the Resurrection could have been accepted before the circumstantial details had been added to the Gospels. The core of event, though ultimately, as we have seen, a 'metaphysical event', had to be retained; but much of the material embarrassing to the Enlightened mind, such as the Virgin Birth, could be considered pagan legend already circulating in the Jewish community before the birth of Christ.

Dupuis seems to have played a particularly crucial role for Coleridge in the period when he was moving away from Unitarianism, by suggesting that the Book of Revelation, in which Coleridge was already so passionately interested, was the vehicle of an accomplished syncretism within the New Testament itself. It was this, then, that we find represented in 'Kubla Khan', where the mystery rite (early known to Coleridge in the full neo-platonic panoply of Iamblichus's *De Mysteriis*) has already begun to assume the proportions of its later role as the Hellenistic ark of revelation.

In Ralph Cudworth, whom he was reading in 1796, Coleridge found a strong statement of the idea that there had been continuous transmission of the same esoteric doctrine from Pythagoras to Plato and from Plato to the neo-platonists, the doctrine he held was contained in the Mysteries.[16] This esoteric doctrine, even in Coleridge's later statements of it, was close enough to the natural moral revelation of Toland and the Unitarian tradition so that the projection of the 'milieu of Jesus' backwards and forwards in time becomes comprehensible.

Coleridge, by adopting the idea of a platonic revelation within the Mysteries which was common to all religions, and locating the Christian version of it within the Book of Revelation, made it possible to place the synthesis of 'unitarian' and gnostic–platonic elements in Christianity very early. Heterodox Judaism and pagan Mysteries met in the Book of Revelation.

Coleridge is scarcely alone in the main lines of his solution. Any mythological approach, whether the radical one of Dupuis and Volney or the moderate one of Eichhorn and Gabler, tended to bring early Christianity closer to the Mysteries. It is now a commonplace of apologetics that the 'experience of the "Christ spirit"' was for the early Christians more important than the 'historical figure of Jesus', just as in the Mysteries there is no pretence of showing the validity of the story as history; the acceptance of this is of course the work of the historical–critical movement. If today most authorities tend to consider the similarities between the Mysteries and early Christianity as less striking than their differences, the same apologetical end has been attained in another way. Coleridge's contemporaries saw the gnostic–platonic accretions in the Gospels as late phenomena and considered the Gospel of John as the last of the Gospels; the most recent Biblical scholarship sees these accretions as very early and indeed already present in the Jewish community, and has once again placed the

Gospel of John among the earliest of the Gospels.[17] Coleridge accomplished the same result by making the Book of Revelation the locus of this synthesis.

The mystery rite was interpreted in a more personal way by Hölderlin. The relationship between the poet and the divinity was his lifelong concern. His conception of it underwent complex changes between *Empedokles* and the late hymns; but the relationship never ceased to be dangerous. The seer – and particularly the poet, whose affair it is to make known to the world his commerce with the divine – is liable to death for his presumption. At times Hölderlin was able to express his presumption with confidence:

> Und daher trinken himmlisches Feuer jetzt
> Die Erdensöhne ohne Gefahr
> Doch uns gebührt es, unter Gottes Gewittern,
> Ihr Dichter! mit entblösstem Haupte zu stehen,
> Des Vaters Strahl, ihn selbst, mit eigner Hand
> Zu fassen und dem Volk ins Lied
> Gehüllt die himmlische Gabe zu reichen.
> Denn sind nur reinen Herzens,
> Wie Kinder, wir, sind schuldlos unsere Hände,
> Des Vaters Strahl, der reine versengt es nicht
> Und tieferschüttert, eines Gottes Leiden
> Mitleidend, bleibt das ewige Herz doch fest.
>
>   ('Wie wenn am Feiertage')

> Wherefore to-day the Children of Earth can drink,
> Without destruction, of heavenly fire,
> Ours, though, O poets, when God's storms break,
> To stand beneath them with heads uncovered,
> To grasp its very self with our mortal hands,
> The bolt our Father hurls, and, wrapt in Song,
> To proffer the heavenly gift to our people.
> For if only we come to meet it,
> Like children, pure of heart and innocent-handed,
> Our Father's fire, in its candour, shall not consume,
> And, quivering now though it be with a god's own sorrow,
> The heart that is ours for ever shall yet withstand.
>
>   ('As when on a Holiday')[18]

But in *Empedokles,* a study of the visionary character, the philosopher says to his followers:

> Ihr dürft leben
> Solang ihr Othem habt; ich nicht. Es muss
> Bei Zeiten weg, durch wen der Geist geredet.

> You may live
> As long as you have breath; I cannot. He must
> Depart early, through whom the spirit has spoken.

Punishment may come simply as a result of contact with sacred things; or it may be interpreted as in the second version of *Empedokles*, 'Der Tod des Empedokles', as a result of imparting them to others, not qualified for divine knowledge ('he loved the people too much'); or again it may be intertwined with personal guilt. In 'The Death of Empedokles', the hero's 'sin' is the profanation of the divine, the revelation to the masses of what has given him by the gods. This is a universal mythological motif; but it is very specifically gnostic (in the *Apocalypse of Adam* we hear of the Word imparted to Adam and kept faithfully by his Sethian posterity) and typical of the range of pietist brotherhoods known to Hölderlin. The efficacy of the Word is lost as it is dispersed:

> Verderblicher denn Schwerd und Feuer ist
> Der Menschengeist, der götterähnliche
> Wenn er nicht schweigen kann, und sein Geheimnis
> Unaufgedeckt bewahren.

> More dangerous than sword and fire is
> The human spirit, so like the divine,
> When it cannot keep silent, and preserve
> Its secret undetected.

The necessity of secrecy and the necessity of revelation were equal and opposite in the period. The conflict represents a political and philosophical uncertainty. Truth depends still on a priestly cult, but also on an entire people; it must not and cannot be kept concealed. In the philosophies of the idealists, notably Fichte and Schelling, there is an alternation between a conception of philosophy as an esoteric cult to be preserved in a special private language and a conception of philosophy as a force for public enlightenment to be uttered in 'popular' form: thus the contrast between Fichte's *Wissenschaftslehre* and his 'Popular Lectures', and between these and the personal, cultic teaching of his later years that he felt could not be committed to paper; thus Schelling's attempt at a conjunction of oracular utterance and accessible form, as in Coleridge's favourite among Schelling's works, the mystic-platonic dialogue *Bruno*. Hegel in his early theological writings especially *Das Leben Jesu, The Life of Jesus*, set two forms of ideal religion, the 'reiner Vernunftglauben', the 'pure faith of reason', of Kant and the Greek national religion, over against positive Christianity, and following the mythological Biblical critics he sketched a *Volksreligion*, a popular form of belief that would have the capacity to develop the whole man out of the primitive fetishism in which he was imprisoned into the pure faith of reason. The conflict between secrecy and general enlightenment, then, expressed precisely that attempt to combine the genuinely primitive response with the genuinely sophisticated gnosis in a new 'evolving' mythology that we have seen as characteristic of the higher criticism.

For Coleridge too, the contents of vision must be enigmatic, but not without general significance; and they are not to be withheld, whatever the penalty. The subjective, esoteric doctrine has its necessary function in relation to public doctrine, as the élite clerisy is an instrument for the equal enlightenment of all men. Prophecy belongs not to the prophet but to the people. The prophet is sacrificed to the transcendent god's need for the world. His 'sin' is his purpose. Even in Coleridge's last, claustrophobic, self-circling years at Highgate, he did not believe that he spoke to or for himself alone. Yet it is symptomatic that 'Kubla Khan' remains a hieroglyph, and voluminous manuscripts remain unpublished.

When Hölderlin felt that he had indeed been struck down by the god (in December 1802 he wrote to his friend, Böhlendorf 'I too can truly say what is said of heroes that Apollo has struck me'), his error, he thought, had been precisely the personal interpretation of guilt, his elegiac lingering over his own suffering. As Szondi puts it, he had feared the self-inflicted rather than the divine wound.

His later poetry, then, is in this sense less problematic: the poet presents his vision with a new impersonality; his concern with his own personal relations with the divine and with his own worthiness or unworthiness is past. He is the servant of the vision. As an individual, he has already been sacrificed.[19] Thus his fundamentally Greek – and mythologically universal – conception of the danger incurred by venturing into the groves sacred to the gods merges with the Christian aspiration of death to self and to the world. The 'false priest' is absorbed into the true.

The conception of a personal sin against the god was close to Coleridge too, and the relation of the sin to creativity was a recurrent theme. Usually this is expressed in something like Christian terms: 'In all modern poetry in Christendom there is an underconsciousness of a sinful nature, a fleeting away of external things, the mind or subject greater than the object, the reflective character predominant.'[20] 'Underconsciousness' in Coleridge's aesthetics has a definite technical meaning: it harbours the motive passion which fixes the attention on an object in nature so intensely that the attentiveness itself becomes an end – passion becomes contemplation.[21] For Coleridge, the Christian was impelled towards God by the underconsciousness of sin, but enabled by the very strength of the impulse to attend to Him free from personal motive. Coleridge's work, whether 'philosophy' or 'poetry', was always the aesthetics of doctrine.

There were times, however, when Coleridge expressed the offence against the god in a more nearly Hellenistic and even Greek way. In the 'Prometheus' lecture, he explicated a Greek version of the myth of creation through reflected Word that he held to be the arcane content of the Mysteries. In Aeschylus's play it takes the form of the 'sublime mythus of the birth of reason in man'.[22] The 'sin' of Prometheus is the sin of the human race: presuming to set up his own intellect against the law of the god. This sin is given in all its complexity and in all the glory which in a Christian context Coleridge hesitated to express so openly. This is an heroic sin: the self-creation of the human race. Moreover, it is necessary to Jove himself, for eventually it will free him from his own natural law. The 'sense for God' is not blind awe, but an assertion of self which nevertheless remains wrong in principle. Creation necessitates rebellion and the consequent feeling of sinfulness. The rebellious act is always impotent, because the law of God is all-powerful; but it serves as a prophecy of the downfall of tyrants (on the political level) and of the need even of God for his rebel people. Again, then, the creative act of the poet is essentially prophetic of the truth (rather than 'effective') and inescapably sinful, but it is 'sin' far removed from the specifics of Christian faith.

Mythology begins, then, at the moment when the human race, by coming to consciousness, asserts its own existence against nature and God; and it ends when the human race delivers its developed consciousness up to God again (in *Prometheus*, when Alcides Liberator (Heracles) – a type of Christ – arises). The joy and sensuous pleasure so fully expressed in 'Kubla' is the joy of self-creation and self-discovery of the race, illicit but splendid, still half-shrouded in natural reverence, and heralding dimly the final conscious self-immolation in God.

For Hölderlin, not only is the vision ultimately independent of the personality or merits of the poet, but it is an indirect vision, for the gods are absent from the contemporary world. The poet can only preserve a memory of the gods, and a promise of their return. This very modesty and indirection is the basis of his most stunning and direct confrontation with the divine, in 'Patmos'. The memory and the promise become a conjuration of the renewed presence of the god.

Hölderlin is a master of the miraculous achieved by non-miraculous means, which is the object of the higher critical mythology. As he put it,

Zuerst werde ich hier von einer Idee sprechen, die, soviel ich weiss, noch in keines Menschen Sinn gekommen ist – wir müssen eine neue Mythologie haben, diese Mythologie aber muss im Dienst der Ideen stehen, sie muss eine Mythologie der *Vernunft* werden.[23]

I wish to speak first here of an idea which as far as I know has not yet occurred to anyone: we must have a new mythology, but this mythology must be in the service of ideas, it must become a mythology of *reason*.

'Patmos' opens with a description of that displaced Edenic landscape that haunted eighteenth-century Biblical poetry, the mountains upon which the dispersed community built its first non-paradisal settlements within sight of Eden: the landscape that is so painfully near and yet so far from the god. Here it expresses at once the psychic condition of the seer and the historical situation of the first Christians:

> Nah ist
> Und schwer zu fassen der Gott.
> Wo aber Gefahr ist, wächst
> Das Rettende auch.
> Im Finstern wohnen
> Die Adler und furchtlos gehn

Die Söhne der Alpen über den Abgrund weg
Auf leichtgebaueten Brücken.
Drum, da gehäuft sind rings
Die Gipfel der Zeit,
Und die Liebsten
Nah wohnen, ermattend auf
Getrenntesten Bergen,
So gib unschuldig Wasser
O Fittiche gib uns, treusten Sinns
Hinüberzugehn und wiederzukehren.

(1–16. See Appendix B for the translation of 'Patmos'.)

Who is 'der Gott?' In this passage, where the Christian reference is uppermost, as it effectively is throughout 'Patmos', the question does not arise with the insistence that has led to so many conflicting exegeses of other late hymns, especially 'Brot und Wein' und 'Friedensfeier'.[24] But the gods of Hölderlin were many, and their presence endures even in 'Patmos'. If the multiplicity of gods in Hölderlin's poetry – the gods of the elements, Air, Earth and Water, Apollo, Dionysus, Heracles, Christ, the *Zeitgeist* and the *Halbgötter* and the heroes (ranging from Kepler to Kant) – can be regarded as Greek, it is more particularly Enlightenment gnostic, for the gods of all the nations are accommodated through successive revelations in history. These revelations are organized geographically according to the theories of the origins of civilization that we have already reviewed. Moreover, the gods are selected and related to one another in a way that is scarcely classical Greek, but reflects rather the current interpretations of Hellenistic texts with regard to the Mysteries.

Dupuis had presented the Book of Revelation not simply as a handbook of Oriental mysticism, but as the type of the pagan Mystery, the initiation rite that dominated Hellenistic religion: 'c'est le seul ouvrage d'initiation, qui soit échappé de l'obscurité des sanctuaires'.[25] The Apocalypse of John is a pagan Mystery. Dupuis, like Coleridge, displays that odd but characteristic eighteenth-century blend of a desire to explicate all mysteries with a special love for the most esoteric of them. The mystical undercurrents of the century were not just a subterranean opposition to *les lumières*; they were fostered and elaborated by the rationalists themselves.

At the heart of all the Mysteries lay a vision of God and to this the

Book of Revelation leads the initiate, after the long journey of the soul. All theologies of resurrection are considered 'mithraic' by Dupuis; 'le théâtre le plus brillant de cette Religion' was Phrygia, in Asia Minor, specifically an isolated island where the visionary sees his re-union with the Eternal Light.[26]

In the centre of the Apocalypse is the vision of 'le génie lumineux':

13. And in the midst of the seven candlesticks *one* like unto the Son of man, clothed with a garment down to the foot, and girt about the paps with a golden girdle.

14. His head and his hairs were white like wool, as white as snow; and his eyes were as a flame of fire;

15. And his feet like unto fine brass, as if they burned in a furnace; and his voice as the sound of many waters.

16. And he had in his right hand seven stars: and out of his mouth went a sharp two edged sword; and his countenance was as the sun shineth in his strength. (Rev. 1, 13–16)

According to Dupuis (borne out by Hyde's *Religion of the Persians*, a book well known to Coleridge), this figure 'perfectly represents the Persian god Mithra'. Dupuis points to Athanasius Kircher's represen-tation of this luminous and etherial god of the universe in the *Oedipus Aegyptiacus* – another book well known to Coleridge. The priestess of Mithra is a Phrygian maid, who in the visionary state might represent not only the spirit of prophecy and the divinity, but also the soul of the initiate on its journey.

Dupuis's comparative mythological excursion does not end there: he was after bigger game. The solar theory of the origin of religion, through which Apollo, Dionysus, Christ, and Buddha were all allegorical representatives of the Sun, the generative cause of all things, was a typical piece of Hellenistic syncretism: Macrobius, especially in the *Saturnalia*, is one of Dupuis's main sources. Dupuis, however extravagant, in no way deserves the scorn sometimes heaped upon 'the solar theory'; he is neither mad nor quaint; he represents a leading intellectual stratagem of the time, a return to Hellenistic thought for a new theory of mythology that would consider Christian-ity simply as one version of the religious constitution of man. Macro-bius ends his 'proof' that all the gods were one and solar (a long, pseudo-etymological excursion of the kind beloved of the Hellenistic thinkers and their late eighteenth-century imitators) with an Orphic hymn:

> Hear me, O you who traverse a brilliant circle
> in space around the celestial spheres and who pursue
> your immense route, brilliant
> Zeus Dionysus, father of the sea, father of
> the earth, sun who has engendered everything,
> in your colours ceaselessly changing,
> in your golden light.[27]

The generative and sexual connotations of 'Kubla', long noted by its critics, were closely connected with the Mysteries. The sensational find of phallic objects at Herculaneum in 1738 had drawn attention to phallus worship within the Mysteries. The notorious work of Richard Payne Knight, *A Discourse on the Worship of Priapus, And its Connexion with mystic Theology of the Ancients* (1786) had been an object of considerable interest in the Wordsworth circle. Payne Knight shows how a universal mythology based on fertility cults was combined with an abstract spiritualized notion of its inner 'symbolic' meaning in the current interpretation of the Mysteries. The 'first principles of ancient religion' are 'contained in the Orphic Fragments, the writings of PLUTARCH, MACROBIUS, and APULEIUS, and the Choral Odes of the Greek Tragedies. These principles were the subjects of the ancient mysteries, and it is to these that the symbols. . .always relate.'[28] Payne Knight prefers the most abstract platonist formulation of the 'true Orphic' system of attraction. The centre is no longer the Sun, but 'their metaphysical Abstraction or incomprehensible Unity, whose emanations pervaded all things and held all things together'.[29] He agrees with Coleridge in despising the popular mythology, though Coleridge's attempt to rediscover a poetic Orphism is beyond him: all other systems than the true Orphic were 'only poetical corruptions of it, which extending by degrees, produced that unwieldy system of poetical Mythology, which constituted the vulgar religion of Greece.'[30] Payne Knight held to the Greek rather than the Hebrew origins of this system (Jehovah he identifies with Bacchus), but he drew the Indian deities, so long considered monstrous in the West, into the grand iconographical circle of Oriental religious expression. In the *Bhagavad-Gita* he is able to find the symbolic meaning of the Indian deities – 'though in a more mystic garb, the same one principle of life universally emanated and expanded'.[31]

Payne Knight gives a description as compelling as Dupuis's of the one true god, the luminous god of Orphism:

In the ancient theology of GREECE, preserved in the Orphic Fragments, this Deity, the ’Ερως πρωτογονος, or first-begotten Love, is said to have been produced, together with Æther, by Time or Eternity, (Κρονος) and Necessity, (’Αναγκη) operating upon inert matter (χαος). He is described as eternally begetting, (ἀειγνητης), the Father of Night, called in later times, the lucid or splendid, (φανης), because he first appeared in splendour of a double nature, (διγενης), as possessing the general power of creation and generation, both active and passive, both male and female. . . He is said to pervade the world with the motion of his wings, bringing pure light; and thence to be called the splendid, the ruling PRIAPUS, and self-illumined (αὐταυγης).[32]

All the apparently disconnected items in one list of Coleridge's poetic plans are suddenly seen in their single context: 'Hymns, Sun, Moon, Elements, Man & God. Destruction of Jerusalem. – Conquest of India by Bacchus in Hexameters. –'[33]

The highest god in Hölderlin's pantheon is the Air, *Vater Äther*. This god of the heavens, the god of day and the sun, who manifests himself most commonly through thunder and lightning, may be Zeus, Jehovah, Indra; but his elemental rather than his cult nature is always uppermost. He is Hölderlin's version of 'the luminous god', the fundamental god of all the peoples, the Orphic creator god of the Mysteries. All his characteristics reappear in the Johannine context of 'Patmos'.

His successive revelations are carried out through the 'saviour god', typified in Hölderlin by Heracles, Dionysus, and Christ. As Wolfgang Binder has pointed out, the divinity is named twenty-two times in the course of 'Patmos', but only in the next to the last strophe does he emerge as 'Vater' and 'Christus', 'Father' and 'Christ'. 'Der Gott', then, in this first strophe is the most general and all-inclusive name for the divinity. 'Clearly', as Binder says, 'the course of the poem is the process through which the true name of the god is won.'[34]

The phrase 'unschuldig Wasser' seems to point back to the state of the element before the descent of the divine into it, a nature that is receptive to the god without guilt, and forwards to a state in which nature may receive the divine without diminishing it. This nature out of time permits the divine to pass back and forth easily between worlds, so reuniting the remnant who await him on earth; it is an apocalyptic condition recurring before each descent of the god.

In the second strophe, Hölderlin, at home in Germany, is transported by a 'genius' to Asia; he has a new vision both of his home, and of Asia, of which the landscapes themselves are the genius. It is hard to do justice to these wonderful transpositions:

> So sprach ich, da entführte
> Mich schneller, denn ich vermuthet
> Und weit, wohin ich nimmer
> Zu kommen gedacht, ein Genius mich
> Vom eigenen Haus. Es dämmerten
> Im Zwielicht, da ich gieng,
> Der schattige Wald
> Und die sehnsüchtigen Bäche
> Der Heimath; nimmer kannt' ich die Länder;
> Doch bald, in frischem Glanze,
> Geheimnisvoll,
> Im goldenen Rauche blühte
> Schnell aufgewachsen,
> Mit Schritten der Sonne,
> Mit tausend Gipfeln duftend,
>
> Mir Asia auf. . .   (17–32)

The poet is passive, he is seized by a minor divinity. But the direct intervention is immediately translated back into nature and human action; 'es dämmerten', 'ich gieng'. Divinity is revealed to be indwelling: the brook is full of desire, the towers of Asia bloom. He becomes aware of the intrinsic quality of these natural scenes, as if he had never before seen even his own homeland: 'nimmer kannt' ich die Länder', like the yearning movement of the rivers everywhere in Hölderlin's poetry, seems to refer back (and forwards) to Germany as well as forwards (and back) to the unknown Asia. And the divinity is possibly his own, for a 'genius' is a divine double. We shall see how this mythology is a self-generating power.

Asia carried an immense charge of meaning in Hölderlin's poetry. Historically he stands just where Coleridge stood, between the Enlightenment and the new romantic conception of the Orient. As Kempter has written,

Simply from a temporal point of view, the romantic fashion for the Orient could not have stimulated Hölderlin's participation in the Oriental movement. Like Novalis he stands as intermediary between the romantic fashion and an older tendency more decisively grounded in religious faith.[35]

Kempter rightly sees this tendency as leading back to Swabian pietism, to Hamann's search for 'die ausgestorbene Sprache der Natur', 'the extinct language of nature', and to Herder's belief that Asia was the original *Völkerheimat*, 'national home', of religion, culture, and poetry.[36] But we can be more explicit: it was the emphasis placed on the Oriental mythological character of Scripture by the higher critical movement in the 1790s, the bridge between Enlightenment and Romanticism, that moved Hölderlin eastwards. And he may well have been familiar with Dupuis's mithraic Asia Minor.

Where is 'Asia'? Hölderlin's historical position in the Oriental movement is precisely illuminated by the answer to this question. He conjures up not a Greek or an Egyptian origin for religious culture, but, like Herder (and afterwards Creuzer, Görres, and Hegel), an Indian origin. The conquest of Bacchus is reversed in its direction: Dionysus, great god of unity and dispersal, comes out of India and sweeps westwards.

Although Hölderlin described the great course of civilization from the Indian temples (then mistakenly held to be among the most ancient buildings of the world) to the Gothic cathedrals of the North, the focus of his interest is not at the origin but at the crossroads of civilizations: Asia Minor, the point of contact and cross-fertilization, the home of the great Hellenistic Mysteries. As Pannwitz has said, 'Asia Minor, which stands often for Asia and is always closely connected with Hellas, faces on the Mediterranean towards Palestine and on the Black Sea towards the Caucasus.'[37] More than once Christ, like Dionysus, is referred to as 'the Syrian'. Hölderlin, like Coleridge, refers simultaneously to all the suggested origins of universal history, the icy Caucasus, Palestine, and Iran, yet giving a sense of an even remoter Indian past, from which civilization is carried to Europe and back again through the great waterways of the Danube and the Rhine.

It is, then, at the geographical centre of universal history, gathering to itself all theories of the origins and progress of civilization, that the poet of 'Patmos' arrives. Hölderlin, like Coleridge, employs a syncretic geography which covers immense distances in time and space; but at the same time he uses specific, identifiable locations in their actual relations to each other. Perhaps the most interesting is the transition from 'Asia', generalized in a golden haze of Oriental vision, to the specific scene in Lydia, and then to the Greek isles:

> Es rauschen aber um Asias Thore
> Hinziehend da und dort
> In ungewisser Meeresebene
> Der Schattenlosen Strassen genug.
> Doch kennt die Inseln der Schiffer. (47–51)

Suddenly we realize – only in the fifth line – that the narrator has embarked again, he is not just describing the Asian scene, he is on his way by boat to Greece. He is lost in the confusion of waters as his ship makes its way from the golden ribbon of the Pactolus to the open sea of the Aegean. And within three more lines we are within sight of Patmos.

Patmos is indeed only 40 miles from the coast of Asia Minor; but this quiet landing by sea is as marvellous as the aerial abduction to the fragrant towers of Asia. For Hölderlin, 'Asia' is above all the home of the gods; it is perhaps his most successful stratagem in his struggle to harmonize his obsession with the forms of Greek divinity with his returning Christianity. The vision of Asia provides the common landscape of the birth of the gods and their daily appearance; Patmos (and thereby all of Greek divinity) is placed within this magic circle by arriving at it with such expedition from the Asian rather than the European side; and the scene shifts again immediately back to Jerusalem, scene of John's communion with the god. The mountainous landscape of the risen Christ's last appearance, although 'accurate', recalls the landscape of the mind in the opening stanza of the poem, the landscape of risk and desired confrontation and the promise of salvation. The landscape of 'Asia', where the gods reveal themselves, has been transferred by the action of the poem out of the mind and back to it again. Inhabit these heights, for the gods too dwell here.

All other landscapes are now bereft of divinity, until the next coming.

In 'Kubla', of course, there is no awkward 'travelling': all of Asia is present in one spot: all realism whatsoever about locations and distances falls away. The apparent attempt to establish a mappable landscape succeeds in disestablishing it utterly. But it is worth noticing the impression of precise 'placing' everywhere in the poem: 'In Xanadu'; 'Where Alph, the sacred river, ran'; 'Down'; 'there were gardens', 'here were forests'; 'amid' (a key word throughout the poem, and used no less than four times, and reinforced also by 'girdled round' and 'Weave a circle round him thrice.') It is almost a sacred geometry, not merely a geography. All the phrases have this quality, even the harmless 'on her dulcimer', which indeed has a simple incantatory quality like a child's quizzing: 'Where did she play?' 'On her dulcimer'. This is achieved through simple inversion. Elsewhere the effect depends on an ambiguity of reference not unlike Hölderlin's: 'I would build that dome in air, That sunny dome! those caves of ice!' The dome would be built to stretch high into the air; or would it be built in the air itself (the New Jerusalem)? 'That sunny dome' may be in apposition with 'that dome in the air' or it may be the myriad heavens themselves. There is not only the traditional tripartite cosmos, there is an upwards thrust of infinitely repeated spheres. 'And all who heard should see them there' – where?

The best and most sustained example is the lines:

> The shadow of the dome of pleasure
> Floated midway on the waves;
> Where was heard the mingled measure
> From the fountain and the caves.

We have to do now not with the dome itself, but with its 'shadow', the dome's double. The shadow 'floats' – but yet it is exactly placed: 'midway on the waves'. Midway vertically or horizontally or both? I have already remarked on the multidimensionality of the scene: midway between fountain and ocean; and midway between the bottomless ocean's depths and the roofless sky's heights. At the reflective intersection is the esoteric centre of the poem, the union of godhead and nature, the omphalos of the universe, the circle whose centre is everywhere. In the hermetic literature, as in Dupuis, this union is described as sexual.

Hölderlin draws on an accurate geography for some of his un-canniest effects. He describes the island:

> Gastfreundlich aber ist
> Im ärmeren Hause
> Sie dennoch,
> Und wenn vom Schiffbruch oder klagend
> Um die Heimat oder
> Den abgeschiedenen Freund
> Ihr nahet einer
> Der Fremden hört sie es gern und ihre Kinder,
> Die Stimmen des heissen Hains
> Und wo der Sand fällt und sich spaltet
> Des Feldes Fläche, die Laute,
> Die hören ihn, und liebend tönt
> Es wider von den Klagen des Manns.   (62–74)

Patmos is impressively split into three volcanic hills that are almost but not quite islands. We may imagine that the sounds are collected in the centre of the tripartite island and echo in a particularly resounding way. There is the catchpool for sound and the extraordinary dispersion of it so that the whole island responds to cries for help. The sense of the island being an animated ear and tongue is increased by the mobile, darting, half-concealed, ubiquitous presence of children (on the island and in the passage). Patmos's homely splendour as nurse to the ship-wrecked, the alien, the bereft, and the visionary is achieved by the odd syntactical collocation of all these perfectly straightforward, accurately rendered details.

Both 'des Feldes Fläche' and 'die Laute' are said to 'split', two entirely diverse objects united in one action by a common verb. This form of grammatical synaesthesia is not arbitrary, but actually displays simultaneously the cause of the echo (the steep decline) and the echo (the sounds split into two). This of course wreaks havoc on at least the common understanding of the eighteenth-century physics that was the bane of so much idealist thought; the result – and Hölderlin often employs the technique – is the suggestion of a radical suspension of normal conditions of space and time.

Equally, it is the landscape of Patmos, echoing to cries of stranded distress and loss on its shore, that conjures up John's companionship with Christ. The poet now disappears, while we are told, in the third person, in the past tense, of John's experience. In several well-marked but beautifully managed stages, the poet has been raised to full impersonal visionary power to recount the final communion of John and His master at the Last Supper:

> . . .es sahe der achtsame Mann
> Das Angesicht des Gottes genau,
> Da, beim Geheimnisse des Weinstocks, sie
> Zusammensassen, zu der Stunde des Gastmahls   (80–4)

The *Gastmahl* is a communal rite which figures largely throughout Hölderlin's poetry; it is the central ritual mystery that sums up the significance of all mythologies. Taking the Last Supper as his example, Hegel in *The Positivity of the Christian Religion* had emphasized the importance of the friendship between Jesus and his disciples. On the one hand, he praised it, like Klopstock, for its humanity:

Anyone whose talent for interpretation has not been whetted by the concepts of dogmatic theology and who reads the story of the last evening or the last few evenings which Jesus spent in the bosom of his trusted friends will find truly sublime the conversation which he had with his disciples about submission to his fate, about the way the virtuous man's consciousness of duty raised him above sorrows and injustices, about the love for all mankind by which alone obedience to God could be evinced. Equally touching and humane is the way in which Jesus celebrated the Jewish Passover with them for the last time and exhorts them when, their duties done, they refresh themselves with a friendly meal, whether religious or other, to remember him, their true friend and teacher who will then be no longer in their midst.[38]

Hegel expressed disapproval of the metaphysical sense of the Eucharist, which he attributes to the Gospel of John; Hölderlin retains the humanity of friendship as the mark of the relationship between Jesus and John. As Kempter has remarked, 'Patmos' is 'durchdrungen von Sätzen aus dem "Messias" ', Patmos is 'thoroughly permeated with themes from Klopstock's *Messiah*'.[39]

Hegel, however, found in this intimacy one of the reasons for the speedy corruption of Christianity after the death of Christ. It was an aspect of the limited nature of the apostles:

Lacking any great store of spiritual energy of their own, they had found the basis of their conviction about the teaching of Jesus principally in their friendship with him and dependence on him. They had not attained truth and freedom by their own exertions; only by laborious learning had they acquired a dim sense of them and certain formulas about them.[40]

On account of the immersion merely in the person of Jesus, Christianity was able to become a public religion, as the Socratic faith never had, for Socrates's followers 'loved Socrates because of his virtue and his philosophy, not virtue and philosophy because of him'.[41] Hölderlin catches just this personal dependence on Jesus, the bewilderment of the apostles after his death, the pietist maintenance of the memory. But for him, as in his own personal life (it is one of the recurrent themes of his letters, and Hegel himself he calls 'mein Genius'),[42] this friendship was an unmitigated good, rather than the source of the corrupt government by élite councils of the early church or of fine-spun argument as to how certain kinds of subjectivity lend themselves to the evils of 'positive' religious government. The language and thought of the poem is found, as often with Hölderlin, in a simpler, more direct form in his prose; as he wrote to his friend Neuffer, 'Ich bin des täglich gewisser, dass Lieb und Freundschaft die Fittiche sind, auf denen wir jedes Ziel erschwingen', 'I grow daily more certain that love and friendship are the wings that carry us to every goal'.[43]

Hegel deplored the transformation of the Last Supper into the equivalent of the pagan Mystery:

This human request of a friend in taking leave of his friends was soon transformed by the Christians, once they had become a sect, into a command equivalent to a divine ordinance. The duty of respecting a teacher's memory, a duty voluntarily arising from friendship, was transformed into a religious duty and the whole thing became a mysterious act of worship and a substitute for the Jewish and Roman sacrificial feast.[44]

Hölderlin, however, makes this parallel his opportunity. Hegel is worried by the fact that 'Jesus's leave-taking from his friends took the form of celebrating a love-feast' and finds it, although no longer allegorical, inadequately symbolic;[45] Hölderlin finds his solution in it.

The movement from allegorical explanation of myths to ritual enactment of them is already completed in Hölderlin's poetry. As

Guardini has remarked, Christ's *Abendmahl* – like the feasts of each
god – celebrates all the gods.[46] It is the shared happiness of the community in its god. As always in Hölderlin, simple words are charged
with meaning: as 'Lächeln', 'smile', in 'Der Rhein' carries the whole
burden of the intense but serene joy of the gods, so 'gastfreundlich',
'hospitable' as applied to the island of Patmos marks it out for its high
ritual purposes. Described in the homeliest terms, it is a sacred island,
the island of the Mystery. In *Hyperion*, Diotima had prophesied 'die
Feste der Heiligen in allen Zeiten und Orten, der Heroen des Morgen-
und Abendlands', 'the festivals of the holy one of all times and places
and of the heroes of East and West'. In 'Friedensfeier', where the god is
so effectively Dionysus, Napoleon, the sun, and Christ at once that
critics have argued for one or the other interpretation with great ac-
rimony and to no possible end, he is given the simple but all-embracing
title, 'Fürst des Fests', 'the prince of the ritual celebration'.[47] The
'gastfreundlich' Patmos reunites West with East, the Symposium with
the Last Supper. The island 'wohnt', 'dwells,' it does not merely 'lie'; it
is a being, as in 'Ister' the stream-god 'wohnt'. Instead of the epic action
of the Gospels or the *Messias*, we have the hymn, the Orphic hymn
which celebrates the rite; in the little epic, the idyllic ritual place
absorbs the complete action into itself.

Now the disciples (the third person plural) have their last sight of
Christ on the cross, the communal vision:

> Es sahn ihn, wie er siegend blickte
> Den freudigsten die Freunde noch zuletzt.   (90–1)

This is the high point of the vision. The simple word 'Freude', 'joy'
carries great weight in Hölderlin's poetry, and here especially, for in
other poems the god in the world had procured 'Freude' for his disciples
but not for himself. The close alliterative alliance of the words 'freudigsten' and 'Freunde' emphasizes the achieved unity in vision.

Gradually then the vision, as it had risen, subsides, but with equal
brilliance. As in Keats's 'Nightingale' ode, the highest point of vision,
the approach to the supernatural is reached early in the poem, but this
is not the end but the inception of the visionary state within natural
experience. First, the meeting with the disciples on the road to Emmaus,
fittingly the most bizarre, striking, even physically shocking passage of
the poem:

> Die Locken ergriff es, gegenwärtig
> Wenn ihnen plötzlich
> Ferneilend zurück blickte
> Der Gott und schwörend,
> Damit er halte, wie an Seilen golden
> Gebunden hinfort
> Das Böse nennend, sie die Hände sich reichten –
>
> (130–6)

This passage offers another example of Hölderlin's skilful parallel mythologizing: 'Die Locken ergriff es' refers to the outpouring of the Holy Spirit described in Acts, but equally to the Iliad where the divinity grasps Achilles by his golden locks.

It is in this community that the once shared vision can be preserved. As Coleridge conceived a clerisy, the idea of a new community based on an enlightened priesthood preoccupied Hölderlin: Petzold has pointed to the influence of Heinse, especially *Ardinghello*, on Hölderlin's early conception of a brotherhood in nature; we hear of 'das Reich Gottes', 'the kingdom of God', of his friends in Tübingen; Diotima's 'göttliche Gemeinde', 'divine community'; Hyperion's 'Pantheon alles Schönen', 'pantheon of all the beautiful'; the 'freie Götterliebe', 'free love of the gods' of Empedocles; and the slogan 'allgemeines Priestertum, Vorspiel des Protestantismus', 'universal priesthood, prelude to Protestantism'.[48] Uppermost is the problem faced by the Biblical critics: in what sense, in the absence of contemporary documentation, can we understand 'the Gospel witness'? The solution is the one we have already seen emerging, slowly and painfully, from the work of the mythological school of Biblical criticism. Hölderlin maintains in name only the identity of the apostle John with the visionary John; the experience given as John's is the communal experience of early Christianity. The whole poem centres on the long series of mediations required for the poet of the present to revive a tenuous memory into its original revelation. As for Coleridge, the maintenance of the memorial community through history is the only means to this. Each step of the distance, each step of the mediating series, is rendered by Hölderlin with such vividness that he entirely succeeds in creating an analogue of that history.

The description of Christ's words is based on the Gospel of John. John retains the privileged visionary humanity with which Klopstock had endowed him, while being invested also with the intense Greek beauty of the *Jüngling* that surrounds all the gods of Hölderlin's poetry. Although Christ's distance is maintained ('der achtsame Mann' *versus* 'Das Angesicht des Gottes'), He too, through the intimacy of the two young men takes on the same Bacchic beauty, reflecting the common mythological sources that lie behind the Christian and the Greek stories.

The intimacy of John with Christ and the direct intensity of John's vision of the presence of Christ establish his traditional credentials; yet the poem conspicuously does not assert the identity of John the Apostle with John the Apocalyptic. Visionary powers are required on the island of Patmos to reconstruct the central communal experience of Christianity – not a new vision of the New Jerusalem, but the life of Christ itself; distance has already created a doubt of the adequacy, indeed of the reality, of the event and of the visionary's powers. Ultimately, the only genuine vision in the poem is the poet's vision of 'Patmos' as the mythological centre of the community of all religions. Paradoxically, the restoration of the Christian vision depends on the poet's insistence that his own visionary powers are the most inadequate of all. Yet finally all the varieties of visionary powers are on a level here in their accomplishment and in their painful inadequacy. The modern poet is at one with the prophets.

The poem descends from the visionary communion to the bereft disciples' search for explanations, and then reverts to the solitary first person again – but who is speaking? John or the poet?

> Wenn aber einer spornte sich selbst,
> Und traurig redend, unterweges, da ich wehrlos wäre
> Mich überfiele, dass ich staunt' and von dem Gotte
> Das Bild nachahmen möcht ein Knecht –
> Im Zorne sichtbar sah ich einmal
> Des Himmels Herrn, nicht, dass ich seyn sollt'
> etwas, sondern
> Zu lernen.   (168–74)

This passage spans the whole range of the apocalyptic poet, from companion of the god to knave and fool, from his presumption to his humility, from his authenticity to his charlatanism. One implied reference here is certainly to Paul on the road to Damascus.

Christ in another passage is referred to as 'Einer'; 'einer' (with a small 'e') may be an angel like the one Jacob wrestled with, a minor form of divinity, a spiritual double like the genius of the first strophe, but Christian instead of Greek. And the visible anger of the god (unspecified despite the Biblical context) may simply be, as so often in Hölderlin, the thunder and lightning.

The *Ich* of the modern poet rapt away to Asia has become the *Ich* of a whole series of visionary and prophetic figures who are seen to have been struck down in the same way, neither nearer to nor farther from *imitatio Dei*. The reinterpretation of the prophetic function of the Greek and the Christian bard is here completed, and thereby the modern poet appears fully in all his ambiguity.

Hölderlin's own experience of being struck down by god is undoubtedly present in the passage. It led to the most extraordinary resolution of the whole series of ideas that had occupied him during his poetic life, not least the significance of Greece for a modern German poetry. It seems, from the famous letter of 1802 to Böhlendorf describing the experience, that while wandering in southern France (the nearest he ever came to the classical mediterranean Greece he dreamed of), he attained first to a new sense of Greece:

Das Athletische der südlichen Menschen, in den Ruinen des antiken Geistes, machte mich mit dem eigentlichen Wesen der Griechen bekannter; ich lernte ihre Natur und ihre Weisheit kennen, ihren Körper, die Art, wie sie in ihrem Klima wuchsen, und die Regel, womit sie den übermutigen Genius vor des Elements Gewalt behuteten. Dies bestimmt ihre Popularität, ihre Art, fremde Naturen anzunehmen und sich ihnen mitzuteilen. . .[49]

The athletic quality of the southern race, among the ruins of antique spirit, made me more familiar with the authentic being of the Greeks; I learned to know their nature and their wisdom, their bodies, the way they developed in their climate, and the regimen whereby they protected the proud genius from the power of the elements. This determines their popularity, the way they absorb alien natures and how they communicate their thoughts to them. . .

Greece, he had written to Böhlendorf in 1801, was fundamentally an Oriental nation, which had, through Homer, learned western sobriety. Greece thus was a model for Germany only in that she was a nation that had successfully assimilated other cultures, as Germany so desperately needed to do:

Das eigentlich Nationelle wird im Fortschritt der Bildung immer der geringere Vorzug werden. Deswegen sind die Griechen des heiligen Pathos weniger Meister, weil es ihnen angeboren war, hingegen sind sie vorzüglich in Darstellungsgabe, von Homer an, weil dieser ausserordentliche Mensch seelenvoll genug war, um die abendländische Junonische Nüchternheit für sein Apollonsreich zu erbeuten, und so wahrhaft das Fremde sich anzueignen.[50]

The real national character will, with the progress of education, become less and less of an advantage. The Greeks are the less masters of holy pathos precisely because it was native to them, and on the other hand they excel in the narrative art from the time of Homer onwards, because this extraordinary man was sufficiently generous of spirit to acquire the western Junonian sobriety for his native Apollonian realm, and so genuinely make the alien his own.

Because Germany's character was fundamentally western, any further slavish imitation of Greek forms could only be disastrous. But by the same token, Greece was more indispensable than ever; for one could only know oneself through comprehending the alien:

Bei uns ists umgekehrt. Deswegen ists auch so gefährlich, sich die Kunstregeln einzig und allein von griechischer Vortrefflichkeit zu abstrahieren. Ich habe lange daran laboriert und weiss nun dass ausser dem, was beiden Griechen und uns das höchste sein muss, nämlich dem lebendigen Verhältnis und Geschick, wir nicht wohl etwas gleich mit ihnen haben dürfen. Aber das Eigene muss so gut gelernt sein, wie das Fremde. Deswegen sind uns die Griechen unentbehrlich. Nur werden wir ihnen gerade in unserm Eignen, Nationellen nicht nachkommen, weil, wie gesagt, der freie Gebrauch des Eigenen das schwerste ist.[51]

The opposite is true of us. For this reason it is so dangerous to abstract the rules of art purely and simply from Greek excellence. I have laboured long on this and know now that apart from what must be the highest aim both for the Greeks and for us, namely, the living proportion and fitness, we may not have anything in common with them. But one's own native quality must be learnt as well as the alien. For this reason the Greeks are indispensable to us. But it is in our own national quality that we shall not succeed in being their true posterity, because, as I have said, the free use of one's own is the hardest of all.

The perception of Greece as Oriental and alien, and therefore to be imitated only in its infinite capacity to assimilate the alien, lies behind his brilliant translations. He wrote to a publisher about his translation of Sophocles, promising to emphasize the neglected Oriental nature of the Greek:

> Ich hoffe, die griechische Kunst, die uns fremd ist, durch Nationalkonvenienz und Fehler, mit denen sie sich immer herumbeholfen hat, dadurch lebendiger als gewöhnlich dem Publikum darzustellen, dass ich das Orientalische, das sie verleugnet hat mehr heraushebe, und ihren Kunstfehler, wo er vorkommt, verbessere.[52]

> I hope to present to the public a livelier image than usual of Greek poetry, which is alien to us, on account of attempts to conform to our national proprieties and through the mistakes with which they have always helped themselves out; and I shall do this by emphasizing the Oriental nature of the poetry, which they have denied, and correcting the mistakes wherever they appear.

Germany, then, whose native character was 'Junonian sobriety', must blend it with the Oriental nature of Christianity, already a part of the civilization, but not fully absorbed as the Greeks had absorbed Homer. Through Christ, the Oriental prophet, lies the solution; alien Christianity will provide the key to self, which one cannot approach directly. Hölderlin advanced the hermeneutic art of 'Vachbildung eines fremden Lebens' to an art of self-knowledge.

Schiller had likened Kant to Moses, and called for the stern moral law to be reinterpreted; as Hölderlin put it, 'Kant ist der Moses unserer Nation, der sie aus der ägyptischen Erschlaffung in die freie einsame Wüste seiner Spekulation führt, und der das energische Gesetz vom heiligen Berge bringt', 'Kant is the Moses of our nation, who leads us out of the Egyptian somnolence into the free, lonely desert of his speculation, and brings the energetic law from the holy mountain.'[53] Hölderlin extends the analogy to the genius of the German nation, that in its Kantian sobriety cries out for the 'heiligen Pathos' of Oriental Christianity. Through belief in the unbelievable miracles of Christ would come the *Anmut*, grace, to mitigate the Kantian *Würde*, dignity. 'Orientalism', then, in this convoluted and profound way, opened the path for Hölderlin to a new *Sangart*, a new bardic poetry, for the modern world.

His glimpse of Greek antiquity in France gave him at the same time a new perception of the highest art:

Der Anblick der Antiken hat mir einen Eindruck gegeben, der mir nicht allein die Griechen verständlicher macht, sondern überhaupt das Höchste der Kunst, die auch in der höchsten Bewegung und Phänomenalisierung der Begriffe und alles Ernstlichgemeinten dennoch alles stehend und für sich selbst erhält, so dass die Sicherheit in diesem Sinne die höchste Art des Zeichens ist.[54]

The sight of the antique gave me an impression which made more comprehensible not only the Greeks but in general the highest kind of art, which even in the highest degree of movement and phenomenalization of concepts and everything seriously intended nevertheless contains everything permanent and self-subsistent, so that certainty in this sense is the highest kind of symbol.

The result of his experience – and it is not surprising that Hölderlin in his wanderings through France appeared to observers to be half-crazed, the seer who like Abaris himself carried the arrow of Apollo within him, who 'wie des Weingotts heilige Priester/Welche von Lande zu Land zogen in heiliger Nacht', 'like the wine god's holy priests/Who travel from land to land in holy night' – was an immensely heightened awareness of the particularities of his home surroundings in Germany, which nevertheless served him as 'a philosophical light' by which to compare all that he knows of men and nature until 'alle heiligen Orte der Erde zusammen sind um einen Ort', 'all the holy places of the earth are gathered round one place':

Die heimatliche Natur ergreift mich um so mächtiger, je mehr ich sie studiere. Das Gewitter, nicht bloss in seiner höchsten Erscheinung, sondern in eben diese Ansicht, als Macht und als Gestalt, in den übrigen Formen des Himmels, das Licht in seinem Wirken, nationell und als Prinzip und Schicksalsweise bilden, dass uns etwas heilig ist, sein Drang im Kommen und Gehen, das Charakteristische der Wälder und das Zusammentreffen in einer Gegend von verschiedenen Charakteren der Natur, dass alle heiligen Orte der Erde zusammen sind um einen Ort, und das philosophische Licht um mein Fenster ist jetzt meine Freude; das ich behalten möge, wie ich gekommen bin, bis hieher![55]

Nature in my homeland grips me the more powerfully the more I study it. The thunderstorm, not only in its divine appearance, but in just this aspect, as power and as form, in the other phenomena of the heavens, the light in its effect, impress themselves, nationally, and as a principle, and even like fate itself, so that for us there is something holy in the intensity of its coming and going, the characteristic of the forests and the encounter in one region of different traits of nature, so that all the holy places in the world are gathered round one place, and the philosophical light round my window is now my joy; may I remember how I have come to this place!

We may surmise that it was this philosophical light that Hölderlin continued all his life to see through the window of his confinement.

This passage in Patmos, then, and indeed the whole poem, is to be understood as accomplishing in German poetry what the Greeks had accomplished in theirs, not a syncretism but a new synthesis of cultures. 'O Insel des Lichts!' 'O island of the light!' Hölderlin called it in a later draft of the poem, the achieved symbol of all the holy places on earth.

Hölderlin leaves the question of the visionary's merit behind him only in that he has become aware that he can have no merit that could justify the expectation of divine revelation. And divine revelation itself tells him this. Only the visionary can fully know his own unworthiness through the contrast between himself and his vision. The identity of the several Johns is reasserted in the moment of being struck down, in that John is both he who comes closest to the god and he who in the lightning knows his own incapacity.

Hölderlin thus encased the objective vision within the subjective vision; Coleridge encased the subjective between two objective visions. 'I' becomes 'he' when the seer achieves objective existence in the eyes of the community. The community in 'Kubla' is wider: it is not the Christian remnant only, but 'all who hear'. For Hölderlin too, of course, the remnant comprises all those who await the re-descent of the god and the new revelation. Some may not be able to hear the harmony of the great mythological composition, but no one is excluded on principle. As a later, unfinished version of 'Patmos' puts it:

> Voll Güt' ist, keiner aber fasset
> Allein Gott.

> Full of good, but no one can grasp
> God alone.

The romantic aim remains the Enlightenment of all the people; there is to be a community of all those who receive and see, and this is not a coterie or a few select spirits only. Thus even when the romantic poet is presented very much as an individual, he retains something of the impersonal bard who embodies the visions of a whole community, and who does it for their sake and for the sake of the vision as objective, not for the sake of his own experience. 'Apocalyptic' lyric retains the epic intention.

The strophes following the death of the god who presided over the evening meal carry out the Dionysian motif of the dismemberment of the god, here also the dismemberment of his community:

> Doch furchtbar ist, wie da und dort
> Unendlich hin zerstreut das Lebende Gott. (122–3)

The Dionysian motif continues to dominate the aftermath. The following strophe speaks of the beauty of 'der Gestalt', and the next presents the great Bacchic image of the thresher:

> Es ist der Wurf des Saemanns, wenn er fasst
> Mit der Schaufel den Weizen,
> Und wirft, dem Klaren zu, ihn schwingend über die Tenne.
>
> (153–5)

This modulates into a promise for the future of restoration of unity, but only little by little, in time:

> Nicht alles will der Höchste zumal. (162)

Out of the Dionysian imagery arises the mythological motif that binds together all the Mysteries: the reflection of the god. As the eyes of the Lord and John mirrored one another at the visionary high point, so now must the god's image be reassembled and reflected by man. The poem returns here abruptly to the first person singular, to the poet, to the solitary individual after the dispersal of the god, and

> So hätt' ich Reichtum,
> Ein Bild zu bilden und ähnlich
> Zu schaun, wie er gewesen den Christ. (165–7)

This mythological mirroring, through a series of refractions, is the principle of the poem, the creative mirroring of the god in the world.

The hermetic-alchemical tradition had come down directly to Hölderlin from Boehme through Oetinger.

The imagery of the mirroring eye, of creative vision, of course dominates the poem: 'Mir Asia auf', the 'Seher', 'es sahe der achtsame Mann/Das Angesicht des Gottes genau', and especially 'Und es sahn ihn, wie er siegend blikte'; 'Denn schon das Angesicht/Der theuern Freunde', 'Ferneilend zurück blickte/Der Gotte': 'Von dem Gotte/Das Bild nachahmen'; and 'Ein Bild zu bilden und ähnlich/Zu schaun, wie er gewesen, den Christ'. The mystical likeness to the image of God is the focus of Christian visionary imagery. Through John's eyes we have the vision of Christ, or rather literally in his eyes, as if it dwelt there, permanently, branded there, unsummoned and ineradicable. And when it is dispersed, it is preserved 'in einfaltigen Augen', like the gnostic conception of the soul, a spark of the divine light. 'Einfaltig' has the force of 'unschuldig Wasser': the reflection of the god is accomplished as if without the Fall. Yet the poet's vision, in being struck down by the god, is of his inability to reconstruct that image within himself.

In both poems, the troubled relation of seer to his vision and seer to his community and community to the vision is represented by the mobility and ambiguity of the personal pronoun. Hölderlin moves from 'I' to John's vision in the third person (we never have John's narration directly), and then to the disciples and the whole Christian community in the third person plural.

There is a pervasive ambiguity in the second half of 'Patmos', after the death of Christ, as to the identity of both the speaker and the audience. From the unambiguous 'Sie' referring to the disciples left in uncertainty and dissension –

> ein Räthsel ewig füreinander
> Sie sich nicht fassen können
> Einander, die zusammenlebten
> Im Gedächtniss, (141–4)

– the enigma of their abandoned condition on earth governs the use and relations of personal pronouns.

The poem goes back to the first person singular for the tortured self-communing with divinity identified only as 'einer': the 'je est' of Rimbaud. Finally, the intimacy of 'Ich' and 'Dich' is established through the gods' love for them:

Und wenn die Himmlischen jezt
So, wie ich glaube, mich lieben,
Wie viel mehr Dich,
Denn Eines weiss ich,
Dass nemlich der Wille
Des ewigen Vaters viel
Dir gilt.   (198–204)

Even here, the love of the gods is very uncertain; what emerges as certain is the knowledge of the speaker of what is important to the person he is addressing. Again it is the intimate personal relationship, as between John and Jesus, and between Jesus and the whole group of disciples, that can bear the most weight. That the gods are after all unfathomable is the strongest of the Greek elements in this poem. Yet this mutual knowledge of 'Ich' and 'Dich' depends on their unity in god.

This is the only appearance of 'you' in the poem. At one level, it may refer to the Landgraf von Homburg, to whom the poem is dedicated; at another level Hölderlin may still be addressing his lost Diotima, but if so, this intimate relationship, like John's with Christ, is only a memory to be preserved through 'the loving darkness'. This condition holds for the entire remnant. As the retiring community of the faithful on earth can still find the likeness they seek in this restored community 'Ich' and 'Dich' can again know one another. And as in 'Patmos' so in 'Kubla', just the one reference to 'you': 'And close your eyes with holy dread': the ancient community of belief is restored. The eyes close; the intense burning vision of 'John', or indeed of the Ancient Mariner in his endless wanderings, on which slender lifeline the piecemeal modern world is strung, returns to a primaeval trust. This reflects the idealist solipsism that can be relieved only by a community of shared perceptions dependent ultimately on the unifying idea of the One: without the mythological bond no man can trust his own perceptions. In this community only can the memory of the beloved dead be preserved. The ritual is the act of preservation.

The apocalyptic time-scheme shows the same complexity as the personal reference. Hölderlin's is not the true apocalyptic time – the prophecy of the past event – for he is prophesying the return of the god in the future; but it is a projection of apocalyptic time into linear history, producing the theory of cyclical return which Nietzsche is said to have derived from Hölderlin. The point to which the apocalyptic returns is in the future because the past repeats itself. Despite the appearance of linearity, this is the annulment of history, corresponding to the theological notion of the timelessness of God.

> Und Einer steht darunter
> Sein Leben lang. Dennoch lebt Christus.
> Es sind aber die Helden, seine Söhne
> Gekommen all und heilige Schriften
> Von ihm, und den Blitz erklären
> Die Taten der Erde bis izt,
> Ein Wettlauf unaufhaltsam. Er ist aber dabei. Denn
> seine Werke sind
> Ihm alle bewusst von jeher. (205–12)

Coleridge too, as we have seen, mythologized history into metaphysical event in order to salvage a vision of Christian revelation. For Hölderlin, the punctuation of the world by the divine is one single event, but despite the emphasis on Christ, a recurring one; the eruption of each hero and god is one of His manifestations. This adoption of the gnostic doctrine of successive reappearances of the divine has the effect of binding together Christianity and paganism in an unorthodox way; the Christian can and must worship Christ in any of His forms, however outlandish. This is a kind of literal application of the mythological theory of original unity, subordinated to Christianity.

But since Coleridge refers to the first and the last mythological events, and Hölderlin refers to the recurring mythological revelation, both are legitimate variations on John's apocalyptic time: the beginning and the end are in the present. In this way a kind of rescue operation is carried out for a modern period apparently without gods. Nietzsche was obliged to use more extreme methods to achieve the same end, and to institute a new theological age by declaring the death of the god. It is characteristic of books of Revelation that the most definitive events – the bang, not the whimper – are the signals for, and guarantee of, cyclical process. The passage explaining Jesus's reappearance to the disciples exemplifies Hölderlin's abolition of time within history itself:

> Denn izt erlosch der Sonne Tag,
> Der Königliche, und zerbrach

Den geradestrahlenden,
Den Zepter, göttlichleidend, von selbst,
Denn wiederkommen sollt' es
Zu rechter Zeit. Nicht wär' es gut
Gewesen, später, und schroffabbrechend, untreu,
Der Menschen Werk, und Freude war es
Von nun an,
Zu wohnen in liebender Nacht und bewahren
In einfältigen Augen unverwandt
Abgründe der Weisheit.   (109–20)

The single, immediate reappearance after death occurred then and has not been repeated, because since then the work and the joy of men must be to dwell in the dark and keep faith. Keeping faith in dedicated memory with the word and vision of God has its own virtues and rewards which would be wholly destroyed by the renewal of the divine presence. But the utter strangeness of this climactic point of history is expressed by the presence side by side of a series of expressions of time negating one another: 'Gewesen, später'; and then with this past–future pairing in mind, 'war es/Von nun an' seems to have the same quality (though like 'izt erlosch' it is really perfectly straightforward). More impressive is the contrast between the event of the Resurrection as sharply breaking off from time and yet initiating a long period of continuity in time. This is accomplished partly through the sense of the passage as a whole, but dramatically by the minute transpositions of reference within the lines quoted. Such a coming would have been disruptive of the work of men; and the work of men would have broken off. And, that being so, it would have been 'the mere work of men', 'ein sterblich Werk', as a variant has it. But then there is a more marked shift: the work of men combines with their joy as double subject of the next clause, and we hear not what had happened or would happen if the god had returned (the point of view is successfully both that of the bewildered disciples and that of the present time), but what must be from now on. Although 'Werk' and 'Freude' belong together, 'Freude' is isolated too (by its punctuation), emphasizing that dedication is not a mere matter of duty. Time has stood still since then; our situation is the same as that of the disciples. Finally, then, the denial of time recreates the sense of imminent apocalypse.

Then the return of the god, the end of the world and the resurrection are envisioned, and here the imagery returns to the great mythological course of the sun through the sky:

> Wenn nämlich höher gehet himmlischer
> Triumphgang, wird genennet, der Sonne gleich
> Von Starken der frohlockende Sohn des Höchsten,
> Ein Losungszeichen   (180–3)

During the long period of waiting, which is at once the historical time from the death of Christ to the present, and the time from the next coming of the god to the end of the world, what has been won from these visions is preserved. The heavenly procession and the resurrection of the dead are actually seen only by the poet in his own person, but they are sustained also by all of expectant Christianity. There is still a grace akin to visionary power that is conferred by the Bible:

> Der Welt vergessen
> Stillleuchtende Kraft aus heiliger Schrift fällt, mögen,
> Der Gnade sich freuend, sie
> Am stillen Blicke sich üben.

'Heilige Schrift' is not identical with, but closely allied with, poetry which preserves the rhythm – we recall Schelling's metaphor of the universal mythological music – and receives the signal for the return of the god.

The 'baton', 'der Stab des Gesanges', has been identified by some critics with the thyrsus of Dionysus. But Hölderlin's imagery is always more widely referential, more complex, and more exact within its own established context than any such identification permits. Macrobius supplies further information on the meaning of the musical instruments carried by the Phrygian god: 'To the sun, under the name of Attis, they give as attributes a flute and a baton.'[56] The unequal stops of the flute remind us that the irregular winds borrow their substance from the sun; the baton 'symbolized the power of the sun, by which everything is conducted'. He explains why Mercury as well as Apollo stands for the sun:

The similarity of Apollo and Mercury results in effect from the fact that among many peoples, the star of Mercury carries the name of Apollo and that Apollo presides over the chorus of the Muses, while Mercury is the giver of the word, present of the Muses.[57]

Hölderlin suppresses the specific names of the pagan gods, the system of attributes, and the elaborate allegorical arguments that link them, but maintains the connections among the sun-like divine power, music, and the Word of poetry. Hölderlin's baton, then, emerges from the same circle of Hellenistic references and has essentially the same significance as Coleridge's dulcimer: the divine revelation is in the keeping of poetry. It is not, after all, that a single 'true name' of god has been discovered, but that the pattern of significance of all the names has emerged: the primitive language of revelation.

These, then, are visions within visions, each mediating the others, so that no special supernatural power is claimed, either by the poet, or by John, or by the other disciples, or even by Christ Himself, whose effect resides in His intimate companionship and His death. Yet the force and conviction of each phase builds up the composite picture of the unifying god; and ultimately, looking back across the successive mirrorings, it is clear that the power of the poet has indeed been asserted at full strength: to think of Patmos is to see Christ.

It is clear, too, that syncretism, with its techniques of simple interleaving, superimposition of images, and failed *figura* as apocalypse, while still visible here, has been transcended. Out of romantic Hellenist syncretism arose a new myth, and this myth was identical with its own technique. It has been remarked of both anthropological and religious philosophical approaches to myth in the twentieth century that 'the cognitive content of myths has been suspended or rejected'. Both commit the 'functional fallacy': myth has function, but no referent.[58] This development had taken place in idealist philosophy of mythology in the first two decades of the nineteenth century, as allegory moved towards ritual; it is as true of Schelling as it is of Eliade that myths are 'symbols of symbols'. Although the poems of Coleridge and Hölderlin represent an earlier stage in which myth still has cognitive content, this 'content' arises from a new comprehension of the functioning of mythology in the syncretist context.

The phenomenon of 'mythological doubling' has been pointed out by Merkelbach in the literature surrounding the Hellenistic Mysteries, in just that literature that for the romantics proved the most fruitful source for their heretical Christian mythologizing; Reitzenstein pointed to the parallel between the Mysteries and the romantic *Doppelempfinden*, the 'double-touch' that Coleridge recurred to more than once as a proof of the existence of the self.[59] What does the initiate find at the end of the ritual Mystery? In syncretist literature, when one system of divinities has borrowed some members from other (equivalent) pantheons, the gods sooner or later encounter each other. The goddess Isis is doubled throughout Apuleius's Psyche story on account of the syncretist incorporation of the Greek Io-myth into the Isis-myth; Isis is not only the same figure as Psyche and Venus in different contexts, but here she is involved in a dramatic action in which she plays all three roles at once. All of Coleridge's favourite myths belong to this same complex: Psyche, Prometheus–Heracles, Genesis, and Plato's Penia/Poros myth from the *Symposium*; and often he re-phrased them in the terms of idealist psychology.

The recognition of doubling requires adopting a standpoint outside any single community's myths. The confrontation with the Greek gods in Apuleius is, according to Merkelbach, a 'burlesque', for to the Egyptians, the Greek gods were only emanations of their own.[60] But from the universal comparative mythologer's point of view, all gods are 'emanations' of all other gods, and the effect is by no means one of burlesque. Rather it can produce, as in Hölderlin's poetry, the electrifying sense of encounter not only with specific divinities but with godhead itself.

The internal meaning of mythology, then, is precisely the unity of meaning of all apparently dissimilar myths. Doubling is not an irony or a witticism, but a disconfirmation of unique revelation. All mythological systems except that of one's own community having been thought of as a heresy (even when the system is syncretist), to 'encounter' another system within one's own is heretical, and produces a slight 'shock'; and to claim that all are reducible to one 'internal' system is regarded as the greatest heresy for all systems. The internal system, however, can have no independent full expression; 'original revelation' is lost. Thus various mythological systems become identified with the internal truth, and are one by one used to explicate an 'internal' system *vis-à-vis* the communal mythology. In this sense, all mythological systems are capable of acting as the 'internal' system of the others. In short, there is internal interchangeability as well as external. It is in this way that Coleridge's gradual formulation of a private system rendered it capable of external validation.

'Internal' explication of this kind might seem to raise again the problem of allegory, of reduction of myth to a separable meaning; but understood as a universally applicable comparative method, one myth explicated in terms of another (and another) becomes an end in itself. It results in a relational, not a reductive gnosis. This is why apocalyptic can be defined by Northrop Frye as 'a world of total metaphor, in which everything is potentially identical with everything else, as though it were all inside a single infinite body'.[61] The self-generating power of romantic mythology – its 'doubling' – is the source of its ultimate success at recreating the spontaneity in necessity of primitive myth-making. Each image becomes itself by gradually passing into another and another until the web is complete and each is every other in the whole which is the end of vision. This is the complete psyche; the creating self at last encounters himself again.

Each central image carries with it its whole context, enriched and confirmed by its syncretist references, exoteric and esoteric. Since by syncretist universalism all the images exist in each other's contexts, the images ultimately meet themselves in the extended context of each other's image. Thus in 'Kubla' the maiden is the poet's muse; yet she is the prophet and the priest, and she is the vision itself, the end, the god revealed; and she is the journeying soul of the initiate. The 'I' meets itself in the form of its human double; and in the form of the god of gods. The 'characters' are different phases of each other.

Doubling in its sharpest form is the meeting of self as antithesis; epic action collapses either into absurdity (in all its romantic senses) or into the cyclical, evolutionary inclusion of all revelation. Doubling of this antithetical sort is a special case, like Schelling's antithetical symbol. The clashes occur, the sharp antitheses arise, just at the point of confirmation (doubling). The relation between allegory and symbolism is clarified fully at this stage: the return to Hellenistic allegory led to the discovery of syncretic doubling, which in its sharpest form produces the antithetical confirmatory nodes we call symbols. But this is not characteristic of myth as such. As Merkelbach has said,

But one must not forget that the mythos of earlier peoples was not so firmly fixed as the sacred history of Christianity. The latter is historical; the mythos of earlier cultures, however, indicated the significance of all the important things in life, in that it traced them back to a higher mythical reality. The views of men on the meaning of their actions alter, and with them alters the mythos. For this reason, then, it is not firmly fixed; it will always be related to what men hold to be the real and true. The result is the strange iridescence of the mythical stories, that run now one way and now another.[62]

Coleridge in 'Kubla' created just this sense of the 'strange iridescence' of primitive myth, and of Christianity understood as primitive myth rather than as historical document. The sharp antithesis is an evolutionary possibility within the poem; that is why it can be not quite inaccurately discussed as 'proto-symbolist'. But the sense of ultimate coherence is created not through dialectic, but through the minute gradations by which the mythological ripple-system of each image approaches and overlaps another.

Coleridge put the point in the historical context of the early history of Christianity. In combating Gibbon's views of the reasons for the triumph of Christianity, he offered in their place first 'the necessity for a religion comprehending the interests of all mankind' (the theme of his projected mythological epic). Second, he said, 'that Christianity being the divine medium between all the opposite doctrines of the different philosophers, and comprehending what was true in each, had them, with few exceptions, all as its pioneers, all as its combatants'.[63] Thus Christianity for Coleridge is the great inclusive medium within which the mythological doubling takes place and thereby brings out at the nodal points the fundamental human pattern of need that the comprehensive religion must fulfil. It was this process of overprinting, of pioneers and combatants meeting, that 'created' Christianity; the true religion develops insensibly, necessarily, from mythological superimposition. Mythological doubling is for Coleridge the process of the creation, the historical evolution of true religion; it is a form of 'gradual revelation' which permits a gnostic inclusiveness and a Christian orthodoxy as to the supremacy, finality, and clarity of the revelation of Jesus Christ.

And in this notion of Christianity as the all-encompassing symbolic medium which is an organizing power of significance we find Coleridge's 'modern gnosticism':

Even so it is with the great moral truths. They show a fitness in the human mind for religion, but the power of giving it is not in the reason; that must be

186

given as all things are given from without, and it is that which we call a revelation. And hence it is that I have ventured to call Christianity the proper
supplement of philosophy – that which, uniting all that was true in it, at the
same time gave that higher spirit which united it into one systematic and
coherent power.[64]

Christianity, then, is Hellenism developed and ordered, the evolved
summary of all mythological revelations from the beginning of experienced time by which the race comes to understand the moral
truths of its own nature; and finally, it is the essence of that spiritual
understanding. For Coleridge too, as for the long line of Enlightenment thinkers modulating into philosophical idealism, Christianity is a
form of gnosticism. 'Kubla Khan' is the image of that symbolic process
of human gnosis.

The god multiplied into all his appearances points beyond appearance to the mystic belief in the unknowable and unnameable God that
lies beyond all His names; that god called by Hölderlin 'der ungenannte
Gott'. Just this, of course, was the historical result of Hellenistic
syncretism. As Kenneth Burke has put it,

Hellenistic imperialism itself also provided a step towards the 'monotheizing
of polytheism' in that it tended to treat all gods simply as regional motives,
each of which could be represented by its appropriate temple in the capital
city. Such convergence of outlying deities provided a visual incentive for the
sort of thinking that could culminate in Paul's assurance to the Greeks that he
represented precisely that God, the *Deus absconditus* of nascent Christian
trinitarian monotheism.[65]

Hölderlin clearly remains closer than Coleridge to the Hellenistic
feeling for the gods in action; but the action of 'doubled' gods is
necessarily not narrative action, but ritual action. Ritual action takes
place at the confirming nodes: the rider is overtaken by vision; the
divinity seizes the hair of the head; the dying god is victorious; the
heavens form a procession of celebration; and in the communion meal
all the gods feast one another. 'Division' is overcome by 'unity'.
Hölderlin realizes the ambition of Tübingen days, and founds a new
Mystery. So successfully does he select his mutually confirming ritual
actions, so carefully are they related to bodies of literature, that it is
almost possible to believe in a set of epic narratives lying behind them

of which they are the epitomes. If Hölderlin's central ritual is the *Gastmahl*, Coleridge's poem can be taken as a ritual of baptism, that baptism that characterized a multiplicity of pre-Christian and non-Christian sects, but which, adopted by Christianity, became one of its characteristic celebrations of the birth into vision. Nevertheless, it is equally a system of images belonging to a newly forming ritual Mystery which will dominate nineteenth-century poetry.

The Mystery is the same in the two poems. The soul of the initiate encounters itself. The myth of the distribution of the god into the world lies behind the motifs of self-recognition; but the final vision of the initiate is of his own self-creation: the fully developed psyche not only embraces all the gods, it has created them. Mythology has expanded with the education of the human race, whose last stage is to recognize it as self-education. Man knows all gods to have sprung from his own potentiality to revere them. He has created the gods in his own image. The great system of all the mythologies is a hall of mirrors: each phase is self-reflection. The triumph of humanity is shattered; the image of god cannot be recreated in man once he is aware of it as self-projection. The visionary must maintain the separateness of God; His presence depends on it. In 'Patmos', the reflection eye-to-eye of divinity and visionary is balanced by the visionary avowal of the impossibility of creating the image of Christ within himself. The existence of God depends on the maintenance of the equilibrium between these antithetical visions, as the whole poem's vision depends on its denial of the possibility of vision. The spuriousness of the romantic visionary, the *Knecht*, guarantees his authenticity. His visions can be given a place in the canon of traditional visions.

In 'Divine Ideas', Coleridge's last manuscript, he expressed his metaphysics in terms of a Hellenistic myth which is like an autumnal version of 'Kubla Khan' and a Christian 'Prometheus'. In a letter of 1833 he described the plan of the 'Opus Magnum', of which this manuscript forms part, in terms reminiscent of his mythological epic; and in the same letter, he mentioned Eichhorn, and a plan to versify the Book of Revelation.[66] The apocalyptic 'throne world' is closely related to the Hellenistic and early Christian 'pleroma', the 'fullness', the bright sphere of divinity with its potencies, aeons, archons, and dominions.[67] We find in this last manuscript, which shows his syncretic prose style at its most highly developed, an attempt to give a modern, romantic version of the 'pleroma'. Coleridge's pleroma is not a platonic emanation system, but a description of the state of those individuals who have separated themselves from God. It therefore has a double character: the particularity of the individual, rebel will is necessarily most valued in the universe of the fallen, for without it they would be at one with God: their existence depends on vivid singularity. At the same time, this is a false position, a position which nullifies their wills, for only the will of God is realized, and with that they are in essential conflict. Thus they exist in a world of self-contradiction, ambivalence, uncertainty, and ambiguity. This state is called 'potentiality': they sway between their own false existence and their true life in God. Their existence nullifies itself. Particularity produces uncertainty. The 'translucence of the general in the particular', in Coleridge's best-known definition of symbol, is also the contradiction of the general by the particular. This sharp opposition, however, Coleridge brought into the open only in the last decade of his life.

From the point of view of the full, ordered, gnostic universe, the romantic system must have a certain melancholy and deserted air. The spaces are vast, hierarchy has collapsed, and though there are crowds they are dim and flitting figures of potentiality that now and again sharpen in an assertive image. We recall Coleridge's dicta on the necessity of obscurity for the sublime.[68] Obscurity is the medium of the sharp sensuous image.

This pleroma, Coleridge's personal mythology, is a late version of the universe of 'Kubla Khan': one in which the sensuous detail of God's creation lives in its first freshness, yet a fallen universe of which the main characteristic is uncertainty produced by a division in created nature itself. They have in common their brilliant ambiguous cosmic particularity. Coleridge, like Hölderlin, in order to maintain Christianity, was obliged to create his own mythology – one that emerged from his art, and came to rest in it.

Warburton, describing the symbolic acts, 'the speaking hieroglyphics', by which the priest of antiquity conveyed to the people the visions and instructions they had received from God, gave the example of 'the voice of the sign' of Ezekiel, who delineated the siege of Jerusalem on a tile.[69] Epic was the art of the encyclopedic minstrel, who maintained the communal memory of the moral and useful knowledge of an oral culture;[70] Coleridge, in a literate culture, gave his sign through a mnemonic hieroglyph referring to all the texts of the communal past, even those that may never have existed. One of Coleridge's favourite quotations was from Statius's *Thebaid*, '*Nec caret umbra Deo* – Nor do the shadows lack a divine power.'[71]

CHAPTER 5

BROWNING'S ST JOHN: THE CASUISTRY
OF THE HIGHER CRITICISM

Coleridge and Hölderlin represent the early phase of the influence of the higher critical movement on nineteenth-century literature. Contemporaneous with the emergence of the mythological school of higher critics, their work has the freshness and the daring of those early days, and at the same time the tentative, testing quality of the originators. The mythologies they created had the spontaneity and the quality of liberation that we rightly associate with the romantics; at the same time they convey a reminiscence of mystery and a sense of things withheld. With Browning and George Eliot, we move into the mid-Victorian age, into the epoch after Strauss, when the mythological school had consolidated its position and expressed its findings fully and publicly. The wider Victorian public, of course, remained largely unaware of the advance of criticism until the *Essays and Reviews* controversy. But the tone of those popular controversies is entirely misleading. The results of the movement were absorbed much earlier by the serious thinkers of the time. There was continuity between the groups of dissenters with whom Coleridge had associated in his Bristol and London days, and the Unitarians of George Eliot's youth; although the Unitarian movement suffered some setbacks during the war years, knowledge of Biblical criticism had not died out among them. Coleridge's mature work had carried his solutions to problems posed by the higher criticism into the hands of the 'Germano-Coleridgeans' Maurice and Hare (though they show much less detailed knowledge of the higher criticism than Coleridge himself). The main figures in the mid-Victorian period are Strauss and Renan, Strauss the more important of the two, the more original and weighty, Renan the popularizer. Yet Strauss himself was only the foremost spokesman of a school stretching back to Eichhorn's earliest publications on Genesis in the 1770s, and Renan was seen as in some respects a serious opponent of Strauss in the interpretation both of the life of Jesus and more generally of the mythological approach. Certainly for literature Renan – himself a man of letters, an essayist, a stylist, as Strauss might have scorned to be – had a powerful attraction. Browning and George Eliot made use of both men's work, to some extent setting them off against each other, to some extent producing unique blends of the two. In the knotty, intricate, 'worked' quality of both Browning and George Eliot we can see the rich maturity of the influence of the higher critical arguments. The movement still has its power to startle, to undermine, to drive to despair and to imaginative reconstruction; but now there is a greater bulk of material to absorb, a heavier weight of reinterpretation, a more difficult task of mythological creation. Through the pressure to accommodate these powerful ideas in literary form a distinctively modern literature emerges. The higher criticism is no longer the concern of a group of linguistic specialists and Oriental scholars, nor the special interest of groups of dissenters seeking support for their own interpretation of early Christian history, nor the poetic province of a handful of especially gifted and prescient intellects, but the medium of a characteristically modern experience of problematic conviction. Indeed, with George Eliot, through her early absorption of Feuerbach, we can see the third phase, the phase of outright secularization, arising from within the mythological movement itself. The emergence of the modern condition is all the more powerful because it works through ancient texts and forms and through minds by no means temperamentally prepared to welcome alteration for alteration's sake. There is no sharp break; but once begun, the process generates its unavoidable conclusions, even while every cranny that might offer refuge is explored, every handhold deepened that offers a moment's respite, and every blind turn in the path welcomed as a delaying action.

Browning has often passed simply for an opponent of the higher criticism.[1] But he was far from this. His own Christian apologetics follow lines laid down within the higher critical movement itself and well, if diversely, trodden by others. Major aspects of his general philosophy (misrepresented by the only philosophers ever to touch them, Santayana and the third-rate British Hegelian Henry Jones) are illuminated by the necessities imposed by the results of the higher criticism; even more, his conception of the role of the poet and his poetic practice, particularly in the 'casuistical' poems, are clearly related to arguments, and modes of argument, employed by the higher critics. All these points emerge from a reading of 'A Death in the Desert', widely recognized as one of his finest poems at the time of its publication in *Dramatis Personae* in 1864.[2] This poem is, like the complex history of the higher critical views of St John, an archetype of nineteenth-century apologetical casuistry.

Browning argued all his life, most fully in 'Parleying with Gerard de Lairesse', against the use of Greek mythology by modern poets; and Douglas Bush declined on those grounds to accord him the 'mythological imagination'. Robert Langbaum has rightly pointed out that 'the modern mythical method challenges and re-establishes mythical pattern precisely through realism and through psychology in the modern sense.'[3] Langbaum, for all his perspicacity, however, fails to mention Browning's 'A Death in the Desert' in his review of works conceivably 'mythological' in the Browning canon; yet it is out of the dramatic realization of the central myth of Christianity – the direct witness to salvation – that Browning extracted a truly modern subject matter: for it had not yet been experienced as 'ancient fable', which had to be 'rendered back/Pallid by fancy as the western rack/Of fading cloud bequeaths the lake some gleam/Of its gone glory!'[4] It was vivid, new, even sensational in a realm where myth had not been suspected. This originating power of criticism is the measure of modern myth-making.

There has been some dispute as to whether Browning used Renan's *Life of Jesus* as well as Strauss's in composing 'A Death in the Desert'; internal evidence points conclusively to the use of Renan, not just incidentally, but for the crux of the poem: John's confession that he was not, as the Fourth Gospel claims, present at the Crucifixion. Although Browning may have conceived the poem much earlier, and may even have drafted some part of it, the form and significance of the poem as we now have it depends on his use of this material. W. O. Raymond rightly felt inclined to believe that Browning had been spurred on by Renan, on the general grounds that the interest which colours Browning's poems is not abstract, but 'focused in a person, writing, or sequence of event', as 'Christmas-Eve and Easter-Day' are in Strauss, as 'Blougram' is in the career of Cardinal Wiseman, 'Cleon' in Arnold's 'Empedocles', 'Mr. Sludge' in the encounter with Home, 'Prince

Hohenstiel-Schwangau' in the opportunism of Napoleon III, 'Dodington' in the political chicanery of Disraeli.[5] The peculiar qualities of Renan's *Life of Jesus* make it fit very well into this pattern. The only objection lay in the unsupported opinion of the Rev. Llewellyn Davies, given in discussion at a Browning Society Meeting in 1887, that Browning had written the poem long before November 1863, when, we know from his letter to Isa Blagden, he read Renan. But Llewellyn Davies's argument really rests not on the dating, but on the quite unfounded opinion repeated to this day by critics that since Strauss was 'more radical' than Renan, Browning's reply needed to be directed at Strauss alone.[6]

The question of who was 'more radical', or who most urgently required answering, is not so quickly resolved, either in general or specifically on the point of the treatment accorded John. It is quite true that Strauss denied the authorship of the Fourth Gospel to the Apostle John, attributing it rather to 'a late Hellenistic writer' of 'Greek or Alexandrian culture' probably of the second half of the second century. Despite his ostensible defence of apostolic authorship, however, or rather by means of it, Renan's treatment of John is notably less sympathetic than Strauss's. Renan indeed bears much more resemblance to the 'rationalist' tradition of Biblical criticism typified by Reimarus and Paulus, indeed to the scoffs of Voltaire, than to the 'myth' tradition of Eichhorn and Gabler that Strauss elaborated. In line with the long series of attacks in the eighteenth century on the probity of religious leaders – Bayle's immoral David, Mohammed 'the Charlatan', Moses 'the Egyptian priest', and finally the vulgar, ignorant, and cunning disciples of Jesus – Renan does not scruple to attack John as dishonest and Jesus as duplicitous.

Strauss had carefully documented the aggrandizement of John in the Fourth Gospel, that is, the claims made for the pre-eminence of John over the other disciples, claims not borne out by any of the other three Gospels; but because Strauss does not hold the author to be John himself, but one of his school, John is not accused of self-aggrandizement. Renan, in contrast, has things both ways: he first implies that the author is not John, but wishes to pass himself off as John; he then proceeds to declare that after all the author must be John, so that the apostle is guilty of the double charge, Strauss's of not being himself, and Renan's of passing himself off as himself. If the author is not the apostle, he is spurious; if he is the apostle, he is doubly spurious. Thus Renan:

The author always speaks as an eye-witness; he wishes to pass for the apostle John. If, then, this work is not really by the apostle, we must admit a fraud of which the author convicts himself. Now, although the ideas of the time respecting literary honesty differed essentially from ours, there is no example in the apostolic world of a falsehood of this kind. Besides, not only does the author wish to pass for the apostle John, but we see clearly that he writes in the interest of this apostle. On each page he betrays the desire to fortify his authority, to shew that he has been the favourite of Jesus; that in all the solemn circumstances (at the Lord's supper, at Calvary, at the tomb) he held the first place... We are tempted to believe that John, in his old age, having read the Gospel narratives, on the one hand, remarked their various inaccuracies, on the other, was hurt at seeing that there was not accorded to him a sufficiently high place in the history of Christ.[7]

Strauss outlined the case soberly, displaying the gradual step-by-step aggrandizement of John as the structural principle of the Fourth Gospel:

The more we approach the catastrophe, the more marked is the subordination of Peter to John. At the last supper, indeed, Peter is particularly anxious for the discovery of the traitor: he cannot, however, apply immediately to Jesus (13. 23ff.), but is obliged to make John, *who was leaning on Jesus' bosom*, his medium of communication. While, according to the synoptists, Peter alone followed Jesus into the palace of the high priest; according to the fourth Evangelist, John accompanied him, and under such circumstances, that without him Peter could not have entered, – John, as one known to the high priest, having to obtain admission for him (18. 15f.). In the synoptical gospels, not one of the disciples is bold enough to venture to the cross; but in the fourth, John is placed under it, and is there established in a new relation to the mother of his dying master: a relation of which we elsewhere find no trace (19. 26f.). On the appearance of the risen Jesus at the Galilean sea (21), Peter, as the θερμότερος, casts himself into the sea; but it is not until after John, as the διορατικώτερος (Euthymius), has recognized the Lord in the person standing on the shore. In the ensuing conversation, Peter is indeed honoured with the commission, *Feed my sheep*; but this honour is overshadowed by the dubitative question, *Lovest thou me?* And while the prospect of martyrdom is held up to him, John is promised the distinction of tarrying till Jesus came again, an advantage which Peter is warned not to envy. Lastly, while, according to Luke (24. 12), Peter, first among the apostles, and alone, comes to the vacant grave of his risen master, the fourth gospel (20. 3), gives him a companion in John, who outruns Peter and arrives first at the grave. Peter goes into the grave before John, it is true; but it is the latter in whose honour it is recorded, that he *saw and believed*, almost in contradiction to the statement of Luke, that Peter went home *wondering in himself at that which was come to pass*. Thus in the fourth gospel, John, both literally and figuratively, *outruns Peter*, for the entire impression which the attentive reader must receive from the representation there given of the relative position of Peter and John, is that the writer wished a comparison to be drawn in favour of the latter.[8]

Thus Strauss does not place any special emphasis on the absence from the cross, indeed, to him the climax of John's steadily rising claims comes at the very end, when John arrives before Peter at the grave of the risen Christ. It is Renan who makes dramatic capital of John's claim to have been present at the cross, in one of his most striking passages of rhetorical aspersion, in which mockery, invective, assumption of the correctness of the synoptical account, and sweeping extension of the significance of John's claim all play a part.

His disciples had fled. John, nevertheless, declares himself to have been present, and to have remained standing at the foot of the cross during the whole time.[9]

Having contradicted John out of the mouths of the other Gospels (despite the authority he is apparently prepared to accord, in his introductory discussion of the authenticity of the Fourth Gospel, to John's word unsupported by the other Evangelists), he gives John's version with a sneer, prefacing it with 'If we must believe John'. Only John claims Mary was at the foot of the cross. 'But we do not understand how the synoptics, who name the other women, should have omitted her whose presence was so striking a feature.'[10] Having shaken John's authority very thoroughly, he then proceeds to fabricate accusations:

This is, in my opinion, one of those features in which John betrays his personality and the desire he has of giving himself importance, John, after the death of Jesus, appears in fact to have received the mother of his master into his house, and to have adopted her (John 19. 27). The great consideration which Mary enjoyed in the early church, doubtless led John to pretend that Jesus, whose favourite disciple he wished to be regarded, had, when dying, recommended to his care all that was dearest to him. The presence of this precious trust near John, insured him a kind of precedence over the other apostles, and gave his doctrine a high authority.[11]

This goes far beyond what any comparison of the Gospels could establish and beyond Strauss's hint. Browning's remarks after reading Renan are not those of an opponent of Biblical criticism, but of a perspicacious literary critic: the book is 'weaker and less honest than I was led to expect'. And 'The want of candour is remarkable: you could no more deduce the character of his text from the substance of his notes, than rewrite a novel from simply reading the mottoes at the head of each chapter: they often mean quite another thing.'[12] Indeed, Renan's alternation between scathing attack and saccharine narrative of the life and times of the 'charming' Jesus ('charming' is his favourite epithet for Jesus, Renan's *doux* and *enchantant* also being rendered as 'charming' by his English translator) is a vulgar debasement, not to say fearful parody of Biblical critical techniques and as such has often been deprecated by sober historians of the movement. But as a parody it brings into relief certain pervasive features of the higher criticism. Browning grasped this immediately, drawing the parallel between the argumentative modes of Renan himself and of the 'John' reconstructed by the higher criticism: 'His admissions & criticisms on St. John are curious. I make no doubt he imagines *himself* stating a fact, with the inevitable license, so must John have done.'[13] Browning's John, with his imagination of facts and his inevitable license, and John's poetic creator, with his own special 'want of candour', owe a great deal to Renan's vulgar dramatic exaggeration and exploitation of the antithetical stratagems of the higher criticism. Browning's John is far from vulgar; but the contrast between his admission of his own guilty trumping-up of tales, and the dignity he achieves in spite of it, is owing to Browning's skilful use of a similar alternation as the dialectical style of post-apostolic Christianity. No one had been more successful than Coleridge as an apologist who adopted a wide range of the critics' damaging findings or inferences while appearing to fend them off; the *Confessions of an Inquiring Spirit* is a masterpiece of the genre. Renan's, one is tempted to say, is a failure of the genre. But Browning rose to the challenge: the shoddy incongruities of Renan's work are transformed by Browning into a masterpiece of convincing casuistry.

At the heart of Browning's poem is John's confession that he was indeed not present at the cross:

> 'Look at me who was present from the first!
> 'Ye know what things I saw; then came a test,
> 'My first, befitting me who so had seen:
> ' "Forsake the Christ thou sawest transfigured, Him
> ' "Who trod the sea and brought the dead to life?
> ' "What should wring this from thee!" – ye laugh and ask.
> 'What wrung it? Even a torchlight and a noise,
> 'The sudden Roman faces, violent hands
> 'And fear of what the Jews might do! Just that,
> 'And it is written, "I forsook and fled":
> 'There was my trial and it ended thus.'   (301–11)

Browning adopts Renan's emphasis on this significant particular. We shall see that John's Christian apologetics are inseparable from his confession of falsehood. But Browning's John is not yet done with his aggrandizement. He makes a claim to have performed a miracle himself:

> 'I cried once, "That ye may believe in Christ,
> 'Behold this blind man shall receive his sight!"
>
> (459–60)

More self-aggrandizing than the claim to have outrun Peter to the empty tomb, or to have stood under the cross with Mary playing son of Christ to Mary's mother of Christ, it has, nevertheless, the same significance. As Strauss notes (speaking not of John but of the whole ancient world),

Elsewhere also we find proof that in those times the power of effecting miraculous cures, especially of blindness, was commonly ascribed to men who were regarded as favourites of the Deity.[14]

Thus John's claim to have cured blindness is another way of asserting his favour with Christ.

Strauss set the stage for Browning's discussion of miracles in the context of the life of John, for he pointed to the heightening of all the miracles that is a feature of the Fourth Gospel, attributing it to John's dogmatic purposes long after the 'events'. Although John relates fewer miracles than the synoptical writers, 'this deficiency in number is compensated by a superiority in magnitude':

Thus while the other Evangelists have simple paralytics cured by Jesus, the fourth gospel has one who had been lame thirty-eight years; while, in the former, Jesus resuscitates persons who had just expired, in the latter he calls back to life one who had lain in the grave four days, in whom therefore it might be presumed that decomposition had begun; and so here, instead of a cure of simple blindness, we have that of a man born blind, – a heightening of the miracle altogether suited to the apologetic and dogmatic tendency of this gospel.[15]

In the perspective of Renan's attack on John, the claim Browning places in the mouth of his John is outrageous. One of Renan's most extreme passages is his incriminating account of the 'miraculous' raising of Lazarus and Jesus's part in it. There was nothing new in the idea that the miracles were simple fraud, the result of collusion between Jesus and the disciples. Strauss did not hesitate to suggest this solution in the case of pagan miracles. But in so far as Renan produced an apology for Jesus, an apparently sympathetic 'psychological' inter-pretation of Jesus's participation in a staged miracle, he casts more doubt on Jesus than any number of such charges.

The contrast with Strauss is again stark; for while Strauss conducts a searching scrutiny of the accounts given of the miracle and concludes that they are grossly unhistorical, he in no way makes this reflect on the character of Jesus or even of the disciples. It was characteristic of the higher criticism that its mythological view of history rendered its accounts of the life of Christ completely unbiographical in tone and intention; from the search for the historical Jesus emerged a figure compact of legend and of doctrine, never of anecdotage and psychology. Renan's popularization is in this respect completely anomalous.

Renan explains the fraud in terms of the gradual alteration and corruption of Jesus's character as his rising claim to divine mission collides with the need to prove it to unbelievers. In Jerusalem, a city always hostile to him, 'Jesus was no longer himself':

Not by any fault of his own, but by that of others, his conscience had lost some of its original purity. Desperate, and driven to extremity, he was no longer his own master. His mission overwhelmed him, and he yielded to the torrent. As always happens in the lives of great and inspired men, he suffered the miracles opinion demanded of him rather than performed them.[16]

Renan imagines that Lazarus and his family staged the miracle, and Jesus, without foreknowledge, acquiesced in it; he allows an element of the genuine only in Lazarus's enthusiastic willingness to be duped by his own fraud. Browning had, of course, already made use of the Lazarus story in 'Karshish' (1856), before knowing Renan, and had put in the mouth of his Arab physician a straightforward rationalist explanation: "'Tis but a case of mania – subinduced/By epilepsy, at the turning-point/Of trance prolonged unduly some three days' (lines 79–81). In the context of the confessions of John, Renan's emphasis on personal fraudulence was decisive. For Strauss, the Lazarus story is a 'myth'; for Renan, it is a perpetrated fraud. Again Renan appears the more 'radical' in the destructive sense, though not in the reconstructive or apologetic sense.

Where the mythological school had built up a new conception of Orientalism and placed the Jewish milieu of Jesus in its historical and geographical setting, Renan offers as a 'defence' of Jesus a view outmoded in the higher criticism since Eichhorn, and stated as the merest popular prejudice: he was 'an Oriental without our conception of truth.'[17]

This is crude enough. But in so far as Renan makes the fraudulent Lazarus miracle the culmination of a pervasive weakness in Jesus, there is a psychological interest in the result that could not fail to appeal to Browning. Jesus is portrayed throughout as pliant, confused, having no sense of his own personality but only of his idea, increasingly insistent on his own superiority and finally divinity, until the idea itself is corrupted by intercourse with men, and Jesus must die to save it. His acquiescence in the Lazarus miracle leads directly to his downfall and death. In Renan's hands, the simple statement of the Fourth Gospel that the miracle caused the authorities to become anxious at Jesus's growing fame [12, 47] becomes the turning-point in the tragic internal drama of the messianic mind. Browning's indignant analysis of Renan's procedure is absolutely accurate:

What do you think of the figure *he* cuts who makes his hero participate in the wretched affair with Lazarus and then calls him all the pretty names that follow? Take away every claim to man's respect from Christ and then give him a wreath of gum-roses and calico-lilies, or, as Constance says to Arthur in King John 'Give Grannam King John and it grannam will give it a plum, an apple and a fig.'[18]

How can this culpable Christ still be praised in the old terms?

Browning, then, is stung into trying to construct an apology for John's claim to have performed a miracle that will seem less discreditable to Christianity than Renan's apology for Jesus. Browning undertakes his task – and it is the more difficult on this account – not on the mythological ground of Strauss, but on the concrete, psychological ground of Renan.

Renan, of course, had a case against the mythological view of Strauss which he stated well and which was widely shared. He praised Strauss for his 'bold advance from the letter to the spirit; a painful decipherment which substitutes for the legend a reality a thousand times more beautiful. Such is the law of modern criticism.'[19] But he felt that the *Leben Jesu* was a book of theology, of sacred exegesis, not easily understood in France where the schism between theology and profane science is much more marked. 'In Germany', he remarks, 'Voltaire would have been a professor in the faculty of theology.'[20] Strauss, exclusively preoccupied by the necessity of substituting one system of exegesis for another, 'took no reckoning of shades'. For this reason, 'The historian finds it too devoid of facts; the critic, too uniform in its processes; the theologian, founded upon a hypothesis subversive of Christianity.'[21] Renan was at one with a host of German critics of Strauss in holding that 'myth was impossible at the epoch when Christianity appeared', because 'the Jewish people always had a power of imagination very inferior to that of the Indo-European people',[22] or because at that period humanity was already too far advanced in historical understanding to admit of myth, or simply because there was not time for the formation of myth between the death of Jesus and the epoch in which his history was related.[23] But even admitting the mythological view, Renan holds, Strauss went too far in his reaction against the euhemeristic interpretation; for some kinds of contradictions as to fact arise precisely when the reports are factual, not mythical. Moreover, Strauss allows too little for the action of Jesus himself in bringing men to believe in his Messiahship, without which belief none of the myths would have been brought to bear on his case. It was this conviction that moved Renan in his own *Life of Jesus*:

Strauss has shown himself to be a rather unphilosophical historian when he neglects to explain how Jesus arrived at, in the view of the society in which he lived, a sufficient realisation of the Messianic ideal.[24]

He insists on the importance of 'the action of a powerful individuality' in the acceptance of Jesus as worthy of the application of existing myths to him. Renan states his own justification:

We can affirm that if France, less gifted than Germany with a sentiment of practical life, and less prompted to substitute in history the action of ideas to the play of the passions and individual characteristics, had undertaken to write in a scientific manner the life of Christ, it would have done so with a more rigorous method, and that by avoiding the taking of the problem, as Strauss has done, into the domain of abstract speculation, it would have approached much nearer the truth.[25]

He summed up his objections: 'The mythological school, quite denying miracles and the supernatural order, preserves a sort of psychological miracle.'[26] Renan, then, set out, and one can see how this would have interested Browning, to show minutely the process by which the 'psychological miracle' came about. The *Vie* was a genre based on Renan's belief that the life of Jesus is legendary, rather than mythological in Strauss's sense; and yet the strong impulse to poetic reconstruction owes much to Strauss's denial that historical fact is anywhere to be found in mythological material. Taking the 'Life of St. Elizabeth' as his model, one of the great legends that he considers were the special gift of the Order of St Francis, Renan says, 'there are legends which have neither biographies nor history (these two words must be limited to positive facts, into which nothing of the supernatural enters), yet are true portraits'.[27] It is clear why Renan began his labours on his many-volumed *Origines du Christianisme* with the *Life of Jesus*, though, as he admitted, it would have been more appropriate to begin with the *Histoire du Peuple d'Israel* which he finished only in 1891.

Browning's interest in 'A Death' was not in the great man around

whom legend gathers, but in the creator of legend; and here the
personality of Renan the critic and artist, the creator of the legendary
Life for his own time, is drawn into the enterprise. Browning was
extremely struck by the character of Renan himself, as his letter
shows; indeed, never has there been a character more suitable for a
Browning monologue than Renan, the *prêtre manqué* (as he styled
himself in his *Souvenirs*), who regarded religion as 'a necessary imposture' on account of the stupidity of the human race, 'a priest officiating
alone in the void of a disused cathedral', as Alphonse Daudet said.
Religious persons, he said, live on a shadow; we live on the shadow of a
shadow; what will people live on after us? His character indeed was
what we would now call a life-style, and in his own day was known as
renanisme: a strange blend of blasphemy and unction, sentiment and
rebellion, asceticism and sensualism. Advocate of *l'esprit de finesse*, his
incantatory prose, seductive and enigmatic, gave him the reputation
of 'the old enchanter'. He was constantly charged with dilettantism.
Romain Rolland, listening to his speech of reception at the Academy
in 1889 for the historian Jules Clarétie, thought that Renan's mockery
lay in the fact that he was telling the truth to men who were incapable
of noticing it. 'There seemed to me to be something of Nero in the
silky irony and feline purring of this old man posing as the flatterer
and entertainer of men at whom he was really jeering.'[28] He was a
Browningesque autobiographer; 'he departs from the literal truth about
himself in so many ways that it would be tedious to list them', his
biographer has remarked. He wrote that he continued his training
for the priesthood despite having lost the faith, on the basis of a
'paradoxical wager' which consisted in rejecting the dogmas of Christianity and keeping its morality in a world for which it was not intended.
Perhaps most characteristic of the false pathos, self-delusion, and sly
vaunting of the man was his comparison of himself to St Francis of
Assisi: in the preface to his *Nouvelles Études* he remarks that like the
patriarch of Assisi he has passed through life without any serious links
with the world and as though he were 'a mere tenant'. Brunschwicg,
writing 'Sur la philosophie de Renan' shortly after his death, saw him
as a representative figure of the century, who lost his faith, rocked the
foundations of orthodoxy, yet still made ambiguous use of the voca-
bulary of faith and transferred to human history the apocalyptic
demand for a new heaven and a new earth. The response to the *Vie de*

Jésus reflected these convolutions. Both denounced and praised, examined and exonerated by Napoleon's public prosecutor, vilified as an atheist and deluged with letters seeking religious advice and consolation, he was representative indeed of the paradoxes of faith as the century experienced them, of the 'double-edged wisdom' of the higher criticism.

Against this background of critical controversy, in which attacks on 'factuality' are woven into the new fabric of Christian belief, it is evident that H. N. Fairchild's notion that Browning always provides a 'giveaway' that convicts his casuists and establishes the proper moral attitude towards them is over-simple.[29] Browning, of course, as Hillis Miller has pointed out, does not always provide a 'giveaway'.[30] In John's admission that he was not at the Crucifix, Browning indeed tells us his own position, what he thought the facts of the case were, but he does not thereby tell us what attitude he or we must adopt towards John's narrative or John's character. In so far as he does, his suggested attitude runs counter to the facts of the case.

The claim to have performed a miracle is in every way more dubious even than the claim to have been present at the Crucifix; the reason why John confesses that his eye-witness account of the Crucifixion was false, and yet produces a supporting argument for his miracle-working goes to the heart of the case that is being presented: John stakes himself on a view of truth that requires that certain kinds of falsehoods be true and certain kinds of truths false. The problem of judging the Browning casuist is placed in the strongest light here, in the Christian context, where the whole credibility of the Gospels is called in question. Those who have seen and been distressed that Browning is a participant in, is implicated in the casuistry of his casuists, have here their best illustration and so their richest distress. Coleridge's late perception that Christian European civilization rests upon a lie is never far from Browning; and both poets learned this from the higher criticism, and learned too how to transform it into something like a virtue, indeed, into a philosophical method.[31] The counter-factual conditional is capable of modulation into a special kind of experiential truth.

How, then, does Browning's apology run? and what is its relation to higher critical apologetics? So far I have spoken of the ways in which Renan figures in 'A Death in the Desert' as an influence on the 'radical' side. But Renan also provided apologetic material. Browning clearly recognized this possibility while finding Renan's explanations unacceptable:

I am glad it is written; if he thinks he can prove what he says, he has fewer doubts on the subject than I, but mine are none of his. As to the Strauss school, I don't understand their complacency about the book, he admits many points they have thought it essential to dispute, and substitutes his explanation, which I think impossible.[32]

To see this possibility in Renan, let us return simply to the question of the identity of the author of the Fourth Gospel. Renan ostensibly defends the authorship of the Evangelist, Apostle, and Apocalyptic John, as does Browning, and as Strauss does not. But the more we press upon the exact form of this claim, the less straightforward it seems. The authenticity of the Fourth Gospel is more doubtful than that of the Synoptic gospels:

Is it indeed John, son of Zebedee, brother of James, (of whom there is not a single mention made in the fourth Gospel,) who is able to write in Greek these lessons of abstract metaphysics to which neither the synoptics nor the Talmud offer any analogy?...for myself, I dare not be sure that the Fourth Gospel has been entirely written by the pen of a Galilean fisherman. But that, as a whole, this Gospel may have originated towards the end of the first century, from the great school of Asia Minor, which was connected with John, that it represents to us a version of the life of the Master, worthy of high esteem, and often to be preferred, is demonstrated, in a manner which leaves us nothing to be desired, both by exterior evidences and by examination of the document itself.[33]

What trace, then, of John the Apostle, the Galilean fisherman, in the Gospel? Renan, like Strauss, finds the discourses of Jesus wholly inauthentic; 'if Jesus spoke as Matthew represents, he could not have spoken as John relates'.[34] He adds:

This by no means implies that there are not in the discourses of John some admirable gleams, some traits which truly come from Jesus. But the mystic tone of these discourses does not correspond at all to the character of the eloquence of Jesus, such as we picture it according to the synoptics. A new spirit has breathed; Gnosticism has already commenced; the Galilean era of the kingdom of God is finished; the hope of the near advent of Christ is more distant; we enter on the barrenness of metaphysics, into the darknesses of abstract dogma. The spirit of Jesus is not there, and, if the son of Zebedee has truly traced these pages, he had certainly, in writing them, quite forgotten the Lake of Gennesareth, and the charming discourses which he had heard upon its shores.[35]

It is one of the striking features of Browning's poems that Jesus does not enter into it at all; the central fact about the poem is not the traditional intimacy of Jesus and John, but its absence, not merely John's absence from the crucifixion, but Jesus's absence from the faith John is promulgating. Browning has fully assimilated the charge of the Tübingen school that the Fourth Gospel is a Hellenistic theology standing far from apostolic experience. But to express it, he used Renan's suggestion that 'John' outlived his first vision of Christ.

Renan, assuming for a moment the authorship of the apostle, conjures up an aged John much like Browning's:

It may be that, after the crisis of the year 68 (the date of the Apocalypse) and of the year 70 (the destruction of Jerusalem), the old apostle, with an ardent and plastic spirit, disabused of the belief in a near appearance of the Son of man in the clouds, may have inclined towards the ideas that he found around him, of which several agreed sufficiently well with certain Christian doctrines.[36]

Browning adopted this picture of John, creating out of it an image of all the generations of Christians for whom the Second Coming was no longer an imminent expectation. But we still seek a trace of the apostle John, of the basis of the claim that he was author of the Fourth Gospel. Renan casts doubt on his own portrait:

If we are to speak candidly, we will add that probably John himself had little share in this; that the change was made around him rather than by him. One is sometimes tempted to believe that precious notes, coming from the apostle, have been employed by his disciples in a very different sense from the primitive Gospel spirit.[37]

In short, Renan is prepared to think that there is an historical core to the Fourth Gospel in the form of some notes probably taken down by followers of John from his account and worked up in the intellectual mode of their day. But in looking more closely still at the evidence within the Gospel for a first-hand account emanating from the apostle, Renan discusses it only in the context of John's fraudulent attempt to appear to have been present at the most important events:

Hence his perpetual desire to recall that he is the last surviving eye-witness, and the pleasure which he takes in relating circumstances which he alone could know. Hence, too, so many minute details which seem like the commentaries of an annotator – 'it was the sixth hour;' 'it was night;' 'the servant's name was Malchus;' 'they had made a fire of coals, for it was cold;' 'the coat was without seam'.[38]

Even the touches of verisimilitude, then, are untrustworthy. But Renan turns round once more:

Hence, lastly, the disorder of the compilation, the irregularity of the narration, the disjointedness of the first chapters, all so many inexplicable features on the supposition that this Gospel was but a theological thesis, without historic value, and which, on the contrary, are perfectly intelligible, if, in conformity with tradition, we see in them the remembrances of an old man, sometimes of remarkable freshness, sometimes having undergone strange modifications.[39]

Renan concludes his discussion with the formula:

On the whole, I admit as authentic the four canonical Gospels. All, in my opinion, date from the first century; and the authors are, generally speaking, those to whom they are attributed; but their historic value is very diverse.[40]

This is characteristic of the casuistry of the higher criticism. The authenticity of the Gospels is reasserted; but the meaning of authenticity has been completely altered. None of the Gospels, least of all the Fourth, is from the hand of the apostle, none is an eye-witness account; authenticity depends rather on a tenuous and elaborate tradition of oral transmission aided by certain limited kinds of written record. This is, of course, the view now fully accepted by scholars. Browning's account of the provenance of his poem, the purported deathbed words of St John, follows faithfully the higher critical analysis of the complex transmission of the Christian story. The 'deathbed words' have four purported auditors, Valens, Xanthus, the Boy, and 'I' (supposed to be Pamphylax the Antiochene); and keeping watch, out of earshot, was a Bactrian convert. Names and vivid description are used to give verisimilitude in the manner ascribed to the author of the Gospel by Renan. The narrator 'I', we learn at the end, is 'tomorrow' to 'fight the beasts' and will tell the story to one 'Phoebas', 'Valens being lost, and the Bactrian but a wild childish man,/And could not read nor speak.' Xanthus was burned at Rome. The result of all this verisimilitudinous detail, then, is that it is left quite unknown, as with the Gospels, by whom the actual manuscript was written down; and as with the Gospels, it is written in Greek, not the language of the apostles. The manuscript was in the possession at one time of one who identifies himself thus: '*Mu* and *Epsilon* stand for my own name', and who signs with a cross; and the manuscript seems to have come down from 'Xanthus, my wife's uncle, now at peace'. This might or might not not be the same Xanthus who was present at the death but died a martyr in Rome before he was able to write the chronicle himself. Again as with the Gospels, the manuscript was somehow preserved among the families of the early Christians; but the exact transmission cannot be established.

There are, moreover, interpolations and additions to the manuscript. An interpolation occurs in the discourse itself, an abstract interpretation of doctrine, based on 'the glossa of Theotypas'. Near the end we hear 'Cerinthus read and mused; one added this:'. So it seems that someone, probably of the school of Cerinthus, added the passage that follows, still believing that Christ will return though after a further delay of ten or twelve years. This acts as a corrective to the long view of John himself, who, as Renan said, had lost his faith in the imminent reappearance of Christ. The poem ends, 'But 'twas Cerinthus that is lost'; whose words are these, as indeed whose words are 'Cerinthus read and mused'? In short, Browning has produced a document that within its brief compass is almost as hard to trace and interpret as the Gospels, and in the same way. How many oral transmissions (whom did Phoebas tell?), how many hands are represented in the writing, and of what school? How many narrators are there? Is the 'I' of the interpolation the same as that of the main narrator, 'supposed Pamphylax' – or another? Was this John? Did he die thus? And did he speak these words, or something like them, or not at all? Thus Browning accepted the main factual contention of the higher criticism as to the uncertain and tenuous link between the documents of Christianity and the apostles' witness, and the interpretation of the surviving documents as 'mosaics' from a variety of sources. The historical basis is slender; it is the tradition of the Christian community itself which becomes the guarantor of authenticity. The Gospels are not authentic because written by the apostles; they are gospels 'according to the apostles' by grace of long acceptance as such. Though this is not new with Renan, his view did serve Browning as support for the imaginative reconstruction of an aged man just within 'the apostolic age'; but Renan's dismissal of apostolic authorship in the literal sense is only more devious and less peremptory than Strauss's.

Browning fully accepted the basic position of the Tübingen school as to the lateness and philosophical gnosticism of the Fourth Gospel, which was disputed by Arnold in *Literature and Dogma* and its sequel, *God and the Bible*. Arnold, for whom style was the main criterion of Biblical criticism, paradoxically doubted the artistry of the author of the Gospel in order to maintain the authenticity of the reports of Jesus. Arnold too based himself on Renan, but rather on Renan's external claims as to the dating than on his internal analysis of the significance of the text. One must conclude that Browning was the subtler reader.

The literary representation of John was thus strikingly altered by the higher criticism from the youthful intimate of Jesus we saw in Klopstock's *Messias* to the strange old man of Browning. Browning's John is so wasted a body, so eerie a spirit, because he is in fact long since dead – only his name, 'according to the apostle John', survives him. He has outlived himself. 'A Death in the Desert' shows the process by which the claim to ocular witness was transformed into the claim to valid Christian spiritual experience. It is Browning's peculiar merit to have exhibited this change, which took place over centuries, which indeed was complete only in his own day, as the experience of 'John'. This 'John', then, is neither the aged apostle nor his gnostic disciples and interpolators, but 'John' as inherited and interpreted by Christians. That he can be taken thus is shown by Browning as the triumph of Christianity over historical fact.

It is a paradox that the so-called 'historical–critical school' was obliged, in order to maintain Christianity, to scrap the appeal to historical evidences. This is the sense of Browning's argument (which is all too often misconstrued as an argument against the higher criticism).

It may not be too much to suggest that these contentions and consequences of the higher criticism influenced Browning's own methods as a poet, not only here in this direct reproduction of the difficulties of the Gospel texts, but in the casuistic monologues and dialogues especially, and notably in *The Ring and the Book*. There he applies the technique to modern history as well, and, as several critics have noted, ultimately undermines the whole structure of witness, report, and judgment. Browning's notorious 'difficulty' as a poet reflects his full grasp of the significance of the higher critical analysis of the untrustworthiness of historical evidence, that is, all human testimony. He did not oppose the higher criticism – he could not – but he feared the diminution in the quality of belief that it might entail in its practitioners, friends, and enemies alike. 'A Death in the Desert' exhibits the power of a belief founded on doubt and denial.

Perceptual scepticism, as we have seen, was closely bound up with higher critical apologetics. The Gospel history, and particularly the miraculous portions of it, came to be taken not as a special case, but as a pattern for all historical events. The inaccessibility, the uncertainty of what really happened, the unreliability of personal witness and of document, the saturation in folk tale and dogmatic expectation characterize all historical events, not simply because they happened long ago, but because we cannot perceive in any other way. At the very moment of 'ocular witness' the fact is lost; it is moulded by the perceiver. Myth need not wait to be formed until long after the event (this was a very important argument in establishing the chronology of the accretion of myth in Christianity, and particularly the place of the myth of Resurrection); perception is instantaneous myth-making.

For Browning too, scepticism provided the assurance of the possibility of continuing belief in miracle. The role of scepticism in Browning's philosophy of faith has been much misunderstood, though he is by no means unique; the main authority on his relation to the higher criticism, W. O. Raymond, found it possible to assert, for example, that 'Browning's sceptical theory of knowledge never shook his faith in the validity of the Christian revelation.'[41] No indeed: his scepticism made the preservation of his faith possible. As Raymond cannot see that the extreme of scepticism is the springboard for the leap of faith, so Betty Miller is quite unable to fathom Browning's friendship with Carlyle. Equally, the standard 'refutation of scepticism' provided by Henry Jones and adopted by several critics is beside the point; before Browning is 'refuted', he must be placed within the fideist tradition to which he belongs, and its uses, poetic and otherwise, clearly understood.

It is perhaps to be wondered at that Santayana, whose own 'philosophy of faith', like Browning's, is based on perceptual scepticism, found it fitting to castigate him for the 'poetry of barbarism'. The reason, no doubt, lies in the fact that Browning is pre-eminently a protestant poet, one who like Luther, like Jacobi, like Kierkegaard, wishes to show forth again and again the leap of faith itself, the moment of exacerbation and exaltation, whereas Santayana, like Newman, having taken the leap of faith to Rome, or like Eliot to Canterbury, wishes only to conceal the saltatory way he came, in order to earn the right to a cultivated serenity, a catholic humanism. Perhaps Browning might care to retort that *this* was the poetry of barbarism. But there is no need to rehearse the old argument between Luther and Erasmus. Browning's celebrated optimism is at the furthest reach from complacency; it is a convulsive protestant faith based on the scepticism of reason. Browning's knowledge of German philosophy has often been disputed; but there can be no doubt that he had grasped it at its protestant root and traced one of its most characteristic flowerings in the contemporary form of the higher criticism. Again the earliest likely sources of his knowledge of the higher criticism were Unitarian, through his close friendship with W. J. Fox, minister at South Place Chapel, where Browning often attended, and where in 1840 Philip Harwood, the minister coadjutor, gave a series of lectures on Strauss, published the next year as *German Anti-Supernaturalism*. By the mid-1840s there was considerable general awareness of Strauss, in part through reviews of George Eliot's translation.[42]

The role of scepticism is displayed with great clarity in the discussion in 'A Death in the Desert'. The discussion is typical of the construction of the whole poem; John, as it were, gropes his way backwards into a lost past by imagining first the future and the doubts of an imaginary interlocutor, who asks for proof of miracles, and thinks that without proof all must be held 'projection from the mind of man'. John finally comes to the nub of his answer:

> 'I cried once, "That ye may believe in Christ,
> ' "Behold this blind man shall receive his sight!"

'I cry now, "Urgest thou, *for I am shrewd*
' "*And smile at stories how John's word could cure* –
' "*Repeat that miracle and take my faith?*"
'I say, that miracle was duly wrought
'When save for it, no faith was possible.   (459–65)

But how was it accomplished? John's devout equivocation is an argument from perceptual scepticism:

'Whether a change were wrought i' the shows o' the world,
'Whether the change came from our minds which see
'Of shows o' the world so much as and no more
'Than God wills for His purpose, – (what do I
'See now, suppose you, there where you see rock
'Round us?) – I know not;   (466–71)

The language of scepticism can be understood here as Christian
humility, as a visionary's vaunt, or as modern doubt, and is utterly
appropriate, for John himself began the long history of the incorporation of Platonism into Christian orthodoxy.

Browning applied his scepticism to the personal history of John.
The way in which John and the external history of Christianity are
rendered equivalent is natural in a sceptical system where the self has
no privileged knowledge of itself, but is in the same position *vis-à-vis*
its own operations as it is *vis-à-vis* the operations of the outside world.
John's experience is a Fourth Gospel to himself, always beyond solid
grasp and fix.

'A Death in the Desert' exhibits fully the sensuous unreality of
modern poetry, often achieved through images of old men – one
thinks of Baudelaire, Rimbaud, Yeats, Stevens – with its displacement
and distortion, its heightening and tenuity, its fine line of spirituality,
grotesque, almost extinguished, but for that reason genuine. 'Le Beau
est bizarre,' as Baudelaire said. And one thinks back to the Ancient
Mariner, Coleridge's transgressing apostle, forever marked out by his
experience of an impossible salvation.

This is not to say that 'history' is abandoned; rather the narrower
conception of 'ocular witness', of historical reportage, is replaced by
the interpretation of history. Scrutiny of isolated events in the Gospels
gave way to Herder's imaginative grasp of the character and tone of

the entire milieu from which they sprang and in which they could be validated. This imaginative effort to return to another time and to grasp from within the principles of its experience (for another community or a later generation simply false) was one of the major apologetic methods of the higher criticism, as it was one of the major preoccupations of Browning's poetry. In 'A Death' he adopts a central apologetic device of the higher criticism: the idea of the 'community' in which an idea has its root. Whether or not these are the deathbed words of John, whether or not the apostle John literally wrote the Fourth Gospel, or any of the works ascribed to him, these confessions represent the experience of the Christian community, of the early Christians in the first instance, and through John as the 'last survivor' the experience of the whole post-apostolic Christian community down to the present. This is not, as a contemporary critic, Robert Buchanan, thought, a lame effort at unconvincing 'prophecy' on John's part (and hence a failure in the poet), but the acceptance of doubt as to the identity of 'John' and the substitution for personal identity of community experience. John represents the attenuation of direct witness, the sense of pervasive loss, the intellectualization of Jesus's teaching that has characterized the Christian community since his death; and John represents the sense in which this condition of deprivation can be grasped as spiritual gain.

Depersonalization, often dated from Baudelaire, we know as one of the main characteristics of modern poetry;[43] it is striking, however, how Browning dramatized the separation between empirical self and its poetry, while yet insisting on the paradoxical romantic unity between the dark, fragmentary self and its capacity to transcend itself. It is not surprising that Browning should have found his subject in the higher criticism, for the solutions of the higher criticism were bound up at their sources with the dialectics of romantic irony.

In sceptical positions one tends to feel a void, or nothingness, as the background of all activity, a sudden dropping away of things and the reduction of consciousness. But in Browning there is something irreducible, a kind of muckiness, never the cleanly pure nothing. Even Hume's 'heap of perceptions' has a touch of this, not void, not just chaos, but a kind of refuse. Thus John's horror of those noises and lights – 'Even a torchlight and a noise' – before which vanished his companionship of Christ in this and another world. As in *The Ring and the Book*, mere circumstantial detail is not trivial, it is the 'sludge' of mediumship.

John has lost faith in his own identity, in his own vision, even in his own presence at the events that formed the significance of his life. John's first words concern personal identity:

> 'If a friend declare to me,
> 'This my son Valens, this my other son,
> 'Were James and Peter, – nay declared as well
> 'This lad was very John, – I could believe!
> '– Could, for a moment, doubtlessly believe:
> 'So is myself withdrawn into my depths,
> 'The soul retreated from the perished brain
> 'Whence it was wont to feel and use the world
> 'Through these dull members, done with long ago. (71–9)

Browning brilliantly equates the personal condition of the dying John with the condition of the Christian community as described by the higher criticism. John himself does not know himself as John. Yet at the same time he is able to reconstruct the earliest community of the disciples from whatever materials are to hand. The disciples do not have personal identity, they exist by virtue of being disciples of Christ; and this office it is open to any Christian to assume and earn. Later on he addresses his companions: 'You are my sons' and 'I am your brother John.' Even kinship relations are blurred and lost in the greater kinship to God where all are kin in every way to one another; and this reflects the strange difficulty in the Gospels of determining who John's father is (is he the son of Zebedee?) and which James is which and why John never mentions James brother of the Lord in his Gospel. Moreover, the three disciples mentioned here are the three most prominent actors in the Gospels, those whom Renan pictures as battling like any courtiers for supremacy and the favour of Christ. Finally this intense competition, at once worldly and spiritual, dies away; was it this Peter, or that John, who arrived first at the tomb? The destitution of the community through its remoteness in time from event and identity creates the possibility of universalizing it.

> 'Yet now I wake in such decrepitude
> 'As I had slidden down and fallen afar,

'Past even the presence of my former self,
'Grasping the while for stay at facts which snap,
'Till I am found away from my own world,
'Feeling for foot-hold through a blank profound,
'Along with unborn people in strange lands,
'Who say – I hear said or conceive they say –
' "Was John at all, and did he say he saw?"   (188–97)

Thus the higher criticism transformed its own minute destructive scrutiny of event and person into a new bulwark of faith. John has his experience still, just because he has it not: and this is the import of the poem. The community has inherited his personal experience in the form of Christian doctrine, though doctrine may once have existed only through the persons of Jesus and his followers.

We may so understand the interpolation on the Trinity. One of the liveliest sources of controversy and scathing attack throughout the eighteenth century had been the history of the doctrine of the Trinity. The Trinity was undeniably a late, neo-platonic and gnostic importation into primitive Christianity; John was alternately praised and blamed for his philosophical qualities. Browning, in effect, makes the doctrine of the Trinity follow from the relinquishing of personal identity. John's ability to reconstitute the community of disciples in every generation, his ability to make Valens Peter, depends on the doctrine of the Trinity:

This is the doctrine he was wont to teach,
How divers persons witness in each man,
Three souls which make up one soul: (82–4)

Depersonalization in the human sense brings forward the spiritual principles that constitute every man. We may thus understand the appearance of Cerinthus in the poem, to whom Voltaire among others ascribed the authorship of the Gospel, for Cerinthus held the more extreme view that Jesus was no man, but only spiritual principle clothed in phenomenal humanity. John verged on this heresy with his doctrine of the Trinity in every man, but did not quite commit it. Browning shrewdly, and in line with the whole strategy of the poem, brings the doctrine into relation with John's personal experience after all: the three prominent disciples, who warred for precedence, James,

Peter, and John, are a model for the doctrine; their absorption into trinitarian doctrine is an aspect of the absorption of personality into community. Browning shows himself a higher critical apologist of considerable subtlety. Ultimately, his is not, as has been suggested by Raymond and, following him, DeVane, a defence of the personality of the Apostle, as against the higher criticism whose technicalities are beyond him, but a reassertion of the unique manner in which person and doctrine are intertwined in Christianity. Personal experience is absorbed and universalized in doctrine, but is not lost there.

The lynchpin of spirituality is betrayal. The depersonalization of the Gospel that is so marked a characteristic of John refers back to his treacherous desertion of Jesus in his last hours, which in the Fourth Gospel forced him to claim that he alone of the disciples was present at the foot of the Cross, and which now he can admit, for the casuistical depersonalization of the synoptic story is complete. The personal has been transformed into a communal spiritual experience. Mrs Glazebrook, discussing the doctrine of the Trinity in 'A Death' at the Browning Society meeting in 1887, pointed out that in the Trinity of 'What Does, what Knows, what Is; three souls, one man', the 'What Does' is the lowest level: 'To him, now, this actual experience seems only the very superficial truth, and much inferior to the true, spiritual, informing knowledge which succeeded it'.[44] Her description of the process of development is accurate, but she misses the engine of it. Not despite John's forsaking of Jesus in his hour of need, but because of it, actual experience 'became material for the soul above', and the fruit of that growth – ripened knowledge – was imparted to others. Because of his desertion in action he lost faith in the historical fact, in the historical record of Jesus; only as spiritual knowledge could it work – could he work. It was his desertion, and his consequent desertion of the fact, that made it possible for 'those who had never known Christ on earth' to believe in Him, through the disciple's teaching, with 'a real, devoted faith'.[45] From this he could proceed to the 'What Is': communion with God. 'So strong, indeed, was this faith, that it became the absolute proof of the reality of Christ's human life;. . .thus "What Is" became the real evidence of "What Does".'[46] Through a lifetime of the development of doctrine John transcended, or, as we might say, sublimated his desertion. His first outright lie evolved into a neo-platonic doctrine of the Christ. His distance from

Christ put him at one with the later Christian community, so that he, above all the other Evangelists, spoke to their need; in this extended sense his false claim to be the favourite among the disciples was validated by his posterity, just as all the false claims of the Gospels were validated in the after-experience of Christians. 'History', itself translated into *Heilsgeschichte*, is indeed the court of last resort. Once again John triumphs over the other disciples. And over all challengers: 'But 'twas Cerinthus that was lost.'

The kinship metaphor is extended to an apocalyptic prophecy of final unity in Christ:

> 'See if, for every finger of thy hands,
> 'There be not found, that day the world shall end,
> 'Hundreds of souls, each holding by Christ's word
> 'That He will grow incorporate with all,
> 'With me as Pamphylax, with him as John,
> 'Groom for each bride! (679–84)

The way to this end-apocalypse, however, lies through progressive revelation, a doctrine characteristic of the higher criticism, indeed essential to its apologetics. Browning in 'Christmas-Eve' derived the idea from 'the Göttingen professor' and characterized it accurately as a doctrine of tolerance stemming from the Enlightenment notion of 'natural religion':

> 'Better pursue a pilgrimage
> 'Through ancient and through modern times
> 'To many peoples, various climes,
> 'Where I may see saint, savage, sage
> 'Fuse their respective creeds in one
> 'Before the general Father's throne!' (XIX, 21–6)

Browning branded that as a 'mild indifferentism' that taught the 'one colour' of different faiths; but his own doctrine serves the same function. Mrs Orr was never more mistaken than when she declared, 'The one consistent fact of Mr Browning's heterodoxy was its exclusion of any belief in Revelation.'[47] Here she displays ignorance not simply of Browning but of the history of the conception of revelation. Revelation was seen by an increasing range of thinkers not as static or once-for-all, not as inspired dictation, but as the *Erziehung des*

Menschengeschlechts, in Lessing's famous phrase, the development of mankind from its primitive response through a series of equally valid yet progressively more civilized and refined formulations of religious experience. It is this conception that makes it possible to slough off the miracles, the prodigies, the 'facts of an unliveable life' and the other accoutrements of primitive faith, and seek the 'idea', or, as Browning calls it in the platonic terms of his John, the 'type' that is left when all the tablets are broken.

The development theory applied not only to the comparative anthropology of religions, but, in the hands of Strauss and especially Baur, to the gradual development of Christian doctrine itself and of pre-existing pagan, Jewish, and other Oriental elements. As Robertson has said, the theory had

> for two generations inspired speculation in every direction, colouring philosophy, sociology, and Biblical criticism, while the solid historic research of the typical German scholars was but providing material for a sounder synthesis. Meantime it was in theologically backward England that there was being built up, in virtue of another order of gift for research, the ordered evidence that made the philosophic theory of Evolution a firm science.[48]

Browning's primitivism shows none of the piety of a Herder or a Coleridge towards 'original monotheism' or primitive religious awe; rather, reinforced by science, Browning sweeps up all the radical Enlightenment accounts of non-edenic primitive states into a dynamic, highly-coloured evolutionary conception of the primal energy of the first phase of development of consciousness, which Hillis Miller has so well described as 'massive substance, a seething diffused energy, a shaping force urging the shapeless bulk toward form'.[49] Browning inevitably takes less pleasure in the generality and universality that German critics brought up on the German classics found both bracing and reassuring; but at bottom he shares, whatever the difference in tone, their doctrine of progressive revelation: the reinterpretation of the meaning of the Gospel story through their own destructive work was justifiable and indeed necessary to the developing mind of man. This conception was so widespread in Browning's day as to be cliché: as the Rev. Llewellyn Davies said at the discussion of the Browning Society, gently correcting Mrs Glazebrook's contention that Browning was opposed to Strauss:

It has been said that the German speculative thought is distasteful to Browning; still, we cannot be blind to its telling character, and the poet took the right line in affirming the *internal* force of the Christianity handed down to us – that which alone commended itself to thoughtful and humble persons in this generation.[50]

Browning did not and could not oppose the idea of progressive revelation, but only the banality and complacency and automatism with which it was sometimes expressed. How complex and tortuous the progression, how much a record of loss as of gain, 'A Death in the Desert' reveals. Indeed, in the view of history based on perceptual scepticism, progressive revelation is accomplished by interpretation, and is in no way patent to the simple observer of the course of events.

Development theory involved both the analogy of Christianity with the myths of other religions and the analysis of the way in which other myths had actually been incorporated into Christianity; at the same time, it maintained the view that Christianity represented the highest point the race could touch. This requires the strategy of Browning's John indefinitely extended: the reading back of man's continuing progress towards reason into the first revelation of Christianity. An apocalyptic's vision is required in order to know not merely the future, but the past. Browning's imaginary interlocutor from the future adduces a range of comparisons with primitive beliefs to which we can no longer lend credence. They are nevertheless identical with Christianity in their genesis and even in their substance. Man has love within him – Christ is but a projection of it, 'With shape, name, story, added, man's old way'. He cites examples of primitive animism:

> ' "Our sires declared a charioteer's yoked steeds
> ' "Brought the sun up the east and down the west,
> ' "Which only of itself now rises, sets,
> ' "As if a hand impelled it and a will, – (391–4)

Then he quotes the Old Testament miracles of the sun, doubting whether anthropomorphic interpretation is essential to them. The process of evolution to a grasp of abstraction is traced through the Greek gods:

> ' "First, Jove's brow, Juno's eyes were swept away,
> ' "But Jove's wrath Juno's pride continued long;

' "As last, will, power, and love discarded these,
' "So law in turn discards power, love, and will.   (415–18)

It is typical of Browning's relation to these ideas that although his John replies to his interlocutor from a Christian standpoint, his replies are simply versions of the same argument, as he himself recognizes in his admission that he is speaking as a pagan might ('This might be pagan teaching, now hear mine'). When the interlocutor takes him to task for manufacturing historical particulars for what was evidently a myth parallel to Aeschylus's Prometheus, John's reply is an extension of the same argument and is itself couched as a platonic myth or extended metaphor: the 'Statuer' employs the form in order to convey the abstract type. He adds that the aim is not to slough off the form, but to realize the myth in the form of the 'angel's law'; but this is described as a Schillerian aesthetic harmony:

> Indulging every instinct of the soul
> 'There where law, life, joy, impulse are one thing.' (632–3)

If this is immortal life, heaven is not named. As so strikingly throughout, John gives the higher critical apology in reply to the higher critical attack.

The call for realization of the myth rather than abstraction or allegory depends on one of the most far-reaching and powerful developments of higher critical apologetics. As we have seen, 'prophet' and 'visionary' had gradually received new definitions in response to critical attacks on the possibility of literal prophecy, on the texts (especially Daniel) which claimed to be so, and on the character of the prophets and apostles. Out of the Enlightenment attacks on the character of the religious leader, rose a new defence. No longer superhuman, these men were, by virtue of being vessels of revelation, more fully aware of their personal inadequacy, their mendacity, their poverty of spirit. The visionary was no longer characterized by confidence in his powers, but by his doubts of them. Early defences of the prophets as artists, by Eichhorn in the 1780s, for example, still bore traces of the notion of simple trickery: art is still artifice, fiction in a pejorative sense. But this was transformed in the romantic conception of the poet as consumed by his own gift, his vision attended by sickness and mortality, illusion and delusion. Simple 'trickery' was transformed into the imaginative condition, 'falsification' into the over-extension and exacerbation suffered by man, whose faculties cannot absorb these powers of divination. The allegorical fiction became the romantic realization of myth, religion indeed a form of poetry. As Arnold wrote, 'Our religion has materialized itself in the fact, in the supposed fact; it has attached its emotion to the fact, and now the fact is failing it. . . The strongest part of our religion today is in its unconscious poetry.'[51] This famous statement, like many of Arnold's 'vague' pronouncements, had a series of precise theological developments behind it. Browning was meeting Strauss on his own ground, contrary to what critics have averred, in so far as the poetic interpretation of the meaning of prophecy was absolutely essential to the apologetic function of Biblical criticism. This was not the vague drift and emptiness that Fairchild and Santayana have seen in Victorian religion, but a positive and subtle reaffirmation of the prophetic character. The nineteenth century is full of such portraits; none is more powerful or subtle, nor more persuasive in defence, than Browning's.

John was naturally the focal point for such considerations in the New Testament, as Isaiah and Ezekiel were in the Old. In the last decade of the eighteenth century, as the mythological interpretation spread, characterizations of John and his style abounded. In so far as the Apostle and the Evangelist and Apocalyptic were still held to be one, there were attempts to harmonize their diverse, perhaps irreconcilable styles into a supreme mode of poetic vision. Klopstock, Herder, Coleridge in the 'Religious Musings', Hölderlin in 'Patmos', Chénier and Ballanche with their progressive histories of orphic revelation, all tried their hands at it. As Evangelist, Apocalyptic, and Apostle separated out, the philosophic qualities of the Fourth Gospel were as much praised for exemplifying the ultimate phase of Christian cultivation as they were decried by Renan for their surrender to an arid and intricate barbarism. Browning inherited a highly elaborate tradition. It is little wonder that St John is Browning's archetypal casuist. We may remark that the other master-casuist of a Victorian poet, Tennyson, achieved with his 'Simeon Stylites' and his 'Ulysses', as Browning did with his John and his Sludge, his Blougram and his Don Juan, just the balance of the heroic and the meretricious arrived at in critical apologetics. Victorianism is an elevating casuistry.

The parallel between Browning's Shelley, 'the subjective poet', and

Browning's St John

his St John is very clear. The private life of such a poet, unlike that of the objective poet, is important to his poetry, and their matter indivisible. Browning grants that there are

certain charges against his private character and life, which, if substantiated to their whole breadth would materially disturb, I do not attempt to deny, our reception and enjoyment of his works, however wonderful the artistic qualities of these. For we are not sufficiently supplied with instances of geniuses of his order, to be able to pronounce certainly how many of its constituent parts have been tasked and strained to the production of a given lie, and how high and pure a mood of the creative mind may be dramatically simulated as the poet's habitual and exclusive one.[52]

As he says of Shelley's letters, in a point of first importance for his own style, 'The musician speaks on the note he sings with; there is no change in the scale, as he diminishes the volume into familiar intercourse.'[53] Browning contrasts this with the case where there is 'jarring between the man and the author', with the

mean discovery of the real motives of a life's achievement, often, in other lives, laid bare as pitifully as when, at the close of a holiday, we catch sight of the internal lead-pipes and wood-valves, to which, and not to the ostensible conch and dominant Triton of the fountain, we have owed our admired waterwork.[54]

It is not that he exonerates Shelley in his private life; on the contrary. But he finds nevertheless a unity of style in Shelley's utterances, from the lowest, the falsest, or the most exaggerated to his finest poetry; and it is this that he finds in John. What he says of Shelley applies to his John: 'It was not always truth that he thought and spoke; but in the purity of truth he spoke and thought always.'[55] For Browning it seems that the impossibility of full vision in this life makes the 'lie' unavoidable. Yet he makes a sharp distinction between the lies and ambiguities absorbed in the unity of style, and the lies that issue in a false poetry,

false under whatever form, which shows a thing not as it is to mankind generally, nor as it is to the particular describer, but as it is supposed to be for some unreal neutral mood, midway between both and of value to

222

neither, and living its brief minute simply through the indolence of whoever accepts it, or his incapacity to denounce a cheat.[56]

These are 'the depths of failure'.

The visionary element of the poem, then, is carried not by the argument as such, but by the pervasive antithetic imagery of 'point' *versus* 'star', which absorbs the argument and creates the unity of John's style. What is a 'fact'? John, explaining how the primitive meaning of events he witnessed developed in his mind and resulted in the version given in his Gospel, declares:

> 'What first were guessed as points, I now knew stars'.   (164)

Both 'point' and 'star' are identified with his state of near-death to the body:

> 'Which wear the thickness thin, and let man see –
> 'With me who hardly am withheld at all,
> 'But shudderingly, scarce a shred between,
> 'Lie bare to the universal prick of light.   (192–5)

John is at the end of his span, he is reduced to that 'spark' which is himself, which is his imaginative vision, which is 'soul' – the exacerbated condition allied to death is the state of vision. Browning elsewhere was able to show how just this tenuousness marks the potent presence of divinity: in 'Christmas-Eve and Easter-Day' he demonstrates to the academic higher critics that their own defence of the religious leader as a poet is correct, demonstrating it as only the poet himself could: the merest hem of Jesus's garment touching him envelops and transports him in his state of sleep and scepticism. A critic has spoken of Rilke's 'skeletal Christianity'; in both poets it is a mortal condition converted to grounds of affirmation.

Again in the complex image of the 'optic glass', it is the very distance from the phenomena that makes it necessary in order to see it to turn vision into a 'point' of fact and so make it expand again from 'point' into 'star':

> 'These are, I see;
> 'But ye, the children His beloved ones too,
> 'Ye need – as I should use an optic glass

'I wondered at erewhile, somewhere i' the world,
'It had been given a crafty smith to make;
'A tube he turned on objects brought too close,
'Lying confusedly insubordinate
'For the unassisted eye to master once:
'Look through his tube, at distance now they lay,
'Become succinct, distinct, so small, so clear!
'Just this, ye needs must apprehend what truth
'I see, reduced to plain historic fact,
'Diminished into clearness, proved a point
'And far away: ye would withdraw your sense
'From out eternity, strain it upon time,
'Then stand before that fact, that Life and Death,
'Stay there at gaze till it dispart, dispread,
'As though a star should open out, all sides,
'Grow the world on you, as it is my world.   (215–33)

This is a superb piece of casuistry, John's final explanation of why descriptions of events in Jesus's life were trumped up as 'plain historic facts'. This passage leads into his confession that he was not present by the Cross. John did not see 'points', 'plain historic facts', nor had he need of them, for he saw the movement of ideas:

'I saw the Power; I see the Love, once weak,
'Resume the Power: and in this word 'I see,'
'Lo, there is recognized the Spirit of both
'That moving o'er the spirit of man unblinds
'His eye and bids him look.   (211–15)

John manufactured factual 'points' for posterity to view through its optic glass of distance; that is, he reduced his visionary world to the clarity required by the non-visionary. Only through a false fact could they believe they saw the star John saw. 'History' is required for those who did not and do not see; 'historical events' are an allegory of the true operative forces. 'Angel's law' is 'fact indeed'. Thus Strauss's Hegelian conception of the power of Jesus as an Ideal, so often criticized as dilute and abstract, is given poetic embodiment in John's dying vision. The very fullness and immediacy of the poetic embodiment of tenuity, distance, and abstraction is the final crown of casuistry.

CHAPTER 6

DANIEL DERONDA AND THE CONVENTIONS OF FICTION

When a great innovator in the form of the novel like Henry James fails to appreciate the innovations of an equally great predecessor, and a first-rate moral critic like F. R. Leavis fails to recognize the moral significance of the mature work of a novelist he himself recognizes as central to the tradition he most values, then one must turn back again to the novelist. George Eliot's formal innovations have never received the consideration they deserve, if only because her intentions are so palpably, so successfully, moral that the reader misses the way in which the structure of each of her novels is wholly dictated by the special moral concerns that govern it. These moral concerns could not exist except for the innovating form that makes them credible. To make moral concerns live in the texture of a whole experience is the work of a formal structure designed for that purpose; this is a fact of the artistic life that has always partly escaped Leavis, blinded by the very tradition he helped to define into the assumption that moral concerns and moral judgments exist in a realm separable from the novel, that they need only be located, pointed to, restated by the affirming novelist and the critic following in his wake. George Eliot wished to bind the community of her readership into the maintenance of this belief; but like the great artist that she was she consciously assumed the burden of creating and recreating structures in which that belief was possible, for no such structure was available in the society around her. 'No matter how empty the adytum, so that the veil be thick enough.'[1] It is the sense in which she hoped to keep her readership unaware of the artistry that was required to maintain what they and she would have liked to take as independently given that perhaps explains James's inability to appreciate her formal achievement; for he wished above all to draw attention to the form precisely as the creation of the artist. What for him was the glory of the artist would have signified for George Eliot the artist's defeat.

225

In *Daniel Deronda*, nevertheless, her real enterprise comes closest to the consciousness of the reader, and forms a deep malaise and even anguish, the more in her most devoted readers, accustomed to immerse themselves in her novels, to rest and work upon the cunningly contrived apparent density of the past society of *Adam Bede*, the ingenious network of apparent cause and effect in *Felix Holt*, the labyrinth of 'historical' destinies in *Romola*, the brilliantly constructed equilibrium of *Middlemarch*. A deep malaise is certainly the right response, the initial (though not the ultimate) response the novel aims at; yet in order to deny the true sources of the malaise and to save himself from the moral attitude it requires – so much more difficult and strenuous than any required by the earlier novels – the reader rejects the call upon him by dismissing in trivial terms the form in which the novel is cast, the form which states the claim of the moral order of the novel upon him. Moral order, *Daniel Deronda* tells us, must be created and maintained by the individual and by the mutual actions of individuals; and life depends on doing so. There is no other source of moral authority. All the novels of George Eliot tell us this; but never before had the tenuousness and uncertainty of the grasp of individual and society on the sources of their moral activity been fully revealed. Here for the first time, as in the last works of so many of the best artists, she lays bare the meaning of her own strategies as a novelist. The theme of the novel is indeed 'gambling'. George Eliot risked her own moral authority in attempting to shift its foundations to what she herself considered higher ground. Her readers have not risen to the challenge.

Daniel Deronda is the story of a love affair which undermines Victorian social convention even while seeming to observe it, which rejects conventions of English fiction defined as 'realistic' in favour of less familiar Continental models, and transforms conventions of the novel which Frank Kermode has seen fit to define as 'irreducible' even in our own times.[2] Leavis, who in *The Great Tradition* went so far as to propose carving out of *Daniel Deronda* an 'English novel' to be called *Gwendolen Harleth* admitted in a new introduction to the novel that the elements are so intermingled as to make this cannibalism at any rate 'much more difficult than I had thought'; even U. C. Knoepflmacher, whose theme in *Religious Humanism in the Victorian Novel* is the development of a philosophical fiction in George Eliot in Pater's *Marius the Epicurean*, and in Samuel Butler, fails to rise to his own insight. For finally, 'realism' is a shibboleth that prevents us from understanding the functioning of this novel, and indeed blinds us to the full scope of the English novel, for despite its Continental philosophical, critical, and literary sources, *Daniel Deronda* reinvents a characteristically English form.

George Eliot's friends, readers, and critics recognized that there was something new about *Daniel Deronda*, something qualitatively different from her previous novels; whether or not they 'liked' it as they had *Adam Bede* or *Middlemarch*, there is a tone of puzzled respect in their comments, public and private. The great novelist had earned her right, of course, to do whatever she liked; this was a 'late' work, a fully mature work, with all the freedom and all the difficulty that implies. But there is a further note of agreement in the response to the book. Edward Dowden wrote to Blackwood regretting that he had not the time to write his proposed book on George Eliot, for *Daniel Deronda* 'seems to me to move in a higher plane of thought and feeling than any other work of its author'.[3] *Daniel Deronda* seemed to be other than a novel, more than a novel; to some, it seemed to be a poem. Not Lewes alone had felt that there was something of the poet in George Eliot; and her *Spanish Gypsy* had been well received by the public, and was still selling well when *Daniel Deronda* appeared. But in this novel whatever was poetic in George Eliot came to fruition.

Blackwood was predictably unhappy about certain aspects of the book (George Eliot wrote to him, 'I thought it likely that your impressions about Mordecai would be doubtful'), yet he was not just producing dutiful praise to order when he exclaimed, 'She is a *Magician*. It is a Poem, a Drama, and a Grand Novel.'[4] But it was not new for George Eliot's readers to perceive the novels as poetry. Browning wrote to her in praise of *Romola* before he had finished it, calling it 'the noblest and most heroic prose-poem that I have ever read'.[5] Frederic Harrison, asked to advise George Eliot on the legal aspects of inheritance in *Felix Holt*, saluted the finished work as a poem:

I find myself taking it up as I take up Tennyson or Shelley or Browning and thinking out the sequence of thought suggested by the undertones of the thought and the harmony of the lines. Can it be right to put the subtle finish of a poem into the language of a prose narrative?[6]

He regrets that the audience cannot consciously observe the fact that 'they have a really new species of literature before them (a romance constructed in the artistic spirit and aim of a poem)'; he predicts that she is to produce a poem – 'not a poem in prose but in measure – a drama'. And on the strength of this perception he proposed to her that she should undertake to realize 'a dream of mine that the grand features of Comte's world might be sketched in fiction in their normal relations though under the forms of our familiar life'.[7] Harrison sketched at length his dream of a novel that should embody the positivist ideal of society, and make it persuasive by using only the material that human nature and our present state of society offer:

Every conflict possible in the breast of man or between classes might be there and yet the humanising powers which govern them sufficiently vigorous and disciplined. There are such forces now in every society even in the worst, but in the best they are hardly enough concerted and harmonious to show their action very clearly. All that would be necessary to invent would be the conditions which would give an organic unity to the good elements. They now fight like untrained heroes without a chief.[8]

George Eliot replied in the warmest terms, and we see the full context of one of her most celebrated and evidently misunderstood aesthetic dicta:

I assure you your letter is an evidence of a fuller understanding than I have ever had expressed to me before. . .

That is a tremendously difficult problem which you have laid before me, and I think you see its difficulties, though they can hardly press upon you as they do on me, who have gone through again and again the severe effort of trying to make certain ideas thoroughly incarnate, as if they had revealed themselves to me first in the flesh and not in the spirit. I think aesthetic teaching is the highest of all teaching because it deals with life in its highest complexity. But if it ceases to be purely aesthetic – if it lapses anywhere from the picture to the diagram – it becomes the most offensive of all teaching. Avowed Utopias are not offensive, because they are understood to have a scientific and expository character: they do not pretend to work on the emotions, or couldn't do it if they did pretend. I am sure, from your own statement, that you see this quite clearly. Well, then, consider the sort of agonizing labour to an English-fed imagination to make art a sufficiently real background for the desired picture, to get breathing, individual forms, and group them in the needful relations, that the presentation will lay hold on the emotions as human experience – will, as you say, 'flash' conviction on the world by means of an aroused sympathy.[9]

George Eliot, then, admits to Harrison that the sort of novel he proposes is just what she has always attempted: an unavowed Utopia, in which the spectacle of human evil and human wretchedness is so ordered as to bring into relief human capacities for good. She starts with an idea, which she attempts to incarnate. As Lukács has said, 'to aspire to a utopia is to affirm the will in what is philosophically the more objective and distilled form of an "ought" [Sollen]'.[10]
Harrison was assured that she would not forget his suggestion:

My whole soul goes with your desire that it should be done, and I shall at least keep the great possibility, (or impossibility) perpetually in my mind as something towards which I must strive, though it may be that I can do something only in a fragmentary way.[11]

George Eliot surely recalled Harrison's plan, in The Spanish Gypsy, which was dubbed 'the Mass of Positivism'; in Middlemarch, where there is just such a microcosm of society with the woman, the physician, and the capitalist at the centre; and in Daniel Deronda, which is dominated by the problem of the secular priest, the 'Priest of Humanity' of Comte's Catéchisme positive, who, as Harrison put it, 'without coming into conflict with the Church or its representatives might practically succeed to the whole influence and spiritual duties of the Catholic priest' (Harrison had suggested a French setting as the most plausible basis for a positivist society).

Representing to herself the almost insuperable difficulties of creating the 'clerisy' in novel form, she insisted that she had exactly the same concerns and the same views as when she had begun Scenes of Clerical Life. Replying to a letter from Elizabeth Stuart Phelps, who had written, 'knowing me to be a believing Christian, you will foresee the points in which I should mourn over your later works', George Eliot affirmed that 'The principles which are at the root of my effort to paint Dinah Morris are equally at the root of my effort to paint Mordecai.' Indeed, 'there has been no change in the point of view from which I regard our life since I wrote my first fiction – the "Scenes of Clerical Life" '.[12]

Daniel Deronda did in fact return her to the concerns that had been fresh in her mind as she embarked on her first fiction, however immense the difference in scope and technique bestowed on her by her fictions since that time and imposed on her by the attempt to portray not the life of clerics, but the idea of a clerisy. It returned her to criticism, to her three-year struggle to translate Strauss, and then to translate Spinoza and afterwards Feuerbach, which for her meant the strenuous labour to possess the whole background and tradition in which Strauss worked, and to place herself fully in the position so slowly and arduously arrived at by German criticism itself.

Mary Ann Evans came to German criticism through the milieu that had always been closest to it in England, provincial dissenting and especially Unitarian circles. It is not surprising or accidental that she should have come to it through Hennell, Bray, and Dr Brabant; nor was it owing to any special virtue on her part. But it is a sign of her own powers that, unlike Hennell and Bray, she learned to know directly and at firsthand the work of Strauss's own predecessors in the mythological interpretation of the Bible, the German culture in which the higher criticism had developed in the previous half-century, and the most important contemporary interpreters of religious philosophy. It was a labour not of translation but of absorption and of transformation, a work of the potential novelist's imagination.

It is important nevertheless to correct the common misapprehension that Charles Hennell knew nothing of German criticism, that he somehow reinvented it spontaneously for the *Inquiry into the Origins of Christianity* (1838) which shook Mary Ann Evans out of her acquired Evangelical piety and her family's Anglican adherence. This misapprehension follows from the failure to take account of the early history of the dissemination of Biblical criticism in England, the history that preceded George Eliot's translation of Strauss. Basil Willey has presented this misapprehension, with all its implications, in his widely-read essay in *Nineteenth Century Studies*, and the biographers have echoed it. It stems from a misreading of history, and it leads to a misreading of Hennell, an exaggeration of Hennell's influence on George Eliot, and a dismissal of Strauss's influence; it makes something like a claim therefore not only for Hennell's independence of

German criticism, but for the independence of George Eliot herself. This in turn leads to a failure to evaluate the use of criticism in her novels.

The fact is that Hennell was perfectly aware of the general results of pre-Straussian German criticism, for as Willey says, he was 'a Unitarian of the school of Priestley and Belsham', and one who was in touch with Unitarian centres, including Manchester (where he was born) and London (where he was brought up). Indeed, it is inconceivable on the face of it that Hennell could have arrived by his own unaided native wit at the whole familiar range of conclusions available in advanced Unitarian circles from the time of Priestley's *Prospectus for the Unitarian Bible* (1788): the late dating and comparison of the Gospels, denial of apostolic authorship (with some lingering doubt about John), the treatment of the Bible as secular history and literature, the denial of miracle, rationalist explanations of apparent miracle, religion as natural rather than divinely revealed, the source of the Gospels in the spontaneous myth-making of the early Christians, the value of the Gospels not as history but as statements of the genuine faith of the early Christians, and even the explanation of their mythical power in terms of 'an eastern and imaginative clime'. When Dr Brabant sent a copy of Hennell's book to Strauss, what impressed Strauss was the apologetic intention, the 'earnest and dignified tone', the tracing of religion not to the machinations of priestcraft but to 'the tendencies and wants of human nature'. Strauss, in his turn, was most familiar with the tone of 'ridicule and scorn' of the English deists, for these had been an important source for German criticism; he was unaware that the new apologetics of Eichhorn had found its way into England. Hennell's enlightened piety is in fact perfectly characteristic of advanced Unitarian circles at the end of the eighteenth century. Despite his surprise at the tone, Strauss was able to give a perfectly accurate, if general, account of the sources of English knowledge:

Not sufficiently acquainted with German to read continuously a learned work in that language, the labours of our theologians were only accessible to him so far as they were written in Latin, or translated into English, or treated of in English writings or periodicals: especially he is unacquainted with what the Germans have effected in the criticism of the Gospels since Schleiermacher's work on Luke.[13]

But as we have seen, such sources as these had been perfectly sufficient fifty years earlier; and the resurgence of Unitarianism in the
1820s had made certain their effects were not lost. Indeed, the leading
Unitarian periodical, *The Monthly Repository*, had made it a primary
purpose from 1827 to present German criticism in a favourable light
as part of its political campaign against the narrowly exclusive and
therefore (they agreed) intellectually debilitated Anglican Establishment.[14] Only the English belief in amateurism could so long have
maintained the notion of Hennell as a kind of instinctive Strauss,
warbling wood-notes wild; and only English snobbery could so disregard the long-standing culture of provincial dissenting circles as to
marvel as Willey does at the possibility that such as Hennell and his
friends, 'a remarkable little intellectual élite', could exist in Coventry
in the middle of the nineteenth century.

Despite Willey's admission of the great differences between Hennell
and Strauss, in particular Strauss's wholly mythological approach
and his Hegelian apologetics, he makes a sweeping claim for George
Eliot's total indifference to Strauss:

The fact was that Strauss, with all his vastly greater learning and philosophical depth, could do little for her that Hennell had not already done; she
no longer needed him, so that the translating was merely a 'soul-stupefying
labour', a heavy duty to humanity, to be discharged with deep sighs and
languishing of spirit.[15]

But no one can read Strauss and remain unmoved, as Willey himself
testifies; Hennell presents a point of view, Strauss carries overwhelming
conviction. In Strauss, criticism becomes an interpretation of experience. No one can read a paragraph of George Eliot and doubt the
lasting effects of such a model of intellectual striving in areas of
emotional stress as Strauss's *Life of Jesus*. More specifically, if Hennell
first opened Mary Ann Evans's eyes, it was Strauss and afterwards
Feuerbach who provided her with the materials for reconstruction.
Willey's view leads him to the feeble conclusion that the effect of
George Eliot's conversion to disbelief and the ensuing years of intellectual labour (so far from a mechanical work of translation) was
that in her novels she 'preferred the heart to the head'. Nothing could
be more characteristic of the impoverishment of what passes for 'his-

tory of ideas' in literary criticism, than this series of unfounded and inconsistent arguments and the vacuous conclusion which implicitly denies the value of the critic's own enterprise.

It is evident how much George Eliot's knowledge of the higher criticism contributed to *Daniel Deronda*. Indeed, the novel is inexplicable without it. The higher criticism had had a devastating effect on the assumptions of the religious and social order, yet at the same time offered a new apologetical basis for the recreation of that same order. *Daniel Deronda* contains the harshest social satire, the most unflinching indictment of English society to be found anywhere in the English novel; yet it searches for and tries to make imaginatively present the sources of that order in such a way as to renew it. These sources are seen, strikingly, as mythological in the sense of the higher criticism; if, as some have argued, the new first-hand knowledge of the Near and the Far East had played a part in the 'realism' of the English novel of the 1840s, *Daniel Deronda* carries on directly in the tradition of the imaginatively more powerful conception of the Oriental roots of religious experience characteristic of the higher criticism and of romantic poetry.

The higher criticism required and offered a searching and far-reaching scrutiny of the grounds of belief on which a man might base his life and action in contemporary history. Like other writers all over Europe, George Eliot made use of these critical and constructive materials in presenting on a vast scale the development of and dissolution of historical civilizations, in examining the nature of historical time and event, and in seeking the forms of the prophetic and poetic imagination. The most general statement of George Eliot's place in a poetic tradition is by a modern critic, Raymond Williams: in George Eliot we have 'the emergence in the novel of that structure of feeling of the greatest Romantic poetry: at once a commitment to a personal vision and a passionate concern with the social experience of ordinary life'.[16] But we can be more specific: *Daniel Deronda* takes its place among the attempts to join East and West again in a new synthesis that assume so many forms in the nineteenth century, whether the epic proposal of *The Fall of Jerusalem*, Goethe's ironic, Islamic syncretism, Hölderlin's complex German Hellenism, the Indian cult of the romantics, the visionary Catholic apologetics of Ballanche's prose epic *La Ville des Expiations*, or Hugo's *Légende des Siècles*.

George Eliot too set out to write a cosmopolitan religious epic. In this book George Eliot is a European writer; English critics have all felt the difficulty of facing and coming to terms with it. This is a novel outside the English tradition as it has been narrowly, and I believe wrongly, defined; it is a novel whose affinities are with *Wilhelm Meister* rather than with *Pride and Prejudice*. Critics grasping in desperation and relief at the superficial resemblances of Gwendolen Harleth to Jane Austen's heroines have made it nearly impossible to comprehend *Daniel Deronda* as a whole, or, even more simply, to understand the character of Daniel Deronda himself. In the novel we feel the breath of a larger society blowing upon the inbred and declining English social scene; we see an attempt to make England aware – an attempt which England systematically rejects – of her larger historical and cultural milieu, the community of European Christianity and its Oriental origins. George Eliot was never less than ambitious; and in this novel she undertook her most ambitious project, to go to the roots of the validity of her society apprehended in the widest sense. Her concern is, as her concern had always been, with how one is to live in England today, but as with other English moralists of European interest and scope, as with a Coleridge or a Carlyle, she understood how far afield it was necessary to go to begin to give any viable answer.

George Eliot absorbed and made use of the major critiques of religion of the nineteenth century, those of Strauss, Feuerbach, and Renan. From Strauss came the foundation of her enterprise in *Daniel Deronda*, the mythological view of history through which she attempts to reveal the nature of her own society. From Feuerbach she took the translation of theology into contemporary secular disciplines which permitted her to put Strauss's insights into current, practical, fictional forms. Renan's influence was less fundamental, yet his legendary life of Jesus had a pervasive effect upon the novel's attempt to portray the relationship between religious leader and disciple and upon the characterization of Daniel Deronda. The work of both Feuerbach and Renan underlies her analysis of the sexual basis of religion, Feuerbach in his theoretical formulation of the I–thou relation and his systematic equation of theology and pathology, Renan in his psychological and literary studies of the sources of religious experience.

As might be expected from her long immersion in Strauss and his predecessors, George Eliot attempted in *Daniel Deronda* to translate into contemporary terms their sense of Judaism as the enabling milieu for Christianity. Like them, she examined the Jewish prophetic character as the groundwork for the possibility of Christian visionary sensibility and for the possibility of a modern spiritual leader; she attempted in her Mordecai a character resembling as closely as possible the sensibility upon which the events of both the Old and the New Testaments had worked, and to do so she drew on the long tradition of experiments in the sublime 'hebraic' style. As in her romantic predecessors, this became, through the medium of the novel itself, the claim to, and the justification for, the poet's power to create the foundations of community.

As historical justification she relied upon the maintenance of the prophetic character as a constant in the post-Christian history of the Jews. She was learned enough in the history of Diaspora cabbalism and hasidism to make this at least plausible, in the light of the claims that it had always been heterodox rather than 'priestly' Judaism which was the repository of spiritual illumination. Indeed, it is in the cabbalist lore that she finds the most convincing and congenial analogue of the humanist spiritual encounter which is such a marked feature of her work from its beginnings in *Scenes of Clerical Life*.

Her account of the Cohen family belongs only incidentally in the annals of realism; more fundamentally, it belongs, with the rest of her characters in *Daniel Deronda*, to the long and varied history of the uses of the Jewish experience and character for Christian polemical purposes. In modern times we have taken this history to start from Bayle's brilliant indictment of the moral character of the Jewish leaders from Moses, Abraham, and David, which was gradually extended to a searching scrutiny of the trustworthiness of the apostles and Jesus himself; the challenge to the privileged position traditionally accorded to Christianity among Oriental religions and literatures; and finally, the painstaking attempts to reconstruct the historical Jewish milieu that, for good or ill, contained the seeds of Christian myth. She knew, of course, the recent work as well, such as Henry Hart Milman's *History of the Jews* (1829), and Heinrich Ewald's *Geschichte des Volkes Israel*, which was translated as the *History of the Jews* (1867–74), and given wider currency through Arthur Stanley's *Lectures on the History of the Jewish Church*. Milman has the special interest for us of having started his career as a poet; in 1820, when Coleridge was still talking of it, Milman wrote *The Fall of Jerusalem*. An Orientalist, a translator of Sanskrit poetry, he carried on the collocation of interests characteristic of Biblical critics since the time of Herder. The poetic subject, the Fall of Jerusalem, naturally emerged from these interests, though Milman's poem scarcely rises to Coleridgean heights.

Milman's *History of the Jews* was first published in 1829, and went into several editions. His mildly stated higher critical views had brought him considerable obloquy. His new preface written for the 1866 edition states his adherence to the school of Eichhorn, De Wette, and Strauss:

I pretend not to have traversed the interminable field of German inquiry relating to the early Hebrew annals, extending from Eichhorn and De Wette to Bleek, one of the latest and best of the school. There has been a strong reaction, it is well known, in Germany against this, vulgarly called Rationalistic, criticism. The school of Eichhorn and De Wette (not to go back to Spinoza), of Rosenmüller, of Gesenius, Schleiermacher, Winer, Ewald (very different men), to say nothing of Paulus, Strauss, and those to whom Strauss is orthodoxy, has been confronted by Hengstenberg, Keil, Hävernick, and others. This reaction has been hailed and welcomed by many devout men, both in Germany and in England, as a complete triumph. I must say that, as far as my knowledge extends, I doubt this.[17]

While accepting the leading ideas of the critics – the categorical rejection of inspiration (he quotes Warburton), the relegation of the supernatural to the realm of fancy ('Men believe in miracles because they are religious: I doubt their becoming religious through the belief in miracles';[18] but he is ambiguous about the Resurrection), the late 'compositor' theory of the Mosaic books, – he takes a characteristically English view of what he considers to be the excesses of critical zeal. He writes of Ewald's *History of the Jews*:

I must acknowledge, as regards the modern German school of criticism, profane as well as sacred, that my difficulty is more often with their dogmatism than with their daring criticism. If they destroy dominant theories, they rarely do not endeavour to compensate for this, by constructing theories of their own, I must say in general on the most arbitrary conjecture, and assert these theories with as much certitude, and even intolerance, contemptuous intolerance, as the most orthodox and conservative writers. This dogmatism appears to me to be the inherent fault of the Geschichte des Volkes Israel.

At best, this is a criticism of method (and Milman always prefers to avow necessary ignorance rather than indulge in what seems to him speculative or ingenious):

Ewald seems to have attempted (he has no doubt of his own success) an utter impossibility. That the Hebrew records, especially the Books of Moses, may have been compiled from various documents, and it may be at an uncertain time, all this is assuredly a legitimate subject of inquiry. There may be some certain discernible marks and signs of difference in age and authorship. But that any critical microscope, in the nineteenth century, can be so exquisite, and so powerful as to dissect the whole with perfect nicety, to decompose it, and assign each separate paragraph to its special origin in three, four, or five, or more, independent documents, each of which has contributed its part, this seems to me a task which no mastery of the Hebrew language, with all its kindred tongues, no discernment, however fine and discriminating, can achieve. . .I must confess that I read Ewald ever with increasing wonder at his unparalleled ingenuity, his surpassing learning, but usually with decreasing conviction. I should like an Ewald to criticise Ewald. Yet Ewald's is a wonderful, I hardly scruple to use the word of Dr. Stanley, a noble work.[19]

Now much bolder in their disintegration of the text, and making stronger claims to 'objectivity', the critics seemed to English observers, even relatively knowledgeable and sympathetic ones like Milman, to have tenuous grounds for their diverse reconstructions. George Eliot, like Milman, shared in this English moderation by virtue of her adherence to the earlier German mythological school culminating in Strauss, whose analysis rested on the unity of the text understood as the religious experience of a community.

On a slightly more popular level, Emanuel Deutsch's widely-read article on the Talmud, first published in the *Quarterly* in 1867, found favour with George Eliot: 'It is written by one of the greatest of Oriental scholars, the man among living men who probably knows the most about the Talmud, and you will appreciate the pregnancy of the argument', she wrote to Sara Hennell.[20] Deutsch, like a number of George Eliot's acquaintances a Biblical Orientalist, German by origin and training, argued that there were 'more vital points of contact between the New Testament and the Talmud than divines yet seem fully to realise', and went so far as to say that 'It is the glory of Christianity to have carried these golden germs, hidden in the school and among the "silent community" of the learned, into the market of Humanity.'[21]

Much recent discussion of the alleged anti-semitism of certain twentieth-century writers which takes Nietzsche, a late example, as its starting-point seems to have been conducted in ignorance of the long established context of discussions of Jewish history. Whether in praise or in blame, the spirited argument as to the quality of hebraic life and thought was part of the movement towards secular tolerance, and subserved the critical reappraisal of the foundations of Christian faith.

For George Eliot's purpose in *Daniel Deronda*, the most important aspects of this extensive literature, with much of which she was acquainted at first hand, were the originating character of the Jewish experience, the subsequent symbiosis of Judaism and Christianity, the sceptical discussion of the nature of religio-political leaders, and the analysis of their 'Oriental' character. It is here that we must look for the beginnings of understanding of Daniel Deronda himself, for to it, Daniel owes whatever is feminine, passive, 'charming', receptive, fantastic, and duplicitous in his character. As Stanley put it:

Like the history of Greece and Rome (only more so) the history of the Jews was veiled until recently by venerability. Its sacred character had deepened the difficulty already occasioned by its extreme antiquity. That earliest of Christian heresies – Docetism, or 'phantom worship' – the reluctance to recognise in sacred subjects their identity with our own flesh and blood – has at different periods of the Christian Church affected the view entertained of the whole Bible. . . Even to speak of any portion of the Bible as 'a history', has been described, within the last few years in our own country, even by able and pious men, as an outrage upon religion.[22]

George Eliot was prepared to 'recognize in sacred subjects their identity with our own flesh and blood', indeed this became her special strength as a novelist. It was Feuerbach who unfolded this possibility for her.

Feuerbach has rightly been considered the most important influence on *Scenes of Clerical Life*, and therefore on George Eliot's later work as well, in so far as her themes and techniques are continuous. A typical literary opinion of Feuerbach's significance simply asserts that he gives 'a totally humanistic interpretation of Christian theology', or, even more unhelpfully, that for Feuerbach 'theology was anthropology.'[23]

Certainly it is difficult to place Feuerbach philosophically, partly because he simply was not a consistent or thorough-going philosopher, but a critic, whose analysis had a liberating, rather than a systematic, intention, and partly because he stands at a crossroads of nineteenth-century thought. Though sometimes hailed as an empiricist, his Hegelian belief in the inadequacy of British empiricism remained as an unworked-out assumption in his later work;[24] for he emphasized that the senses cannot distinguish appearance from reality – only thought can. Sometimes hailed (or castigated) as a materialist, he marshalled a number of arguments against absolute or reductive materialism. Feuerbach had no doubt, even by 1838, that thinking was a product of physical processes, but he was insistent that the product could not be reduced to its cause or *sine qua non*; having been produced, it became an independent thing, functioning in its own right. It is true that there can be no mind without a body 'but the body acts as a vehicle for an activity that is higher than itself'.[25]

By far the best way to understand Feuerbach is to recognize his historical place in the gradual devolution of idealism. He himself saw his philosophy as the culmination of the idealist tradition – 'substitute *man* for self-consciousness, and you translate the old philosophy into the new'.[26] Feuerbach took it for granted that the eighteenth-century Enlightenment, especially and finally Kant, had shown that there is no God; accordingly, the principle of his devolved idealist philosophy was atheism. 'Anthropology', the analysis of the natural foundations of morality, is his reconstructive method. George Eliot, as Mallock wrote in *Atheism and the Value of Life*, is 'the first great *godless* writer of fiction that has appeared in England'.

An often quoted dictum of Feuerbach is that 'the essence of Christianity is the essence of human feeling'.[27] But what is the context of this dictum?

Feeling is the oblique case of the *ego*, the *ego* in the accusative. The *ego* of Fichte is destitute of feeling, because the accusative is the same as the nominative, because it is indeclinable. But feeling or sentiment is the *ego* acted on by itself and by itself as another being – the passive *ego*. Feeling changes the active in man into the passive, and the passive into the active. To feeling, that which thinks is the thing thought, and the thing thought is that which thinks. Feeling is the dream of Nature; and there is nothing more blissful, nothing more profound than dreaming. But what is dreaming? The reversing of the waking consciousness. In dreaming, the active is the passive, the passive the active; in dreaming, I take the spontaneous action of my own mind for an action upon me from without, my emotions for events, my conceptions and sensations for true existences apart from myself. I suffer what I also perform. Dreaming is a double refraction of the rays of light; hence its indescribable charm. It is the same *ego*, the same being in dreaming as in waking; the only distinction is, that in waking, the *ego* acts on itself; whereas in dreaming, it is acted on by itself as by another being. *I think myself* – is a passionless, rationalistic position; *I am thought by God*, and think myself only as thought by God – is a position pregnant with feeling, religious. Feeling is a dream with the eyes open; religion the dream of waking consciousness: dreaming is the key to the mysteries of religion.[28]

This is a succinct statement of that self-reflecting, yet authentically productive and objectifying power that we have seen to be at the basis of romantic mythologies. Later in the chapter Feuerbach identifies this with the specifically Christian imagination. 'Christianity is distinguished from other religions by this, that in other religions the heart and imagination are divided, in Christianity they coincide.'[29] Whereas 'with the orientals, with the Greeks, imagination, untroubled by the wants of the heart, revelled in the enjoyment of earthly splendour and glory[30]. . .in Christianity, the imagination does not wander, left to itself; it follows the leadings of the heart; it describes a circle, whose centre is feeling'.[31] In a strikingly Coleridgean statement, arising out of the same movement towards the disciplined exploration of the nature of human consciousness, Feuerbach concludes:

Imagination is here [in Christianity] limited by the wants of the heart, it only realizes the wishes of feeling, it has reference only to the one thing needful; in brief, it has, at least generally, a practical, concentric tendency, not a vagrant, merely poetic one.[32]

Any discussion of Feuerbach that loses sight of the context in which 'human feeling' is equivalent to Christianity is grossly misleading.

'Human feeling' is spoken of precisely because, as Kant had shown in his refutation of the ontological proof, 'Human reason cannot constitute itself an object of sense.'[33] Feuerbach does not reduce god to man, but raises man to god. To grasp this subtlety rather than reading it as anthropomorphic reductionism, is, according to Feuerbach himself, the next and higher stage of man's religious development out of positive primitive religion. 'The course of religious development which has been generally indicated, consists specifically in this, that man abstracts more and more from God, and attributes more and more to himself.'[34]

> The Israelite trusted himself to do nothing except what was commanded by God; he was without will even in external things; the authority of religion extended itself even to his food. The Christian religion, on the other hand, in all these external things, made man dependent on himself, i.e. placed in man what the Israelite places out of himself, in God. Israel is the most complete presentation of positivism in religion. In relation to the Israelite, the Christian is an *esprit fort*, a free-thinker. Thus do things change. What yesterday was still religion, is no longer such to-day; and what to-day is atheism tomorrow will be religion.[35]

Thus the gradual attribution of divine things to man is a clear advance, in no sense a degeneration or a loss; and the Hegelian view of the 'positivity' of the Jewish religion is turned not, as in Hegel himself, to an examination of Christian spirituality, but to an equation of true Christianity with free-thinking.

We begin to see how the attacking and the apologetical aspects of the higher critical enterprise emerged into open paradox: in the new eschatology, atheism and true faith were one. But the justification for this was the hard-pressed insistence so common among the Victorians – Mill's certainty that the moral gains of Christianity were permanent, Arnold's that Puritanism could now be dispensed with, for it had done its work of civilizing the body – that divine things, justly perceived as human, still retained all their divinity.

The misunderstanding of Feuerbach has led to serious misjudgements of George Eliot's art. Knoepflmacher, in *The Early Novels of George Eliot*, thinks 'Amos Barton' in certain respects over-idealizing (Milly's madonna-like qualities, Amos's repentance at her death); but this is the result of looking back on the events of 'Amos Barton' from a fully idealized and dogmatic viewpoint, whereas George Eliot is concerned to show the very stuff out of which the idea of a madonna arises (physical beauty in striking contrast to circumstances, groundless and inexhaustible love, suffering and early death), the very stuff of repentance in the perfectly ordinary sense of having done too little for someone in life. She is not showing 'a failed conversion', but giving a delicate adumbration of the primitive, originating material of experience in which theology has its roots, and at the same time constructing a carefully controlled vision of the future of religion. The past and the future can only be grasped at the advanced point of history when men have become become sufficiently developed religiously to be conscious of the materials and the process, and only so can the past be gathered up into the future. As Cassirer has said,

Not the world, not objective existence and happenings are the scene of myth and religion, nor do religious tales pretend to be giving information on that score. What else is historical criticism of these Biblical stories doing if not following through to the end Schelling's thought that the active subject of mythology is to be sought in human consciousness itself and not somewhere outside it?[36]

George Eliot, like many nineteenth-century poets, displays the gap between positive parroted institutional doctrine and private religious experience in process, while locating in genuinely common experience the germ of all dogma. As humanist tolerance extends, the opposition of 'primitive' and 'advanced' becomes a source of irony. In short, it is just because the idealist element in Feuerbach is underestimated that the idealizing element in George Eliot is overestimated and isolated out from the texture of her *Scenes of Clerical Life*.

The attempt to see 'Janet's Repentance' as more successful than the earlier stories in *Scenes of Clerical Life* is another such misjudgement with more pervasive consequences. George Eliot does not, as Knoepflmacher argues, 'narrow the gap' between actual and ideal (she had already narrowed it as much as she ever could), but rather, since now she does attempt to show a full-blown conversion, the whole story takes place on a different level of religious consciousness. The difficulty of where to set a Feuerbachian religion (or a Comtian society) dogged George Eliot: should it be set in, as it were, a Feuerbachian milieu, a milieu of high religious consciousness among *esprits forts*, or should it, as in 'Amos Barton', occur at a primitive level, where only the author was aware of the relation of experience to doctrine, where the growth of consciousness was all unconscious? She was always exceedingly good at the latter, and it is this which has earned her the accolade of 'realist'; but this is to see her enterprise in a false light. Not only was such a primitive portrait equally, as we have seen, a vision of a Utopian future; but in all her portraits, the question is, at which point will it be most effective to intersect the evolutionary scale of spirit? What degree of consciousness is to be depicted?

In practical terms, the novelist's difficulty is that specific religious experiences like conversion ordinarily take place within a specific doctrinal context. In 'Janet's Repentance', the need is to show the human potential for specific, not general religious experience – here evangelicalism; and this is theologically awkward as well as novelistically demanding. The harsh portrait of Dempster and of the town of Milby, in conjunction with Mr Tryan's selflessness – 'the mixture of satire and hagiography' deplored by Knoepflmacher – catches the special conditions and tone out of which a specific spiritual remedy will grow. Thus the resemblances of the story to a temperance tract represents George Eliot's usual attention to the accurate setting of emotions, and in wider terms it is evident that this mixture characterizes the Feuerbachian position itself. 'The utopian perspective', Lukács has said (and he locates it in Goethe and Balzac, Stendhal and Tolstoy), 'serves a double function: it enables the artist to portray the present age truthfully without giving way to despair.'[37]

Daniel Deronda poses and resolves the same problem, not of any 'gap' between actual and ideal (for the mythological view of history copes with it), but of matching specificities, now over the whole range of consciousness, at the highest as at the lowest. George Eliot should be given credit for deliberately weighting her descriptions towards the unfamiliar in order to bring the reader's knowledge up to something like the density of what he knows by experience of his own milieu. This is the justification for *Romola*; it is a failure of the readers' imagination, not of George Eliot's, that Florence is not as alive to them as Victorian England. In *Daniel Deronda* a special difficulty is created by the disparity in knowledge needed to be supplied to the English reader in the 'English' and the 'Jewish' portions. The more one considers this disparity, however, the better George Eliot seems to have succeeded. From one point of view, no doubt, there is much more that the reader needs to begin to understand her Jewish milieux; from another point of view, she has already supplied more than her readers can in their frailty bear. But in fact, the Jews supplied George Eliot with a solution to the problem of specificity, for the Jews' historical relationship to Christianity was a permanent aspect of Christian doctrine, and, in the modern world, they represented precisely those emancipated, liberalized, nationalized, secularized religious beings, those *esprits forts* of Feuerbach who formed the avant-garde of Christian spirituality. Neither in their ideal, unchanging relationship to Christianity, nor in their present historical position, were they 'specific' in the awkward manner of Mr Tryan the Evangelical. 'Zionism' summed up for George Eliot this double significance of Judaism: the conservation of the historical experience of the race symbolized by the 'homeland' (and she had the most profound respect for this conservation), and the recognition of its modern secular form by the advance to nationhood. From both these points of view she had at last, after many attempts, found the right Feuerbachian milieu: one saturated with religion, yet essentially secular and modern, where she could unite the primitive ground of religion with the most advanced consciousness of it. The modern Christian is to be immersed in a memorial community of consciousness by now alien and unfamiliar, which constitutes his own capacity for religious experience. Gwendolen Harleth, although she undergoes the most lengthy and authentic 'conversion' to be found in the pages of George Eliot, is not converted to a specific religion, to the church of the Rev. Mr Barton, or Tryan, or Rufus Lyon, or Irwine, but to the Christian version of the religion of humanity. At last George Eliot has got the balance right on the largest scale, as in 'Amos Barton' she had got it right on the most minute.

George Eliot spoke of

my yearning affection towards the great religions of the world which have reflected the struggles and needs of mankind, with a very different degree of completeness from the shifting compromise called 'philosophical theism'.[38]

Feuerbach put succinctly the problem posed by this *nostalgie de la foi* and suggested a solution:

When a belief has departed from the reason, the intelligence, when it is no longer held spontaneously, but merely because it is a common belief, or because on some ground or other it must be held; in short, when a belief is inwardly a past one; then externally also the object of the belief is referred to the past. Unbelief thus gets breathing space, but at the same time concedes to belief at least an historical validity. The past is here the fortunate means of compromise between belief and unbelief: I certainly believe in miracles, but, *nota bene*, in no miracles which happen now – only in those which once happened, which, thank God! are already *plus quam perfecta*.[39]

The historical novel, which dominates the century's prose, exploits the past as 'the fortunate means of compromise between belief and unbelief'. More exactly, the novel of the present was written as a historical novel, and the historical novel as a novel of the present, thus playing out the compromise in dramatic terms. The milieu of belief was still, though with great pain, portable. In *The Mill on the Floss* the return is a psychic one, to a paradisal spot of childhood time where the life of the mind began, and ends; the symbolic treatment of this poetic *topos* is perfectly in order. But at the same time, the complexity of the historical treatment of *Adam Bede*, for example, has sometimes been lost in appreciation of its 'pastoral' aspect: this novel, with its tenuous links between the anonymous modern narrator, the old Adam Bede as informant, and the actual events related with apparent omniscience, turns on the very intermittence of omniscience, on the nostalgia for the possibility of direct narration of immediately accessible events.[40] The compromise is worked out in all its fullness as a technique of the novel's narration: what we know we do not know, what we do not believe we believe. The half-concealed, half-revealed awareness of compromise issues in an affirmation: like Browning's St John, the critical reader is still just barely within living memory of credulous community. But only a critical technique can achieve a value for credulity.

Within living memory of what? Certainly not of 'miracles *plus quam perfecta*'. Feuerbach's I–thou analysis had fundamental epistemological implications. For Feuerbach, 'man's dependence' is at the centre of religion; but he emphasizes that it is not as in Schleiermacher a 'mystical, indeterminate, abstract feeling', but the concrete empirical dependence of man on nature and other men. Religion is a projection of man as a *Gattungswesen*, a species-being. As species-being 'Man is both I and Thou.' Man is the 'ground and focal point' of what Feuerbach sees as a dialectical unity, a logical interdependence of the subject and object of knowledge.'[41] Feuerbach vacillated between the view that common human agreement was a check on truth or objectivity and the quite different view that it constituted truth or objectivity. On the constitutive side, he often quoted the Protagorean dictum that 'man is the measure of all things'. As Kamenka remarks,

There are overtones in Feuerbach as in Marx, of Vico's famous *verum factum*, of the view that man can know completely and with certainty only that which he has fashioned himself. Idealism, indeed, tried to make nature transparent by making it a product of mind.[42]

In short, Feuerbach still speaks of subjectivity, though no longer of the abstract ego, but of the whole man as species-being. This puts him at one with the higher critical analysis of the knowability of historical event, in which Vico, and following him Herder, had indeed played an influential role; at the same time, it removes him a step from his affiliations with idealism, and so makes comprehensible the sense in which Feuerbach could be at once a materialist and an idealist. Feuerbach typically used 'objectivity' in a variety of senses. His thought often turns on his aphoristic style, and Kamenka has pointed to the element of punning in Feuerbach, an extreme but illuminating way of describing the mental acrobatics by which the 'objectivity' of religion was justified by its roots in the subjective need of man; this view was often not consistently maintained by those who employed it, precisely because they wanted ultimately to claim that objectivity in this subtle extended sense was after all a foundation for religious 'fact' in a naive sense.

The view of 'fact' that developed in the context of rational disbelief of miracle has extended itself fully to all fact: the wheel has come another full circle, for Feuerbach uses the mythological view of historical fact as a weapon against the mythological school of apologists themselves:

O ye short-sighted religious philosophers of Germany, who fling at our heads the facts of the religious consciousness, to stun our reason and make us the slaves of your childish superstition, – do you not see that facts are just as relative, as various, as subjective, as the ideas of the different religions?

Were not the Gods of Olympus also facts, self-attesting existences?. . .A fact, I repeat, is a conception about the truth of which there is no doubt, because it is no object of theory, but of feeling, which desires that what it wishes, what it believes, should be true. A fact is that, the denial of which is forbidden, if not by an external law, yet by an internal one. A fact is every possibility which passes for a reality, every conception which, for the age wherein it is held to be a fact, expresses a want, and is for that reason an impassable limit of the mind. A fact is every wish that projects itself on reality: in short, it is everything that is not doubted simply because it is not – must not be – doubted.[43]

'Fact', then, so far from being a privileged kind of event in the world, is identified with the objectifications of the 'vagrant, merely poetic' imagination, which in Christianity, unlike other religions, Feuerbach found subject to a discipline of the essentials of feeling. We must, I think, see a certain inconsistency in Feuerbach between his desire on the one hand to see all religions as equivalent, as based equally on the needs of human feeling, and his desire still to protect the claim of Christianity to have attained an especially high degree of religious culture. He sways between a thorough-going, iconoclastic relativism and a nostalgia for the privileged position of his own culture. An apologetical aura still clung to him which Marx was to dispel. But inconsistent or not in this respect, 'fact' has been thoroughly internalized and historicized. In dealing with George Eliot, it must always be remembered that this view of 'fact' was part of her intellectual equipment and part of her technique as a novelist, and that just the inconsistency we spy in Feuerbach makes possible the novelist's range from the subjective, the vagrant, merely poetic, interpretation of fact as part of the pathology of her characters to the fully justified imaginative circle of essential human need as determinative of the 'external world' of the novel. To put it another way, complete license is granted to the imagination, and then circumscribed again in the light of old arrangements. Within this view, the passage from what a modern might recognize as a fact and what he might prefer to call a symbol is facilitated, expected. Attacks on George Eliot for 'sentimentality', wishful immaturity, and the like (Leavis: 'day-dream self-indulgence') are completely misplaced until her art is discussed within the right frame of reference. The possibilities open to her as a nineteenth-century novelist were infinitely greater than some modern critics have been able to recognize, despite their general acclaim (on the wrong grounds) for the superiority of the nineteenth-century novel.

The power of the novelist in the nineteenth century stems from his awareness that 'realism' is but one moment of the whole development of consciousness which it is his function to reconstruct. His creative power and range arise not from adherence to 'reality' however defined, but, quite the contrary, from his new sense, derived from the romantics, of the full range and *disponibilité* of all of human experience. Objects in the world, events in history, and divine things were ranged along the same continuum; they were objectified by human feeling. Human feeling was not, however, a 'mere, vagrant poetic fancy', but was indeed moulded by milieu, by historical tradition within a given society, by the myths of the larger community. Realism arises at the intersection of human feeling with fact interpreted through established myth, and we know with what toughness George Eliot insisted on the inescapability of these forces. But the frame of reference was always the ordered structure of possible human consciousness. By going to the roots in *Daniel Deronda* of the myths of her society, George Eliot was attempting a critique of the often impoverished view of 'reality' (one that identifies readily with 'realism') that dominated Victorian England and has unfortunately continued to dominate criticism of the English novel. She rarely spoke of 'realism', preferring the 'truth' of fiction. Let us be clear: 'realism' there is in George Eliot's novels, even a realism that can associate itself with Dutch painting, with 'Rembrandtish' effects; but it is enacted within a different philosophical setting than that so admirably delineated by Ian Watt in *The Rise of the Novel*.

The novel took a fresh start from the model of *Wilhelm Meister*. As it was profoundly interpreted by Friedrich Schlegel, the novel came to be seen not simply as one genre among many, but as *Universalpoesie*. The silent disregard of Goethe (broken only by the occasional dismissive aside)[44] is a scandal of English criticism of the novel and makes interpretation of George Eliot almost impossible. As Lord Acton said of her, 'If Lessing was the favourite, Goethe was the master.'[45] There is little more reason for disregard of the pervasive influence of the German novella. 'The Lifted Veil', felt to be a puzzling aberration in George Eliot's corpus, has been little discussed; but in fact, this novella, written on her return from several months in Munich, and drawing openly and specifically (like 'Brother Jacob') on the example of the German novella, gives a glimpse of the full range within which her fiction was at all times conducted, even when she chose to touch the highest and lowest chords only by implication.[46] This quotation, were it not so familiar, might seem more likely to derive from 'The Lifted Veil' than from *Middlemarch*:

If we had a keen vision and feeling of all human life it would be like hearing the grass grow and the squirrel's heart beat, and we should die of that roar which lies on the other side of silence.

The novel reabsorbed the traditional elements it had seemed to slough off in its early days, elements of mythopoeic story, of universal type, of spiritual intention, and high art. In reaching maturity, it assumed the stature of the drama and the epic; it ceased to be merely local, particular, bourgeois, domestic, personal, practical – it ceased to be 'feminine' in the sense that Ian Watt has defined it. Mary Ann Evans became George Eliot, and to her must go the main credit for the transformation of the English novel, from an innovating precursor, into a form capable of standing beside the creations of the great Continental practitioners of the nineteenth century. Dickens is the greatest 'English' novelist in the narrowest sense; George Eliot, in the widest.

Goethe's 'structuring irony' occupies an absolutely central place, historically and theoretically, in the modern novel; as Lukács has said, it maintains a delicately fluctuating equilibrium between 'abstract idealism' and the 'romanticism of disillusionment'.[47] 'The novel', he points out, 'is the dialectical form of the epic.'[48] Lukács sees the novel as indeed moving into epic again, with Tolstoy (and Leavis is prepared to call George Eliot 'Tolstoyan'); but this view, guided by a Hegelian definition of the realism of the Greek epic, misses the fact that the epic of the novel is the modern, subjective, non-Greek epic of Dante and Milton, not the epic of Schiller's 'naif' Homer. Ian Watt, in summing up the differences between epic and novel in such a way as to make them seem as far apart as possible (in order to keep at bay the 'epic' interpretation of Fielding's novels), nevertheless produces a definition of epic that strikingly applies to *Daniel Deronda*:

The epic is, after all, an oral and poetic genre dealing with the public and usually remarkable deeds of historical or legendary persons engaged in a collective rather than individual enterprise; and none of these things can be said of the novel.[49]

On the contrary: *Daniel Deronda* is concerned with the collective enterprise of the Jews to maintain their community and with a much broader collective enterprise through which Christian society too is to be renewed and continued; the main characters are not merely types of these societies but consciously modelled on the historical and legendary figures of their religious literature, the Old Testament prophets, the Christian saints and martyrs, and not least Jesus himself. Its language, though not 'oral', is one of many attempts to capture a spontaneous, primitive level of experience identified with oral cultures, while adapting it to an advanced, rationalizing, literate culture; we are dealing already with a modern 'art of quotation' as it was practised *in extremis* by Walter Benjamin and recently traced by Herman Meyer through the European novel.[50] It is not at all surprising that in England one of the earliest and most effective exponents of this mosaic technique of reconstruction from débris was Coleridge. All of these characteristics came to George Eliot through her preoccupation with the higher criticism with its emphasis on the oral and legendary springs of the religions of the Book. *Daniel Deronda* was intended to be an epic poem in modern terms, and it adheres to a new set of epic rules and epic 'machinery' based on the nature of Biblical history. The breakdown of the boundaries between prose and poetry is one of the most significant aspects of Victorian writing. The novel stands in the middle between the 'philosophical fiction' of the great Victorian prose stylists Carlyle, Ruskin, Newman, Arnold, and the syncretic strategies of Victorian poetry, and it is enriched from both sides. We have heard much of *The Ring and the Book* as a novel; we have heard less often of the poetry of the novel (though the continuity of *Wuthering Heights* with the Gondal poetry has been shown, and comparison of Blake with Dickens has been mooted). Only by forging a language capable of moving between the lyrical and the abstruse scientific, between the private and the public, could the web of consciousness be made whole.

The 'particular', the 'innovatory', and the 'critical', certainly (in Watt's terms); but, as this book has attempted to show throughout, these were balanced by and absorbed into systems of philosophical idealism. Watt has attempted to draw such conspicuous practitioners of the later art of the novel as Henry James and Proust and Joyce into his realist net by referring to the tradition of 'philosophical dualism' stemming from Descartes. But while this is broadly true (for all philosophy since Descartes stands in the dualist shadow), in the local history of the modulation from the eighteenth- to the nineteenth-century novel, it is mere sleight-of-hand: one cannot so easily wish away the idealist movement in poetry and criticism that, as René Wellek has shown, was disseminated all over Europe in the first half of the nineteenth century. In the history of philosophy since Descartes, post-Kantian idealism, though it was hag-ridden by the problems of dualism and ultimately founders on them, attempted a unified solution. It can be said from the point of view of idealism itself that the human mind has a nostalgia for naive realism; and all the sophisticated treatments of Christianity which we have seen take place in the context of the higher criticism are shadowed by an uneasy sense of loss, duplicity, and ingenuity in their revaluation of the significance to be attached to 'facts'. But the enterprise is clear: whether through providential history, or Straussian myth, or Feuerbachian I–thou, to carry into the novel the whole range of human consciousness, and thereby to 'place' realism as a moment of that consciousness.

In *The Essence of Christianity*, Feuerbach distinguished man from animals by his possession of religion, but religion, in its positive content, was no other than consciousness of infinity:

Consciousness in the strict or proper sense is identical with consciousness of the infinite; a limited consciousness is no consciousness; consciousness is essentially infinite in its nature. The consciousness of the infinite is nothing else than the consciousness of the infinity of the consciousness; or, in the consciousness of the infinite, the conscious subject has for his object the infinity of his own nature.[51]

George Eliot's conception of God, Hillis Miller has remarked, is Feuerbach's 'essence of man', and the narrator of *Middlemarch* is precisely that all-inclusive 'consciousness of the species' which was Feuerbach's definition of Christ.[52] Miller makes the general point that the Victorian novelist is not omniscient like a transcendent God, but like an immanent God who has knowledge not of what He Himself has created but of what some other God has created. There are 'no or few' claims made to be the creator; the novelist is part of his community.[53] This is not quite accurate. Just because 'George Eliot is the most explicit example of the Victorian transformation from a view of society as based on a transcendent ground to a view of it as generating itself',[54] the novelist is indeed within his own community, but he is fully aware that the community must generate, and regenerate, itself from within; and the artist has a specially powerful role in this. Moreover, the transcendent God, in Feuerbach's analysis, is nothing else but the hypostasis of the *Gattungswesen*'s consciousness of itself and its separation off from society in the artificial, rigid form of theology. The transcendent God and the omniscience of the author, then, have not disappeared, they have been reabsorbed into the original creative power of man. It is not in *Middlemarch*, but in *Daniel Deronda*, that this final phase of the restoration of God to man is completed, the consciousness attained that the transcendent God Himself is created by man. It is through the gradual interpenetration of the several series of I–Thou relationships in *Daniel Deronda* that the novel fully articulates its claim to be not merely one subjective interpretation of the world, nor a succession of them in turn, but the consciousness of the *Gattungswesen* itself, the 'narrator's transindividual vision of the whole truth'.[55] This is the meaning of the circularity of the book's structure, signalled by the opening epigraph from *Faust*:

No retrospect will take us to the true beginning; and whether our Prologue be in heaven or on earth, it is but a fraction of that all-presupposing fact with which our story sets out.

The 'fact' is the fully-formed consciousness of the race, to be comprehended only through the analysis of its development which the novel presents. Vast though the scale of *Daniel Deronda* is, and long the roll of minutiae, this is the circularity of 'Kubla Khan'. In the parable of the candle-flame in the scratched pier-glass in *Middlemarch*, the scratches appear to arrange themselves in concentric circles when approached by a candle. 'The scratches are events, and the candle is the egoism of any person. . .', George Eliot says. This view of event, of course, she always maintained; and it is, as Hillis Miller says, the consistency of her commitment to this form of subjectivism in which she differs from other Victorian novelists.[56] But only in *Daniel Deronda* do we see the full extent of this egoism (the multiple mirrors in which

Gwendolen sees herself), and the candle-flame of the 'general consciousness' which makes one set of concentric circles of all the different
sets of concentric circles of the individual egos. Henry James never
improved, in theory or in practice, on the 'organic form' of this novel.

At the same time, in this process of enlargement and transformation
of the novel into the modern reflective epic, the local, bourgeois,
domestic, and personal elements to which Watt has pointed came into
their own. With whatever astounded admiration we may observe the
tour de force of critical provincialism in which Q. D. Leavis sets
Dickens's treatment of themes of love and marriage in *David Copperfield* above Tolstoy's in *War and Peace*,[57] it is to George Eliot we must
look for the most adequate and searching treatment of these themes in
English. In *Daniel Deronda* these themes achieve their fullest expression.

For the means, we must return to Feuerbach's equation of theology
and pathology. In the chapter on 'The Mystery of Mysticism, or of
Nature in God', he wrote, 'Mysticism is deuteroscopy – a fabrication
of phrases having a double meaning.'[58]

Thus here, in the mystical doctrine of the two principles in God, the real
object is pathology, the imaginary one, theology; i.e. Boehme's light and
darkness, pathology is converted into theology. There would be nothing to
urge against this, if, consciously, real pathology were recognized and expressed as theology; indeed, it is precisely our task to show that theology is
nothing else than an unconscious, esoteric pathology, anthropology, and
psychology and that therefore real anthropology, real pathology, and real
psychology have far more claim to the name of theology, than has theology
itself.[59]

He proceeds accordingly to analyse theology in terms of the sexual
constitution of man. 'And the strongest of the impulses of Nature, is
it not the sexual feeling?'[60]

He who lives in the consciousness of the species, and consequently of its
reality, lives also in the consciousness of the reality of sex. He does not regard
it as a mechanically inserted, adventitious stone of stumbling, but as a inherent quality, a chemical constituent of his being. He indeed recognises
himself as a man in the broader sense, but he is at the same time conscious of
being rigorously determined by the sexual distinction, which penetrates not
only bones and marrow, but also his inmost self, the essential mode of his
thought, will, and sensation.[61]

How thoroughly George Eliot agreed we know: writing to Emily Davies in 1868, *à propos* of her attempt to set up the college for women that was to become Girton, she commented:

1. The physical and physiological differences between women and men. On the one hand, these may be said to lie on the surface and be palpable to every impartial person with commonsense who looks at a large assembly made up of both sexes. But on the other hand the differences are deep roots of psychological development and their influences can be fully traced by careful well-instructed thought. Apart from the question of sex, and only for the sake of illuminating it, take the mode in which some comparatively external physical characteristics such as quality of skin, or relative muscular power among boys, will enter into the determination of the ultimate nature, the proportion of feeling and all mental action, in the given individual. This is the deepest and subtlest sort of education that life gives.[62]

Feuerbach places the essence of community in the 'I' and the 'Thou' and emphasizes the dependence of the very self on this community, which for him as for Hölderlin derives from Fichte; but he gives it a specifically sexual cast:

Where there is no *thou*, there is no *I*; but the distinction between *I* and *thou*, the fundamental condition of all personality, of all consciousness, is only real, living ardent, when felt as the distinction between man and woman. The *thou* between man and woman has quite another sound, than the monotonous *thou* between friends.[63]

All George Eliot's work centres on this relation between the thou and the I of male and female, intimate and indispensable in the theological, the philosophical, the moral, and the pathological senses. How her own life and experience corroborates and underlies this view her biographers have abundantly revealed. In her adoption of the I–thou analysis as the core of her thinking on individual and communal relations, she stands in a tradition carried on by Scheler, Berdyaev, Heidegger, Buber, and Sartre.

Everywhere George Eliot explored this essential relationship, the unit of individual being and of society – in Caterina's moral convalescence through Gilfil, in the relationship between Janet and Mr Tryan, with its overt sexual outcome of his spiritual consolations; in the intellectual admiration of Dorothea Brooke for Mr Casaubon which she disastrously accepts as a basis for marriage; in the single face-to-face encounter of Dorothea and Lydgate, which carries all of *Middlemarch*'s ironies of waste; in the distant yet powerful relationship between Savonarola and Romola, whose face-to-face meeting is the turning point in Romola's life. Nowhere does she do so more powerfully or in a more sustained way than in *Daniel Deronda*. The mirror-imagery pointed out by Barbara Hardy in *The Novels of George Eliot* is not 'mirror-imagery' simply but one of the richest elaborations we have of the romantic myth of reflection. *Daniel Deronda* abounds in 'Narcissus' reflections in another face, from Daniel's first sight of Gwendolen at the gaming table in Leubronn, through the whole series of their intense encounters, to Gwendolen's last sight of the face of her husband as he drowns; and presiding over them all, the encounter of Mordecai and Daniel on the river, which for Mordecai was the appearance of the Son of Man in the clouds.

The mystical basis of the I–thou unity is the gnostic-cabbalistic notion of Adam as the soul that contained all souls. Adam Ha-Rishon, the Adam of the Bible, corresponds on the anthropological plane to Adam Kadmon, the ontological primary man: his fall scattered the sparks of soul everywhere, and they became diffused in matter. The moral task of man in the Jewish cabbala is to restore his primordial spiritual structure, and so contribute to the restoration of the spiritual structure of mankind. This was combined with a doctrine of metempsychosis, facilitating the passage of souls. In *Daniel Deronda*, the mystical substratum is expressed directly through the fraternal relation of the master and his disciple, Mordecai and Daniel. The experience of the exile as migration of the body became a symbol for the exile of the soul in Jewish popular belief. The release from exile, according to Isaac Luria, the great sixteenth-century cabbalist, depends on the relationship between certain souls, which corresponds to the place they originally occupied in the undivided soul of Adam. There are relationships between souls and even families of souls that have a special aptitude for assisting each other and setting a whole group on the return journey. The true history of the world is the history of the migrations and interrelations of the souls; and the true interpretation of the Bible reveals the interrelations of souls expressed through their mundane stories. The mystical transference of the name of God from the master to the disciple, which traditionally took place over water, achieves a portion of the restoration of unity to the severed parts of mankind through the special relationship of certain souls.[64]

The relationship of Gwendolen Harleth and Daniel Deronda carries an immense charge of meaning. The vividness of these personal encounters from first to last in the novel is not, and cannot be, independly given; any critical attempt to treat this 'vividness' as separable from what Leavis is pleased to call 'the mass of fervid and wordy unreality' is mistaken.[65] George Eliot did not lightly make the claim: 'I meant everything in the book to be related to everything else there.'[66]

The vividness is all of George Eliot's own making, all, that is, of the making of her idea. *Daniel Deronda* explores to the full the Feuerbachian equation of theology and pathology, with all the tensions that implies. Marcel Mauss in his essay 'The Techniques of the Body' (1935) offered a modern version: he held that the study of bodily techniques would have to take place within a study of symbolic systems. We may see this as an extension of the association of sexuality with religious symbolism, often using anthropological material, common to the radical debunkers of religion and to the enthusiastic defenders of symbolic systems of religious ritual. *The Essence of Christianity* is an extended exercise in this double-edged mode. George Eliot gives us in *Daniel Deronda* her own version of the luminous god, priapic and etherial, of Payne Knight and Dupuis. In George Eliot the critical material is so fully absorbed, and so grounded in Lewes's physiological and psychological investigations, that the tone of bravado and risk typical of the earlier writers in this mode is no longer evident.

But bravado and risk are both there. From the point of view of Victorian convention, we may observe something like a developmental theme, whereby sexuality is gradually transmuted into spiritual experience; but in fact the vehicle of spiritual enlightenment remains sexual throughout (this is still part of George Eliot's programme, for Gwendolen Harleth is an 'ordinary woman' in the same sense as Amos Barton was an ordinary man). Our sense of development is based on the gradual heightening of an adulterous passion that passes through all the stages of a secular liaison. These are the stages of a spiritual progress: just as Thomas à Kempis is used in the *The Mill on the Floss* (rather more rudely and literally and externally) as a guide to Maggie's gradual articulation in her own personal terms of the contradiction between the world and the spirit, so here sexuality flowers into the full range of human feeling.

The whole novel is conducted in terms of the equation between theology and pathology, developing both sides and persisting in the equation along the whole scale of consciousness. The sexual pathology of marriage and the sexual pathology of Christianity are both revealed through the medium of an intense liaison between a married woman and a young man she chooses to make her 'confessor', and together form the basis of a searching analysis of the valid emotional sources of religious experience from which doctrine arises. The 'doctrine' that emerges, as so often in the higher criticism, is at once an interpretation of history and a conscious new manifesto for modern times.

Under the aegis of Feuerbach – and we may recall that if Marx took up one aspect of Feuerbach's teaching, Freud took up another – she had begun in *Scenes of Clerical Life* to explore the theme of mismating. This had, of course, always been a theme of the novel; only Richardson and Trollope outstrip her in conveying the considerations of class, position, and property that govern marriage; and neither can approach her in conveying the complex interaction of physical incongruities with moral and intellectual disparities. Richardson's portrayal of Clarissa's distaste for her suitor Solmes is remarkably awkward and unpersuasive; Trollope, though powerfully attracted to the theme, remains external in his treatment. George Eliot gives a finer shade to the sexual plight of women in her society. Here, indeed, the comparison is rather with D. H. Lawrence than with any of her predecessors or contemporaries. Her Feuerbachian explorations of the relation between pathology and theology, quite beyond Trollope, are more persuasive both as generalized analysis and as inward experience than Lawrence's fantasia of the unconscious.

In 'Amos Barton', the sense of the incongruity, physical and temperamental, between Barton and his wife is strong, and only barely repressed by the author through the tranquil, loving acceptance of the fictional wife. In 'Janet's Repentance', the melodrama of wife-beating and strong drink only a little obscures the fine rendering of Janet Dempster's bewildered fear that her husband should not be pleased. In 'Mr Gilfil's Love-Story', which in many respects foreshadows *Daniel Deronda*, the tiny Caterina is to be married off to the stocky curate Gilfil, the immensity of whose calves and ability to take five-foot fences are stressed. She is in love with her social superior Captain Wybrow, of whom George Eliot gives a full page of physical description, emphasizing his exquisite dandy's daintiness, and ending with a comparison between him and Gilfil, respectively a 'peach' and 'the largest vegetable marrow'. Wybrow, who resents the curate's calves and suffers from palpitations of the heart, is to be married off for reasons of social propriety to Miss Assher, whose height and power and imperious temper and abundance of hair and redness of cheek and carved nose and noble profile and firm seat on horseback are alluded to throughout. These details are presented in a way that makes it impossible not to think in sheerly physical terms about the incongruity of the prospective mates. George Eliot conveys a sense of shock and imposition, as she does at the uncomplaining death of Amos Barton's wife, at thirty-five, in childbed (her seventh). The callous kindness of Sir Christopher Cheverel, who controls the bodies of his social dependents, is conveyed in a repulsive mixed metaphor of animal breeding between different species: 'The little monkey is quite old enough. It would be pretty to see her a matron, with a baby about the size of a kitten in her arms.'[67]

This hybrid image carries all that need be said. In this story, the further connection between theology and pathology is ill-managed. It is through Mr Gilfil's loving ministrations that Caterina recovers, physically and morally, from her intention to murder her trifling lover Wybrow. (Like Gwendolen, she has a concealed knife and the desire to do a man to death; unlike Gwendolen, she sets out with the knife intending actually to carry out the deed, only to find Wybrow already dead.) As she gradually recovers, she begins to be dependent on his presence and his moral consolation, as Gwendolen will later depend so much more powerfully on Daniel's. Yet when she marries Gilfil, the earlier, grotesque, unwilled mismatching is not fully overcome or integrated; she too dies in childbirth. George Eliot resorts to an apparently very different sort of imagery to get over this awkwardness: 'But the delicate plant had been too deeply bruised, and in the struggle to put forth a blossom it died.'[68] This apparently tame euphemism suggests, in its resort to the reproductive imagery not of animals but of flowers, that the question was no longer one of breeding specificities but of a solitary woman's fate; the pregnant woman is, to the imagination, parthenogenetic: the Virgin Mother. Bruised in the conflict, so graphically presented, between the passionate and the grateful love, she died as it were by her own hand (as Gwendolen cannot rid herself of the sense that she is responsible, by the very strength of her wish, for Grandcourt's actual death). Her death is an act of moral parthenogenesis.

One might perhaps wish that the mature George Eliot had undertaken to explore the tragic irony, just sketched in the early story, of the conflict between the physical forces and the morally restorative tenderness. In *The Mill on the Floss*, indeed, mismating rises to something like tragedy: the deformed Philip Wakem's intellectual and emotional rapport with Maggie as against Stephen Guest's vigorous but coarse-grained physical prowess is an insoluble dilemma for the young woman. This is well within the scope of Feuerbach's analysis; one need think only of his famous account of the contradiction between faith and love. A thorough appreciation of her use of Feuerbach extirpates Leavis's double error about George Eliot, his contempt for the basis of her art in the emotional life, and his incomprehension of the level at which her intellectual life moulded it.

Much has rightly been said in praise of George Eliot's description of the Casaubons' Roman honeymoon, in which Dorothea's disappointment suffuses her response to the ancient city. The Grandcourt wedding night is brilliant and terrifying, as befits this book. The wedding-day opens with a Lawrentian passage between the people:

The miller's daughter of fourteen could not believe that high gentry behaved badly to their wives, but her mother instructed her – 'Oh, child, men's men: gentle or simple, they're much of a muchness. I've heard my mother say Squire Pelton used to take his dogs and a long whip into his wife's room, and flog 'em there to frighten her; and my mother was lady's-maid there at the very time.'

'That's unlucky talk for a wedding, Mrs Girdle,' said the tailor. 'A quarrel may end wi' the whip, but it begins wi' the tongue, and it's the women have got the most o' that.'

'The Lord gave it 'em to use, I suppose,' said Mrs Girdle; '*He* never meant you to have it all your own way.'

'By what I can make out from the gentleman as attends to the grooming at Offendene,' said the tailor, 'this Mr Grandcourt has wonderful little tongue. Everything must be done dummy-like without his ordering.'

'Then he's the more whip, I doubt,' said Mrs Girdle. '*She's* got tongue enough, I warrant her. See, there they come out together!' (*Daniel Deronda*, pp. 400–1)[69]

As the previous chapter has shown us Grandcourt at home with his mistress Mrs Glasher, enforcing upon her the need to hand back her diamonds to the lawful wife, the reader is under no illusions: Grandcourt is indeed 'the more whip'.

Gwendolen is still under illusions. The state of her sensibility is carefully described: we know more of the nervous organization of this woman than we do of the Brangwen sisters. At the same time it is a description of her moral condition in the metaphorical terms that govern the book's structure:

Gwendolen, in fact, never showed more elasticity in her bearing, more lustre in her long brown glance: she had the brilliancy of strong excitement, which will sometimes come even from pain. It was not pain, however, that she was feeling: she had wrought herself up to much the same condition as that in which she stood at the gambling-table when Deronda was looking at her, and she began to lose (p. 401).

Next we hear of her moral condition, of the 'intoxication of youthful egoism', but the passage moves to isolate this as a physical state present to herself: 'there was an under-consciousness in her that she was a little intoxicated' (p. 402). The precise quality of her excitement is rendered in this passage of George Eliot's mature art:

Gwendolen had been at her liveliest during the journey, chatting incessantly, ignoring any change in their mutual position since yesterday; and Grand-court had been rather ecstatically quiescent while she turned his gentle seizure of her hand into a grasp of his hand by both hers, with an increased vivacity as of a kitten that will not sit quiet to be petted. She was really get-ting somewhat febrile in her excitement; and now in this drive through the park her usual susceptibility to changes of light and scenery helped to make her heart palpitate newly. Was it at the novelty given to her girlish dreams of being 'somebody' – walking through her own furlong of corridors and under her own ceilings of an out-of-sight loftiness, where her own painted Spring was shedding painted flowers, and her own fore-shortened Zephyrs were blowing their trumpets over her; while her own servants, lackeys in clothing but men in bulk and shape were as nought in her presence, and revered the propriety of her insolence to them: – being in short the heroine of an admired play without the pains of art? Was it alone the closeness of this fulfilment which made her heart flutter? or was it some dim forecast, the insistent penetration of suppressed experience, mixing the expectation of a triumph with the dread of a crisis. Hers was one of the natures in which exultation inevitably carries an infusion of dread ready to curdle and declare itself (p. 404).

George Eliot catches throughout the book this element of animal superstition, now fully removed from the 'natural state' of primitive man and rendered as the substrate of civilized consciousness. She presents the more radical of the eighteenth-century analyses of the roots of religion, founding it in savage fear rather than natural piety. Natural piety and nobility of character exist for George Eliot, and she is at pains to depict them; but they are not unanalysed 'givens' of human nature (and are only presented as such when the total character, action, or milieu calls them utterly in question).

Grandcourt leads Gwendolen into her boudoir – 'an open doorway sending out a rich glow of light and colour' – and leaves her to prepare for an early dinner. While she is alone, the packet of diamonds from Lydia Glasher is delivered, with her letter.

In this moment of confused feeling and creeping luxurious languor she was glad of this diversion – glad of such an event as having her own diamonds to try on (p. 406).

She is struck down by Mrs Glasher's curse: her 'eyes were spell-bound'; a 'new spasm of terror' made her burn the paper; the diamonds rolled on the floor. 'She took no notice, but fell back in her chair again helpless.' She can no longer see her reflections in the multi-faceted mirror.

She sat so for a long while, knowing little more than that she was feeling ill, and that those written words kept repeating themselves in her.

'After that long while, there was a tap at the door and Grandcourt entered, dressed for dinner,' George Eliot continues.

The sight of him brought a new nervous shock, and Gwendolen screamed again and again with hysterical violence. He had expected to see her dressed and smiling, ready to be led down (p. 407).

We need not say that this scene 'stands for' the one that will be enacted later that evening between the husband and wife in order to feel that no modern novelist has told us more fully what the physical relationship between a particular man and woman is like. We know fully what sends Gwendolen down on her knees to Daniel Deronda. Underlying her adoption of the role of acolyte to his 'secular priesthood' is a frank analysis of the hysterical desire occasioned by sexual deprivation. George Eliot's treatment of it is quite open and uncompromising. What can match the sexual deprivation, what the intensity of hysteria, caused not by chastity but by enforced conjugal relations with a man for whom his wife felt only loathing? George Eliot struck this note again and again in her studies of mismating, as it is this which in a haunting form is freely re-enacted by Hardy's 'emancipated' woman Sue Bridehead.[70]

The equation between pathology and theology has been established; Gwendolen's guilt at having stepped into Mrs Glasher's place – the germ of her religious development – is brutally reinforced on her wedding night. The equation is maintained throughout by casting the theme of mismating in traditional apocalyptic animal imagery, the reptilian and beastly natures of Revelation.

George Eliot often worked in this unsparing spirit on her own creations, including her 'Saints of Humanity', Dorothea, Romola, and Daniel Deronda. This has been completely misconstrued by her critics. Leavis, telling us that 'the weakness' of *Middlemarch* is 'in Dorothea', glosses: 'We have the danger-signal in the very outset, in the brief "Prelude" with its reference to St. Teresa.'[71] Leavis is apparently unaware of the already long history of probing analyses of St Teresa's religious gift. We may recall Coleridge's physiological and psychological analyses of St Teresa (part of a Protestant debunking of Catholic phenomena):

Combine these causes only and you will see how almost impossible it was that a woman so innocent and so susceptible, of an imagination so lively by nature, and so fever-kindled by disease and its occasions, (and this so well furnished with the requisite images and pre-conceptions), should not mistake, and often, the less painful and in such a form the sometimes pleasurable approaches to bodily deliquium, and her imperfect fainting-fits, for divine transports and momentary union with God. Especially if, with a thoughtful yet pure psychology, you join the force of suppressed instincts stirring in the heart and bodily frame, of a mind unconscious of their nature, and these in the keenly sensitive body, in the innocent and loving soul of Teresa, with 'all her thirsts, and lives, and deaths of love', and what remains unsolved, for which the credulity of the many and the knavery of a few will not furnish ample explanation?[72]

George Eliot sets out carefully to create the temperamental prerequisites, the physical and psychic make-up, which given the right milieu and training could have led to the experiences of a Teresa. The inappropriateness of the image of the Catholic nun to the religious possibilities open to a citizen of *Middlemarch* serves to reveal the incongruity of Middlemarch with such a temperament, as before she had shown the 'fit' between Milby and evangelical experience. In ironic contrast to Dorothea's experiences with Casaubon and Ladislaw stands, distant but vividly notorious, Teresa's intercourse with Christ.

In Gwendolen, with her 'large discourse of imaginative fears', George Eliot approaches more boldly the nervous hysteria, the literal fainting-fits which form the basis of ecstatic religious experience of this kind. No more effective use has been made of the Gothic convention than in the fainting scene early in the novel, the first inkling of Gwendolen's nervous organization: George Eliot, as we would expect of her, returns not simply to Burke's formulation of the origin of the feeling of the sublime in elemental terror, but to Kant's mature version of this aesthetic doctrine in the third *Critique*, his grounding of religious awe in the feeling of fear. As George Eliot wrote in a review article,

Fear is earlier born than hope, lays a stronger grasp on man's system than any other passion, and remains master of a larger group of involuntary actions. A chief aspect of man's moral development is the slow subduing of fear by the gradual growth of intelligence, and its suppression as a motive by the presence of impulses, less animally selfish; so that in relation to invisible Power, fear at last ceases to exist, save in that interfusion with higher faculties which we call awe.[73]

This theme governs Gwendolen's development. The 'dread' of her wedding day modulates into the specific fear and need of retribution occasioned by a specific guilt. The central Christian doctrines depend on this complex of feeling. In the course of the novel, elemental fear is transmuted, not only into the Kantian 'sublime' but into the modern form of this analysis, the religious *Angst* of Kierkegaard, the experience of nothingness which for Gwendolen centres on the pallid face of her husband in imagined death.

The ill-effects of religious belief had already been a commonplace of Enlightenment medical practice, and had wide currency. The *Encyclopédie* naturally presents these views:

The intemperate impressions made by certain extravagant preachers, the excessive fears they inspire of the pains with which our religion threatens those who break its laws, produce astonishing revolutions in weak minds. At the hospital of Montelimar, several women were reported suffering from mania and melancholia as a result of a mission held in that city; these creatures were ceaselessly struck by the horrible images that had thoughtlessly been presented to them; they spoke of nothing but despair, revenge, punishment, etc., and one of them absolutely refused to undergo any cure, convinced that she was in Hell and that nothing could extinguish the fire she believed was devouring her.[74]

Sometimes religion was considered only as an element in the transmission of error, but, as Foucault has pointed out, 'there had been analyses of a more rigorous historical nature, in which religion appeared as a milieu of satisfaction or repression of the passions'.[75] This was particularly a German view: a strong religion was able to impose order, but

if, on the contrary, religion loosens its hold but maintains the ideal forms of remorse of conscience, of spiritual mortification, it leads directly to madness; only the consistency of the religious milieu can permit man to escape alienation in the excessive delirium of transgressions.[76]

Both these views agreed that 'religious beliefs prepare a kind of landscape of images, an illusory milieu favourable to every hallucination and every delirium'. For a literary analysis of a perfervid pietism one need look no further than Goethe's famous account of the 'schöne Seele' in *Wilhelm Meister*, in which ecstasy and irony are brilliantly balanced.

George Eliot presents just that milieu in which religion loosens its hold but maintains the ideal forms of conscience, a landscape of images in which hallucination and delirium flourish and assume both their social form of wayward passion and their private form of rootless devotion seeking new rites. It is the milieu that Thomas Mann isolated in *Der Zauberberg, The Magic Mountain.*

The relationship between Gwendolen and Daniel has all the earmarks of a liaison, and is seen throughout as such by a series of worldly observers, Sir Hugo Mallinger, Hans Meyrick, Lush, Grandcourt, and intermittently by Deronda himself. It passes through the conventional stages: their dramatic meeting over the gambling table; the reunion after her marriage to a man Deronda dislikes; their increasing interest in one another; their series of meetings in public places where they must dissemble that interest and signally fail to do so; the confrontation between the two women, first publicly, later privately; the arranged meeting to which the deceived but suspicious husband unexpectedly returns; the removal abroad to separate the wife from her lover; the coincidental meeting abroad, which indirectly leads to the husband's death; the full declaration; the gradual, painful parting over a long period; a final scene of revelation.

The emotional intensity of these meetings is unequalled in the English novel. It depends on the complexity of the structure formed by the continuous commentary of pathology and theology on one another. The conventional pattern of an *amour* is both relied upon and ironically criticized by comparing it with the greater power generated by the conjunction of sexual and metaphysical motive. Only the suffocating Protestant virginities of Richardson's *Shamela* generate analogous sexual power.

The maintenance of the equation between pathology and theology through every step of the affair with Daniel is aided by George Eliot's use of Renan, who in his *Life of Jesus* had already carried it into the central action of the Christian faith. Through the relationship of Daniel and Gwendolen, George Eliot recapitulates and refines Renan's critical and artistic enterprise in the *Life of Jesus*: the minute scrutiny of the 'psychological miracle' left unsolved by Strauss, the process whereby traditional messianic expectations came to be applied to a specific living man.

George Eliot had long been acquainted with Renan's work, and made the acquaintance of the man in Paris in 1866; her admiration for the early essays, however, the *Essais de morale et de critique* and the *Études d'histoire religieuse* which she and Lewes had read aloud to each other in 1859 and 1861 (the *Essais* she had reviewed favourably in 'Maga') gave way to disapprobation of the *Life of Jesus*, mingled with a somewhat grudging recognition of its compelling, essentially fictional interest. As Strauss's translator, her first response to the news of Renan's *Life of Jesus* was cool. It could have nothing to tell her:

Renan is a favourite with me. I feel more kinship with his mind than with that of any other living French author. But I think I shall not do more than look through the Introduction to his 'Vie de Jesus' – unless I happen to be more fascinated by the constructive part than I expect to be from the specimens I have seen. For minds acquainted with the European culture of this last half-century, Renan's book can furnish no new result; and they are likely to set little store by the too facile construction of a life from materials of which the biographical significance becomes more dubious as they are more closely examined.[77]

The rejection of the possibility of biography is of course in accordance with the tradition in which Strauss wrote. The letter continues in a Straussian vein:

It seems to me the soul of Christianity lies not at all in the facts of an individual life, but in the ideas of which that life was the meeting-point and the new starting-point. We can never have a satisfactory basis for the history of the man Jesus, but that negation does not affect the Idea of the Christ either in its historical influence or its great symbolic meanings. Still such books as Renan's have their value in helping the popular imagination to feel that the sacred past is of one woof with that human present which ought to be sacred too.[78]

It is, in short, illegitimate and impossible to attempt the life of Christ. This anti-biographical bias has a history in the German novel in particular. Hermann Hesse, in telling the story of the life of Joseph Knecht, the *Magister Ludi*, the Master of the Glass Bead Game, head of the cultural priesthood, wrote a long attack on the biographical and a justification of the legendary:

Wenn wir den Versuch machen, Knechts Leben nachzuzeichnen, so machen wir damit auch einen Versuch zu seiner Deutung, und wenn wir als Historiker es tief bedauern müssen, dass über den letzten Teil dieses Lebens beinahe alle wirklich verbürgten Nachrichten fehlen, so gab uns doch gerade der Umstand zu unserem Unternehmen Mut, dass dieser letzte Teil von

Knechts Leben Legende geworden ist. . .Wir gestehen sogar, dass das Entsch-
weben dieses Lebens in die Legende uns organisch und richtig scheint, so
wie uns das Fortbestehen eines Gestirns, das unsern Augen entschwindet und
für uns 'untergegangen' ist, keinerlei Glaubensskrupel schafft.[79]

In attempting to trace the course of Knecht's life we are also attempting to
interpret it, and although as historians we must deeply regret the scantiness
of authenticated information on the last period of his life, we were nevertheless encouraged to undertake the task precisely because this last part of
Knecht's life has become a legend. . . We go so far as to admit that the
manner in which his life drifts gently off into legend appears to us organic
and right, just as it imposes no strain on our credulity to believe in the continued existence of a constellation that has vanished below the horizon.[80]

We cannot doubt that George Eliot's intention was to bring the
history of Daniel Deronda up to the point where his life 'drifts gently
off into legend', as Romola did in her boat. Criticism of the 'vagueness'
of Deronda's Zionist mission is misplaced. Hesse says, 'we must not
forget that the writing of history – however dryly it is done and however sincere the desire for objectivity – remains literature. History's
third dimension is always fiction.'[81]

Daniel Deronda, of course, like Christ, is also outfitted with a
legendary birth and secret parentage; for the higher criticism held that
the life drifted off into legend, interpolated from Jewish tradition, at
its beginning as at its end. George Eliot, as she transformed a stock
'Gothic' mode into a critique of religion, transformed a romance
convention widely used in the Victorian novel into a legendary birth-
right, knowledge of which is Deronda's initiation into his vocation.

Yet George Eliot felt that one can trace in the present the same
human process which created and received a Christ, rendering the
past accessible and the present sacred. How was it to be done?

As one eminently well 'acquainted with the European culture of the
last half-century', she continued to be indifferent to the *Life of Jesus*,
as to other belated excursions into Biblical criticism by English authors
and public. She wrote to Sara Hennell,

And perhaps you have felt inclined, as I have, to be impatient at the 'fuss'
made about Renan's book, as well as Colenso's doings by an English public
which supposes that these men are finding out new heresies. However, such
impatience is unreasonable.[82]

Despite Renan's lack of originality, however (and Colenso's book on the Mosaic question is, however affecting from the point of view of his personal history, no more than the rankest provincial amateur might have penned in a lonely vicarage a hundred years previously), George Eliot did read the whole of Renan's *Life*, and had much the same mixed reaction as Browning, of condemnation and fascination:

I have read Renan's book, however, which has proved to be eminently in the public taste. It will have a good influence on the whole, I imagine; but this 'Vie de Jesus' and still more Renan's Letter to Berthelot in the Revue des Deux Mondes have compelled me to give up the high estimate I had formed of his mind. Judging from the indications in some other writings of his I had reckoned him amongst the finest thinkers of the time. Still his Life of Jesus has so much artistic merit that it will do a great deal towards the culture of ordinary minds by giving them a sense of unity between that far-off past and our present. I have witnessed this effect in our own Charlie, who is now reading Strauss on the strength of the interest which Renan created.[83]

Renan's 'artistic merit': George Eliot, like Browning, was drawn into the 'old enchanter's' net. Her own enterprise in *Daniel Deronda* was the Feuerbachian one of showing the roots of religion not in history but in the human psyche; yet Renan's account of the gradual stages by which the charming and duplicitous 'Oriental' came to an understanding of his mission has had a pervasive effect on the novel.

Renan presents in Jesus, despite the delicate, conciliating touches of his eloquent pen, something like a case history in the pathology of messianic claims. Those who have found Daniel Deronda merely priggish have misread George Eliot and will find enlightenment in Renan: for the very sensibility and receptivity that is the ground of Jesus's greatness is also a moral flaw which leads to his downfall. His impressionability, his willingness to be swayed form the basis for the concoction of a series of fraudulent miracles by Jesus's followers, in particular the Lazarus 'miracle', which Jesus does not himself plan, but permits to be made public. This psychological account is itself an advance on the blatant imposture theories of the eighteenth century; George Eliot refines it still further, eliminating altogether the publicly staged imposture dear to the French Enlightenment, but clearly delineating the elements of it in private personal imposture.

In Renan's account, Jesus's sensibility practises on itself as he becomes more and more persuaded of and possessed by the conviction of his divine mission, and, finally, divine origin. In the history of Daniel Deronda we have only the earliest stages, the pre-history of the messianic character, the organic basis on which the later condition might grow. Whatever remains of the crude, mechanistic rationalism of Renan's predecessors in his version of Jesus's Oriental malleability, his acquiescence in his disciples' machinations, his dependence on female susceptibilities, his obsession with his own mission is portrayed by George Eliot at its psychic threshold, as conversion is in 'Amos Barton', at its first most delicate implantation, almost before potentiality itself. She makes her own contribution to the long discussion as to the origins of Christianity and the course of the early life of Jesus: the creative influence of a personality works in the first instance without any conscious intention on its part, and begins to become conscious of itself through its observed effect on those around it. The disciples form their leader as he forms them. In Daniel's relations with others, especially Gwendolen, George Eliot renders both the nature of religious power of this kind and the duplicity to which such a character is subject. As in Lazarus, as in Jesus, the deluding of others is bound up with self-delusion. The widespread critical opinion that George Eliot presents a one-sided, overly idealized picture of Daniel Deronda could not be further from the mark. On the contrary, her critique of the religious sensibility of the proto-messianic Daniel Deronda is perhaps the most searching she ever made.

George Eliot is at pains to establish that Deronda's interest in Gwendolen is at all times the interest of a young man in an attractive woman. His interest is in no way rarefied, indeed it can be defined by popular adage: 'Whenever a marriage of any mark takes place, male acquaintances are likely to pity the bride, female acquaintances the bridegroom' (p. 456). Even while he evinces interest, however, he denies it. Partly these are public denials in response to the continued admonitions and innuendoes of Sir Hugo:

'I hope you are not playing with fire, Dan – you understand me.'
'I believe I do, sir,' said Deronda, after a slight hesitation, which had some repressed anger in it. 'But there is nothing answering to your metaphor – no fire, and therefore no chance of scorching.'
'So much the better. For between ourselves, I fancy there may be some hidden gunpowder in that establishment' (p. 510).

The pattern of interest and denials of interest governs his own inward attitude; the denials enable him to become more and more deeply entangled in the affair:

Undeniably Deronda's growing solicitude about Gwendolen depended chiefly on her peculiar manner towards him; and I suppose neither man nor woman would be the better for an utter insensibility to such appeals. One sign that his interest in her had changed its footing was that he dismissed any caution against her being a coquette setting snares to involve him in a vulgar flirtation, and determined that he would not again evade any opportunity of talking with her (p. 489).

His hypocritical refusal to admit to others or himself what is going on enables him to draw and to hold Gwendolen always more passionately to him. Deronda 'certainly did not avoid her; rather he wished to convince her by every delicate indirect means that her confidence in him had not been indiscreet, since it had not lowered his respect' (p. 647).

His hypocrisy, rising to self-delusion, enables him to engage directly and even recklessly with her. He permits himself to become completely absorbed and forgets where he is:

Deronda forgot everything but his vision of what Gwendolen's experience had probably been, and urged by compassion let his eyes and voice express as much interest as they would (p. 494).

George Eliot throughout emphasizes the beauty of his face; so seductive is it in the full bloom of interest that he succeeds in irritating Grandcourt by the mere act of taking off his hat. 'Gwendolen had slipped onto the music stool, and looked up at him with pain in her long eyes, like a wounded animal asking help' (p. 495). It is not surprising that Sir Hugo, observing this intense *tête-à-tête*, puts his hand on Deronda's shoulder 'with a gentle admonitory pinch'. His self-delusion is supported and fed by her view of him as he conceives it:

Sir Hugo's hints had made him alive to dangers that his own disposition might have neglected; but that Gwendolen's reliance on him was unvisited by any dream of his being a man who could misinterpret her was as manifest as morning, and made an appeal which wrestled with his sense of present dangers, and with his foreboding of a growing incompatible claim on him in her mind (p. 625).

George Eliot's irony at the expense of this hebraic humbug is implicit in 'manifest as morning'. For such a nature as Deronda's, the theological quality of her passion has an irresistible charm. Hans Meyrick, observing them from across a room, has no difficulty in identifying their conversation as 'a quarrel', adding, 'Oh, about theology, of course; nothing personal' (pp. 625–6).

Gwendolen's supporting view of him undergoes a crisis, classically in the confrontation with another woman. The tension between pathology and theology increases as the sexual relation rises to its highest pitch, and as the disparity threatens, the ironic view must be acknowledged, employed, and yet overcome. Grandcourt in his role of wronged husband imposes a vulgar recognition of the disparity and leads naturally to irony of the kind George Eliot indignantly rejected as peculiarly 'French'. His insinuation to Gwendolen that Mirah is of course Deronda's mistress leads to one of George Eliot's most brilliant solutions of the difficulty of maintaining the equation of theology and pathology throughout this romance. For a moment, through Gwendolen's own eyes, usually blinded with necessitous trust, we see Deronda in worldly terms as a deceiver and a humbug:

Deronda unlike what she had believed him to be, was an image which affected her as a hideous apparition would have done, quite apart from the way in which it was produced. It had taken hold of her as a pain before she could consider whether it were fiction or truth; and further to hinder her power of resistance came the sudden perception, how very slight were the grounds of her faith in Deronda – how little she knew of his life – how childish she had been in her confidence. His rebukes and his severity to her began to seem odious, along with all the poetry and lofty doctrine in the world, whatever it might be; and the grave beauty of his face seemed the most unpleasant mask that the common habits of men could put on (p. 650).

The scene of confrontation between the two women is a convention of amorous intrigue; but George Eliot's handling of it is beyond the range of any other English novelist. Simple jealousy of another woman and an abstract despair that the one good man might be like all the rest are perfectly blended, and conduce to the same end. The intensity of Gwendolen's desire that the good should not be untrue (though she has no claim) results in her complete vindication of Deronda, although the fact that he is actually in Mirah's house when she calls might rather seem a confirmation of Grandcourt's charge.

Deronda himself gradually comes to confirm his duplicity, though not in Grandcourt's terms. Only after Grandcourt's death and only after his full commitment to Mirah does he admit to himself that his relation to Gwendolen had been of the same kind:

Anyone who knows him cannot wonder at his inward confession, that if all this had happened little more than a year ago, he would hardly have asked himself whether he loved her: the impetuous determining impulse which would have moved him would have been to save her from sorrow, to shelter her life for evermore from the dangers of loneliness, and carry out to the last the rescue he had begun in that monitory redemption of the necklace (p. 835).

This passage alone is sufficient to prove how wholly inextricable the so-called 'two parts' of this novel are from one another.

In his last visits to Gwendolen, not able to bring himself to confess to her, he still maintains his old duplicitous relationship. He continues to hold out to her only 'the hardness of easy consolation', yet 'Any one overhearing his tones would have thought he was entreating for his own happiness' (p. 839). This sums up his behaviour throughout; he has seemed to answer her need, while only increasing it. Finally, after three visits to Offendene in full consciousness of his fault, he tells her the truth. Throughout, her impulse has been to go down on her knees to him; now he goes down on his knees to her. She blames herself, her habitual gesture; she has been a cruel woman and deserves at last to be forsaken. He confesses that he too has been cruel: and the confession has the more weight for being uncharacteristic. The price of his tenderness was cruel deception and a pervasive self-deception. At the same time, this final exchange, this final symmetry in their relationship, is the confirmation of the I–thou bond; and on this duplicity depends the modulation, for both of them, from the amorous to the religious experience. Deronda is not 'likeable'; no more than Will Ladislaw is he meant to be 'satisfactory' or (as Raymond Williams has put it) 'one of us'.

This streak of ardent hypocrisy and tender cruelty does not exhaust Renan's contribution to the 'Oriental' Deronda. From boyhood, his appearance is slightly exotic:

He wore an embroidered holland blouse which set off the rich colouring of his head and throat, and the resistant gravity about his mouth and eyes as he was being smiled upon, made their beauty the more impressive (p. 207).

This same appearance, in young manhood, causes Grandcourt in a fit of jealous pique to pronounce him a '*fat*', fop (p. 475). As he dances with old Lady Pentreath, 'her partner's young richness of tint against the flattened hues and rougher forms of her aged head had an effect something like that of a fine flower against a lichenous branch' (p. 497). George Eliot is giving us a portrait of Semitic beauty to set beside her portrait of Tito's Greek beauty in *Romola*, and the parallel extends further, for Tito's tragic enmeshment is an ironic commentary on Greek heroism, as well as on the history of post-Renaissance Graeco-philia.

The sensuous grace of Renan's Jesus stands behind Deronda, and, behind the Jesus, Renan's celebrated conception of Celtic poetry, whose character he identified with that of early Christianity. Renan had no sympathy with Jewish mythology – as a Catholic, he found monotheism arid, unimaginative, forced to resort to 'miracle', the harsh intervention in, and suspension of, natural process; and as we have seen, he considered Jewish mythology in any case unable to account for the character of early Christianity. In the Celts, on the contrary, he found the true spirit of the poetry of primitive races, legendary, marvellous, the spirit of all religions at their birth:

Peu de races ont eu une enfance poétique aussi complète que les races celtiques: mythologie, lyrisme, épopée, imagination romanesque, enthousi-asme religieux, rien ne leur a manqué.[84]

Arnold, following Renan in his essay 'On the Study of Celtic Liter-ature', which, like George Eliot's novel, attempted to broaden the range of temperament available to the English nation, found that the supremely Celtic quality is 'to react against the despotism of fact'. Underlying Deronda's sensibility is this conception of the Celtic race, 'une race essentiellement feminine':

Aucune famille humaine, je crois, n'a porté dans l'amour autant de mystère. Nulle autre n'a conçu avec plus de delicatesse l'idéal de la femme et n'en a été plus dominée. C'est une sorte d'enivrement, une folie, un vertige.[85]

The woman as conceived by chivalry, he says, 'cet idéal de douceur et de beauté posé comme but suprême de la vie, – n'est une creation ni classique, ni chrétienne, ni germanique, mais bien réellement celtique'. In this set of identifications, so curious in itself yet so typical of the

accomplished syncretism of the nineteenth century, we must understand Deronda. Those who have been mystified and annoyed by the
contrast between their conception of religious leadership in the heroic
mould and the character of Daniel Deronda would do well to consult
not only Renan but the vast literature standing behind his *Life of Jesus*
before they attribute what seems to them the 'effeminacy' of Deronda
simply to George Eliot's own sex. Leavis might as well have said of
Renan's Jesus what he said of George Eliot's Deronda: 'He, decidedly,
is a woman's creation.'[86]

Renan wrote not a little on normal and abnormal religious psychology. George Eliot thought that Renan, like herself, could be
characterized by the combination of 'science' and 'faith', and this is the
main tenor of Frazer's eulogy on Renan in 1923. Frazer's own work,
of course, goes back to the levelling of Christianity to fertility cults
that was such a feature of eighteenth-century critiques of religion. As
Renan himself put it in his eulogy on Claude Bernard, whom he
succeeded in the Academy in 1870: 'The triumph of science is in
reality the triumph of idealism.' Arnold carried this note into his *St.
Paul and Protestantism*:

To popular religion, the real kingdom of God is the New Jerusalem with its
jaspers and emeralds; righteousness and peace and joy are only the kingdom
of God figuratively. . .Science exactly reverses this process. For science, the
spiritual notion is the real one, the material notion is figurative.[87]

The blend of scientific debunking and piety was translated into the
psychological sphere. Like William James, Renan insisted on the
importance of the illusion whose sources he laid bare. In the *Nouvelles
Études*, he included a pathological study of the medieval saint Christina
of Stommeln, whose piety is traced to her mental disturbance. Martyrs
are dupes of their bodies. This is not a disgrace, just as the origin of the
idea of Christ's resurrection in the Magdalen's hysterical sexuality does
not lessen its importance; he wished simply to search out the unconscious roots of religion.

Elements of Renan's own sexual pathology had found their way
into his Jesus, and are reflected in Deronda. The relationship between
Daniel and Gwendolen owes much to Renan's description of Jesus's
attraction for his feminine followers. Renan found it possible not only
to compare himself to St Francis, but to identify with Jesus. The *Life*

was written during an archaeological expedition to Byblos, which gave Renan the opportunity to retrace Jesus's steps through Palestine. Accompanied by his wife and his sister Henriette, with whom he had a (spiritually) incestuous relationship, he traversed the Holy Land, conceiving the pastoral of the young Jesus at Lake Gennasareth which is one of the most distinctive aspects of the *Life*, and remarking at Jerusalem that the past was 'translucid at every step'.[88]

Renan felt there was a distinct parallel between Jesus's relation to his female disciples and his own. The susceptibility of women to Jesus in the *Life* (and his to them) is noteworthy. They form the inner circle of his disciples, and in the celebrated passage already quoted, the Magdalen's passionate ravings at the tomb (a note Gwendolen often approaches) are responsible for the rumour that Jesus had risen. Renan is poised between ridicule, scientific analysis of the sources of religious experience, and self-gratifying autobiography.

In his essay on Feuerbach, he protested against Feuerbach's German Hellenism and defended the abnormal spirituality of Christian art:

Castor and Pollux, Diana and Minerva are to us cold images, because they represent nature in its healthy and normal state. Yet we must be on our guard: these grand airs of abstention and sacrifice are often only a refinement of instincts which feed on their opposite qualities. Christian spiritualism is, at bottom, much more sensual than what is called the materialism of antiquity, and sometimes resembles weakness.[89]

The relations of Jesus and his female followers in the *Life*, then, offer Renan an ideal aesthetic portrait of the sensuality of Christianity: the allure of chastity. It is the Greeks, he holds, who have the true chastity, and he contrasts a figure in the Vatican Museum, 'an antique Modesty, half nude, but veiled by its severe beauty' with a figure in the chapel Della Pietà de Sangri in Naples. 'A *Pudiciʒia* covered with a long veil, which clings to her whole person in a manner to suggest beneath the marble folds, the form rendered more seductive by mystery.'[90] Christian chastity, then, is specifically unchaste; for Renan, it is sensual, and this speaks in its favour. To him, the nun is the expression of female sexuality. In *L'Antéchrist*, recounting the charms that the Christian virgin martyrs had for Nero, he goes so far as to say that the 'charming paradox' of Nero's aesthetic rests on the principle that 'la pudeur est une volupté'; and this is 'the love-philtre of Christianity'.[91]

Arnold, despite his admiration for Renan, was led to say that Renan did his devotions before that typical French idol, Aselgeia, goddess of Lubricity.

George Eliot hardly shared Renan's real perversity, and her Deronda, as befits Jewish tradition, is presented as frankly heterosexual, both in his flirtation with Gwendolen and in his engagement to Mirah. Nevertheless, Daniel Deronda has just this trait of aesthetic *pudeur* that allures and maddens and does not, cannot satisfy ordinary sexuality; this is one source of his spiritual power, of whose nature he is as yet only half-conscious. We cannot doubt that George Eliot believed with Renan that female sexuality flourished in the religious and especially the Christian context (if only because there it was in some sort condoned and encouraged). Renan supplied her with the missing link: the male sexuality of Christianity that was the counterpart and the occasion of female sexual religiosity. Like Renan, she affirms it, although she takes it out of the context of Catholic aestheticism, and places it in the English context of hebraic puritan hypocrisy. But surely here we have one of the main sources of readers' uncomfortable feelings about Daniel Deronda. He is a Christ debunked, in terms looking forward to Freud. Yet rightly understood, this should cause the modern reader no discomfort. For George Eliot, exposure and espousal of the sexual sources of religious feeling and action was explicitly demanded by her Feuerbachian formula.

The climax of all these themes occurs in the scene of Gwendolen's confession to Daniel of her part in Grandcourt's death. This is the most intense of their encounters because now the husband who has stood between them is gone. The theme of gambling which has from the opening scene dominated George Eliot's description of a society in which one man's gain is another man's loss is replaced by a gamble of mutuality in which the religious myth of moral responsibility is adopted by both parties in relation to one another.

George Eliot establishes the whole basis of the scene as mythical in the sense of Strauss. The spiritual enactment depends on the ambiguity as to the nature of witnessed event that we have become accustomed to in the broader application of the higher critical attempts to justify the Christian story. As Barthes has said, 'The teleology common to the Novel and to narrated History is the alienation of the facts.'[92]

What part did Gwendolen play in Grandcourt's death? and how is it to be judged? Very little was known about the accident. The nearest eyewitnesses were some fishermen at a distance – and Gwendolen herself.

Meanwhile, he [Deronda] employed himself in getting a formal, legally-recognised statement from the fishermen who had rescued Gwendolen. Few details came to light. The boat in which Grandcourt had gone out had been found drifting with its sail loose, and had been towed in. The fishermen thought it likely that he had been knocked overboard by the flapping of the sail while putting about, and that he had not known how to swim; but though they were near their attention had been first arrested by a cry which seemed like that of a man in distress, and while they were hastening with their oars, they heard a shriek from the lady, and saw her jump in (p. 752).

She had wished him dead, never more than on that day when she had seen Deronda again; and it came to pass: 'I only know that I saw my wish outside me.'

I saw him sink, and my heart gave a leap as if it were going out of me. I think I did not move. I kept my hands tight. It was long enough for me to be glad and yet to think it was no use – he would come up again. And he was come – farther off – the boat had moved. It was all like lightning. 'The rope!' he called out in a voice – not his own – I hear it now – and I stooped for the rope – I felt I must – I felt sure he could swim and he would come back whether or not, and I dreaded him. That was in my mind – he would come back. But he was gone down again, and I had the rope in my hand – no, there he was again – his face above the water – and he cried again – and I held my hand and my heart said, 'Die!' – and he sank; and I felt 'It is done – I am wicked, I am lost!' – and I had the rope in my hand – I don't know what I thought – I was leaping away from myself – I would have saved him then. I was leaping from my crime, and there it was – close to me as I fell – there was the dead face – dead, dead. It can never be altered. That was what happened. That was what I did. You know it all. It can never be altered (p. 761).

What do we learn from this account? Did she jump in to save him, or to save herself from having to throw him the line? He came up twice, and both times he cried out, the first time she stooped for the rope, the second she held her hand, did not throw the rope. He sank; she jumped. One cannot know whether throwing him the line would have helped;

277

but it appears that she delayed in giving him what both regarded as the means to salvation. But this eyewitness report is not decisive. All that is decisive is the construction she places on it based on her knowledge of her own wishes. She has a visionary experience of her own guilt. The facts are forever unclear; the imaginative interpretation is firm. This is the more powerful because, unlike in Lord Jim's long leap from the deck of the 'Patna', we already know, and feel we know, everything about Gwendolen that we need to resolve the question. Deronda believes it 'almost certain that her murderous thought had had no outward effect'. At the same time he judges the desire as if it were the act. And he accounts her remorse more valuable than her probable innocence.

Her visionary experience of guilt and his response to it are governed by their previous relationship. His ethical demands on her give rise to her assumption of guilt; her emotional demands on him lead him beyond his own ethical position. At the beginning of the scene, before having told him the story, Gwendolen, 'sheathed in a white shawl, her face and neck not less white, except for a purple line under her eyes', had asked him not to forsake her. The analogy with Jesus is stressed, in that he accepts moral responsibility for a future of as yet unidentified crimes, and suffers in so doing:

Deronda could not answer; he was obliged to look away. He took one of her hands, and clasped it as if they were going to walk together like two children: it was the only way in which he could answer, 'I will not forsake you'. And all the while he felt as if he were putting his name to a blank paper which might be filled up terribly. Their attitude, his averted face with its expression of a suffering which he was solemnly resolved to undergo, might have told half the truth of the situation to a beholder who had suddenly entered (p. 755).

For her part – and the analogy with the Magdalen is inescapable here – and so is the difference from the vulgarity of Renan's pathology –

That grasp was an entirely new experience to Gwendolen: she had never before had from any man a sign of tenderness which her own being had needed, and she interpreted its powerful effect on her into a promise of inexhaustible patience and constancy.

Again there is a meeting of their eyes which carries the full weight of their relationship:

But his eyes met hers sorrowfully – met hers for the first time fully since she had said, 'You know I am a guilty woman;' and that full glance in its intense mournfulness seemed to say, 'I know it, but I shall all the less forsake you' (p. 759).

The resemblance to 'the man of sorrow' grows stronger, and indeed, 'Gwendolen was pierced, as she had been by his face of sorrow at the Abbey with a compunction less egoistic than that which urged her to confess.'

Fully to understand the transformation that Daniel undergoes in this scene we must recall the nature of the injunctions he has, under pressure of Gwendolen's demands, laid upon her in the past. He had said to her:

Take your fear as a safeguard. It is like quickness of hearing. It may make consequences passionately present to you. Try to take hold of your sensibility, and use it as if it were a faculty, like vision (p. 509).

This injunction, which guided the romantic conflation of the poetic and prophetic roles, is a characteristic move in the post-Kantian attempt to break down the strict limits Kant had placed on the employment of the reason. For Kant, neither sensibility nor vision could be a faculty. Hegel among others drew a parallel between Kantian ethics based on reason and Old Testament legalism. To overcome this rigidity, the far reaches of the organization of man, his elemental sensibility and his visionary capacity, must be brought back into a structure of the faculties. This is at once an acceptance of Kantian limits and an attempt to bring back some part of what he had excluded into his account of the possibilities of human experience. We know Coleridge's lifelong attempts to do this. And we know from his attempts the pathos and the terror of this impossible voluntarism whereby control of the involuntary becomes a moral imperative whose necessary failure is a scourge to the conscience. But this is exactly what Daniel enjoined on Gwendolen, and she in her innocent unregeneracy confronted him with the impossibility:

'But if feelings rose – there are some feelings – hatred and anger – how can I be good when they keep rising? And if there came a moment when I felt stifled and could bear it no longer –' She broke off, and with agitated lips looked at Deronda, but the expression on his face pierced her with an entirely new feeling. He was under the baffling difficulty of discerning, that what he had been urging on her was thrown into the pallid distance of mere thought before the outburst of her habitual emotion. It was as if he saw her drowning while his limbs were bound.

But through his emotion Gwendolen suddenly grasped the impossibility as the possibility:

The pained compassion which was spread over his features as he watched her affected her with a compunction unlike any she had felt before, and in a changed imploring tone she said – 'I am grieving you. I am ungrateful. You *can* help me. I will think of everything. I will try. Tell me – it will not be a pain to you that I have dared to speak of my trouble to you? You began it, you know, when you rebuked me.' There was a melancholy smile on her lips as she said that but she added more entreatingly, 'It will not be a pain to you?' 'Not if it does anything to save you from an evil to come,' said Deronda, with strong emphasis; 'otherwise, it will be a lasting pain.'

He took her pain on himself, but only in the form of a threat. George Eliot's attempt to give the prehistory of Christian consciousness is immensely effective here. The imperative form and the sacrificial content of his prevision of unspecified offences stands exactly between the Old and the New Testaments. That prehistory moves a step forward as Gwendolen replies, ' "No – no – it shall not be. It may be – it shall be better with me because I have known you." She turned immediately, and quitted the room' (pp. 758–9).

The parallel drawn by Hegel and others between Kantian ethics and Old Testament legalism rendered this attempt to incorporate vision within the bounds of human faculties parallel to the movement in the early Christian period towards a Christian interpretation of the history of Jesus. Thus in the scene following Grandcourt's death, Daniel arrives for the first time at his vocation:

He was completely unmanned. Instead of finding, as he had imagined, that his late experience had dulled his susceptibility to fresh emotion, it seemed that the lot of this young creature, whose swift travel from her bright rash girlhood into this agony of remorse he had had to behold in helplessness, pierced him the deeper because it came close upon another sad revelation of spiritual conflict: he was in one of those moments when the very anguish of passionate pity makes us ready to choose that we will know pleasure no more, and live only for the stricken and afflicted (p. 762).

Deronda now, instead of manufacturing ethical advice and issuing imperatives backed by threats (not the least of which is the withdrawal of his own presence), moves to acceptance of a messianic role conceived in Christian terms. The recurrent use of images of 'piercing' in this chapter rises to its climax as George Eliot gives us her version of the crucifixion, moralized after the manner of Kant. For Kant, Jesus is 'the Archetype of Humanity', and crucifixion represents the willing assumption of moral responsibility for one's own evil; for George Eliot, adopting the fraternal imagery of the cabbala and the revolutionary egalitarianism of Feuerbach's I–thou, it is the mutual assumption of moral responsibility for each other's evil. And indeed, in this crucifixion of human feeling, Daniel and Gwendolen now exchange places, as he takes on her guilt and she crucifies herself. The imagery of piercing is now attached not to him but to her (community of imagery is characteristic of the novel). This exchange is the climax of the I–Thou relationship in which they are united:

Deronda could not utter one word to diminish that sacred aversion to her worst self – that thorn-pressure which must come with the crowning of the sorrowful Better, suffering because of the Worse (p. 762).

They are each other's master, each other's disciple. The early non-institutional history of religious movement is complete. The inward experience is non-factual but real, it is a myth based on an experience capable of being universalized and capable also of developing into a sectarian dogma.

Strauss and Feuerbach are equally important here, Strauss in understanding religious experience as myth, Feuerbach in understanding the unity of man to reside not in the solitary ego but in the species-being, in the sexual man and woman taken as one. Renan is important too, but in the negative sense that his early life of Jesus is corrected and rewritten in accordance with a deeper grasp of the principles of the higher criticism and a novelist's power of searching out the intricacies of mutual dependence. How newly we now understand the 'acquiescence' of Jesus in the demands of his disciples, seen by Renan as 'Oriental' weakness and guile. No novelist in English has matched these passages in George Eliot; none has her intellectual grasp and none her ability to make these movements of thought live in art – which, in its own view, was the highest act of apologetics of which the nineteenth century was capable.

The gambling imagery has now modulated into a new religious context. The Pascalian wager on the probability of the existence of God receives a more extreme and paradoxical formulation in the nineteenth century: the gamble of faith is a gamble on an impossibility. Kierkegaard of course formulated this most completely. But the outlines of the religious dilemmas of the nineteenth century are clear in *Daniel Deronda*: the premises are atheistic; the assumption of moral responsibility is a myth; belief in the myth is an unmitigated good. Gwendolen's victory at Mrs Glasher's expense becomes the groundwork of her moral gamble on embracing the guilt for her husband's death, which on one level is to relinquish her ill-gotten gain, on another, a transcendence of the worldly terms of the original transaction. Moreover, the power of the myth is affirmed, in that although Gwendolen's certainty of guilt is a compulsion for her, for Deronda it is evident that she has made a moral choice. Both are possible because she has been struggling in moral terms. The freedom of the will (on which the assumption of moral responsibility is based) is the central myth of our civilization, as Coleridge had seen in his last writings. The myth is reaffirmed in full knowledge that the gamble is on an impossibility. By embracing the terminology of belief despite its falsehood, the empty gaming of life in which every gain is at the expense of others is transformed into a gamble on faith such that all may gain. George Eliot still preserves a sense of development, of *Bildung*, of gradual transition from the gambling of this world to the gamble on faith. Yet the gamble is presented in the imagery of death by drowning, and even of the Kierkegaardian 'leap'. Theology and pathology are united in this central experience, the culmination of the book's endeavour to present their equation.

In her attempt to bring East and West together in a quasi-historical quasi-psychological synthesis, George Eliot was one in the line of thinkers and poets who attempted to analyse the relation of European to Greek culture, of both to the Orient, and of the ancients to the moderns. As the Germans tried to grasp the character of a modern Germany by a series of comparisons with other civilizations, so George Eliot tried to create a modern English religious culture.

In one of their aspects, of course, Deronda and Gwendolen represent Jew and Christian, and the physical and temperamental opposition is stressed: she the Nordic, the cool, the 'Water-nixie' of 'The Lifted Veil' (a reference, surely, to Fouqué's celebrated story *Undine*, the mermaid who sought a human soul through suffering); he the Oriental, with a dark liquidity, a patriarchal gravity. George Eliot wishes to present the characters, Jewish and Christian, that were at the basis of religious experience in her culture; in the symbolic contrasts and similitudes of physical forms and cultural natures again we have a tradition deep-rooted in German literature down to Hesse and Mann. As she points a contrast, so she points out specific affinities of the English nation with the Jewish nation. The connections are not only on the basis of a shared religious experience at the root of both religions, but on the basis of national characteristics and experiences in modern times.

In *The Impressions of Theophrastus Such*, she wrote,

Every nation of forcible character – i.e., of strongly marked characteristics, is so far exceptional. The distinctive note of each bird-species is in this sense exceptional, but the necessary ground of such distinction is a deeper likeness. The superlative peculiarity in the Jews admitted, our affinity with them is only the more apparent when the elements of their peculiarity are discerned.[93]

What are the affinities of the English with the Jews? Like them, with their

sense of corporate existence, unique in its intensity, – it has been held that we have a peculiar destiny as a Protestant people, not only able to bruise the head of an idolatrous Christianity in the midst of us, but fitted as possessors of the most truth, and the most tonnage to carry our purer religion over the world and convert mankind to our way of thinking.

It is between the Puritans and the Jews that she makes the strongest links. The Puritans assert 'their liberty to restrain tyrants' on the basis of the Hebrew scriptures themselves, 'equal in arrogance, resistance to oppression, and self-confidence of supreme moral value'. It is, then, on this Arnoldian analysis of the 'Hebraism' of the English that George Eliot founds her claim of the 'affinities of disposition between our own race and the Jewish'.[94]

George Eliot, of course, did not share Renan's views of Jewish mythology; following the Tübingen school, she stressed the continuity of Jewish mythology (through the Old Testament prophetic character of Mordecai) and in effect defended it against Renan's charges by attributing to it in the person of the Jew Deronda just those qualities which Renan attributes to Celtic mythology and to his Celtic Jesus. She thus accomplishes one of her ends: the welding of the Jewish mythological and the early Christian character. Daniel's character represents that transitional Jewish character out of which Christianity – over a period of centuries – arose, just that period of flux and growth that Renan himself (like so many of the Biblical critics) described: his *Origines* stopped short at the death of Marcus Aurelius because, as he said, after that there was no longer a history of the religious spirit of a people to write, but only ecclesiastical history. There is, of course, an ambiguity here, in that Daniel has actually been given the upbringing of a Christian gentleman; but this emphasizes that her aim is not to relate the rise of Christianity, but to describe what it would be like to grasp these roots again from the point of view of the present.

From this point of view, Daniel and Gwendolen come to represent this welding. The match between Mirah and Daniel seems unsatisfactory, for it is a formal accreditation of what he learns through his affair with Gwendolen. It is with England, after all, that Deronda is as a youth most engaged; it is in intimate alliance with England that he learns to measure his strength and to see where it leads him, just as one might say that Christ's religion finds its role only when Paul has taken it to the Gentiles.

Yet George Eliot's concern was not to defend the Judaic or the Hebraic; Knoepflmacher misunderstands both George Eliot and Arnold in exaggerating their attachment to Hebraism on the basis simply of Arnold's famous dictum that 'conduct is three-fourths of life' and the sheer quantity of Jewish matter in *Daniel Deronda*. More than twenty-five years earlier George Eliot had been able to write:

The fellowship of race, to which D'Israeli so exultingly refers the munificence of Sidonia, is so evidently an inferior impulse, which must ultimately be superseded, that I wonder even he, Jew as he is, dares to boast it. My Gentile nature kicks most resolutely against any assumption of superiority in the Jews, and is almost ready to echo Voltaire's vituperation. I bow to the supremacy of Hebrew poetry, but much of their early mythology, and almost all their history, is utterly revolting, Their stock has produced a Moses and a Jesus; but Moses was impregnated with Egyptian philosophy, and Jesus is venerated and adored by us only for that wherein He transcended or resisted Judaism. The very exaltation of their idea of a national deity into a spiritual monotheism seems to have been borrowed from the other oriental tribes. Everything specifically Jewish is of a low grade.[95]

This was in the context of her contempt for Disraeli's novels, and in defending the character Mordecai to Blackwood she still proudly disclaimed the ability to produce a Sidonia. But we can trace this view in the synthesis she attempts in *Daniel Deronda*: for finally she wishes to present a Judaism impregnated with the ideas of other Oriental tribes, and as altered by early Christian experience. It is to the fusion of cultures at the crucial moment of the formation of European Christianity that she, like Coleridge, wished to point, though for her it was the moment of first fusion, not the period of full, systematic, neo-platonic assessment.

Arnold called for a return to the Orientalizing style of St Paul, an abandonment of the weak hebraizing element in his thought which has been rigidly legalized by the philistine Puritan, who 'reserved all his imagination for Hell and the New Jerusalem'.[96] We should construe Paul's Oriental language for what it is, 'the vivid and figured ways' of conveying Jesus's words 'within the sphere of religious emotion':

The figured speech of Paul has its own beauty and propriety. His language is, much of it, eastern language, imaginative language; there is no need for turning it, as Puritanism has done, into the methodical language of the schools. But if it is to be turned into methodical language, then it is the language into which we have translated it that translates it truly.[97]

Arnold, then, in accordance with the higher critical revision of conceptions of 'Oriental' primitivism, values the imaginative language of religious emotion for itself; he does not refrain, however, from translating it, if not, as Augustine did, into 'the formal propositions of western dialectics', then into the language of a rationalized, humane morality.

Arnold, as *God and the Bible* shows, was not a good Biblical critic; he
was not only derivative, but slack and fanciful, relying too much on
considerations of style and 'moral' translations. George Eliot, on the
contrary, though no more original, by her very quality of fidelity to
her masters, was well-grounded, weighty, and succeeded in making
a real transference of their leading ideas into an imaginative mode
which could fairly be called the Orientalizing style of modern religious
experience.

The style of *Daniel Deronda* seems to have been completely misunderstood, even by such a helpful and sensible critic of George Eliot
as W. J. Harvey. He complains of the 'far-fetched irrelevancies' of the
metaphorical style of the late works, especially *Daniel Deronda*. He
especially singles out for adverse criticism a passage in the last book of
the novel, 'Fruit and Seed', describing the inward state of Rex (Gwendolen's rejected suitor):

In Rex's well-endowed nature, brief as the hope had been, the passionate
stirring had gone deep, and the effect of disappointment was revolutionary,
though fraught with a beneficent new order which retained most of the old
virtues: in certain respects he believed that it had finally determined the bias
and colour of his life. Now, however, it seemed that his inward peace was
hardly more stable than that of republican Florence, and his heart no better
than the alarm-bell that made work slack and tumult busy (p. 777).

Harvey particularly objects to the reference to 'republican Florence'.
Yet this passage states in little the theme of the novel: the establishment
of that modern temper in which 'the effect of disappointment was
revolutionary though fraught with a beneficent order which retained
most of the old virtues'; and it epitomizes the form of the novel in its
movement from individual psychology to the community. Moreover,
this is a time-honoured comparison between macrocosm and microcosm, platonic in origin, and here appropriately translated to the main
traditional, literary context of the novel, Dante's *Commedia*. There is
constant reference to Dante throughout the book, both in chapter
headings and in the text. Her use of extended comparisons which lead
out of the immediate context and are wholly just and apposite in the
fuller context is simply a use of epic simile; it represents her adaptation
of Dante's own use of simile to the demands of prose. Indeed, one
might say that the use of this central theme to illuminate the state of

mind of a minor character is just the 'organic', Shakespearean use of imagery pointed out by a series of romantic critics from Herder onwards. The reference to Florence, of course, points also to the geographical span of this novel, which accomplishes in prose what Hölderlin did in poetry. George Eliot grounds her geographical and temporal witchery on the history of the Diaspora. The encounter of Daniel and Gwendolen at Leubronn and again at Genoa, or Daniel and Joseph Kalonymos in Frankfurt, are not coincidental, but are based on the historical experience by which the Spanish, the Italian, and the German, and the learned 'Arab' Jews are linked, the geography of the carriage of eastern experience into modern Europe. They are succinctly expressed in the fact that 'Deronda' as well as 'Charisi' is the family name – and 'Halm-Eberstein' by marriage. There can be little doubt that George Eliot regarded this novel as her *Divina Commedia*, her religious epic, her cultural *summa*, as Dante had made the internecine squabbles of Florence the vehicle of political order and religious illumination.

It is worth noticing that Hesse refers the intricacies of the glass bead game, the highest art of the cultural mystery of his hieratic élite, back to Albrecht Bengel's interpretation of the Book of Revelation. Bengel hoped ' "in einem enzyklopädischen Werk alles Wissen seiner Zeit symmetrisch und synoptisch auf Zentrum hin zu ordnen und zusammenzufassen. Das ist nichts andres, als was das Glasperlenspiel auch tut." '[98] Bengel hoped ' "to arrange and sum up all the knowledge of his time symmetrically and synoptically around a central idea. This is precisely what the Glass Bead Game does." '[99]

The conversation between Knecht and Father Jacobus pursues the matter of Bengel and of 'organic order':

'Es ist der enzyklopädische Gedanke, mit dem das ganze achtzehnte Jahrhundert gespielt hat', rief der Pater.

'Er ist es', meinte Josef, 'aber Bengel hat nicht bloss ein Nebeneinander der Wissens- und Forschungsgebiete angestrebt, sondern ein Ineinander, eine organische Ordnung, er was unterwegs auf der Suche nach dem Generalnenner. Und das ist einer der elementaren Gedanken des Glasperlenspiels. Und ich möchte noch mehr behaupten, nämlich: Wäre Bengel im Besitz eines ähnlichen Systems gewesen, wie unser Spiel eines ist, so wäre ihm wahrscheinlich der grosse Irrweg mit seiner Umrechnung der prophetischen Zahlen und seiner Verkündigung des Antichrist und des Tausendjährigen

Reiches erspart geblieben. Bengel fand für die verschiedenen Begabungen, die er in sich vereinigte, die ersehnte Richtung auf ein gemeinsames Ziel nicht ganz, und so ergab seine mathematische Begabung, in der Zusammenarbeit mit seinem Philologenscharfsinn, jene wunderlich aus Akribie und Phantastik gemischte "Zeiten-Ordnung", die ihn so manche Jahre beschäftigt hat.'[100]

'After all, the whole eighteenth century toyed with the encyclopedic idea,' Father Jacobus protested. 'So it did,' Joseph agreed. 'But what Bengel meant was not just a juxtaposition of the field of knowledge and research, but an interrelationship, an organic denominator. And that is one of the basic ideas of the Glass Bead Game. In fact, I would go further in my claims: if Bengel had possessed a system similar to that offered by our Game, he probably would have been spared all the misguided effort involved in his calculation of the prophetic numbers and his annunciation of the Antichrist and the Millennial Kingdom. Bengel did not quite find what he longed for: the way to channel all his various talents toward a single goal. Instead his mathematical gifts in association with his philological bent produced that weird blend of pedantry and wild imagination, the "order of the ages," which occupied him for so many years.'

George Eliot attempted to do with a secularized but wholly public myth what Hölderlin did with his private revelations and Hesse with his hieratic, supra-public 'Castalian' élite: create a unique product of the encyclopaedic knowledge of the whole culture, a modern epic.

Arnold attempted in *Culture and Anarchy* to temper English Hebraism not with Orientalism but with 'Hellenism'. The syncretic patterning of his own poetry has not been estimated at its true value. But Arnold's Hellenism was Greek in the style of Winckelmann; George Eliot's, like Hölderlin's, is rather a version of Orientalism which more readily permits the alliance of Judaic, Greek, and Christian culture. Knoepflmacher is wrong in claiming George Eliot's and Arnold's ideas of culture to be 'identical'. George Eliot's 'Hellenism' – the 'Oriental' susceptibility, receptivity, the 'negative capability' of romantic poetry – she brilliantly locates not only in the 'Oriental' Jews, but in the 'hebraic' English. And it is here she successfully makes the synthesis that Arnold failed to achieve.

For, as she portrays them, these are the qualities not simply of the receptive primitive translating his hopes and fears into divine promises and threats, but the qualities of the cultivated, the gentle life; the qualities making for the civilized brilliancies of English social life (never better rendered than in this novel, not for their own sake, but for the sake of these complex themes). They have an intense attractiveness, a kind of vividness united with languor – the draperies of women, the shade of sun upon green grass at the archery meeting and the 'feast of sunset lights' along the glades, the sleek flanks of thoroughbreds, the ancient Abbey, the musical evening at Lady Mallinger's ('all white, gold, and crimson'), – which in the attempt to draw a parallel within the English scene to the Oriental susceptibilities of Daniel brings George Eliot closer than anyone, even Henry James, to defining that character in English social life that has so enchanted, mesmerized, and duped alien observers. What Jane Austen achieved through provincial instinct, 'that sense of special belonging' which George Eliot agreed was 'the root of human virtues, both public and private', George Eliot herself achieved through a difficult and indirect nostalgia for 'Loamshire' and a long-suffered and hard-won cosmo-politan intellectual empathy. It is not thereby 'better'; but it is the process of *Bildung* completed, the primitive rootedness brought out fully into consciousness. Loamshire makes place for Sion.

Gwendolen is George Eliot's supreme achievement: not because she is 'local', indigenous, but because finally she carries the full sense of George Eliot's synthesis. To be sure, she is 'Christian' and 'Female'; she is 'Nordic', she is 'English', in the self-defining, isolating sense which makes Deronda her foil; but she also displays the affinities of the English disposition with the Jewish. Her nervous, half-hysterical sensibility is at the basis both of her coldness and her passion, her theatrical self-presentation and her vulnerability. This primitive sen-sibility, rightly presented in English terms as 'Gothic', sensational and full of dread, develops into the religious awe that for Kant is hebraic and sublime and underlies the assumption of moral responsibility that is the essence of the categorical imperative, and then, through the complex transaction in the climactic scene between Gwendolen and Deronda, into the assumption of moral responsibility understood in Christian terms as imaginative crucifixion. Not only does she absorb this religious history within herself, her appearance carries all of these significances, just as the brilliant superficies of English social life carries all its values, unstated yet flaunting. This book has perhaps a better claim to the title 'The Tragic Muse' than Henry James's novel, though both clearly link the Jewish histrionic capacity to the intensely theatrical element in English society.

There is a form of symbolism here which makes *Daniel Deronda* a 'philosophical novel' in a specifically English mode. For it restores the central claim of the English novel, that social life can express the intellectual and moral values of an informing culture.

In the novels of the 1870s the social structure is seen not to reflect the ethical order. To maintain the reflection, the symbolic system of the novel needed to be completely revised. In order that ethical values should continue to be experienced as one with the very gesture and manner of the social system, George Eliot had to create an alternative social structure. Realism is employed only to go beyond itself. What had been an unexamined English assumption becomes a mode of a specifically modern art. Henry James is the only other novelist who achieved a like revision, in which imaginative value was able still to reside in the social gesture. As for James this was only possible through his alien system of American transcendentalism, so for George Eliot it was possible only through a German transcendental system which was historically anterior to the American versions but came to her in its most modern form. Only an alien cosmopolitan consciousness essentially poetic in its operations was able to restore the characteristic stance of the English novel; and so to court permanent misunderstanding and disparagement from English society. No English novelist has succeeded in restoring it since then. The modern novel has passed into other hands.

The distinction between the external doctrine and institutions of Christianity and the internal spiritualist revelation – the distinction that plagued the romantics and drove them to create a mythology in which internal and external relations were interchangeable – was overcome again in the fully public social sphere where institutions and doctrines have been subject to reinterpretation and theology can be understood as pathology without loss of value.

In her very attempt to resurrect religious culture, George Eliot had so to bend and obliterate convention as to exhibit the base of atheism on which all future religious culture in that society would rest; the constructive and destructive aspects of the higher criticism work here in a new, more dissonant concert. Kermode has written, 'the careful meaninglessness' of Meursault's life in Camus's *L'Étranger* is 'exactly antithetical to the fullness of the concordances found in the life of Jesus'.[101] True enough; but if in *Daniel Deronda* we have a 'life of Jesus' with its fullness of concordances we have also an exploration of the fictive nature of those concordances. If Coleridge was forced to invent a new dialectical logic to preserve moral responsibility, if Browning perceived religious culture to rest upon a lie and a condition contrary to fact, in George Eliot's last work the refuge in art of those transcendental ideas which Kant had found at the basis of religion and of morality was itself invaded. The refuge is no longer a refuge, but an exposed position; the conventions of fiction are after all implicated in the conventions of morality and of religion which have already been shown to diverge from canons of truth; the very closeness of poetic and religious techniques as shown by the higher criticism did not merely put religion on a new apologetical basis, but had a corrosive effect on art itself. Poetry was not a separate realm where these ideas could take refuge, just in the degree to which religion and poetry were necessarily seen to belong to the same realm. For their own message was that myth – the union of poetry and religion – could not be re-enacted in an age of criticism. If for Coleridge and Hölderlin the method of mythological synthesis was still available as a poetic technique, in *Daniel Deronda* the poetic technique indicts itself, exhibits its sheer virtuosity in a context of unavowed Utopia and so reveals the hopeless plight of humanism.

It was the fullness of George Eliot's comprehension of the higher criticism that led to this unlooked-for result; yet as all her art depended on this virtuosity, perhaps it was her unconscious desire, like John on his deathbed, to sacrifice her own constructed humanism to a confession and a boast of the triumph of her unaided deceiving art.

EICHHORN'S OUTLINE OF THE POETIC ACTION
OF THE BOOK OF REVELATION

———

Here is Eichhorn's division of the Book of Revelation into acts and scenes:

Thus, in Act One, the fall of Jerusalem is exhibited in prophecies of the destruction of Judaism by signs and figures, after which the reign of Jesus Christ is brought to view, weak and infirm in its beginnings.

In Act Two, Rome, image and symbol of the Gentiles, is conquered, after which the reign of Christ grown to full power through the double triumph can be shown, which, all difficulties and dangers having been happily overcome, will endure to the end of the world.

In Act Three, the joys of future life appear, under the image of the heavenly inhabitants of Jerusalem, the joys to be expressed through symbols and mysteries.

Thus far the drama itself. In order, however, that the poet may describe it fully and fitly, he prefixes another vision, in which he hands on in the letters to the churches that message from Jesus Christ himself which he wished to stand as the Prologue.

Now, in truth, the poem does not consist of equal parts, unless the peculiar Epilogue be included, which the poet used almost of necessity to confirm the certainty and truth of the things foretold by dramatic arts.

We have therefore divided the oracle for performance according to this rule and in this order of parts:

TITLE, c. i. 1–3.

PROLOGUE, c. i. 4–c. iii. 22.

in which the dramatic argument is declared to pertain to Christians:

(a) The churches are greeted. c. i. 4–8.

(b) It is narrated to the churches, in what time and place John received his visions of the future, and the enjoined duty is performed of transmitting the visions through these letters c. i. 8–20; at the same time he is ordered

(c) to admonish Christians by letter to the duties of virtue and piety, when things revealed in visions shall be expounded to them. c. ii. 1–3, 22.

The letters to the churches follow, which in the symbolical style of the poem are brought up to the number of seven. . .

The Drama Itself

PRELUDE c. iv–c. viii. 5.

The Scene is set.

(a) God is seen sitting upon the throne. c. iv. 1–11.

(b) Jesus Christ is seen enthroned with God and in addition a volume is seen containing future changes of things sealed in letters, and at the same time it is declared, no one but God and his companion on the throne knows the argument of the volume. c. v. 1–14.

(c) A beginning is made at explaining the volume. As the first four of the seals are opened, the argument of the volume was permitted to predict great misfortune. c. vi. 9–11.

(d) The fateful argument of the volume pertained to the adversaries of the Christian religion.

(e) The horror of the omens increases, portending evils to the adversaries of the Christian religion. c. vi. 12–17.

Conclusion. The Christians gathered from the Jews and from the Gentiles are immune from the dangers, from the horrifying omens thus far prophesied; and indeed

(α) the Christians from among the Jews, c. vii. 1–8.

(β) the Christians from among the Gentiles, c. vii. 9–17.

(f) The preparations for the unfortunate events just declared are seen. c. viii. 1, 2.

Conclusion. The train of miseries commences next. c. viii. 3–5.

ACT I c. viii. 6–c. xii. 17.

Jerusalem falls, or Judaism is conquered by the Christian religion.

(a) Public calamity is prophesied. c. viii. 6–12.

Conclusion. The triple woe is proclaimed. c. viii. 13.

The first state of the Christian church is described, how infirm it was thought after the overthrow of Judaism; then, the wretched condition of the Jews who are still adherents to Judaism, improved nevertheless through the hope that at some time, converted to the Christian discipline, they may receive the fruit of happiness. c. xii. 1–17.

ACT II c. xii. 18–c. xx. 10.

Rome falls, or the Gentiles are conquered by the Christian religion.

(a) To what destruction is it now to proceed? The superstition of the Gentiles is expressed in clear symbols and signs. c. xii. 18–c. xiii. 18.

(α) Rome, the seat of idolatry, is described under the image of a sea monster, in order that an idea of idolatry should be excited in the souls of the readers. c. xii. 18–c. xiii. 10.

(β) The preceding scene is set with another monster emerging from the earth which counterfeits the prophet, who, having arranged prodigies and miracles to deceive mankind, aids the sea-monster. c. xii. 11–18.

Conclusion. The happiness of the worshippers of God and the contented state and condition of their souls is contrasted with the rage of the profane Gentiles and the tumult of spirit with which they burn. c. xiv. 1–5.

(b) The fall of Rome, or the rooting out of the Gentiles, is prophesied and accomplished. c. xiv. 6–c. xvi. 21.

(α) The fall of Rome is proclaimed. c. xiv. 6–13.

(β) The same fall is expressed in symbols of the harvest and the vendange. c. xiv. 14–20.

(γ) Seven plagues rage furiously upon Rome for the destruction of the city. c. xv.–xvi. 16.

Angels come forth as omens of evil events. c. xv. 1.

Conclusion. It is declared to the Gentiles that they are to look upon these omens of future evils. c. xv. 2–4. The omens are confirmed by the event. c. xv. 5–16, 21.

(a) Angels receive the mandate to rage with ills against Rome. c. xv. 6–c. xvi. 1.

(b) They carry out the mandate. c. xvi. 2–21.

(α) Public calamity is shadowed forth. c. xvi. 2–9.

(β) The prophesied calamity has to do with the extinguishing of idolatry (idolatrous Rome). c. xvi. 10, 11.

(γ) All difficulties vanish which could impede so great a matter. c. xvi. 12–16.

(δ) Rome at last falls. c. xvi. 17–21.

Conclusion. Rome and the Roman rule, seat of idolatry, is shown by these strange things and by indubitable signs. c. xvii.

(c) Lament over conquered Rome. c. xviii. 1–24.

(d) Triumphal song. c. xix. 1–10.

(e) Triumphal march. c. xix. 11–c. xx. 3.

The Christian religion reigns. c. xx. 4–10.

ACT III c. xx. 11–c. xxii. 5.

The heavenly Jerusalem descends from the sky, or the bliss of future life which will endure forever is described.

(a) The scene is set: namely, the dead are resurrected and honest men are assembled among the citizens of the heavenly republic. c. xx. 11–14.

(b) The New Jerusalem, seat of the rule of the Messiah and of the happiness of future life, is described. c. xxi. 1–c. xxii. 5.

EPILOGUE. c. xxii. 6–11.

   (a) Angels. c. xxii. 6.

   (b) Jesus Christ. c. xxii. 1–16.

   (c) John. c. xxii. 16–21.

     (α) He admonishes them to concern themselves with the realizing of the oracle. c. xxii. 16–20.

He bids the churches farewell.

A TRANSLATION OF HÖLDERLIN'S 'PATMOS'

———

Near us
And hard to grapple is God.
But where there is risk, there sprouts
Our salvation too.
In darkness household   5
The eagles and fearless stride
The children of the Alps over the abyss out
On lightly suspensive bridges.
So, since high-piled peaks of time
Ring us round,   10
And the best-beloved
Live so close, wearying out
Atop the deepest-divided peaks,
Give us innocent water
O give us wings, trustfully   15
To cross over and to return again.

So much had I said, when snatched up
From my hearth with a rapidity
Far flown beyond imagining
To places I had scarcely dreamt to see   20
By a genius' hand. In the twilight
As I went dawned
The shade-chequered wood
And the longing, reminiscent streams
Of my homeland; never had I known these lands;   25
But soon, shimmering
Secret-laden
In a golden haze unfolded
On the steps of the sun up-shooting
Full-blown   30
A thousand towers of fragrance

296

Asia I saw: dazzled,
I groped, seeking one known thing, unfamiliar
In these broad avenues, where down
From Tmolus flows   35
The gold-braceleted Pactolus
And where Taurus stands and Messogis
And the garden is full of flowers,
A sculptured fire. But the silver snow
Blooms above on a stalk of light;   40
And witness of immortal life
On inaccessible walls
Age-old the ivy grows and, borne up
By sentient pillars, cedars and laurels,
Are the ceremonious,   45
The god-built palaces.

  Around the arches of Asia murmuring
Tides drawing in and out
Criss-cross the traceless routes
Of the tilting sea-top.   50
But the helmsman knows these islands.
And when I heard
That of the many lying near us
One was Patmos
I above all longed   55
To land there and harbour there
And draw nearer the dark grotto.
For it is not like Cyprus
Fountain-flowing, nor
Like any of the others,   60
Glorious Patmos,

  Hospitable, though,
In the needy houses,
This island,
And if from shipwreck or crying out   65
For homeland or for
The departed friend
One of the outcast nears,
A stranger, she hears it gladly, and her children,
The voices from the burning grove,   70

At the point where the sand drops away
And the smooth pasture and the sounds are cleft,
All hear him, and lovingly
All echo the outcries of the man. So once
Patmos fostered god's friend,   75
The visionary, who in joyous young manhood strolled

   Arm in arm
With the son of the Almighty, inseparable, for
The thunder-bearing God loved his simplicity
And the intent young man feasted his eyes and saw   80
The face of the god directly
When, in the mystery of the vine, they
Sat together, at the hour of the feast,
And the great foreboding soul looking inwards
Spoke calmly of death and the extremity of his love,   85
For no words ever
Were enough for him then to tell of goodness
Or to quiet, as he saw it, the world's quarrelling.
For everything is good. On that he died. A long story
Might be told of it. And they saw him, as he triumphing gazed,   90
Thus most contented, his companions, to the very last.

   Yet they mourned, as the plummeting sun
Blacked, lumining
In their astounded eventful souls
For the future was within them   95
Yet they clung to the life and day they loved
Loath to abandon the face of the Lord
And their homeland. Like fire in iron
They were furnaced in him,
And the shadow of the loved one   100
Walked at their sides.
Therefore he sent
The Spirit down on them, and indeed the house
Quaked in the thunder of God from far rolling
Over the divining heads, deeply inclined, as   105
Death's heroes were bonded together,

   Now, as in parting
He appeared to them once more.

For now the imperial sun was snuffed
And now snapped the scepter,   110
The straight-streaming noon on its cross-beam,
Suffering like a god, of itself,
For it should return
At the right time. It would not have been good
Later, but disruptive, unfaithful,   115
Human work, and joy it was
From now on
To dwell in loving night and perpetuate
In innocent unswerving eyes
Abysses of wisdom. And even   120
Deep in mountain recesses grow verdant images,

   Yet it is terrible, how far and wide
God forever scatters the living limbs.
For already abandoning
The face of friends   125
To pass over the mountains alone,
Twice recognized
But single-hearted
In parting was divine spirit; and it was not prophesied, but
Suddenly present   130
He seized them by the hair of their heads
As hurrying on
Suddenly the god looked back and swearing,
That he might hold as on golden threads
Bound to him from now on   135
Exorcising evil, they clasped outstretched hands, –

   But if he dies then
To whom beauty most clung
So that a miracle shaped round him, and the gods
Marked him out, and if,   140
An eternal puzzle for one another
They could not grasp
One another, who lived together
Only in the community of memories of him; and not
The wasteland only nor the grazingland   145
Is seized nor the temple only
Is shaken to the root

When the worship of the demi-god and his followers wanes
And even the god of gods turns
His face away, so that nowhere one   15c
Immortal more is to be seen in heaven or
On the green earth, then what does this mean?

    This is the toss of the seedsower, when he turns
With his shovel to gather the wheat
And flings it, skywards, in an arc over the threshing-floor.   155
The husks heap up at his feet, but
At the far end sifts down the corn.
And no harm is done, if some goes astray
As from speech the living seed of sound
Falls whispering away,   160
For God's work is like our own.
He does not require everything at once.
Yet the blast-furnace bears the iron in its womb
And Aetna bears glowing resins,
And so should I carry rich ores within   165
To shape an image of myself
Like Christ as He was.

    But if one spurred himself,
And sadly talking, along the way, when I was defenceless,
Ambushed me, so that I marvelled and would wish   170
To imitate the image of the god – I, a knave –
In the visible anger of heaven's master that once
I saw that I was not to be, but
To learn. The gods are benevolent, but abhorrent to them
As long as they rule is falsehood, and so   175
What is accounted human among men is nothing to them.
For men do not rule, immortal fate rules
And the work of gods sets its own pace
And hastens to its end.
For when higher climbs the triumphal procession   180
Of heaven, sunlike he will be named
By the strong, the exulting son of the highest,

    The watchword: and here is the baton
Of poetry, descending,
For nothing is common. He awakens   185

The dead, for whom the raw earth
Is no longer a prison. But many
Are the light-shy lids
That tremble to open. Not gladly
Will they bloom on the sharp ray's thorn,   190
Although that shining light-bridle contains courage
But when, as
By the raised eyebrows of the world
Forgotten,
Still power lights on them from Holy Scripture, may   195
They, delighting in grace
Exercise quiet sight.

   And if the heavenly powers now
Love me so, as I believe,
How much more they love you,   200
For I know one thing
Only, that the will
Of the eternal Father
Weighs with you. Quiet is his sign
In thundering skies. And One stands beneath it   205
His whole life long. For Christ still lives.
But all the heroes, his sons, have come
And all Holy Writ has come
From him, and the deeds of the earth till now
And the lightning clarify one another   210
In unceasing rotation. But he is present. For his works
Are all known to him from eternity.

   Too long, too long already
Has the glory of the gods been invisible.
We can scarcely move a finger   215
Without them, and shamefully
Our hearts are torn out of us by one power or another.
For each of the gods demands sacrifice,
And whenever one has been left out
It has led to no good.   220
We have a long time served our mother Earth
And most recently have served the sunlight
Unwittingly, but the Father loves most
Who rules over all

That the enduring letter be cared for and
All that subsists well augured and interpreted.
German poetry hearkens to his word.

PATMOS

Nah ist
Und schwer zu fassen der Gott.
Wo aber Gefahr ist, wächst
Das Rettende auch.
Im Finstern wohnen   5
Die Adler und furchtlos gehn
Die Söhne der Alpen über den Abgrund weg
Auf leichtgebaueten Brücken.
Drum, da gehäuft sind rings
Die Gipfel der Zeit,   10
Und die Liebsten
Nah wohnen, ermattend auf
Getrenntesten Bergen,
So gib unschuldig Wasser,
O Fittiche gib uns, treuesten Sinns   15
Hinüberzugehn und wiederzukehren.

So sprach ich, da entführte
Mich schneller, denn ich vermutet
Und weit, wohin ich nimmer
Zu kommen gedacht, ein Genius mich   20
Vom eigenen Haus. Es dämmerten
Im Zwielicht, da ich ging,
Der schattige Wald
Und die sehnsüchtigen Bäche
Der Heimat; nimmer kannt' ich die Länder;   25
Doch bald, in frischem Glanze,
Geheimnisvoll
Im goldnen Rauche, blühte
Schnellaufgewachsen,
Mit Schritten der Sonne,   30
Mit tausend Gipfeln duftend,

Mir Asia auf, und geblendet sucht'
Ich eines, das ich kennete, denn ungewohnt
War ich der breiten Gassen, wo herab

Vom Tmolus fährt   35
Der goldgeschmückte Paktol
Und Taurus stehet und Messogis,
Und voll von Blumen der Garten
Ein stilles Feuer; aber im Lichte
Blüht hoch der silberne Schnee;   40
Und Zeug' unsterblichen Lebens
An unzugangbaren Wänden
Uralt der Efeu wächst und getragen sind
Von lebenden Säulen, Zedern und Lorbeern
Die feierlichen,   45
Die göttlichgebauten Paläste.

   Es rauschen aber um Asias Tore
Hinziehend da und dort
In ungewisser Meeresebene
Der schattenlosen Strassen genug,   50
Doch kennt die Inseln der Schiffer.
Und da ich hörte
Der nahegelegenen eine
Sei Patmos,
Verlangte mich sehr   55
Dort einzukehren und dort
Der dunkeln Grotte zu nahn
Denn nicht, wie Cypros,
Die quellenreiche, oder
Der anderen eine   60
Wohnt herrlich Patmos,

   Gastfreundlich aber ist
Im ärmeren Hause
Sie dennoch,
Und wenn vom Schiffbruch oder klagend   65
Um die Heimat oder
Den abgeschiedenen Freund
Ihr nahet einer
Der Fremden, hört sie es gern, und ihre Kinder,
Die Stimmen des heissen Hains,   70
Und wo der Sand fällt und sich spaltet
Des Feldes Fläche, die Laute,
Sie hören ihn, und liebend tönt

Es wider von den Klagen des Manns. So pflegte
Sie einst des gottgeliebten,   75
Des Sehers, der in seliger Jugend war

  Gegangen mit
Dem Sohne des Höchsten, unzertrennlich, denn
Es liebte der Gewittertragende die Einfalt
Des Jüngers und es sahe der achtsame Mann   80
Das Angesicht des Gottes genau,
Da, beim Geheimnisse des Weinstocks, sie
Zusammensassen, zu der Stunde des Gastmahls,
Und in der grossen Seele, ruhigahnend den Tod
Aussprach der Herr und die letzte Liebe, denn nie genug   85
Hatt' er von Güte zu sagen
Der Worte, damals, und zu erheitern, da
Ers sahe, das Zürnen der Welt.
Denn alles ist gut. Drauf starb er. Vieles wäre
Zu sagen davon. Und es sahn ihn, wie er siegend blickte,   90
Den Freudigsten die Freunde noch zuletzt,

  Doch trauerten sie, da nun
Es Abend worden, erstaunt,
Denn Grossentschiedenes hatten in der Seele
Die Männer, aber sie liebten unter der Sonne   95
Das Leben und lassen wollten sie nicht
Vom Angesichte des Herrn
Und der Heimat. Eingetrieben war,
Wie Feuer im Eisen, das, und ihnen ging
Zur Seite der Schatte des Lieben.   100
Drum sandt' er ihnen
Den Geist, und freilich bebte
Das Haus und die Wetter Gottes rollten
Ferndonnernd über
Die ahnenden Häupter, da, schwersinnend   105
Versammelt waren die Todeshelden,

  Izt, da er scheidend
Noch einmal ihnen erschien.
Denn izt erlosch der Sonne Tag,
Der Königliche, und zerbrach   110
Den geradestrahlenden,

Den Zepter, göttlichleidend, von selbst,
Denn wiederkommen sollt es
Zu rechter Zeit. Nicht wär' es gut
Gewesen, später, und schroffabbrechend, untreu,   115
Der Menschen Werk, und Freude war es
Von nun an,
Zu wohnen in liebender Nacht und bewahren
In einfältigen Augen unverwandt
Abgründe der Weisheit. Und es grünen   120
Tief an den Bergen auch lebendige Bilder,

Doch furchtbar ist, wie da und dort
Unendlich hin zerstreut das Lebende Gott.
Denn schon das Angesicht
Der teuern Freunde zu lassen   125
Und fernhin über die Berge zu gehn
Allein, wo zweifach
Erkannt, einstimmig
War himmlischer Geist; und nicht geweissagt war es sondern
Die Locken ergriff es, gegenwärtig,   130
Wenn ihnen plötzlich
Ferneilend zurück blickte
Der Gott und schwörend,
Damit er halte, wie an Seilen golden
Gebunden hinfort   135
Das Böse nennend, sie die Hände sich reichten –

Wenn aber stirbt alsdenn
An dem am meisten
Die Schönheit hing, dass an der Gestalt
Ein Wunder war und die Himmlischen gedeutet   140
Auf ihn, und wenn, ein Rätsel ewig füreinander
Sie sich nicht fassen können
Einander, die zusammenlebten
Im Gedächtnis, und nicht den Sand nur oder
Die Weiden es hinwegnimmt und die Tempel   145
Ergreift, wenn die Ehre
Des Halbgotts und der Seinen
Verweht und selber sein Angesicht
Der Höchste wendet
Darob, dass nirgend ein   150

Unsterbliches mehr am Himmel zu sehn ist oder
Auf grüner Erde, was ist dies?

   Es ist der Wurf des Säemanns, wenn er fasst
Mit der Schaufel den Weizen,
Und wirft, dem Klaren zu, ihn schwingend über die Tenne.   155
Ihm fällt die Schale vor den Füssen, aber
Ans Ende kommet das Korn,
Und nicht Ubel ists, wenn einiges
Verloren gehet und von der Rede
Verhallet der lebendige Laut,   160
Denn göttliches Werk auch gleichet dem unsern,
Nicht alles will der Höchste zumal.
Zwar Eisen träget der Schacht,
Und glühende Harze der Atna,
So hätt' ich Reichtum,   165
Ein Bild zu bilden und ähnlich
Zu schaun, wie er gewesen, den Christ,

   Wenn aber einer spornte sich selbst,
Und traurig redend, unterweges, da ich wehrlos wäre
Mich überfiele, dass ich staunt' und von dem Gotte   170
Das Bild nachahmen möcht ein Knecht –
Im Zorne sichtbar sah ich einmal
Des Himmels Herrn, nicht, dass ich sein sollt' etwas, sondern
Zu lernen. Gütig sind sie, ihr Verhasstestes aber ist,
So lange sie herrschen, das Falsche, und es gilt   175
Dann Menschliches unter Menschen nicht mehr.
Denn sie nicht walten, es waltet aber
Unsterblicher Schicksal und es wandelt ihr Werk
Von selbst, und eilend geht es zu Ende.
Wenn nämlich höher gehet himmlischer   180
Triumphgang, wird genennet, der Sonne gleich
Von Starken der frohlockende Sohn des Höchsten,

   Ein Losungszeichen, und hier ist der Stab
Des Gesanges, niederwinkend,
Denn nichts ist gemein. Die Toten wecket   185
Er auf, die noch gefangen nicht
Vom Rohen sind. Es warten aber
Der scheuen Augen viele,

Zu schauen das Licht. Nicht wollen
Am scharfen Strahle sie blühn,   190
Wiewohl den Mut der goldene Zaum hält.
Wenn aber, als
Von schwellenden Augenbrauen
Der Welt vergessen
Stillleuchtende Kraft aus heiliger Schrift fällt, mögen   195
Der Gnade sich freuend, sie
Am stillen Blicke sich üben.

        Und wenn die Himmlischen jetzt
So, wie ich glaube, mich lieben,
Wie viel mehr Dich,   200
Denn eines weiss ich,
Da nämlich der Wille
Des ewigen Vaters viel
Dir gilt. Still ist sein Zeichen
Am donnernden Himmel. Und Einer steht darunter   205
Sein Leben lang. Denn noch lebt Christus.
Es sind aber die Helden, seine Söhne
Gekommen all und heilige Schriften
Von ihm, und den Blitz erklären
Die Taten der Erde bis izt,   210
Ein Wettlauf unaufhaltsam. Er ist aber dabei. Denn seine Werke sind
Ihm alle bewusst von jeher.

        Zu lang, zu lang schon ist
Die Ehre der Himmlischen unsichtbar.
Denn fast die Finger müssen sie   215
Uns führen und schmählich
Entreisst das Herz uns eine Gewalt.
Denn Opfer will der Himmlischen jedes,
Wenn aber eines versäumt ward,
Nie hat es Gutes gebracht.   220
Wir haben gedienet der Mutter Erd
Und haben jüngst dem Sonnenlichte gedient,
Unwissend, der Vater aber liebt,
Der über allen waltet,
Am meisten, dass gepfleget werde   225
Der feste Buchstab, und Bestehendes gut
Gedeutet. Dem folgt deutscher Gesang.

NOTES

INTRODUCTION

1 L. Goldmann, *Sciences humaines et philosophie* (Paris, 1966), trans. as *The Human Sciences and Philosophy* (London, 1969), p. 63.
2 Goldmann, *Le Dieu caché* (Paris, 1955), trans. as *The Hidden God* (London, 1964), p. 12.
3 *The Human Sciences and Philosophy*, p. 31.
4 *The Hidden God*, p. 12n.
5 Michel Foucault, *Histoire de la folie* (Paris, 1961), trans. as *Madness and Civilization: A History of Insanity in the Age of Reason* (London, 1967).
6 Raymond Williams, 'The Analysis of Culture', in *The Long Revolution* (London, 1961), p. 62.
7 *The Anatomy of Criticism* (Princeton, N.J., 1957), p. 315.
8 Ed. Hans Eichner (Manchester, 1970).
9 M. H. Abrams, *Natural Supernaturalism: Tradition and Revolution in Romantic Literature* (London, 1971), p. 256.

CHAPTER I
The Fall of Jerusalem: Coleridge's unwritten epic

1 Coleridge, marginal note in J. G. Eichhorn, *Commentarius in Apocalypsin Joannis* (Göttingen, 1791), Copy B 1-2— -1. References to Coleridge's marginalia are given in the style adopted by the editor of the marginalia for *The Collected Coleridge*: flyleaves are numbered backwards from the first printed page and forwards from the last printed page; hence 'minus' numbers refer to front flyleaves, 'plus' numbers to back flyleaves. This should facilitate reference both to the original texts and to the authoritative edition of them. Copy A refers to a two-volume set of the *Commentarius* made up of Volume II of an edition acquired by Coleridge on 19 February 1826 bound together with Volume I which Coleridge reports having had in his possession 'for years'. Copy B is Volume I of the set bought in 1826. Both copies are in the possession of the British Museum.

The dating of Coleridge's knowledge, acquisition, and annotation of any particular work is difficult to establish precisely, as he often annotated several copies of the same work or reread, adding new annotations which he sometimes but not always dated. Copy A 1 is most probably the first volume of Eichhorn's works acquired by Coleridge. On dating see also Chap. 2, n. 31 and 3, n. 106.

2 *Ibid.*, Copy A1 –1. Coleridge's summarizing note indicates his agreement with Eichhorn's interpretation of 'this grand prophetic Drama', though also indicating, in accordance with Coleridgean custom, that he was familiar with it from an earlier source, Joannes Cocceius (1603–69), 'the first rational commentator on the Apocalypse'. After requesting Crabb Robinson to procure him a copy of Eichhorn's *Commentarius*, Coleridge refers, in several letters of 1826, to the commentary he is using as 'Cocceius'.

See Appendix 1 for a translation of Eichhorn's outline of the action of the drama.

3 Kenneth Burke, ' "Kubla Khan", Proto-Surrealist Poem', *Language as Symbolic Action* (Berkeley, 1966), p. 218.

4 Earl Leslie Griggs, *The Collected Letters of Samuel Taylor Coleridge* (Oxford, 1956–71), II, To Thomas Wedgwood, 20 October 1802.

5 G. Wilson Knight, 'Coleridge's Divine Comedy', *The Starlit Dome* (London, 1941). 'The Book of Revelation supplied numerous footnote quotations. Indeed, his religious poetry is distinguished pre-eminently by its apocalyptic tendencies' (p. 129). 'The Destiny of Nations' presents 'a single, objectively conceived personality, Saint Joan, able to bear and transmute the burden of world-evil. Such a dramatic projection alone can approach the synthesis most perfectly accomplished in *Zapolya*: hence the high place to be accorded dramatic literature and the supreme importance of dramatic action in the New Testament' (p. 143). Thus Wilson Knight perceived the connections of 'Kubla Khan' with apocalyptic religious poetry, dramatic action based in the New Testament, and epic saviours.

6 Coleridge, *Table Talk*, 4 September 1833, quoted in T. M. Raysor, *Miscellaneous Criticism* (Cambridge, Mass., 1936), p. 429.

7 Helen Adolf, *Visio Pacis: Holy City and Grail* (Pennsylvania, 1960), p. 175.

8 De Quincey, 'The Death of a Great Man', *Monthly Repository* (1830), quoted in B. Q. Morgan and A. R. Hohlfeld, *German Literature in British Magazines 1750–1860* (Madison, 1949).

9 Herder was well-known and widely reviewed in British periodicals: 'Herder and Lessing shared a place of honor close behind that of Goethe and Schiller in the esteem of the British magazines.' (Morgan and Hohlfeld, *German Literature in British Magazines*, p. 108.) There were no substantial translations, however, until the end of the eighteenth century: *Oriental Dialogues; containing the Conversation of Eugenius and Alciphron on the. . .sacred Poetry of the Hebrews* (1801) was drawn from the first volume of *Vom Geist der ebräischen Poesie* (1782) (slightly rearranged); the *Outlines of a Philosophy of the History of Man*, trans. T. Churchill (1800) is a translation of one of Herder's most important works, the *Ideen zur Philosophie der Geschichte der Menschheit. A Brief Commentary on the Revelation of Saint John* (1821) renders *Johannes Offenbarung* (1774); *The Spirit of Hebrew Poetry* was translated in full only in 1833, by

James Marsh, the American transcendentalist who also did much to make Kant and Coleridge known in New England.

Coleridge had very considerable early knowledge of Herder. It has been established that he had read the *Briefe, das Studium der Theologie betreffend, Kalligone, Von der Auferstehung,* and two other volumes by December 1804, and had known *Von der Auferstehung* and probably other books of Herder's well before that date. See the discussions by Merton Christensen under the individual titles in the volume of *The Collected Coleridge* containing the marginalia on Herder.

10 The study of Semitic languages was encouraged in the first instance by the orthodox insistence of the Reformation on the letter of the text. This led to the study of the other languages associated with the Bible, Arabic, Syrian, Chaldean, Samaritan, and Ethiopian, and to the great polyglot lexicons of the seventeenth century which were the basis of comparative linguistics. From this work A. Schultens in 1733 drew the conclusion that the 'holy language' Hebrew was not the original, but only a twig on the Semitic language tree, and he especially praised Arabic as the clearest and purest of semitic languages, as against the obscure and ambiguous Hebrew. This broke the hold of the 'inspiration' theory of the Bible, and led to an immense increase in the study of Arabic as well as the other related languages. Michaelis and Eichhorn emphasized Arabic. The 'primitivism' of Hebrew was shortly turned to good account by Herder who held that it particularly well represented the expressive *Bildersprache* of the infancy of the human race (H. J. Kraus, *Geschichte der historisch-kritischen Erforschung des alten Testaments* (Neukirchen-Vluyn, 1969).

If language study undermined the inspiration theory, even more telling were the new editions of the Bible that recorded not only variant readings but parallel passages from other sources, from classical Greek, then from Jewish–Hellenistic literature (Grotius) and rabbinical literature (Lightfoot), and as in Johann Jakob Wettstein's New Testament of 1751–2 published them all directly under the accepted text, so that the result, however unintentional at first, was a comparative mythology.

11 Friedrich Meinecke, *Die Entstehung des Historismus* (München u. Berlin, 1936), p. 27.

12 Pierre Bayle, 'Réponse aux questions d'un provincial', ch. 134, quoted in Paul Hazard, *The European Mind 1680–1715* (Aylesbury, 1964), p. 137.

13 Voltaire, *Dictionnaire philosophique portatif* (Londres [Geneva?], 1764).

14 T. K. Cheyne, *Founders of Old Testament Criticism* (London, 1893), p. 14.

15 *Ibid.*, pp. 14–15.

16 *Herders sämmtliche Werke*. Dritter Teil. Erste Abteilung. (Berlin, 1877–1913), p. 121. In 'Von den deutsch-orientalischen Dichtern', 'On the German-Oriental Poets', is the subheading '4. Geist der Religion: christliche Lieder in orientalischen Geschmack (Klopstock)', '4. The Spirit of Religion: Christian Poems in the Oriental Taste (Klopstock)'. Not only Klopstock's epic, but his odes are referred to here, for he made an effort to found a new Protestant mythology to set up against the Greek.

17 B. Price and L. M. Price, *The Publication of English Humaniora in Germany in the Eighteenth Century* (Berkeley and Los Angeles, 1955), p. xxiii. Lowth sent Michaelis his work on the Hebrew Bible (Michaelis having heard one of the lectures while in England), and Michaelis's notes to the German edition were translated for the English edition of 1784. Percy sent Michaelis his 'The Song of Solomon newly translated' (1764). This by no means exhausts Michaelis's acts of mediation. One more example: Robert Wood sent his 'Essay on the Original Genius of Homer' to him, and he showed it to Heyne, who wrote an enthusiastic review (1770); Michaelis's son translated it. The enthusiasm of the Germans in the eighteenth century for English literary phenomena has long been acknowledged and documented; the record of the reciprocal interest in England in the German literary renascence, however, is buried in rather specialized bibliographies of translations or in 'comparative' monographs, and has hardly found its way into English criticism.

18 Duncan Forbes, *The Liberal Anglican Idea of History* (Cambridge, 1952). Forbes is fully aware that behind the views of history he is discussing lies 'the German historical movement', but he declines to discuss it: 'It is not the primary object of this study to examine the influence of the German historical movement. . .so that it is not necessary in sketching the main outlines of the Liberal Anglican idea of history, to trace back each separate strand of thought to its origin' (p. 12). At the same time he holds that 'in Germany the new historical outlook was established by the end of the eighteenth century; but in England it was not until the decade 1820–30, or thereabouts, that the attempted construction by Coleridge of a new system. . .brought about a real revolution in historical thinking' (p. viii). It therefore becomes imperative to examine the roots of Coleridge's 'new system' in the German eighteenth century.

Maurianne S. Adams, 'Coleridge and the Victorians: Studies in the Interpretation of Poetry, Scripture, and Myth', is built upon the premise that Coleridge's 'new system' is an indigenous product that 'can be set off against German importations. Unpublished Ph.D. thesis (University of Indiana, 1967).

19 J. Robert Barth, *Coleridge and Christian Doctrine* (Cambridge, Mass., 1969), p. 56n.

20 *Collected Letters*, IV, To Derwent Coleridge, 28 March 1819.

21 'Eichhorn's lectures on the New Testament were repeated to me from notes by a student from Ratzeburg', Coleridge recalled in the *Biographia* (I, 138). Charles Parry explained the reason for Coleridge's non-attendance at Eichhorn's lectures. 'Coleridge was an able vindicator of these important truths [Christian Evidences], is well acquainted with Eichhorn, but the latter is a coward, who dreads his arguments and his presence' (*Early Years and Late Reflections*, I, 100n, quoted in Lawrence Hanson, *The Life of S. T. Coleridge, The Early Years* (London, 1938), p. 332). Coleridge also reported that 'the Professors here are exceedingly kind to all the Englishmen, but to me they pay the most flattering attentions, especially Blumenbach and Eichhorn' (*Biographia*, I, 138–41).

22 R. C. Fuller, 'Dr Alexander Geddes: A Forerunner of Biblical Criticism', Unpublished Ph.D. thesis (Cambridge, 1969), pp. 33–4.

23 *Ibid.*, pp. 189–90.

24 *Collected Letters*, I, To Robert Southey, 11 September 1794.

25 *Ibid.*, To George Dyer, Late February 1795; To John Prior Estlin, 30 December 1796.

26 Fuller, 'Geddes', p. 62.

27 Geddes refers to Eichhorn's paper, *Urgeschichte – ein Versuch* (1779), but, surprisingly, not to his review of Stendal, *Die ältesten Urkunden der Ebräer* (in the *Allgemeine Bibliothek* (1788)) nor even to the new edition of the *Urgeschichte* edited by Johann Philipp Gabler (1790), which carried out the mythological analysis more boldly than the earlier paper. Whether or not Geddes was acquainted with these, however, his criticisms of the earlier paper are very much in the spirit of the newer position of Eichhorn and Gabler (Fuller, 'Geddes', pp. 94–5).

28 Carl August Weber, 'Bristols Bedeutung für die englische Romantik und die deutsch-englischen Beziehungen', *Studien zur englischen Philologie* (Halle, 1935).

29 *The Watchman*, 17 March 1796.

30 *Collected Letters*, III, To Humphrey Davy, 30 January 1809.

31 *Collected Letters*, I, To Thomas Poole, 5 May 1796, announces his intention to go to Jena, to translate Schiller's works, to study chemistry and anatomy, and to bring back the works of Semler and Michaelis and Kant, 'the great German metaphysician'.

32 'A Memorial concerning the State of the Bodleian Library. . .by the Chemical Reader' (1787), quoted in Weber, 'Bristols Bedeutung', p. 104.

33 *Ibid.*

34 John Edmonds Stock, *Memoirs of the Life of Thomas Beddoes, M.D.* (London, 1811). 'He was master of the French, Italian, Spanish, and German languages; with the polite and the scientific authors in the last, in particular, he was equally conversant, and his library contained a rich collection of works of both descriptions.' Moreover, 'he left no stone unturned' in obtaining periodicals especially on medical subjects, from abroad (p. 409).

Beddoes shows definite knowledge of the following German periodicals (apart from purely medical journals): *Lichtenbergs und Forsters Göttingisches Magazin* (this contained Heyne's criticism of English classical education); the *Göttingische Gelehrte Anzeigen* (this reviewed Beddoes's publications, including the whole of the number for 23 October 1794); *Wielands Teutscher Merkur* (this praised Beddoes for his championship of Kant in 'Über das Gedeihen der Kantischen Philosophie in England' (II, 436–50)); *Commentationes Societatis Regiae Scientiarum Gottingensis* (Heyne was for many years editor of this publication, and many of his articles appeared there); *Neue Orientalische und Exegetische Bibliothek* (edited by Michaelis, this is a major source of information about Biblical criticism and Oriental studies generally); *Voss'sches und Göttingisches Musenalmanach* (Southey and his friends modelled their *Annual*

Anthology on this; it published Beddoes's poem, *Alexander's Expedition to the Indian Ocean*).

Given Beddoes's interest in Göttingen, it is highly probable that he subscribed to the *Göttingische Bibliothek der neuesten theologische Literatur* (ed. C. F. Stäudlin) in which Gabler's articles were published during the 1790s and the *Philosophische Bibliothek*, eds. J. G. H. Feder and C. Meiners. Eichhorn's *Repertorium für biblische und morgenländische Litteratur*, carried on from 1790 after Eichhorn's departure from Jena by Dr Paulus as the *Neues Repertorium*, etc., was certainly known to him. This list could easily be extended and amplified.

35 *Critical Review*, 19 (1797), 194–200.
36 Weber, 'Bristols Bedeutung', p. 41.
37 *Collected Letters*, I, To Benjamin Flower, 1 April 1796.
38 Thomas McFarland, *Coleridge and the Pantheist Tradition* (Oxford, 1969) gives a full account of Lessing's controversy with Jacobi over Spinoza's 'atheism'. He seems to have overlooked or been uninterested in the fact that Coleridge's earliest concern with Lessing centred on the *Wolfenbüttel Fragmente* and their attack on the credibility of the Gospels. Although he undoubtedly knew of the *Atheismusstreit*, he began to read Jacobi only after he went to Germany, and Spinoza's *Ethics* only after his return. Coleridge's earliest knowledge of Spinoza may well have been of the *Tractatus*, the name of the author being too dreaded to mention, as Leslie Stephen pointed out long ago, even while it served as the source of many of the deists' arguments.
39 Hermann Samuel Reimarus, *Fragments, consisting of brief critical remarks on the object of Jesus and his disciples as seen in the New Testament*, trans. and ed. Charles Voysey (London and Edinburgh, 1879), p. 19.
40 George Henry Lewes, *The Life and Works of Goethe*, 2nd rev. ed. (Leipzig, 1858), I, 227.
41 Herbert Butterfield, *Man on his Past: the Study of the History of Historical Scholarship* (Cambridge, 1955), p. 33.
42 *Ibid.*, p. 60.
43 *Ibid.*, pp. 15–16.
44 Acton, quoted in Butterfield, *ibid.*, p. 16n.
45 A. D. Momigliano, *Studies in Historiography* (London, 1966), pp. 20–1.
46 *Ibid.*, p. 81.
47 Coleridge, *Table Talk*, 4 September 1833, quoted in Raysor, *Miscellaneous Criticism*, p. 429.
48 Raysor, *Miscellaneous Criticism*, p. 161.
49 *Ibid.*
50 *Anima Poetae*, ed. Ernest Hartley Coleridge (London, 1895), pp. 290–1.
51 *Collected Letters*, I, To Robert Southey, 25 September 1799.
52 *Ibid.*
53 *The Notebooks of Samuel Taylor Coleridge*, ed. Kathleen Coburn (New York, 1957), I, 1245[k].
54 *Notebooks*, I², 1245[f].

55 Voltaire, *Essai sur la poésie épique* (Paris, 1724; rev. ed. 1764), p. 400.
56 *Ibid.*, pp. 374–5.
57 *Ibid.*, p. 383.
58 *Ibid.*, p. 353.
59 *Notebooks*, 1, 687 10.49. The passage is from Henry Foulis, *The History of the Wicked Plots and Conspiracies of our Pretended Saints* (Oxford, 1662), pp. 103–4.
60 MS Notebook 41, quoted in Kathleen Coburn, ed., *Inquiring Spirit: A New Presentation of Coleridge from his Published and Unpublished Prose Writings* (New York, 1951), p. 164. It is worth noticing how even in Coleridge's very last years the doubts cast on the character of the apostles by Reimarus and others encourage their use as *dramatis personae*:
'We are all too apt to forget the dark and fleshly state of all the Apostles during our Lord's sojourn with them. What were the expectations and imaginations of the Sons of Zebedee when they were quarrelling about the places, they should hold in the new Court – Which should be the Grand Vizier? Hence the character of Judas appears to be far more incomprehensible and strange than in a fair view of all the circumstances it ought to do' (*Ibid.*).
61 *Ibid.*, p. 165.
62 Josephus was particularly highly regarded from the time of Scaliger onwards. He represented the nearest to a Biblical authority, for the simple reason that he had recapitulated Biblical history, and thus two texts appeared to corroborate each other; at the same time, he ranked as a valuable independent source, since according to his own testimony, he had a whole archive of ancient Tyrian records which give him special authority to speak about any 'Eastern' nation. To recapitulate the Bible with the appearance of independence was the aim of the school of euhemerizing Judaeophiles typified by Newton; Newton's protégé William Whiston made an English translation of many of Josephus's works. From the many quotations and references to Josephus (in the Latin versions), in Coleridge's early Notebooks, it is clear that Coleridge, though he was neither a euhemerizer nor a Judaeophile in any simple sense, inherited the sense of the historian's importance. For Coleridge's poetic purposes, the combination of a nearly sacred authority and a reputation for independence through access to eyewitness accounts (we shall see how important this was for Eichhorn's theory of the transmission of Gospel accounts) was ideal. The secular historian who stands nevertheless in the brilliant presence of divinity represents the position of the last poet of the epic fall of Jerusalem.
63 Josephus, *The Jewish War*, trans. William Whiston (London, 1737), p. 513.
64 *Ibid.*, p. 555.
65 *Ibid.*, pp. 547–8.
66 *Ibid.*, p. 569.
67 *Ibid.*, p. 570.
68 *Ibid.*, p. 565.
69 *Lectures 1795: On Politics and Religion*, eds. Lewis Patton and Peter Mann (London, 1971), p. 155.

70 Samuel Johnson, 'Life of Milton', *Lives of the English Poets* (London, 1925), II, 105.
71 Friedrich Gottlieb Klopstock, *Ausgewählte Werke* (München, 1962), p. 1007. This essay was prefixed to the translation of cantos 1–10 of the *Messias* by M. Collyer in 1763. The translation was reprinted in 1769 and 1808, without the introductory essay; cantos 11–15 were added. The translation is more accurate, but no indication of the translator is given.
    For a full account of all translations, see Price, *English Humaniora in Germany*. The translation in the text is my own.
72 Gotthold Ephraim Lessing, *Kleine Schriften, Sämmtliche Schriften* (Berlin, 1791), V, 121.
73 Coleridge, marginal note on Lessing, *Kleine Schriften*, V, 123–5.
74 Fritz Strich, *Die Mythologie in der deutschen Literatur von Klopstock bis Wagner* (Halle, 1910), I, 143. The study of the Old Testament led Herder to the view that every system of science is at bottom a mythology, and that therefore a modern mythology is possible (p. 140).
75 Lessing, *Nathan the Wise*, trans. Andrew Wood (London and Edinburgh, 1877), p. 111.
76 *Fragments*, p. 114.
77 René Wellek, *Immanuel Kant in England* (Princeton, 1931) gives an inaccurate account of the reception of Kant in England. Kant's ideas began to be current earlier, and through quite different channels than he describes. I hope to return to this elsewhere. Here it is sufficient to point out that Wellek does not even mention Beddoes.
78 *Collected Letters*, I, To George Coleridge, 11 February 1794.
79 *Ibid.*, To George Coleridge, 30 March 1794.
80 *Ibid.*, To John Thelwall, Late April 1796.
81 Hartley's role has been cogently and accurately described by J. A. Appleyard, S.J., *Coleridge's Philosophy of Literature: The Development of a Concept of Poetry 1791–1819* (Cambridge, Mass., 1965), pp. 22–42.
82 *Ibid.*, To Benjamin Flower, 2 November 1796; To Thelwall, 31 December 1796.
83 *Ibid.*, To Thomas Poole, 30 March 1796.
84 Nathaniel Lardner, *A Letter written in the Year 1730, concerning the Question, whether the Logos supplied the Place of an Human Soul in the Person of Jesus Christ* (London, 1788), pp. 6–7.
85 *Collected Letters*, I, To Thelwall, 13 May 1796.
86 Priestley, *An History of the Corruptions of Christianity*, General Conclusion, Pt I (2 vols., Birmingham, 1786), II, 456, quoted in *Lectures 1795*, p. 113n.
87 *Lectures 1795*, pp. 112–13.
88 *Notebooks*, I, 1010, November 1801.
89 *Lectures 1795*, p. 111. Georg Wilhelm Friedrich Hegel, *Early Theological Writings*, trans. T. M. Knox (New York, 1948) holds mere legalism to be religious imposture.
90 *Lectures 1795*, p. 144.
91 *Collected Letters*, I, To Poole, 1 November 1796.

92 Coleridge borrowed Ralph Cudworth's *True Intellectual System of the Universe* (1678) in the edition of 1743 from the Bristol Library in 1795 and 1796, and took notes from it. C. Meiners (mentioned by Beddoes in his *Memorial*) had already pointed out analogies between Cudworth and Kant.

93 Coleridge declared himself a Berkleian in a letter to Thelwall (17 December 1796) rejecting a body–soul theory 'not that I am a Materialist; but because I am a Berkleian', and in the Gutch Notebook, where he proposes a poem which will make 'a bold avowal of Berkeley's System!!!!!' (*Notebooks*, I, 174. G. 169 f. 25^v.)

94 Gian N. G. Orsini, *Coleridge and German Idealism: A Study in the History of Philosophy* (Carbondale, Illinois, 1969), pp. 29–33, minimizes the influence of Berkeley, and subordinates the early subjective idealist Berkeley of *The Principles of Human Knowledge* and the *Dialogues between Hylas and Philonous* to the later, neo-platonic Berkeley of the *Siris*, which Coleridge certainly preferred in his later years, in order to preclude the argument that Coleridge had already received from Berkeley all that he later found in Kant. But this is to ward off one crudity with another. Kant's subtle transcendentalist position is not to be found in Berkeley, or in any other predecessor.

95 *Table Talk*, 28 April 1832, quoted in Raysor, *Miscellaneous Criticism*, p. 409.

96 J. G. Eichhorn's *Urgeschichte*, hsgb. mit Einleitung und Anmerkungen von Dr J. P. Gabler (Altdorf, 1790–3) offers a full account of Genesis as myth.

97 Reimarus, *Fragments*, p. 73.

98 *Ibid.*, p. 118.

99 Nathaniel Lardner, *The Credibility of the Gospel History* (13 vols., London, 1730–55), XII, 3.

100 *Poetical Works*, I, 124.

101 A. J. Arberry, *Oriental Essays* (London, 1960).

102 Warburton's book was primarily concerned to combat Newton's insistence that the Israelites, the nation of the Bible, were the oldest civilized nation on earth; he argues at length for the superior antiquity of Egyptian civilization, and shows that Moses adopted the means of the Egyptian sacerdotal class, the mysteries and the hieroglyphics, to oppress the masses. Coleridge supported Warburton until 1795, then turned against him.

103 *Collected Letters*, I, To Thomas Poole, 7 November 1796.

104 William Jones, *The Works of Sir William Jones* (6 vols., London, 1799), III, 56.

105 *Ibid.*, p. 55.

106 *Ibid.*, pp. 27–8.

107 *The Life and Correspondence of Robert Southey*. Edited by his son, the Rev. Charles Cuthbert Southey, M.A. (6 vols., London, 1849–50), II, 47–8. See M. Ahmad, 'Oriental Influences in Romantic Poetry'. Unpublished Ph.D. thesis (University of Birmingham, 1959). I owe much to Dr Ahmad's discussion of the genesis of the epic *Mohammed*, and to Professor T. J. B. Spencer for drawing the thesis to my attention.

108 *Poetical Works*, p. 329.

109 Donald Sultana, *Samuel Taylor Coleridge in Malta and Italy* (Oxford, 1969)

has shown that some of the metrical notes assigned to October 1804 were in fact written in 1801–2.

110 The MS of the sketch plan for the *Mohammed* is in the Mitchell Library, Sydney. See note in *Collected Letters*, I, 531.

111 *Life and Correspondence of Robert Southey*, II, 48.

112 Coleridge, marginal note on Lessing, *Theologische Aufsätze, Sämmtliche Schriften* (Berlin, 1791), VII, 95. Coleridge comments that some Unitarians had heard the argument that since the Koran had texts similar to some in the Gospel of John, and in the Koran 'These high phrases were mere metaphors & mystic hyperboles' in the mind of Mahomet, why should they have been more to Jesus? But Coleridge argues in rebuttal that at one period in his life Mahomet meant to present himself as 'the Paraclete, or Holy Ghost'. In short, for both 'Oriental prophets', Jesus and Mahomet, these hyperboles were genuine claims, not mere delusive window dressing.

113 Charles Lamb, *The Letters of Charles Lamb*, ed. E. V. Lucas (3 vols., London, 1935), I, 85.

114 H. J. Hunt, *The Epic in Nineteenth-Century France* (Oxford, 1941).

115 John Warden Robberds, *A Memoir of the Life and Writings of the Late William Taylor of Norwich* (London, 1843), I, 357.

116 *Table Talk*, 4 September 1833, quoted in Raysor, *Miscellaneous Criticism*, p. 429.

117 Josephus, *Jewish War*, p. 520.

118 *Ibid.*, p. 541.

119 Coleridge, marginal note on Eichhorn, *Commentarius*, Copy A11 – 2, referring to 1110.

120 *Ibid.*

121 Johann Wolfgang von Goethe, quoted and translated in Lewes, *Goethe*, I, 250–2. For accounts of the widespread use of the theme, see Werner Zirus, *Ahasverus, der Ewige Jude*. Stoff-und Motivgeschichte des deutschen Literatur, no. 6 (Berlin und Leipzig, 1930); Peter Thorslev, Jr, *The Byronic Hero* (Minneapolis, 1962); and Léon Cellier, *L'Épopée humanitaire et les grands mythes romantiques* (Paris, 1971).

122 Jean Paul [Richter], *Rede des toten Christus, Siebenkäs* (1791–7), Erstes Blumenstück. Dr Beddoes was the first in England to take up Jean Paul, and praised him highly. This particular piece was well known and widely translated, for example in Mme de Staël's *De l'Allemagne* and by Carlyle (whose translation this is) in 'Jean Paul Richter Again' (1829), his third essay on Jean Paul. There were, moreover, two complete Victorian translations of *Siebenkäs*.

123 Coleridge, marginal note on Poole's copy of Thomas Adam's *Private Thoughts on Religion*, quoted in Coburn, ed., *Inquiring Spirit*, p. 391.

CHAPTER 2
The visionary character: Revelation and the lyrical ballad

1 Quoted in G. B. Tennyson, *Sartor Called Resartus* (Princeton, 1965), p. 291.

2 John Milton, *Paradise Regained, The Minor Poems and Samson Agonistes,* ed. Merritt Y. Hughes (New York, 1937), p. 538f.

3 Quoted in Léon Cellier, *L'Épopée humanitaire,* p. 11.

4 Ernst Robert Curtius, *European Literature and the Latin Middle Ages,* trans. W. R. Trask (London, 1953), Excursus VI, pp. 451–2.

5 *Statesman's Manual,* p. 23.

6 J. G. Herder, *Briefe an Johann Georg Hamann* (Berlin, 1889), p. 8.

7 Barbara Lewalski, *Milton's Brief Epic* (Providence, R.I., and London), 1960, p. 51.

8 Coburn, ed., *The Inquiring Spirit,* p. 151. Note on Luther, *Colloquia Mensalia* (London, 1652), p. 362.

9 Lowth, *Lectures on the Sacred Poetry of the Hebrews,* trans. G. Gregory (London, 1787), II, 400.

10 Paul Haupt, ed., *Biblische Liebeslieder. Das sogenannte Hohelied Salomos* (Leipzig, 1907), p. x.

11 *Ibid,* p. vii.

12 John Beer, *Coleridge the Visionary* (New York, 1962), pp. 282–3.

Coleridge executed and continued to propose all his life works of art based on these theories of Biblical genres. In 1799 he made a paraphrase of Psalm XLVI in hexameters. In 1815 he hoped 'soon to present. . .a series of Odes and Meditations, in different metres, on each clause of the Lord's Prayer: as the first, on the word *Our*: the second, on *Our Father*: the third, on "which *art* – in the Heaven" &c.' (*Collected Letters,* IV, To Thomas A. Methuen, 2 August 1815). To Derwent he proposed 'a biblical work, containing 1. a literal and 2. a metrical translation of all the Odes and fragments of Odes scattered throughout the Pentateuch and the Historical works of the O. Testament' (*Collected Letters,* IV, 8 January 1818).

13 *Collected Letters,* I, To Thelwall, 17 December 1796.

14 See complete translation of Eichhorn's outline in Appendix A.

15 Kraus has written:

'Einen radikalen Umbruch in der Auslegung der Prophetie hat erst Herder eingeleitet, indem er die Propheten ausschliesslich in ihrer Menschlichkeit, also unter Ausschaltung jedes supranaturalen a priori, sieht, ihre poetischen Verkündigungen aufnimmt und in begeisterter Ergriffenheit den 'göttlichen Inhalt' der menschlichen Poesie deutet. . .[A]lles das, was Herder anleitend und wegweisend mitgeteilt hatte, bei Eichhorn nun zur beherrschenden Norm der Hermeneutik wird' (Kraus, *Geschichte der historisch-kritischen Erforschung,* p. 131).

'A radical upheaval in the interpretation of prophecy was introduced by Herder, in that he views the prophets exclusively in their humanity, that is, ruling out *a priori* everything supernatural, he takes up their poetic prophecies and with enthusiastic emotion expounds the 'divine content' of human poetry . . .All that the pioneering Herder had intimated became in Eichhorn's hands the commanding norm of hermeneutics.'

They laid the foundations of the aesthetic-psychological categories that dominated the nineteenth-century view of prophecy.

16 Johann Jakob Griesbach's Greek New Testament (1774–5) was used by the Unitarians as the basis for their new Bible; it is still the basis of *Textkritik*. Even Michaelis had, like William Whiston in England, still given a harmony of the four Gospels, despite his denial of canonicity to Mark and Luke; Griesbach separated the Fourth Gospel from the others and printed them in parallel columns under the title 'Synopse der Evangelien', thus originating the term 'Synoptic Gospels'. His aim was to make possible a comparison of the Gospels, because a harmony was impossible, as none offers a reliable chronological order. (Werner Georg Kümmel, *Das Neue Testament: Geschichte der Erforschung seiner Probleme* (Freiburg u. München, 1958), p. 88.)

17 Klopstock, *Ausgewählte Werke*, Letter 'An Meta', p. 111.

18 *Klopstocks Werke* (Leipzig, 1798–1813), III, 44, lines 62–5.

19 Friedrich Gottlieb Klopstock, *The Messiah. A New Edition in One Volume.* (Bungay, 1808), p. 27.

20 *Messias*, p. 46, lines 100–6. Again these lines are slightly at variance with the preferred text.

21 *Messiah*, p. 29.

22 *Messias*, p. 49, lines 153–4.

23 *Messiah*, p. 31.

24 *Werke*, IV, 194, lines 1166–79.

25 *Messiah*, p. 121.

26 Quoted in Kümmel, *Das Neue Testament*, p. 92.

27 Eichhorn treated the question first in his 'Über die drey ersten Evangelien' in 1794, postulating 'eine gemeinschaftlichen Quelle', 'a common source' for the Gospels that had existed in various forms. In his *Einleitung in das Neue Testament* (Leipzig, 1804–18) his hypothesis grew even more complex. Eichhorn pointed out that whatever documents Matthew and Luke had used, they related nothing of the conception, birth, and youth of Christ; these later accretions are mere 'sagas' with which tradition had decked out the life of Jesus. Coleridge, with his anti-Catholic bias, went even further than Eichhorn in dismissing the miracles of the conception. Thus the historical investigation of the life of Jesus reduced the materials for the life as 'biography'.

28 J. G. von Herder, *Herders sämmtliche Werke*, hrsg. Bernhard Suphan, XIX (Berlin, 1880), 418–19.

29 *Ibid.*

30 *Confessions of an Inquiring Spirit*, ed. H. St J. Hart (London, 1956), p. 53. The book was first published posthumously in 1840, but was read by Thomas Arnold and others in manuscript.

31 Coleridge, MS Notebook 23 f. 42ᵛ. This notebook contains long transcriptions from Eichhorn and from an anonymous work, *Characteristik der Alten Mysterien für Gelehrte und Ungelehrte, Freimaurer und Fremde, aus den Original-Schriften* (Frankfurt und Leipzig, 1787). It was written about 1822, when Coleridge was entering the phase of his religious thinking recorded in the *Aids to Reflection*, then at the planning stage. It is interesting to remark that he never changed his opinion, recorded on the margins of Eichhorn's *Einleitung in das Alte Test-*

ament, as to the fragmentary and non-Mosaic origins of the Pentateuch. The theological lectures of 1795 still defended the Mosaic origins. In general, Coleridge seems not to have accepted deist contentions until they came to him from the German apologists.

The dating of Coleridge's notes is always hazardous. In the three volumes, two of the fifty-three notes are dated (1812 and 1827). The editors of the marginalia place the earliest notes at about 1807, and attempt to classify the rest on the doubtful evidence of handwriting as 'early' or 'late'. Whatever the dates, they tell us little about the date of Coleridge's first acquaintance with the work or its purport.

32 He was willing to accept that earlier documents had been used by Moses.

33 Thomas Hobbes, *Leviathan* (London, 1651), Pt 3, chapter 33.

34 Fuller, 'Geddes', p. 113.

35 Coleridge, marginal note on Eichhorn, *Einleitung in das Alte Testament*, (Leipzig, 1780–3), III, 338. William Whiston had attempted to harmonize the prophecies quoted in the New Testament with the Old Testament. Anthony Collins's *Discourse of Freethinking* (1713) had used the elaborate ironic technique of the period, arguing that the truth of Christianity must stand or fall by its fulfilment of prophecy, and then showing that the prophecies did not bear the meaning attributed to them in the New Testament; allegorization was therefore essential, and Collins's satiric allegory shows that by allegory anything in the Old Testament can be twisted into a prophecy of New Testament events.

36 Coleridge, marginal note on Eichhorn, *Einleitung AT*, III, 388.

37 Coleridge, marginal note on Eichhorn, *Einleitung AT*, II, 341.

38 *Confessions of an Inquiring Spirit*, p. 46. This was a common opinion among the critics. In the edition of Genesis published by Eichhorn and Gabler in 1790, Gabler remarks on how this Jewish superstition of inspiration had obscured the real character of the Pentateuch:
'Das Hauptlabyrinth in das der christliche Theologe sich verirrte, war die jüdische Superstition, dass Moses diese ganze Urgeschichte aus unmittelbarer göttlicher Offenbarung erhalten habe. Hatte man keine so übertriebenen Begriffe von Theopneustie der Heiligen Schrift gehabt, so hätte man sich in dieser Urgeschichte nie so sehr von der Natur verirren können' (*Urgeschichte*, III, 7 n. 2).
'The main labyrinth in which Christian theology lost itself was the Jewish superstition that Moses received the whole of Genesis by direct divine revelation. If one had had no such exaggerated conception of the theopneusty of the Holy Scriptures, one would never have been able so to wander from the true nature of Genesis.'

Thus, once the doctrine of inspiration was amended, the mythical character of Genesis seemed obvious.

39 Coleridge agreed that the life of Christ must be regarded as doctrinal, not biographical. Speaking of the infancy narratives in Matt. 1–2, he asks: 'Is it possible, that at a very early period, as early as A.D. 80 or 90 a poetic Romance,

allegorico-cabalistic, a Christopaedia, could have been written?' (Notebook 30 (1823–4), ff. 29–29ᵛ). His marginalia on Eichhorn point scathingly to the legendary nature of all the material that has served Mariolatry. Belief in the devil was likewise a matter of 'popular faith' that arose during the 'Intersilentium of the O. and N. Testament' (Notebook 30, ff. 4–7).

40 'Religious Musings', lines 45–63, *Poetical Works*.

41 Herder, *A Brief Commentary on the Revelation of Saint John* (London, 1821), pp. 275–6.

42 It is clear that 'primitive expressiveness' even in Herder is far more complex than it is given credit for by critics, e.g. the influential book by M. H. Abrams, *The Mirror and the Lamp* (New York, 1958), p. 90.

43 *Herders Werke*. Dritter Teil. Erste Abteilung, p. 144.

44 *Ibid.*, p. 139.

45 The alternatives presented themselves succinctly to Michaelis: either Revelation is a circumstantial historical account of the Fall of Jerusalem, or it is a forgery: 'But if it be really a forgery, if it contains prophecies of the Jewish war made after the events themselves had taken place, we have reason to wonder, that the author did not prophesy more circumstantially, & that he appears so little acquainted with the events of that war' (John David Michaelis, *Introduction to the New Testament*, trans. Herbert Marsh (6 vols., Cambridge, 1801), IV, 528). Semler had attributed Revelation to Cerinthus, and denied its canonicity. Lessing, in his *Historische Einleitung in die Offenbarung Johannis*, agreed that the inclusion of Revelation showed how planlessly the canon of the NT had been formed, 'wie planlos sich der Kanon des Neuen Testaments gebildet!' (See Leopold Zscharnack, *Lessing und Semler; ein Beitrag zur Entstehungsgeschichte des Rationalismus und der kritischen Theologie* (Giessen, 1905), p. 102.)

46 Lardner, *The Works of Nathaniel Lardner* (11 vols., London, 1788), III, 130.

47 Austin Farrer, *The Revelation of St. John the Divine* (Oxford, 1964), p. 50.

48 S. N. Mukherjee, *Sir William Jones: A Study in Eighteenth Century British Attitudes to India* (Cambridge, 1968), p. 7.

49 Lewalski, *Milton's Brief Epic*, pp. 11–12.

50 Sir Thomas Herbert, *Some Years' Travels into Divers Parts of Africa and Asia the Great, etc.* (1677), pp. 31–3, quoted in Beer, *Coleridge the Visionary*, p. 226.

51 C. H. Dodd, *The Interpretation of the Fourth Gospel* (Cambridge, 1953), pp. 97–114. Gnosticism may be understood in the special limited sense as referring to the group of religious systems described by Irenaeus and Hippolytus in their works against heresy; or it may be understood in a more extended sense as referring to a way of thought widely prevalent both before Christianity and much later. Writers in the eighteenth century tended to take it in a variety of extended polemical senses. Some modern authorities have carried on the practice of the earlier Biblical critics and have included in gnosticism such sects as the Iranian sect of John the Baptist known as 'Mandaism', whose sacred book of John and other writings – discovered only in this century – are held to be closer to primitive Christianity than the Synoptic

Gospels themselves, which are the product specifically of Jewish reaction. This is clearly a continuation of the efforts to restore closeness to Jesus through understanding his milieu. C. H. Dodd dismisses the theory that Mandaean books can tell us anything about the mythology of early Christianity; their date is too late, they contain no new historical nor legendary material about John or Jesus. But it has been strongly supported by the continuators of the German tradition, Lidzbarski, Reitzenstein, and Bultmann, and has recently won the support in a modified form of some English writers as well.

52 Isbon T. Beckwith, *The Apocalypse of John: Studies in Introduction with a Critical and Exegetical Commentary* (New York, 1919).

53 'Vom dogmatischen Gesichtspunkt aus darf die Frage als offen gelten.' See 'Apokalypse', *Lexikon für Theologie und Kirche*, p. 695.

54 Eichhorn, *Commentarius*, p. xlvii.

55 Quoted in Kümmel, *Das Neue Testament*, p. 100. Coleridge had apparently been prepared to entertain the possibility of abandoning the idea of canonicity altogether, for in the *Confessions* he defends the necessity of preserving some form of canonical test:
'. . .on the one hand, to prevent us from sinking into a habit of slothful, undiscriminating, acquiescence, and on the other to provide a check against those presumptuous fanatics, who would rend the *Urim* and *Thummim from the breastplate of judgment*, and frame oracles by private divination from each letter of each disjointed gem, uninterpreted by the Priest, and deserted by the Spirit, which shines in the parts only as it pervades and irradiates the whole' (p. 65).
Semler had concluded from his historical examination of the formation of the canon that the only test must be 'practical present need' (Zscharnack, *Lessing und Semler*, p. 103).

56 Semler, quoted in Kümmel, *Das Neue Testament*, p. 79.

57 Coleridge's views on the authenticity of the Apocalypse reflect the complex new apologetics. He doubts its authenticity on the old grounds; but finds new grounds for reinstating 'John'. He often expressed his 'doubts', which amount to a denial, without reservation (*Literary Remains*, pp. 512–21, and 115). He holds to the canonicity of the book in the new fashion: 'I myself believe the Evangelist John to have been the author of the Apocalypse; but still in controversy I should content myself with demonstrating it's Apostolic *Age*' (*Collected Letters*, IV, 2 August 1815). That is to say merely that it was composed within the period traditionally assigned to the life of the apostles; the traditional date of A.D. 81–96 corresponds well enough with Eichhorn's date of A.D. 95 or 96 and with modern opinion, which holds that the events refer generally to the fall of Jerusalem but in detail to events under Domitian and possibly even Trajan (putting the date into 98), though Jewish apocalyptic material of an earlier date may be included. If Coleridge's phrase reflects the new, broader definition of what might be taken to define 'apostolic' in terms of history, a late statement adds the argument equally characteristic of the movement, the argument from literary value: Coleridge described himself as

'without the least sympathy with Luther's suspicions on this head, but on the contrary receiving this sublime poem as the undoubted work of the Apostolic age' (*On the Constitution of Church and State*, ed. Shedd, VI, 113n).

58 *Principles of Biblical Interpretation*, translated from the *Institutio Interpretis* of J. A. Ernesti, by Charles H. Terrot, Fellow of Trinity, Cambridge (Edinburgh, 1832), p. 6. There was also a translation by Moses Stuart in 1827.

59 F. D. E. Schleiermacher, *Hermeneutik*, hrsg. von Heinz Kimmerle (Heidelberg, 1959). This is the first complete edition of Schleiermacher's writings on hermeneutics.

60 Wilhelm Dilthey, 'Die Entstehung der Hermeneutik', *Gesammelte Schriften* (Leipzig, 1924), V, 326–7.

61 Momigliano, 'Friedrich Creuzer and Greek Historiography', in *Studies in Historiography*, p. 83.

62 Ernesti, *Institutio Interpretis*, p. 210.

63 See the searching discussion of the problem by the modern philosopher of history, R. G. Collingwood in 'History as Re-enactment of Past Experience', Epilegomenon to *The Idea of History* (London, 1946). See also Alan Donagan, *The Later Philosophy of R. G. Collingwood* (Oxford, 1962).

64 Dilthey, *Gesammelte Schriften*, p. 331.

65 Frank Kermode, *The Sense of an Ending: Studies in the Theory of Fiction* (New York, 1967), p. 5.

66 Beckwith, *Apocalypse of John*, pp. 168 and 292f.

67 Eichhorn, *Einleitung AT*, III, 188. Similarly, Eichhorn wrote of Jeremiah: 'Diesem einfachen Stoff prophetische Würde zu geben, bedient sich Jeremia der Dichtung einer Unterredung mit Jehova.' 'In order to give this simple stuff prophetic dignity, Jeremiah made use for his poetic fiction of a conversation with Jehovah.'

68 Coleridge, marginal note on Eichhorn, *Einleitung AT*, III, 188–9.

69 Eichhorn, *Einleitung AT*, III, 38.

70 Coleridge, marginal note on Eichhorn, III, 38.

71 *Confessions*, p. 77.

72 *Notebooks*, I, 191 G. 187 (1796).

73 The note on the Crewe MS reads:
'This fragment with a good deal more, not recoverable, composed, in a sort of Reverie brought on by two grains of Opium taken to check a dysentery, at a Farm House between Porlock & Linton, a quarter of a mile from Culbone Church, in the fall of the year, 1797.'

74 *Confessions*, p. 68.

75 Letter to Paul Demeny, 1871, quoted in R. Ellmann and C. Feidelson, *The Modern Tradition* (London, 1965), p. 203.

76 *Ibid.*, p. 205.

77 Albert Friedman, *The Ballad Revival* (Chicago, 1961), p. 251.

78 Preface, *Lays of Ancient Rome* (London, 1828), p. 16.

79 Friedman, *The Ballad Revival*, p. 254.

80 *Collected Letters*, To Derwent Coleridge, 8 January 1818.

81 *Some Longer Elizabethan Poems,* p. 406.
82 Donald Davie, *Ezra Pound: Poet as Sculptor* (London, 1965), p. 15.

CHAPTER 3
The oriental idyll

1 Friedrich Schiller, 'Über Naive und Sentimentalische Dichtung', *Schillers Werke* (Berlin und Darmstadt, 1956), II, 724.
2 H. M. McLuhan, 'Tennyson and Picturesque Poetry', *Critical Essays on the Poetry of Tennyson,* ed. John Killham (London, 1960), p. 84.
3 Eichhorn, *Commentarius,* p. v.
4 David Friedrich Strauss, *The Life of Jesus,* trans. George Eliot (London, 1892), 2nd ed., p. 329.
5 McLuhan, 'Tennyson and the Romantic Epic', in Killham (ed.), *Critical Essays,* p. 93.
6 Eichhorn, *Commentarius,* II, 35.
7 Coleridge, marginal note on *Commentarius,* Copy AII – 1, referring to II 11. Eichhorn attributes the 'four' disasters to Old Testament tradition, as well as their collocation into one: 'Therefore shall her plagues come in one day, death, and mourning, and famine; and she shall be utterly burned with fire: for strong is the Lord God who judgeth her' (Rev. 18, 8).
8 Coleridge, marginal note on *Commentarius,* II $^{+1-+2}$, referring to II 35.
9 Coleridge, marginal note on *Commentarius,* II, 33.
10 Farrer, *Revelation of St John,* p. 18.
11 Lowth, *The Poetry of the Hebrews,* p. 213.
12 Farrer, *Revelation of St John,* p. 171.
13 Herder, *Oriental Dialogues,* p. 159.
14 The contrast between the two women takes us back to the earliest appearance of the technique of *figura,* to Paul, Gal. 4, 21–31. Through the opposition between Hagar–Ishmael and Sara–Isaac, Paul develops the distinction between law and grace, slavery and freedom, whereby Genesis is *figura* for Isa. 54, 1. (Erich Auerbach, 'Figura', *Gesammelte Aufsätze zur Romanischen Philologie* (Bern, 1967), p. 75).
    Origen developed this treatment of the two women in his allegorical interpretation of Genesis, which interested Coleridge very much, as his later notebooks show.
    Revelation itself, of course, offers the most striking example of the two women as representative of their communities, the community of bondage and the community of grace.
    'The celestial bodies, the sun and moon, are replaced by the glory of God (21.23), yet the prophet continues to visualize this glory in terms of trees, streets, rivers, and a city. It is the city which binds this new heaven and its earth together, for it is the place where God dwells with his people. The strategic difference between the first and the new creation is thus defined by the community which dwells there. The mark of one community is idolatry

(vs. 8), the mark of the other is victorious faithfulness (vs. 7)' (Paul S. Minear, 'The Cosmology of the Apocalypse', *Current Issues in New Testament Interpretation: Essays in Honor of Otto A. Piper*, eds. William Klassen and Graydon F. Snyder (London, 1962), p. 27).

15 Lilith, Adam's concubine, is one of the three Queens of the Demons of Jewish popular lore, and was thought to have given birth to demons. ('Demonology', *The Jewish Encyclopedia*, ed. I. Singer (New York and London, 1903), IV.

16 Alice D. Snyder, 'The MS of "Kubla Khan"', *Times Literary Supplement*, 2 August 1934, 541. For Coleridge's note, see my chapter 1, p. 59.

17 On 'war' and the prophets, a modern commentator is instructive:
'In every vision the prophet sees this heaven and this earth as the home of the idolaters. But in every vision he also sees this home as a realm under attack, as a battlefield on which these lords and their servants are decisively defeated. 'War broke out in heaven' and as a result no place is left in heaven for the devil and his angels (12. 7,8). We must therefore cope with the picture of this heaven and earth as passing away because of the incursion of a powerful conqueror. The transience of one is the measure of the power of the other. The aggressors are clearly identified: the declaration of war proceeded from God and from his throne. His emissary, who judged and fought in righteousness, was the Lamb that was slain. In the prosecution of his campaign he used his prophets and apostles, his kings and priests, his virgins and lampstands – the whole retinue of servants' (Minear, 'Cosmology of the Apocalypse', pp. 28–9).

This eschatological war of the last days, the divine destruction of the realm of the idolatrous, has been seen by each of the prophets in his own day.

18 Curtius, *European Literature*, p. 504. See Excursus XV, 'Numerical Composition' and Excursus XVI, 'Numerical Apothegms'; and F. Dornseiff, *Das Alphabet in Mystik und Magie* (Leipzig and Berlin, 1925).

The Book of Wisdom was probably produced at Alexandria in the first century after Christ: 'The thoroughly Jewish core is embellished with all manner of traits derived from Greece, or rather from Hellenistic–Egyptian syncretism' (Otto Eisfeldt, *Einleitung in das Alte Testament* (1934), p. 656). Once again, the source of Orientalism in the eighteenth century is Hellenistic syncretism.

19 Gershom G. Scholem, *Major Trends in Jewish Mysticism*, 3rd rev. ed. (New York, 1961), p. 42.

20 This is the more likely because of the attempts in the eighteenth century to reconstruct the architecture of the Temple; Newton's drawings of the Temple were published in the well-known *Chronology*, and attention had been drawn particularly to these figures in Ezekiel by Newton's attempt to determine the actual dimensions of the reed and the 'sacred cubit' in 'A dissertation upon the Sacred Cubit of the Jews and the Cubits of the Several Nations; in which, from the dimensions of the greatest Egyptian Pyramid, as taken by Mr. John Greaves, the ancient Cubit of Memphis is determined' (1737) (Frank Manuel, *Isaac Newton Historian* (Cambridge, 1963), pp. 161–2).

Coleridge had read Newton's *Opera*, ed. S. Horsley (5 vols., 1779–85), by 1796, and there are mentions of him in several contexts in that year.

21 For an Arabist's allegory of 'Kubla Khan' see Mahmoud Manzalaoui, 'Some English Translations of Arabic Imaginative Literature (1704–1838): a Study of their Portrayal of the Arab World, with an Estimate of their Influence on Nineteenth Century English Literature'. Unpublished B.Litt. thesis (Oxford, 1947).

22 Goethe, 'Hebräer', Notes to *Der West-östlicher Divan* (Nördlingen, 1961), p. 123.

23 *Ibid.* Goethe's sense of the Bible as a second world, in which we find and create ourselves is not far from Coleridge's:

'Und so dürfte Buch für Buch das Buch aller Bücher dartun, dass es uns deshalb gegeben sei, damit wir uns daran wie an einer zweiten Welt versuchen, uns daran verirren, aufklären und ausbilden mögen' (*ibid.*, p. 124).

'And so, book by book, the Book of books might make it evident that it was given to us in order that we may prove ourselves on it as on a second world, lose ourselves, enlighten and educate ourselves in it.'

24 I follow here the reconstruction given by Mark L. Reed, *Wordsworth. The Chronology of the Early Years 1770–1799* (Cambridge, Mass., 1967), pp. 208–210. Reed in turn bases his account on Mary Moorman, disagreeing with her only on the date of 'Kubla'. The date in late November is preferable to the September or early October date which E. K. Chambers, Moorman, and Griggs, supported by Wylie Sypher, favour, because it makes it possible for Coleridge's quarrel with Charles Lloyd already to have reached its full height, so that the evidence connecting 'Kubla' with the time of the quarrel with Lloyd is accounted for without placing the poem in the spring of 1798.

Elisabeth Schneider in *Coleridge, Opium, and 'Kubla Khan'* (Chicago, 1953), was surely right in calling attention to Landor's *Gebir* (1798), in that it clearly belongs to the group of mythological poems which attempted a kind of classical-Oriental syncretism based on a Hellenistic geography. *Gebir*, however, since it is so far from being an isolated example, was hardly necessary to 'Kubla Khan' and adds little if any support to the argument for a later date for the writing of 'Kubla'.

25 Goethe, 'Hebräer', p. 123.

26 Newton, New College MSS, 11, f.186, quoted in Manuel, *Isaac Newton Historian*, p. 128. Among the works of Newton that Coleridge had read was the *Observations upon the Prophecies of Holy Writ*, which together with the *Chronology* constitute 'a fairly complete universal history of mankind, both sacred and profane, since the Creation' (Manuel, *Isaac Newton Historian*, p. 163).

27 *Ibid.*, p. 128.

28 *Ibid.*, p. 163.

29 *Der Tod Abels. Gessners Werke.* Auswahl. Herausgegeben von Prof. Dr Ad. Frey (Berlin und Stuttgart, n.d.), Zweiter Gesang, p. 121, lines 18–20.

'Siehst du jenen Fluss durchs grüne Thal zu winden? Dort scheinet ein Hügel einen Garten voll Bäum' auf grasreichem Rücken zu tragen.'

30 *Ibid.*, p. 122.

'Itzt wandelten wir wieder dem Hügel zu, wir gingen durch das fruchtbare Gesträuche, das seinen Fuss umkränzte; auf seiner Stirne stund eine Zeder aus den kleinen Fruchtbäumen empor und streute hoch herunter weit verbreitete Kühlung, und in ihrem Schatten floss eine Quelle durch Blumen. Da lag eine unabsehbare Gegend in offener Aussicht vor uns und verlor sich dem zu schwachem Auge in neblichter Luft.' (lines 15–19)

> 'Dies ist ein Schatten des Paradieses,
> eine bequeme Wohnung, ein Paradies werden
> wir hier nicht finden; nimm uns in deinen
> schützenden Schatten auf, hohe Zeder!'   (lines 20–4)

31 Klopstock, *Ausgewählte Werke*, p. 784.

32 Klopstock, *The Death of Adam. A Tragedy in Three Acts.* (Dublin, 1763). B. Q. Morgan, *A Critical Bibliography of German Literature in English Translation, 1481–1927* (Stanford, Calif., 1938), rev. 2nd ed., identifies the translator as B. Lloyd.

33 Klopstock, *Ausgewählte Werke*, pp. 784–5.

34 *Death of Adam.* The English version is unpaginated.

35 *Ausgewählte Werke*, p. 891.

36 *Death of Adam.*

37 *Ausgewählte Werke*, p. 797.

38 *Death of Adam.*

39 *Messias, Werke* (1798–1813), G. v, 186–203.

40 *Messiah*, pp. 135–6. The cedar motif is again conspicuous. Yet another example of it appears in an impressive scene in Bodmer's *Noah*. The race of giants mass below Eden to attack it with a thousand pair of elephants: 'Troops of giants, with sturdy limbs, appear'd with axes to fell the venerable cedars at the foot of the mountain, that stand with trunks enormous, raising their stately heads above all the trees of the forest' (*Noah*, trans. J. Collyer (London, 1767), i, 99).

> 'Es standen
> Schaaren Giganten, gerüstet mit scharf geschliffenen Veilen,
> An dem Fuss des Gebirges, den Schmuck der Zedern zu fällen,
> Die vor dem Menschen wurden, das dritte Tagewerk des Schöpfers.'

(J. J. Bodmer, *Die Noachide* (Basel, 1781), Dritter Gesang, p. 66).

41 *Life and Correspondence of Robert Southey*, ii, 16.

Coleridge's interest in the poetry of the Flood in the context of Revelation continued. In the Notebooks of 1801 we read: 'But in the last Judgment by Fire how can the Salamander die? This & Drayton's Noah's ark a fine elucidation of an idea *spectrally* & at once given – Grand-awful! analysed–devilized–rational – Most exquisitely ludicrous on Salamanders idealy / Third Hour – 9th Stanza (*Notebooks*, i, 1026 6.33).

Coleridge is referring, as Kathleen Coburn's note points out, to the seventeenth-century cosmic epic *Doomes-day* by William Alexander, written in eight-line stanzas divided into twelve hours. This is just the sort of epic Coleridge would have read in preparation for his *Fall of Jerusalem*.

42 Bodmer, *Die Noachide*, Neunter Gesang, pp. 244–5. Bodmer, *Noah*, trans. J. Collyer, II, 82–3. Bodmer's German reads:

> 'Als der folgende Morgen ein stummes, erstorbenes Licht bracht,
> Das mit mühsamer Angst durch Wolkenberge sich durchschlang,
> Waren die Felder in Assur nur Eine Verwüstung, das Land war
> Itzt ein Meer von unabsehbarer Breite vereinet.
> Alle Gürtel der Erd in ihrem vielfarbigten Schmucke
> Lagen da unter der wässernen Decke.'

This was a commonplace of eighteenth-century Orientalism, based on Voltairean notions of 'Oriental despotism'.

Thus Gessner too, praising the poet who consecrates his talents to virtue and to innocence:

'His reputation shall bloom with unfading verdure, while the trophies of the proud conqueror shall moulder in the dust, and the superb mausoleum of the tyrant shall stand unknown in the midst of a desart, where human feet have made no path' (Gessner, *The Death of Abel*, trans. M. Collyer (London, 1761), p. 3).

Towards the end of the century this convention tended to pass into more specific accounts that owed something to Bruce's descriptions of Arab nomadism and the desert 'simoom', of which Coleridge, among many others, made use.

43 Werner Beyer in *The Enchanted Forest* (Oxford, 1963) makes out a convincing case for Coleridge s knowledge of *Oberon* in the original, in part at least, by 1797; but the interpretation as a whole is another example of the critics' tendency to succumb to the tyranny of a single source.

44 Bodmer, *Noah*, I, 73.
Die Noachide, Zweiter Gesang, p. 52:

> 'ihr übet Gewaltthat und Morden,
> Tugenden Satans, der sie in die Herzen die Priester
> gehaucht hat.'

It will be evident that the translation is very free, expanding, contracting and altering the text at will.

45 Bodmer, *Noah*, II, 8.
Die Noachide, Siebenter Gesang, pp. 183–4:

> 'Aber auch an der Decke des Saals, im goldenen Kranze,
> Hängt ein krystallener Himmel mit feurigen Farben gezeichnet,
> Mitten darinn ein Stuhl von Saphir auf Rädern erhaben
> Rad in Rade, belebt mit einem einwohnenden Geiste,
> Und umgeben von vier cherubisch gebildeten Hütern,
> Flugel und Räder voll Augen, die Augen der Räder Berille.
> Feuer zur Rach entflammt hielt wartend zwischen den Rädern;
> Auf dem Stuhl sitzt richterlich einer von göttlichem Ansehn,

Schrecken gieng von der Stirne des Stuhls hervor, in den Rädern
Wälzten sich Donnerkeile.'

46 Bodmer, *Noah*, II, II.
Die Noachide, Siebenter Gesang, p. 185:
'Wie schlägt mir das Herz, ich halte ihn für unsere Hofnung!'

47 Bodmer, *Noah*, II, 163.
Die Noachide, Elfter Gesang, pp. 288–9:
'ich kam im Traume zu einem Gefilde,
Wo ein verparadieseter Grund mit blumigten Gärten
Leuchtet, getränkt aus Nektarbächen von silbernen Fluten,
Und erhöhet mit Hügeln, die, dunkel von Cinnamomus
Und von Orangenschatten, die liebliche Wohnung bedecken,
Mit halböfnendem Zirkel, die vollen Ströme der Sonne
In dem mittäglichen Himmel zu fassen.'
The translator's 'autumn' seems to be an error.

48 Klopstock, *Messias*, G. XII, 870–3. This is another example of the badness of
the text of the edition of 1798–1813. A more satisfactory reading is that of the
Ausgewählte Werke.

49 *Messiah*, p. 355.

50 William Beckford, *Vathek* (London, 1970). For these motifs see pp. 1–23.
Lowes pointed to them, and to the lack of firm evidence that Coleridge
was acquainted with them, remarking typically, 'That a reminiscence of
it flashed through the interweaving fancies of the vision is well within
the bounds of possibility.' As always, he failed to see the imaginative context
(John Livingston Lowes, *The Road to Xanadu* (New York, 1927), p. 364).

51 André Parreaux, *William Beckford, Auteur de Vathek (1760–1844)*, (Paris,
1960), p. 324.

52 Humphrey Prideaux, *The True Nature of Imposture Fully Display'd in the
Life of Mahomet* (London, 1697), p. 13, quoted in Byron Porter Smith,
Islam in English Literature (New York, 1939), p. 35.

53 Quoted in Cellier, *L'Épopée humanitaire*, p. 50.

54 The main works of Jones were as follows:
*Poems, consisting chiefly of translations from the Asiatick Languages. To which
are added two Essays: I. On the Arts commonly called Imitative* (Oxford, 1772);
*The Moallakat or the Seven Arabian Poems which were suspended on the Temple
at Mecca* (London, 1782); *The Asiatic Miscellany consisting of Original
Productions, Fugitive Pieces, Imitations and Extracts* (Calcutta, 1785–6);
Asiatick Researches (Calcutta, 1794).
For all these, see *The Works of Sir William Jones* (6 vols, London, 1799).
See also *The Letters of Sir William Jones*, ed. Garland Cannon (Oxford, 1970),
2 vols.

55 Parreaux, *William Beckford*, p. 332.

56 Jones, 'A Discourse on the Institution of a Society, for Inquiring into the
History, Civil and Natural, the Antiquities, Arts, Sciences, and Literature of
Asia', *Works*, I, I.

57 *Ibid.*, p. 3.
58 *Ibid.*, p. 4.
59 *Works*, I, 93–4.
60 Quoted in Raymond Schwab, *La Renaissance orientale* (Paris, 1950), p. 83.
61 Jones, 'On the Hindu's', *Works*, I, 31.
62 *Ibid.*, p. 115.
63 *Ibid.*, p. 110.
64 *Einleitung AT*, III, 513. Lowth, in speaking of the Book of Job, held that while the scene is laid in Arabia, 'yet the poem abounds so much in imagery borrowed from Egypt, that it is plain that country must have been extremely well known to the author' (Lowth, *The Poetry of the Hebrews*, p. 363n). Herder too, varying the formula, spoke in *Vom Geist der ebräischen Poesie* of Edom as 'a magazine of Oriental, i.e., Arabian wisdom' (Herder's point being the intermingling of Hebrew and Arabian culture in the Book of Job) (*Oriental Dialogues*, p. 205).
65 Jones, *Works*, I, 130.
66 Jones, 'The Palace of Fortune', *Works*, IV, 425.
67 'The Poem of Amriolkais', *Moallakat*, *Works*, IV, 249. Jones too avoided in his pastiches the rank strangeness of these poems, though his prose rendering of them holds its place to this day as the finest English translation, despite some errors.

In this, of course, both Jones and Coleridge are representative of the successful use of Oriental themes and imagery in English in the eighteenth century. As Martha Pike Conant has pointed out in *The Oriental Tale in England* (New York, 1908), the moral and philosophical, rather than the fairy-tale and satiric tale of France, predominated, from Addison's 'Vision of Mirza' through Goldsmith and Johnson; and by the same token, the 'Oriental style' conceived as simple and grave, rather than extravagant, ornate, and coloured, was more successful, for Biblical language and figures could be used as a kind of native Orientalism.

Coleridge was able to combine the extravagant and the grave; he admired the *Moallakat* and compared its sublimity with the Book of Job, echoing Herder: 'The Book of Job is pure Arab Poetry of the highest and most antique cast' (*Table Talk*, pp. 72–3).

The *Moallakat* influenced Rogers's 'Pleasure of Memory', Landor's *Poems from the Arabic and Persian*, Browning's 'Muléykeh', a 'Dramatic Idyl', and, according to Hallam Tennyson's *Memoir*, it gave Tennyson the idea of 'Locksley Hall'.
68 Jones, *Works*, I, 145.
69 *Ibid.*, p. 136.
70 *Ibid.*, p. 137.
71 *Ibid.*
72 *Ibid.*, p. 233.
73 *Ibid.*

74 *Ibid.* p. 277.
75 Strauss, *Life of Jesus*, p. 66. Strauss gives the example of Eichhorn's interpretation of the tree of knowledge as a poisonous plant, an interpretation better received by the orthodox than his own.
76 Jones, *Works*, I, 30.
77 *Ibid.*, pp. 230–1.
78 F. Manuel, *The Eighteenth Century Confronts the Gods* (Cambridge, Mass., 1959), gives a good account of the principal parties.
79 *Urgeschichte*, I, 256, and *Einleitung AT*, I, 383–4. Hartlich–Sachs point out in this the influence of Robert Wood's *Essay on the Original Genius of Homer*, reviewed by Heyne in 1770 in the *Göttinger Gelehrten Anzeigen*; in 1773, Michaelis's son published a translation of Wood, with Heyne's review. Beddoes's library contained the *Göttinger Gelehrten Anzeigen*, but we do not know from what date; his admiration for Heyne and Michaelis, however, makes it likely that he procured the review in book form.
80 For Coleridge's version of this process, see Elinor S. Shaffer, 'Coleridge's Theory of Aesthetic Interest', *Journal of Aesthetics and Art Criticism*, XXVII/4 (Summer, 1969), 399–408.
81 *Einleitung AT*, p. 282.
82 J. P. Gabler, *Neues Theologisches Journal* (1790), 331n.
83 J. P. Gabler, *Urgeschichte*, II, 627.
84 *Ibid.*, 630–1.
85 Christian Hartlich und Walter Sachs, *Der Ursprung des Mythosbegriffes in der modernen Bibelwissenschaft* (Tübingen, 1952), p. 65.
86 Strauss, *Life of Jesus*, p. 47. The most extended application of the notion of the philosophical or dogmatic mythus to the Gospel histories before Strauss was, as Strauss himself pointed out, *Über Offenbarung und Mythologie, Revelation and Mythology* (Berlin, 1799), a response by an anonymous author to Kant's *Religion innerhalb der Grenzen der reinen Vernunft, Religion within the Bounds of Reason Alone*, with which Coleridge extensively concerned himself in the *Aids to Reflection*. I have not been able to find any evidence that Coleridge knew the *Offenbarung*, often attributed to Schleiermacher, but now credited to J. C. A. Grohmann.

The author argued that the whole life of Jesus had an ideal existence in the Jewish mind long prior to his birth, and that those elements in the Gospels that did not coincide with Jewish anticipations were not historical, but the result of popular response to the disparity. Some reviewers condemned the book for 'sweeping scepticism', despite its apologetic intention.

The mythical interpretation was carried further by G. L. Bauer's *Hebräische Mythologie* (1802), reviewed approvingly by Gabler as another step towards the demise of rationalist explanation (*Journal für auserlesene theologische Literatur*, II (1805), 39–59). Strauss was also impressed by a short anonymous article of 1816 on the life of Jesus that argued that the Gospel stories were mythical, and adduced a series of parallels from heathen myth and the Judaic myths of the Old Testament. ('Die verschiedenen Rücksichten in welchen und für welche der Biograph Jesu arbeiten kann', *Kritisches Journal der neuesten theologischen Literatur*, ed. Berthold, v (1816), 225–45. See Horton Harris, *David Friedrich Strauss and his Theology* (Cambridge, 1973), for an account of Strauss's development.)

87 Hartlich–Sachs, p. 67.
88 J. P. Gabler, *Neuestes Theologisches Journal* (1798), 235–9.
89 Coleridge, marginal note on Eichhorn, *Einleitung AT*, ii, 339.
90 *Ibid.*
91 Coleridge, marginal note on Eichhorn, *Einleitung AT*, iii, 513.
92 *Urgeschichte*, ii, 373.
93 MS. 'Logic', p. 10.
94 *Ibid.*, p. 9.
95 *Aids to Reflection*, ed. Shedd, pp. 251–2n.
96 Herder, *Oriental Dialogues*, p. 46.
97 *Ibid.*, p. 54.
98 *Ibid.*, p. 46.
99 *Notebooks*, i^2, 1245(h).
100 Coleridge's early sympathy for Hinduism is fairly well documented, and sometimes castigated by critics prepared to acquiesce in stereotypes of 'Oriental indolence'.
101 'Divine Ideas' MS, p. 273. An extract was printed as an appendix in J. H. Muirhead, *Coleridge As Philosopher* (London, 1930), pp. 283–4.
102 *Miscellaneous Criticism*, ed. Raysor, p. 409.
103 Herder, *Oriental Dialogues*, p. 11.
104 *Ibid.*, p. 24.
105 *Ibid.*, p. 25.
106 Coleridge, marginal note on Herder, *Briefe, das Studium der Theologie betreffend* (Frankfurt und Leipzig, 1790), 2nd corrected ed., – 3 The annotations in this volume have been dated by the editors of the marginalia as '?c autumn 1814' on the grounds that a long quotation from the *Briefe* that appears in a notebook entry of October 1814 was used in the *Biographia Literaria*; they point out, however, that Coleridge had read the *Briefe*, *Kalligone*, and *Von der Auferstehung*, and some other unspecified works by Herder by December 1804 (according to Coleridge's note in *Kalligone*), and there is good reason to believe he had known both the *Briefe* and *Von der Auferstehung* in the 1790s.
107 MS Notebook 23, ff. 43^v–44.
108 *Ibid.*, f. 44.
109 See R. P. C. Hanson, *Allegory and Event: A Study of the Sources and Significance of Origen's Interpretation of Scripture* (London, 1959) for a modern Christian rejection of Origen's allegorical method (in favour, ironically enough, of 'historical-critical' method):
'The step from Paul's allegorization to Origen's, a step into the non-historical world of Hellenistic allegory, can only be taken with the aid of Philonic exegesis. And that is precisely how Origen does achieve this step. The distinction between "moral" (= Philonic) and "spiritual" (= Christian) inter-

pretation (if it ever existed) disappears in Origen's exposition, and the balance between "objective" and "subjective" interpretation is never struck. All is merged in a morass of spiritualizing exposition which has no legitimate ground in historical reality. Origen certainly opened the way to the discovery in the text of the Bible of the deepest secrets of the spiritual life, but the only tools which he provided for the operation were those of theological fantasy' (pp. 282–3).

110 *Notes on English Divines*, I, 337.
111 Quoted in Hanson, *Allegory and Event*, p. 128.
112 Friedrich Wilhelm Joseph von Schelling, *Schellings sämmtliche Werke*, VI (München, 1946–59), 64. These lectures, first delivered in 1821, were published too late for Coleridge to have seen them; Schelling, however, quotes Coleridge, and it is not unlikely that Coleridge knew of them.
113 *Ibid.*, pp. 22–3.
114 *Ibid.*, p. 64.
115 *Ibid.*, p. 244.
116 *Ibid.*, p. 223.
117 Schelling refers to 'dem bekannten Coleridge', 'the well-known Coleridge' in a long footnote (p. 198): The word 'tautegory' he has found in Coleridge's 'Prometheus' lecture, which he intimates derives from his own *Die Gottheiten von Samothrake*, which Coleridge understands better than any of Schelling's own countrymen. He takes issue on one point: 'Coleridge braucht übrigens das Wort tautegorisch als gleichbedeutend mit *philosophem*, was freilich meinem Sinn nicht gemäss wäre, allein er will vielleicht nur sagen, die Mythologie müsse gerade ebenso eigentlich genommen werden, wie man ein Philosophem zu nehmen, pflegt und diess hat er aus der obenerwähnten Abhandlung ganz richtig herausgefühlt.' 'Coleridge uses the word "tautegory" as meaning the same as "philosopheme", which certainly would not accord with my sense of it, but perhaps he merely wishes to say that mythology must be taken as real in just the way we are accustomed to take a philosopheme and this he has quite correctly perceived in the above-mentioned essay [*Die Gottheiten*].'
118 Jean Pépin, *Allégorie et Mythe; les origines grecques et contestations judaeo-chrétiennes* (Paris, 1958), p. 60.
119 Schelling, *Einleitung in die Philosophie der Mythologie*, p. 91 n. 2.
120 *Letters*, III, To Joseph Cottle, 7 March 1815.
121 Kathleen Raine, 'Thomas Taylor, Plato and the English Romantic Movement', *British Journal of Aesthetics* (April, 1968), 99–123.
122 Gershom G. Scholem, *Zur Kabbalah und ihren Symbolik* (Zürich, 1960), trans. Ralph Manheim (London, 1965). See especially Chapter I, 'Religious Authority and Mysticism', p. 15.
123 William Empson, *Some Versions of Pastoral* (London, 1935), p. 186.
124 *Ibid.*, pp. 189–90.
125 Wallace Stevens, *Opus Posthumus* (London, 1959), p. 211.

Hölderlin's 'Patmos' ode and 'Kubla Khan': mythological doubling

1 E. H. Stahl, *Hölderlin's Symbolism, an Essay* (Oxford, 1945), p. 8.
2 Lothar Kempter, 'Hölderlin und die Mythologie', *Wege zur Dichtung*, Bd. vi (1929), 66.
3 P. H. Gaskill, 'Christ and the Divine Economy in the Work of Friedrich Hölderlin', Unpublished Ph.D. thesis (Cambridge, 1971), especially Chapter I, 'Hölderlin's contacts with Pietism'.
4 Dr Gaskill has pointed to the importance of Bengel's Biblical exegesis, especially *Gnomon*, which Hölderlin had among his books. He also draws attention to the fact that he is known to have borrowed from the library of the Tübinger Stift a commentary on Isaiah by Campegius Vitringa, the Dutch theologian whose interpretation of Revelation was respected by Bengel. But Dr Gaskill ignores the range of more recent and influential exegetical works and examples of *Einleitungswissenschaft* that were available to Hölderlin.
5 The evidence as to Hölderlin's reading is scanty, and mainly to be found in his correspondence and in the catalogue of books in his possession at his death (printed in Ernst Muller, *Hölderlin. Studien zur Geschichte seines Geistes* (Stuttgart, 1944)); the *Grosse Stuttgarte Ausgabe* contains much useful documentation; information about his school curriculum is also available. I am grateful to P. H. Gaskell for his help in these matters.
6 Gaskill, 'Christ in the Work of Hölderlin', p. 25.
7 Albrecht Ritschl, *Geschichte des Pietismus* (Bonn, 1880–6), iii, 169.
8 Schleiermacher, *Über die Religion: Reden an die Gebildeten unter ihren Verächtern* (Göttingen, 1920), p. 10.
9 *Lectures 1795*, pp. 197–8.
10 *Ibid.*, p. 199.
11 *On the Prometheus of Aeschylus*, p. 6.
12 *Notes on English Divines*, i, 134. See also p. 131; and ii, 211.
13 MS Notebook 23, ff. 44ᵛ–45.
14 G. A. Wells, 'Stages of New Testament Criticism', *Journal of the History of Ideas*, xxx (April–June 1969).
15 *Lectures 1795*, p. 183.
16 Orsini has made the attractive suggestion that Coleridge had come across this idea early, in Thomas Taylor's translation (1787) of the Sixth Book of Plotinus's First Ennead, on the Beautiful, which he may very well have read as a schoolboy. (Orsini, *Coleridge and German Idealism*, p. 13.)
17 See, e.g., John Marsh, *Saint John* (Harmondsworth, 1968) for a review of the evidence and present views on the dating of the Gospel. The most authoritative statement of the case for holding John to be based on 'an ancient Palestinian tradition' independent of the synoptic gospels and therefore possibly as early as A.D. 70 is to be found in C. H. Dodd, *Historical Tradition in the Fourth Gospel* (Cambridge, 1963). Many would not accept such an extreme view, but in general the estimates of the date have been revised downwards from the

335

middle of the second century to a little later or a little earlier than A.D., 100 depending on how much use John is judged to have made of the Synoptics. The granting of historical primacy to the most 'theological' of the Gospels represents the final triumph of the theological over the biographical interpretation of the Gospels.

18 *Friedrich Hölderlin: Selected Poems*, trans. J. B. Leishman (London, 1944), p. 105.

19 Peter Szondi, *Der andere Pfeil: zur Entstehungsgeschichte von Hölderlin's hymnischen Spätstil* (Frankfurt, 1963), p. 29.

'Das Elegische mündet also nicht eigentlich ins Hymnische, ein qualitativer Sprung trennt die beiden Formen; der von der Erlebnislyrik zum selbstlosen Preis der Götter. Wer aber das Hymnische betritt, ohne das Elegische ganz abgestreift zu haben, erscheint Hölderlin als "falscher Priester".' 'The elegiac, then, does not really flow into the hymnic; a qualitative leap divides the two forms: the leap from the lyric of experience to the selfless praise of the gods. Anyone who enters upon the hymnic without having completely stripped himself of the elegiac appears to Hölderlin as a "false priest".'

20 *Miscellaneous Criticism*, p. 164.

21 Elinor S. Shaffer, 'Coleridge's Theory of Aesthetic Interest', *Journal of Aesthetics and Art Criticism*, XXVII/4 (Summer, 1969).

22 *On the Prometheus of Aeschylus*, p. 7.

23 'Das Älteste Systemprogramm des deutschen Idealismus', *Sämtliche Werke* (Berlin und Darmstadt, 1967), p. 1090. This brief manifesto was in Hegel's possession, but may have been drafted by Schelling, or by all three men together, in 1796. Hölderlin is generally credited with the ideas on mythology, and some scholars see Hölderlin as having played an active part in the formation of the new philosophy. For the view that it was written by Hegel, see Otto Pöggeler, 'Hegel, der Verfasser des ältesten Systemprogrammes des deutschen Idealismus', *Hegel-Studien*, Beiheft 4 (1969), 17–32, and H. S. Harris, *Hegel's Development: Toward the Sunlight 1770–1801* (Oxford, 1972), Appendix, pp. 249–51. Even Harris hesitates, and finally accounts for the 'tone of prophetic enthusiasm' by suggesting that Hegel wrote it in a letter to Hölderlin!

24 See 'Friedensfeier – Die Krise in der Hölderlin-Forschung', in Allessandro Pellegrini, *Friedrich Hölderlin: Sein Bild in der Forschung* (Berlin, 1956).

25 C. F. Dupuis, *Origine de tous les Cultes, ou Religion universelle*, VI (Paris, 1791), 65. Lowes dismissed Dupuis's *Origine* simply as 'a mad performance'. We may surmise from his saying 'I have sedulously turned some hundreds of his pages' and referring in the text only to the first two volumes ('a riot of genii, daemons, guardians, and tutelary spirits of every feather') that unlike Coleridge, Lowes never read as far as the sections on Revelation. In a footnote he is a little more charitable: the work 'foreshadows, in wildly unscientific fashion, the modern scientific study of Comparative Religion' (p. 489). Lowes did point out the reference to Dupuis on the angels of the planets (II[1], 63–103) in the 'Ode to the Departing Year' which again underlines the

importance that the Book of Revelation had for Coleridge during this period:
Throughout the blissful throng,
Hush'd were harp and song:
Till wheeling round the throne the Lampads seven,
(The mystic Words of Heaven)
Permissive signal make.

(*Road to Xanadu*, pp. 489–90)

26 Dupuis, *Origine*, VI, 60.
27 Quoted in Macrobius, *Saturnalia*, trans. and ed. Henri Bornecque (Paris, n.d.), I, 239.
28 Richard Payne Knight, *A Discourse on the Worship of Priapus, and its Connexion with the mystic Theology of the Ancients* (London, 1786), pp. 79–80.
29 *Ibid.*, p. 69.
30 *Ibid.*, p. 76.
31 *Ibid.*, p. 82.
32 *Ibid.*, pp. 29–33.
33 *Notebooks*, I, 1646 21. 392 f. 84.
34 Wolfgang Binder, 'Hölderlin's Patmos-Hymne', *Hölderlin-Jahrbuch* (1967–8), 96–7.
35 Kempter, 'Hölderlin und die Mythologie', p. 69.
36 *Ibid.*
37 Rudolph Pannwitz, 'Hölderlin's Erdkarte', in *Hölderlin: Beiträge zu seinem Verständnis in unserm Jahrhundert* (Tübingen, 1961), p. 279.
38 Hegel, *Early Theological Writings*, pp. 90–1.
39 Kempter, 'Hölderlin und die Mythologie', p. 42.
40 Hegel, *Early Theological Writings*, p. 81.
41 *Ibid.*, p. 82.
42 'Du warst so oft mein Genius', he wrote to Hegel, 10 July 1794. *Briefe von Friedrich Hölderlin* (Weimar, 1922). See also *Grosse Stuttgarter Ausgabe*, 6, 1.
43 To Neuffer, 28 November 1791.
44 Hegel, *Early Theological Writings*, p. 90.
45 *Ibid.*, p. 248.
46 R. Guardini, *Hölderlin; Weltbild und Frömmigkeit* (München, 1955), p. 571.
47 Binder thinks that the 'Erarbeitung des rechten Namens' of the god applies to 'Patmos' only; the same process seems to me to work in 'Friedensfeier', and indeed to characterize Hölderlin's cumulative and progressive use of mythic material throughout the body of his work.
48 Emil Petzold, *Hölderlin's Brod und Wein: Ein exegetischer Versuch* (Sambor, 1896 and Darmstadt, 1967).
49 To Casimir Ulrich Böhlendorf, 2 December 1802.
50 To Böhlendorf, 4 December 1801.
51 *Ibid.*
52 To Friedrich Wilmans, 28 September 1803.
53 To his brother, 1 January 1799.
54 To Böhlendorf, 2 December 1802.

55 *Ibid.*
56 Macrobius, *Saturnalia*, p. 219.
57 *Ibid.*, pp. 203, 205.
58 Hans H. Penner, 'Myth and Ritual', in 'On Method in the History of Religion', *History and Theory*, Beiheft 8, p. 57.
59 Richard Reitzenstein, *Die Hellenistischen Mysterienreligionen* (Leipzig u. Berlin, 1927), pp. 401–3. His examples are drawn from Hoffmann. There is, of course, a continuity between modern scholars of this school and the Biblical and classical scholars who were Coleridge's contemporaries.
60 Reinhold Merkelbach, *Roman und Mysterium in der Antike* (München, 1962), p. 51.
61 Frye, *Anatomy of Criticism*, p. 146.
62 Merkelbach, *Roman und Mysterium*, p. 67.
63 *Philosophical Lectures*, p. 232.
64 *Ibid.*, pp. 233–4.
65 Burke, *Language as Symbolic Action*, pp. 207–8.
66 *Unpublished Letters*, ed. E. L. Griggs, To Sterling, 30 October 1833.
67 Scholem quotes a wonderful description from Baldensperger, *Die messianisch-apokalyptischen Hoffnungen des Judentums*:
'Not only have the seers perceived the celestial hosts, heaven with its angels, but the whole of this apocalyptic and pseudepigraphic literature is shot through with a chain of new revelations concerning the hidden glory of the great Majesty, its throne, its palace...the celestial spheres towering up one over the other, paradise, hell, and the containers of the souls.' (Scholem, *Jewish Mysticism*, p. 43).
68 *Notebooks*, I, 1016 and 383.
69 William Warburton, *The Divine Legation of Moses*, 4th ed. (5 vols., London, 1764–5), III, 108–9.
70 Eric Havelock, *Preface to Plato* (Oxford, 1963), p. 89. Havelock is very illuminating on the topic of the social function of the epic bard.
71 *Notebooks*, I, 1179.

CHAPTER 5
Browning's St John: the casuistry of the higher criticism

1 Perhaps the most balanced essay is by Kingsbury Badger, ' "See the Christ Stand!": Browning's Religion', in *Robert Browning: A Collection of Critical Essays*, ed. Philip Drew (London, 1966), pp. 72–95.
2 The *Athenaeum* for 4 June 1864, reviewing *Dramatis Personae*, thought 'A Death in the Desert' 'on the whole, the finest poem in the book'. The *Quarterly* reviewer was even more lavish, calling it 'one of Mr. Browning's finest poems'. Both construe it, as has often been noted, as a reply to Renan.
3 Robert Langbaum, 'Browning and the Question of Myth', *The Modern Spirit: Essays on the Continuity of Nineteenth- and Twentieth-Century Literature* (London, 1970), p. 96.

338

4 'Parleying with Gerard de Lairesse', lines 386–9.
5 W. O. Raymond, *The Infinite Moment* (Toronto, 1950), p. 109.
6 See the report of the eighth Meeting of the Browning Society, 25 February 1887, for the Rev. Llewellyn Davies's statement that 'Browning wrote the poem long prior to the publication of Renan's work' and for the full context of his conclusion that Browning is concerned with Strauss rather than Renan (*The Browning Society's Papers* (2 vols., London, 1888), II (pt III), 185).
7 Ernest Renan, *The Life of Jesus* (London, 1864), p. 15.
8 Strauss, *The Life of Jesus*, p. 329.
9 Renan, *The Life of Jesus*, pp. 288–9.
10 *Ibid.*, p. 289.
11 *Ibid.*, p. 289n.
12 Letter, 19 November 1863, *The Letters of Robert Browning to Miss Isa Blagden*, arr. by A. Joseph Armstrong (Waco, Texas, 1923), p. 100.
13 *Ibid.*
14 Strauss, *Life of Jesus*, p. 445n.
15 *Ibid.*, p. 452.
16 Renan, *Life of Jesus*, p. 250.
17 *Ibid.*, pp. 186–7.
18 *Letters to Isa Blagden*, p. 101.
19 Renan, 'The Critical Historians of Jesus', *Studies in Religious History* (London, 1886), p. 73.
20 *Ibid.*, p. 187.
21 *Ibid.*, p. 192.
22 *Ibid.*
23 *Ibid.*, p. 198.
24 *Ibid.*, p. 196.
25 *Ibid.*, p. 197.
26 *Ibid.*, p. 205.
27 Renan, 'Francis of Assisi', *Studies in Religious History. First Series: Leaders of Christian and Anti-Christian Thought*, p. 109.
28 Quoted in Harold W. Wardman, *Ernest Renan: a Critical Biography* (London, 1964), pp. 202–3.
29 Hoxie N. Fairchild, 'Browning the Simple-Hearted Casuist', in Boyd Litzinger and K. L. Knickerbocker, eds., *The Browning Critics* (University of Kentucky, 1965), pp. 218–28.
30 J. Hillis Miller, *The Disappearance of God* (Cambridge, Mass., 1963), p. 105n.
31 See Elinor S. Shaffer, 'Metaphysics of Culture: Kant and Coleridge's *Aids to Reflection*', *Journal of the History of Ideas*, XXXI, no. 2 (April–June 1970), 199–218.
32 *Letters to Isa Blagden*, p. 101.
33 Renan, *Life of Jesus*, p. 14.
34 *Ibid.*, p. 16.
35 *Ibid.*, p. 17.
36 *Ibid.*, p. 18.

37 *Ibid.*
38 *Ibid.*, p. 16.
39 *Ibid.*
40 *Ibid.*, p. 21.
41 Raymond, *The Infinite Moment*, p. 47. Other similar remarks by Raymond: 'Yet it is evident that Browning's abnegation of reason continually sprains his argument whenever he is dealing with the historical bases of Christianity. For, if the incidents of the gospel narrative are placed beyond the pale of reason, it is difficult to show how they possess objective validity' (p. 40). But it is when they are placed *within* the pale of reason that it is difficult to show they possess objective validity. As he himself admits, 'In laying exclusive stress on love, he [Browning] is inclined to regard the historical evidence of Christianity, not merely as unproven, but as embodying a narrative of events which are absolutely inconceivable from the point of view of reason' (p. 41). Raymond simply does not see the necessary relationship between the denial of reason and the affirmation of faith.
42 G. C. Goyne, 'Browning and the Higher Criticism.' Unpublished Ph.D. thesis (Vanderbilt University, 1967), p. 22.
43 See, for example, Hugo Friedrich, *Die Struktur der modernen Lyrik* (Hamburg, 1960), p. 36.
44 Mrs M. G. Glazebrook, 'A Death in the Desert', *The Browning Society's Papers*, II, 157.
45 *Ibid.*
46 *Ibid.*, p. 160.
47 Mrs Orr, 'Religious Opinions of Robert Browning', *Contemporary Review*, December 1891, 880.
48 J. M. Robertson, *A History of Freethought in the Nineteenth Century* (London, 1929), p. 162.
49 Hillis Miller, *Disappearance of God*, p. 84.
50 *The Browning Society's Papers*, II, 185.
51 Matthew Arnold, 'The Study of Poetry', *Essays in Criticism*, 2nd series (London, 1888), pp. 1–2.
52 'On the Poet: Objective and Subjective', *The Browning Society's Papers* (London, 1888), I, 12.
53 *Ibid.*, p. 13.
54 *Ibid.*
55 *Ibid.*
56 *Ibid.*, p. 10.

CHAPTER 6
Daniel Deronda and the conventions of fiction

1 'The Lifted Veil', *The Works of George Eliot*, (Edinburgh, 1897), p. 318.
2 Kermode, *The Sense of an Ending*, pp. 138–40.
3 *Letters*, ed. Gordon S. Haight (London, 1954–6), VI, Edward Dowden, To

Blackwood, 13 January 1877. Dowden was one of George Eliot's most perceptive and appreciative critics.

4 *Letters*, VI, 2 March 1876.

5 *Ibid.*, IV, 2 August 1863.

6 *Ibid.*, 19 July 1866.

7 *Ibid.*

8 *Ibid.*

9 *Ibid.*, August 1866.

10 Georg Lukács, *History and Class Consciousness* (London, 1971), p. 160.

11 *Letters*, IV, August 1866.

12 *Ibid.*, VI, 16 December 1876.

13 Basil Willey, 'George Eliot: Hennell, Strauss, and Feuerbach', *Nineteenth Century Studies* (London, 1949), p. 229. Willey, by contrast, writes: 'Hennell shows a remarkable instinctive command of the technique of textual criticism – remarkable, above all, because when he wrote the book he knew next to nothing of what had already been done in Germany' (*Ibid.*, p. 221).

14 See Francis Edward Mineka, *The Dissidence of Dissent: the Monthly Repository, 1806–38, under the Editorship of Robert Aspland, W. J. Fox, R. H. Horne, and Leigh Hunt; with a Chapter on Religious Periodicals 1700–1825* (Chapel Hill, N.C., 1944), pp. 207–8, for an account of the *Repository's* full and favourable coverage of German criticism.

15 Willey, 'George Eliot', p. 230.

16 Raymond Williams, *The English Novel from Dickens to Lawrence* (London, 1970), p. 75.

17 Milman, *History of the Jews*, pp. xxv–xxvi.

18 *Ibid.*, p. xx.

19 *Ibid.*, pp. xxiii–xxiv.

20 George Eliot, *The Letters of George Eliot*, ed. Gordon S. Haight (6 vols., London, 1954–6), 12 October 1867.

21 Emanuel Deutsch, *Literary Remains of the Late Emanuel Deutsch* (London, 1874), pp. 25–6. George Eliot's acquaintances also included such men as Theodor Goldstücker, Professor of Sanskrit at University College, who wrote on Indian subjects for the *Westminster* and the *Athenaeum*; his pupil, Nikolaus Trübner, the publisher of 'Trubner's American Oriental Record' from 1865. The most eminent of them was of course Max Müller.

22 Arthur Penrhyn Stanley, *Lectures on the History of the Jewish Church*, 3rd ed. (3 vols., London, 1883). Preface to Original Edition, I, 21.

23 Derek and Sybil Oldfield, '*Scenes of Clerical Life:* the Diagram and the Picture', in B. Hardy (ed.), *Critical Essays on George Eliot* (London, 1970), p. 2.
   Bernard J. Paris, *Experiments in Life: George Eliot's Quest for Values* (Detroit, 1965) offers a more elaborate discussion of Feuerbach, but presents him as 'consistently empirical' (p. 93).

24 Eugene Kamenka, *The Philosophy of Ludwig Feuerbach* (London, 1970), p. 104.

25 *Ibid.*, pp. 107–8.
26 Quoted in Kamenka, *Philosophy of Feuerbach*, p. 120.
27 Ludwig Feuerbach, *The Essence of Christianity*, trans. George Eliot (London, 1854), p. 139.
28 *Ibid.*, p. 140.
29 *Ibid.*, p. 147.
30 *Ibid.*, p. 147–8.
31 *Ibid.*, p. 147.
32 *Ibid.*
33 *Ibid.*, p. 200.
34 *Ibid.*, p. 30.
35 *Ibid.*, p. 31.
36 Ernst Cassirer, *The Problem of Knowledge* (New Haven, 1950), p. 304.
37 Georg Lukács, *The Meaning of Contemporary Realism* (London, 1962), p. 61. Lukács holds that 'The possibility of realism. . .is bound up with that minimal hope of a change for the better offered by bourgeois society' (p. 68). In modernist art, this perspective disappears. But Lukács himself finds that Flaubert in *L'Éducation sentimentale* anticipates this development. The realistic part of the novel, he tells us, ends during the night on the barricades, and Moreau begins his *temps perdu*. Equally in *Daniel Deronda* the utopian elements become an aspect of despair, of the flight to the past and to art, through the very largeness of the claim to renewal, the immensity of the *recherche* necessary to maintain hope.
38 *Letters*, IV, To Clifford Allbutt, August 1868.
39 Feuerbach, *Essence of Christianity*, p. 191.
40 W. J. Harvey pointed out 'the double remove in time', but tried to wrench it into a means to 'objectivity' and a 'stable relationship with the reader'. The result is that he finds her handling of the tense shifts merely an 'infuriating lapse' ('The Treatment of Time in *Adam Bede*', *A Century of George Eliot Criticism*, ed. Gordon S. Haight (London, 1968), pp. 300–1).
41 Kamenka, *Philosophy of Feuerbach*, p. 109.
42 *Ibid.*, p. 110.
43 Feuerbach, *Essence of Christianity*, p. 204.
44 For example, one simply cannot agree with the judgment that Goethe's contribution to the tradition of *Weltliteratur* (whether or not this is to be identified with 'the works of nineteenth-century European realism', as J. P. Stern thinks) is 'hardly very significant' (Stern, 'Reflections on Realism', *Journal of European Studies* (March, 1971), 16). For a full discussion of the term *Weltliteratur* (coined by Goethe) and of his contribution to it, see Fritz Strich, *Goethe and World Literature* (London, 1949).
45 Lord Acton, 'George Eliot's Life', *The Nineteenth Century* (March, 1885), in *A Century of George Eliot Criticism*, p. 158.
46 The sources of this story are surely German, and not, as Knoepflmacher thinks, at second hand from Mary Shelley; they are the novellas early translated into English and widely read through the Victorian period. Schiller's *Geister-*

seher is invoked (Latimer is described as 'a miserable ghost-seer, surrounded by phantoms in the noonday, trembling under a breeze when the leaves were still, without appetite for the common objects of human desire, but pining after the moonbeams' (p. 323)). The name 'Bertha' recalls Tieck's story, *Der Blonde Eckbert*, whose theme, like that of 'The Lifted Veil', is solitude; and the comparison of Bertha with a cold water-nixie is surely a reference to La Motte-Fouqué's *Undine*.

47 Georg Lukács, ' "Les Années d'Apprentissage de Wilhelm Meister" Comme Tentative de Synthèse', *Théorie du Roman* (Paris, n.d.).

48 L. Goldmann, 'Introduction aux premiers écrits de Georges Lukács', *Théorie du Roman*, p. 171.

49 Ian Watt, *The Rise of the English Novel* (London, 1957), p. 250.

50 Hannah Arendt, 'Introduction: Walter Benjamin: 1892–1940', in Walter Benjamin, *Illuminations* (London, 1970), trans. H. Zohn, describes Benjamin's crucial art of quotion.

51 Feuerbach, *Essence of Christianity*, pp. 2–3.

52 J. Hillis Miller, *The Form of Victorian Fiction* (London, 1968), p. 84.

53 *Ibid.*, p. 140.

54 *Ibid.*, p. 113.

55 *Ibid.*, p. 118.

56 *Ibid.*, p. 117.

57 Q. D. Leavis, 'David Copperfield', in F. R. and Q. D. Leavis, *Dickens* (London, 1970).

58 Feuerbach, *Essence of Christianity*, p. 87.

59 *Ibid.*, pp. 87–8.

60 *Ibid.*, p. 90.

61 *Ibid.*, p. 169.

62 *Letters*, IV, To Emily Davies, 8 August 1869.

63 Feuerbach, *Essence of Christianity* p. 91.

64 Scholem, *Jewish Mysticism*, pp. 278–86 on the soul of Adam; 'Tradition and New Creation in the Ritual of the Kabbalists', in *On the Kabbalah*, pp. 136–7, on the water rituals.

65 F. R. Leavis, *The Great Tradition* (London, 1948), p. 93.

66 *Letters*, To Mme Eugene Bodichon, 2 October 1876.

67 'Mr Gilfil's Romance', *The Works of George Eliot* (London and Edinburgh), IV, 144.

68 *Ibid.*, p. 181.

69 *Daniel Deronda*, ed. with an introduction by Barbara Hardy (Harmondsworth, 1967).

70 It is a striking fact that only Edward Dowden, of all George Eliot's critics, seems to have understood these aspects of her art.

Steven Marcus, the analyst (in *The Other Victorians* (New York, 1964)) of Victorian sexual mores, scarcely mentions her; and his disciple, the self-styled apostle of female emancipation, has nothing but a sneer, founded on the grossest misconception:

'Living in sin, George Eliot lived the revolution as well perhaps, but she did not write of it. She is stuck with the Ruskinian service ethic and the pervasive Victorian fantasy of the good woman who goes down into Samaria and rescues the fallen man – nurse, guide, mother, adjunct of the race' (Kate Millett, *Sexual Politics* (New York, 1970), p. 139).

How very much more accurate is Dowden:

'The conscience of George Eliot asserts itself so strongly because there are in her nature other powers strong also, and urging great claims upon the will. Her senses are framed for rich and varied pleasure. The avenues between the senses and the imagination are traversed to and fro by swift and secret intelligencers. There are blind notions in her blood, which respond to vague influences, the moral nature of which may be determined by a contingency; there are deep incalculable instincts, the heritage from past generations, which suddenly declare themselves with an energy that had not been surmised. There are zeals and ardours of the heart, eager demands and eager surrenders. There is the grasping, permitted or restrained, of a richly endowed nature after joy, – after joy from which to avert the eyes for ever is better as the sundering of flesh and soul. This nature, in which conscience must needs be stern, is a nature of passionate sensibility' ('George Eliot', *The Contemporary Review*, August 1872, in *A Century of George Eliot Criticism*, pp. 66–7).

71 Leavis, *The Great Tradition*, p. 86.
72 Coleridge, *Philosophical Lectures*, pp. 315–16.
73 'The Influence of Rationalism', *Fortnightly Review*, I (1865), 47.
74 Quoted in Michel Foucault, *Madness and Civilisation*, p. 215.
75 *Ibid.*, p. 216.
76 *Ibid.*, pp. 216–17.
77 *Letters*, IV, To Mrs Peter Alfred Taylor, 30 July 1863. George Eliot's boredom with the belated furore seems justified by the account Owen Chadwick gives in *The Victorian Church*, 2nd ed. (2 vols., London, 1970–2), of the state of opinion in the 1860s:

'Until the sixties the Bible had not received accurate examination. Most of England assumed without inquiry that the Bible was still true as history, even if educated England was abandoning the precise accuracy of the earlier parts of Genesis. But once a lack of accuracy was conceded, the historians must attempt to determine the extent of error or of myth, the reliability, the dating, and the authorship of the various books' (pp. 57–8).

The fact that this describes precisely the state of affairs at the beginning of the 1790s reminds us that an institutional history of the acceptance of the higher criticism such as Chadwick's, although justified in its own terms, is completely misleading as to the real rate and locus of knowledge and acceptance of the movement in England. No indication is given of the date of the origin of these ideas, no indication of their early entry into England in the eighteenth century. The presumption throughout is that the Church's rate of acceptance (Chadwick dates acceptance in 1892) is the right one, that moderate men of good judgement all rightly acquiesced in this pace, and that 'serious non-

Christians' like George Eliot deserved the pillorying they got for forcing the pace.

78 *Ibid.*
79 *Das Glasperlenspiel. Versuch einer Lebensbeschreibung des Magister Ludi Josef Knecht samt Knechts hinterlassenen Schriften.* Herausgegeben von Hermann Hesse (2 vols., Zürich, 1943), 1, 69–70.
80 *The Glass Bead Game*, trans. Richard and Clara Winston (London, 1970), p. 49.
    The whole passage, too long to quote, is of interest (pp. 67–71 in Hesse, and in Winston pp. 47–50).
81 *The Glass Bead Game*, p. 48.
82 *Letters*, IV, To Sara Hennell, 23 August 1863.
83 *Ibid.*, 26 December 1863.
84 Renan, 'La Poésie des Races celtiques', *Essais de morale et de critique* (Paris, 1860), p. 455.
85 *Ibid.*, p. 385.
86 Leavis, *The Great Tradition*, p. 96.
87 Matthew Arnold, *St. Paul and Protestantism*, 3rd ed. (London, 1875), p. 90.
88 Wardman, *Ernest Renan*, p. 74.
89 Renan, 'M. Feuerbach and the New Hegelian School', *Studies in Religious History*, pp. 42–3.
90 *Ibid.*, p. 43.
91 Wardman, *Ernest Renan*, p. 137.
92 Roland Barthes, *Writing Degree Zero* (London, 1967), pp. 38–9.
93 *Impressions of Theophrastus Such*, 4th ed. (Edinburgh, 1879), p. 324.
94 *Ibid.*, pp. 327–8.
95 J. Cross (ed.), *Life of George Eliot* (3 vols., Edinburgh, 1885), To J. Sibree, beginning of 1848.
    Of course she made many notably more generous statements, but again they bear primarily on the moral state of her own countrymen:
'Moreover, not only towards the Jews but towards all oriental peoples with whom we English come in contact, a spirit of arrogance and contemptuous dictatorialness is observable which has become a national disgrace to us.'
(To Harriet Beecher Stowe, 29 October 1876.) Note her use of the term 'oriental'.
96 *St. Paul and Protestantism*, p. 117.
97 *Ibid.*, p. 114.
98 Hesse, *Das Glasperlenspiel*, 1, 254–5.
99 Hesse, *The Glass Bead Game*, p. 166.
100 *Ibid*, p. 255.
101 Kermode, *The Sense of an Ending*, p. 143.

Adams, Maurianne S. 'Coleridge and the Victorians: Studies in the Interpretation of Poetry, Scripture, and Myth', Ph.D. thesis, Indiana, 1967.

Adolf, Helen. *Visio Pacis: Holy City and Grail*, Pennsylvania, 1960.

Ahmad, M. 'Oriental Influences in Romantic Poetry', Ph.D. thesis, University of Birmingham, 1959.

Appleyard, J. A. *Coleridge's Philosophy of Literature: The Development of a Concept of Poetry 1791–1819*, Cambridge, Mass., 1965.

Arberry, A. J. *Oriental Essays*, London, 1960.

Arnold, Matthew. *The Complete Prose Works of Matthew Arnold*, ed. R. H. Super, Ann Arbor, Michigan, 1968.

Essays in Criticism, 2nd series, London, 1888.

St. Paul and Protestantism, 3rd ed., London, 1875.

Auerbach, Erich. *Gesammelte Aufsätze zur Romanischen Philologie*, Bern, 1967.

Barth, J. Robert. *Coleridge and Christian Doctrine*, Cambridge, Mass., 1969.

Barth, Karl. *Die protestantische Theologie im 19. Jahrhundert*, Zürich, 1947. ET (in part): *From Rousseau to Ritschl*, London, 1959.

Bayle, Pierre. *Dictionnaire historique et critique*, Rotterdam, 1697. ET: *The Dictionary historical and critical of P. Bayle*, trans., P. Des Maizeaux, 2nd ed., 5 vols., London, 1734–8.

Beck, Lewis White. *Early German Philosophy*, Cambridge, Mass., 1969.

Beckwith, Isbon T. *The Apocalypse of John: Studies in Introduction with a Critical and Exegetical Commentary*, New York, 1919.

Beer, John. *Coleridge the Visionary*, London, 1959, New York, 1962.

Benjamin, Walter. *Schriften*, Frankfurt, 1955. ET (in part): *Illuminations*, ed. and intro. Hannah Arendt, trans. H. Zohn, London, 1970.

Benz, Ernst. *Adam; der Mythos vom Urmenschen*, München, 1955.

Beyer, Werner. *The Enchanted Forest*, Oxford, 1963.

Bodmer, Johann Jakob. *Die Noachide*, Basel, 1781.

Noah, trans. Collyer, 2 vols., London, 1767.

Boeckh, August. *On Interpretation and Criticism,* trans. and ed. John Paul Pritchard, Norman, Oklahoma, 1968.

Borsch, Frederick Houk. *The Son of Man in Myth and History,* London, 1967.

Boulger, James, D. *Coleridge As Religious Thinker,* New Haven, 1961.

Browning, Robert. *The Letters of Robert Browning to Miss Isa Blagden,* arr. A. Joseph Armstrong, Waco, Texas: Baylor University Press, 1923. *Poetical Works,* London, 1968.

The Browning Society's Papers, 2 vols., London, 1888.

Bryant, Jacob. *A New System; or, an Analysis of Ancient Mythology,* 3 vols., London, 1774–6.

Burke, Kenneth. *Language as Symbolic Action,* Berkeley, 1966.

Butterfield, Herbert. *Man on his Past: the Study of the History of Historical Scholarship,* Cambridge, 1955.

Cassirer, Ernst. *The Problem of Knowledge,* New Haven, 1950.

Cellier, Léon. *L'Épopée humanitaire et les grands mythes romantiques,* Paris, 1971.

Chadwick, Owen. *The Victorian Church,* 2nd ed., 2 vols., London, 1970–2.

Cheyne, T. K. *Founders of Old Testament Criticism,* London, 1893.

Coleridge, Samuel Taylor. *Anima Poetae,* ed. Ernest Hartley Coleridge, London, 1895.

Biographia Literaria, ed. with his Aesthetical Essays by J. Shawcross, 2 vols., London, 1907.

Collected Letters of Samuel Taylor Coleridge, ed. Earl Leslie Griggs, 6 vols., Oxford, 1956–71.

The Collected Works of Samuel Taylor Coleridge, ed. Kathleen Coburn, 16 vols., Princeton and London, 1971–.

The Complete Poetical Works of Samuel Taylor Coleridge, ed. Ernest Hartley Coleridge, Oxford, 1912.

The Complete Works of Samuel Taylor Coleridge, ed. W. G. T. Shedd, New York, 1853.

Confessions of an Inquiring Spirit, ed. H. St. J. Hart, London, 1956.

Enquiring Spirit: A New Presentation of Coleridge from his Published and Unpublished Prose Writings, ed. Kathleen Coburn, New York, 1951.

Literary Remains, ed. H. N. Coleridge, 4 vols., London, 1836–9.

Miscellaneous Criticism, ed. T. M. Raysor, Cambridge, Mass., 1936.

The Notebooks of Samuel Taylor Coleridge, ed. Kathleen Coburn, New York, 1957–.

Notes on English Divines, ed. D. Coleridge, 2 vols., London, 1853.

Omniana, by R. Southey and S. T. Coleridge, ed. R. Giddings, Fontwell, 1969.

On the Prometheus of Aeschylus: an Essay, preparatory to a series of Disquisitions respecting the Egyptian in connection with the Sacerdotal Theology and in Contrast with the Mysteries of ancient Greece, London, 1825. Private Edition.

The Philosophical Lectures of Samuel Taylor Coleridge, ed. Kathleen Coburn, London and New York, 1949.

Specimens of the Table Talk of the Late Samuel Taylor Coleridge, ed. H. N. Coleridge, 2 vols., London, 1835.

Manuscripts:
'On the Divine Ideas' MS, Henry E. Huntington Library, San Marino, California.
MS Notebooks 20, 23, *et seq.* British Museum Additional MSS 47, 517, 47, 521, *et seq.*
MS 'Treatise on Logic,' British Museum Egerton 2825, 2826.
MS 'Opus Maximum,' Victoria College Library, University of Toronto, VCL MS 1.

Marginalia: *see under individual entries for books annotated by Coleridge.*

Collins, Anthony. *A Discourse of the Grounds and Reasons of the Christian Religion*, London, 1724.

Conant, Martha Pike. *The Oriental Tale in England*, New York, 1908.

Corpus Hermeticum, ed. A. D. Nock and trans. A. J. Festugière Paris, 1945.

Cottle, Joseph. *Reminiscences of Samuel Taylor Coleridge and Robert Southey*, London, 1847.

Cross, J. (ed.). *Life of George Eliot*, 3 vols., Edinburgh, 1885.

Curtius, Ernst Robert. *European Literature and the Latin Middle Ages*, trans. W. R. Trask, London, 1953.

DeLaura, D. J. *Hebrew and Hellene in Victorian England: Newman, Arnold, and Pater*, Austin, Texas, 1969.

Deutsch, Emanuel. *Literary Remains of the late Emanuel Deutsch*, London, 1874.

Dilthey, Wilhelm. *Gesammelte Schriften*, Leipzig, 1914–.
Leben Schleiermachers, Berlin, 1870.

Dockhorn, Klaus. *Der deutsche Historismus in England.* Göttingen, 1950.

Dodd, C. H. *Historical Tradition in the Fourth Gospel*, Cambridge, 1963.
The Interpretation of the Fourth Gospel, Cambridge, 1953.

Drew, Philip (ed.). *Robert Browning: A Collection of Critical Essays*, London, 1966.

Dupuis, C. F. *Origine de tous les Cultes, ou Religion universelle*, 12 vols., Paris, 1791.

Eichhorn, Johann Gottfried. *Allgemeine Bibliothek der Biblischen Litteratur*, vol. III, Leipzig, 1790.

Commentarius in Apocalypsin Johannis, Göttingen, 1791. Annotated by S. T. Coleridge. (Copy in the possession of the British Museum.)

Einleitung in das Alte Testament, 3 vols., Leipzig, 1780–3. Annotated by S. T. Coleridge. (Copy in the possession of the British Museum.)

Einleitung in das Neue Testament, Leipzig, 1804–18. Annotated by S. T. Coleridge. (Two copies in the possession of the British Museum.)

Einleitung in die Apokryphischen des Alte Testament, Leipzig, 1795. Annotated by S. T. Coleridge. (Copy in the possession of the British Museum.)

J. G. Eichhorn's Urgeschichte, hsgb, mit Einleitung und Anmerkungen von Dr J. P. Gabler, 3 Bde, Altdorf, 1790–3.

Eliot, George. *The Works of George Eliot*. London and Edinburgh, 1897.
Daniel Deronda, ed. and intro. Barbara Hardy, Harmondsworth, 1967.
Impressions of Theophrastus Such, 4th ed., Edinburgh, 1879.
The Letters of George Eliot, ed. Gordon S. Haight, 6 vols., London, 1954–1956.

Empson, William. *Some Versions of Pastoral*, London, 1935, New York, 1960.

Engels, Frederick. *Ludwig Feuerbach and the Outcome of Classical German Philosophy*, ed., C. P. Dutt, London, n.d.

Ernesti, Johann August. *Institutio Interpretis Novi Testamenti* (1761). ET: *Criticism and Interpretation*, trans. Moses Stuart, Philadelphia, 1827; *Principles of Biblical Interpretation*, trans. Charles H. Terrot, Edinburgh, 1832.

Everard, John. trans. *The Divine Pymander*, London, 1650.

Ewald, Heinrich. *Geschichte des Volkes Israel*, 3. Aufl., 8 Bde, 1864–8. ET: *The History of Israel*, 8 vols., London, 1867–86.

Farrer, Austin. *The Revelation of St. John the Divine*, Oxford, 1964.

Feuerbach, Ludwig. *Ludwig Feuerbachs sämmtliche Werke*, Leipzig, 1846–1866.
The Essence of Christianity, trans. George Eliot, London, 1854.

Forbes, Duncan. *The Liberal Anglican Idea of History*, Cambridge, 1952.

Foucault, Michel. *Histoire de la folie*, Paris, 1961. ET: *Madness and Civilization: A History of Insanity in the Age of Reason*, trans. R. Howard, London, 1967.

Friedman, Albert. *The Ballad Revival*, Chicago, 1961.

Friedrich, Hugo. *Die Struktur der modernen Lyrik*, Hamburg, 1960.

Fuller, R. C. 'Dr Alexander Geddes: A Forerunner of Biblical Criticism', Ph.D. thesis, Cambridge, 1969.

Gaskill, P. H. 'Christ and the Divine Economy in the Work of Friedrich Hölderlin', Ph.D. thesis, Cambridge, 1971.

Gessner, Solomon. *Schriften*, 2 Bde, Zürich, 1777–8. ET: *The Death of Abel*, trans. M. Collyer, London, 1761.

The Death of Abel: A Sacred Poem, trans. Thomas Newcomb, London, 1763.

Goethe, Johann Wolfgang. *Der West-östliche Divan*, Nordlingen, 1961.

Goldmann, Lucien. *Le Dieu caché*, Paris, 1955. ET: *The Hidden God*, London, 1964.

Sciences humaines et philosophie, Paris, 1966. ET: *The Human Sciences and Philosophy*, trans. Hayden V. White and Robert Anchor, London, 1969.

Gooch, G. P. *History and Historians in the Nineteenth Century*, 2nd rev. ed., London, 1952.

[Grohmann, J. C. A.] *Über Offenbarung und Mythologie*, Berlin, 1799.

Guardini, R. *Hölderlin: Weltbild und Frömmigkeit*, München, 1955.

Haight, Gordon S. (ed.). *A Century of George Eliot Criticism*, London, 1968.

Hanson, L. *The Life of S. T. Coleridge, The Early Years*, London, 1938.

Hanson, R. P. C. *Allegory and Event: A Study of the Sources and Significance of Origen's Interpretation of Scripture*, London, 1959.

Hardy, B. (ed.). *Critical Essays on George Eliot*, London, 1970.

Hare, Julius. *The Mission of the Comforter and Other Sermons*, 2 vols., London, 1846.

Harris, Horton. *David Friedrich Strauss and his Theology*, Cambridge, 1973.

Harris, H. S. *Hegel's Development: Toward the Sunlight 1770–1801*, Oxford, 1972.

Hartlich, Christian and Sachs, Walter. *Der Ursprung des Mythosbegriffes in der modernen Bibelwissenschaft*, Tübingen, 1952.

Harvey, A. E. *The New English Bible Companion to the New Testament*, Oxford and Cambridge, 1970.

Haupt, Paul. (ed.). *Biblische Liebeslieder. Das sogenannte Hohelied Salomos*, Leipzig, 1907.

Havelock, Eric. *Preface to Plato*, Oxford, 1963.

Hazard, Paul. *The European Mind 1680–1715*, Aylesbury, 1964.

Hegel, Georg Wilhelm Friedrich. *Theologische Jugendschriften*, hrsg. von H. Nohl, 2 Bde, 1907. ET: *Early Theological Writings*, trans. T. M. Knox, New York, 1948.

Hennell, Charles. *Inquiry Concerning the Origin of Christianity*, London, 1838.

Herder, J. G. von. *Herders sämmtliche Werke*, hrsg. Bernhard Suphan, Berlin, 1877–1913.

A Brief Commentary on the Revelation of Saint John, London, 1821. Annotated by S. T. Coleridge. (Copy in the possession of the British Museum.)

Briefe, das Studium der Theologie betreffend, 2. verbesserte Aufl., Frankfurt u. Leipzig, 1790. Annotated by S. T. Coleridge. (Copy in the possession of the British Museum.)

Vom Geist der ebräischen Poesie, Sämmtliche Werke, Leipzig, 1782. ET (in part): *Oriental Dialogues: containing the Conversation of Eugenius and Alciphron on the. . .sacred Poetry of the Hebrews*, London, 1801.

Hesse, Hermann. *Das Glasperlenspiel. Versuch einer Lebensbeschreibung des Magister Ludi Josef Knecht samt Knechts hinterlassenen Schriften*, 2 vols., Zürich, 1943. ET: *The Glass Bead Game*, trans. Richard and Clara Winston, London, 1970.

Hölderlin, Friedrich. *Sämtliche Werke*, hrsg. von F. Beissner, Stuttgart, 1946 –.

Sämtliche Werke, Berlin und Darmstadt, 1967.

Sämtliche Werke und Briefe, hrsg. von G. Mieth, München, 1970.

Briefe von Friedrich Hölderlin, Weimar, 1922.

Friedrich Hölderlin: Selected Poems, trans. J. B. Leishman, London, 1944, 2nd ed. rev. 1954.

Poems and Fragments, trans. M. Hamburger, London, 1966.

Hunt, H. J. *The Epic in Nineteenth-Century France*, Oxford, 1941.

Johnson, Samuel, *Lives of the English Poets*, 2 vols., London, 1925.

Jonas, Hans. *The Gnostic Religion*, Boston, 1958.

Jones, William. *The Works of Sir William Jones*, 6 vols., London, 1799.

Josephus, Flavius. *The Genuine Works of F. Josephus*, trans. William Whiston, London, 1737.

Kamenka, Eugene. *The Philosophy of Ludwig Feuerbach*, London, 1970.

Kempter, Lothar. 'Holderlin und die Mythologie', *Wege zur Dichtung*, Bd. VI (1929).

Kermode, Frank. *The Sense of an Ending: Studies in the Theory of Fiction*, New York, 1967.

Killham, John (ed.). *Critical Essays on the Poetry of Tennyson*, London, 1960.

Klassen, William and Snyder, Graydon F. *Current Issues in New Testament Interpretation: Essays in Honor of Otto A. Piper*, London, 1962.

Klopstock, Friedrich Gottlieb. *Ausgewählte Werke*, München, 1962.

Klopstocks Werke, Leipzig, 1798–1813.

The Death of Adam. A Tragedy in Three Acts, Dublin, 1763.

The Messiah, A New Edition in One Volume, Bungay, 1808.

Knight, Frida. *University Rebel: The Life of William Frend*, (*1757–1841*), London, 1971.

Select bibliography

Knight, G. Wilson. *The Starlit Dome*, London, 1941.

Knight, Richard Payne. *A Discourse on the Worship of Priapus, and its Connexion with the mystic Theology of the Ancients*, London, 1786.

Kraeling, Emil Gottlieb Heinrich. *The Old Testament since the Reformation*, London, 1955.

Kraus, H. J. *Geschichte der historisch-kritischen Erforschung des alten Testaments*, Neukirchen-Vluyn, 1969.

Kümmel, Werner Georg. *Das Neue Testament: Geschichte der Erforschung seiner Probleme*, Freiburg u. München, 1958.

Lardner, Nathaniel. *The Works of Nathaniel Lardner*, 11 vols., London, 1788.

    The Credibility of the Gospel History, 13 vols., London, 1730–55.

    A Letter written in the Year 1730, concerning the Question, whether the Logos supplied the Place of an Human Soul in the Person of Jesus Christ, London, 1788.

Leavis, F. R. *The Great Tradition*, London, 1948.

Leavis, F. R. and Leavis, Q. D. *Dickens*, London, 1970.

Lessing, Gotthold Ephraim. *Sämmtliche Schriften*, Berlin, 1791. Annotated by S. T. Coleridge. (Copy in the possession of the British Museum.)

    Sämtliche Schriften, hrsg. von K. Lachmann. 3. Aufl., 23 Bde, Stuttgart, 1886–1924.

Lewalski, Barbara. *Milton's Brief Epic*, Providence, R.I. and London, 1960.

Lewes, George Henry. *The Life and Works of Goethe*, 2nd rev. ed., Leipzig, 1858.

Litzinger, Boyd and Knickerbocker, K. L., *The Browning Critics*, Lexington: University of Kentucky Press, 1965.

Lowes, John Livingstone. *The Road to Xanadu*, New York, 1927.

Lowth, Robert. *Lectures on the Sacred Poetry of the Hebrews*, trans. G. Gregory (1753), 2 vols., London, 1787.

Lukács, G. *History and Class Consciousness*, London, 1971.

    The Meaning of Contemporary Realism, London, 1962.

    Théorie du Roman, Paris n.d.

Macaulay, George Babington. *Lays of Ancient Rome*, London, 1828.

McFarland, Thomas. *Coleridge and the Pantheist Tradition*, Oxford, 1969.

Mackay, R. W. *The Tübingen School and its Antecedents*, London, 1863.

Macrobius. *Saturnalia*, ed. and trans. Henri Bornecque, Paris, n.d.

Manuel, Frank. *The Eighteenth Century Confronts the Gods*, Cambridge, Mass., 1959.

    Isaac Newton Historian, Cambridge, 1963.

Manzalaoui, Mahmoud. 'Some English Translations of Arabic Imaginative Literature (1704–1838): a Study of their Portrayal of the Arab World,

352

with an Estimate of their Influence on Nineteenth Century English Literature', B.Litt. thesis, Oxford, 1947.

Marcus, Steven. *The Other Victorians*, New York, 1964.

Marsh, John. *Saint John*, Harmondsworth, 1968.

Meinecke, Friedrich. *Die Entstehung des Historismus*, München u. Berlin, 1936.
ET: *Historism: The Rise of a New Historical Outlook*, London, 1972.

Merkelbach, Reinhold. *Roman und Mysterium in der Antike*, München, 1962.

Michaelis, John David. *Introduction to the New Testament*, trans. Herbert Marsh, 6 vols., Cambridge, 1801.

Miller, J. Hillis. *The Disappearance of God*, Cambridge, Mass., 1963.
The Form of Victorian Fiction, London, 1968.

Milman, Henry Hart. *The History of the Jews*, 2nd rev. ed., London, 1865.

Mineka, Francis Edward. *The Dissidence of Dissent: the Monthly Repository, 1806–38, under the Editorship of Robert Aspland, W. J. Fox, R. H. Horne, and Leigh Hunt; with a Chapter on Religious Periodicals 1700–1825*, Chapel Hill, N.C., 1944.

Mitter, Partha. 'European Attitudes to Indian Art from the Mid-Thirteenth to the End of the Nineteenth Century', Ph.D. thesis, London, 1970.

Momigliano, A. D. *Studies in Historiography*, London, 1966.

Morgan, B. Q. *A Critical Bibliography of German Literature in English Translation, 1481–1927*, 2nd rev. ed., Stanford, 1938.

Morgan, B. Q. and Hohlfeld, A. R. *German Literature in British Magazines 1750–1860*, Madison, 1949.

Muirhead, John H. *Coleridge As Philosopher*, London, 1930.

Mukherjee, S. N. *Sir William Jones: A Study in Eighteenth Century British Attitudes to India*, Cambridge, 1968.

Muller, Ernst. *Hölderlin. Studien zur Geschichte seines Geistes*, Stuttgart, 1944.

Müller, Max. *Lectures on the Science of Language*, 2nd series, London, 1864.

Neil, W. 'The Criticism and Theological Use of the Bible, 1750–1959', *The Cambridge History of the Bible: The West from the Reformation to the Present Day*, Cambridge, 1963.

Orsini, Gian N. G. *Coleridge and German Idealism: A Study in the History of Philosophy*, Carbondale, Illinois, 1969.

Pannwitz, Rudolph. *Hölderlin: Beiträge zu seinem Verständnis in unserm Jahrhundert*, Tübingen, 1961.

Paris, Bernard J. *Experiments in Life: George Eliot's Quest for Values*, Detroit, 1965.

Paulus, H. E. G. *Das Leben Jesu*, Heidelberg, 1828. Annotated by S. T. Coleridge. (Copy in the possession of the British Museum.)

Pellegrini, Allessandro. *Friedrich Hölderlin: Sein Bild in der Forschung*, Berlin, 1956.

Pépin, Jean. *Allégorie et Mythe; les origines grecques et contestations judaeo-chrétiennes*, Paris, 1958.

Petzold, Emil. *Hölderlin's Brod und Wein: Ein exegetischer Versuch*, Sambor, 1896 and Darmstadt, 1967.

Pfleiderer, O. *The Development of Theology in Germany Since Kant*, trans. J. Frederick Smith, London, 1890.

Price, B. and Price, L. M. *The Publication of English Humaniora in Germany in the Eighteenth Century*, Berkeley and Los Angeles, 1955.

Priestley, Joseph. *A Comparison of the Institutions of Moses with those of the Hindoos and Other Ancient Nations*, Northumberland, Pa., 1799.

 An History of the Corruptions of Christianity, 2 vols., Birmingham, 1786.

 An History of Early Opinions concerning Jesus Christ, 4 vols., Birmingham, 1786.

 The Theological and Miscellaneous Works of Joseph Priestley, ed. John Towill Rutt, 25 vols., London, 1817–31.

Raymond, W. O. *The Infinite Moment*, Toronto, 1950.

Reed, Mark L. *Wordsworth. The Chronology of the Early Years 1770–1799*, Cambridge, Mass., 1967.

Reimarus, Hermann Samuel. *Fragments, consisting of brief critical remarks on the object of Jesus and his disciples as seen in the New Testament*, trans. and ed. Charles Voysey, London and Edinburgh, 1879.

Reitzenstein, Richard. *Die Hellenistischen Mysterienreligionen*, 3. Aufl., Leipzig u. Berlin, 1927.

Renan, Ernest. *Oeuvres complètes*, ed. H. Psichari, 10 vols., Paris, 1947–61.
 Essais de morale et de critique, Paris, 1860.
 Studies in Religious History, trans. Wm M. Thompson, London, 1886; 2nd series, 1896.
 Vie de Jésus, Paris, 1863. ET: *The Life of Jesus*, London, 1864.

[Richter,] Jean Paul. *Siebenkäs*. 1791–7.

Ritschl, Albrecht. *Geschichte des Pietismus*, 3 Bde, Bonn, 1880–6.

Robberds, John Warden. *A Memoir of the Life and Writings of the Late William Taylor of Norwich*, 2 vols., London, 1843.

Robertson, J. M. *A History of Freethought in the Nineteenth Century*, London, 1929.

Sanders, Charles Richard. *Coleridge and the Broad Church Movement; Studies in S. T. Coleridge, Dr. Arnold of Rugby, J. C. Hare, Thomas Carlyle, and F. D. Maurice*, Durham, N.C., 1942.

Schelling, Friedrich Wilhelm Joseph von. *Schellings sämmtliche Werke*, München, 1946–59.

Schiller, Friedrich. *Schillers Werke*, 2 Bde, Berlin und Darmstadt, 1956.

Select bibliography

Schleiermacher, Friedrich. *Friedrich Schleiermachers sämmtliche Werke,* Berlin, 1834–64.

Hermeneutik, hrsg. von Heinz Kimmerle, Heidelberger Akademie der Wissenschaften, Heidelberg, 1959.

On Luke, trans. Connop Thirlwall, London, 1825. Annotated by S. T. Coleridge. (Copy in the British Museum.)

Soliloquies: an ET of the *Monologen* (1800), trans. H. L. Friess, Chicago, 1926.

Über die Religion: Reden an die Gebildeten unter ihren Verächtern, Göttingen, 1920. ET: *On Religion: Speeches to its Cultured Despisers,* trans. of 3rd German ed., J. Oman, London, 1893; New York, 1965.

Schmidt, Carl Benjamin. *Auszug aus Dr. Robert Lowth's 'Vorlesungen' über die heilige Dichtkunst der Hebräer, mit Herder's und Jones's Grundsätzen verbunden. Ein Versuch, zur Beförderung des Bibelstudiums des alten Testaments, und insbesondre der Propheten und Psalme,* Danzig, 1793.

Schneider, Elisabeth. *Coleridge, Opium, and 'Kubla Khan',* Chicago, 1953.

Scholem, Gershom G. *Major Trends in Jewish Mysticism,* 3rd rev. ed., New York, 1961.

Zur Kabbala und ihren Symbolik, Zürich, 1960. ET: *On the Kabbalah and its Symbolism,* trans. R. Manheim, London, 1965.

Schwab, Raymond. *La Renaissance orientale,* Paris, 1950.

Schweitzer, A. *Von Reimarus zu Wrede,* Tübingen, 1906. ET: *The Quest of the Historical Jesus,* London, 1910.

Shaffer, Elinor, S. 'Metaphysics of Culture: Kant and Coleridge's *Aids to Reflection*', *Journal of the History of Ideas,* XXXI, no. 2, April–June, 1970, 199–218.

Snyder, A. D. 'Books borrowed by Coleridge from the library of the University of Göttingen, 1799', *Modern Philology* XXV (1928), 377–80.

Southey, Charles Cuthbert. *The Life and Correspondence of Robert Southey,* 6 vols., London, 1849–50.

Southey, Robert. *The Poetical Works of Robert Southey,* 10 vols., London, 1837–8.

Spinoza, Benedict de. *The Chief Works of Benedict de Spinoza,* trans. and intro., R. H. M. Elwes, 2 vols., London, 1883.

Opera, hrsg. von Carl Gebhardt, Heidelberg, 1925.

Stahl, E. H. *Hölderlin's Symbolism, an Essay,* Oxford, 1945.

Stanley, Arthur. *Lectures on the History of the Jewish Church,* London, 1863–1876.

Stephen, Leslie. *History of English Thought in the Eighteenth Century,* 3rd ed., 2 vols., London, 1962.

Stock, John Edmonds. *Memoirs of the Life of Thomas Beddoes, M.D.,* London, 1811.

Select bibliography

Storr, Vernon Faithfull. *The Development of English Theology in The Nineteenth Century, 1800–60*, London, 1913.

Strauss, David Friedrich. *Gesammelte Schriften*, hrsg. von Eduard Zeller, 1876–8.

The Life of Jesus, trans. George Eliot, London, 1892.

Strich, Fritz. *Goethe and World Literature*, London, 1949.

Die Mythologie in der deutschen Literatur von Klopstock bis Wagner, 2 Bde, Halle, 1910.

Szondi, Peter. *Der andere Pfeil: zur Entstehungsgeschichte von Hölderlin's hymnischen Spätstil*, Frankfurt, 1963.

Taylor, Thomas. *A Dissertation on the Eleusinian and the Bacchic Mysteries*, Amsterdam, 1790.

The Mystical Hymns of Orpheus, London, 1896.

Thomas Taylor the Platonist: Selected Writings, ed. K. Raine and G. M. Harper, London, 1969.

Tennyson, G. B. *Sartor Called Resartus*, Princeton, 1965.

Todland, John. *Christianity Not Mysterious*, London, 1702.

Nazarenus: or Jewish, Gentile, and Mahometan Christianity, London, 1718.

Volney, C. *The Ruins of Empire*, London, 1792.

Voltaire. *Dictionnaire philosophique portatif*, Londres [Geneva?] 1764.

Essai sur la poésie épique, Paris, 1724, rev. ed. 1764.

Warburton, William. *The Divine Legation of Moses*, 2 vols., 1738–41. 4th ed., 5 vols., London 1764–5.

Wardman, Harold W. *Ernest Renan: a Critical Biography*, London, 1964.

Watt, Ian. *The Rise of the English Novel*, London, 1957.

Weber, Carl August. 'Bristols Bedeutung für die englische Romantik und die deutsch-englischen Beziehungen', *Studien zur englischen Philologie*, Halle, 1935.

Welch, Claude. *Protestant Thought in the Nineteenth Century, I, 1799–1870*, New Haven and London, 1972.

Wellek, René. *Immuanuel Kant in England*, Princeton, 1931.

Wells, G. A. 'Stages of New Testament Criticism', *Journal of the History of Ideas* xxx (April–June 1969).

Whalley, George. 'The Bristol Library Borrowings of Southey and Coleridge, 1793–8', *The Library* iv (September 1949), 114–31.

Willey, Basil. *Nineteenth Century Studies*, London, 1949.

Williams, Raymond, *The English Novel from Dickens to Lawrence*, London, 1970.

Zscharnack, Leopold. *Lessing und Semler; ein Beitrag zur Entstehungsgeschichte das Rationalismus und der kritischen Theologie*, Giessen, 1905.

INDEX

Index